Content Networking Fundamentals

Silvano Da Ros

Cisco Press

800 East 96th Street
Indianapolis, IN 46240 USA

Content Networking Fundamentals

Silvano Da Ros

Copyright© 2006 Cisco Systems, Inc.

Cisco Press logo is a trademark of Cisco Systems, Inc.

Published by:
Cisco Press
800 East 96th Street
Indianapolis, IN 46240 USA

Printed in the United States of America 1 2 3 4 5 6 7 8 9 0

First Printing   March 2006

Library of Congress Cataloging-in-Publication Number: 2005922508

ISBN: 1-58705-240-7

Warning and Disclaimer

This book is designed to provide information about the fundamentals of content networking. Every effort has been made to make this book as complete and as accurate as possible, but no warranty or fitness is implied.

The information is provided on an "as-is" basis. The authors, Cisco Press, and Cisco Systems, Inc., shall have neither liability nor responsibility to any person or entity with respect to any loss or damages arising from the information contained in this book or from the use of the discs or programs that may accompany it.

The opinions expressed in this book belong to the author and are not necessarily those of Cisco Systems, Inc.

Trademark Acknowledgments

All terms mentioned in this book that are known to be trademarks or service marks have been appropriately capitalized. Cisco Press or Cisco Systems, Inc., cannot attest to the accuracy of this information. Use of a term in this book should not be regarded as affecting the validity of any trademark or service mark.

RealNetworks images and information in Chapter 13 provided courtesy of RealNetworks, Inc.:

Copyright © 1995–2005 RealNetworks, Inc. All rights reserved. RealNetworks, Helix, Helix Proxy, RealProxy, RealPlayer, and RealMedia are trademarks or registered trademarks of RealNetworks, Inc.

Feedback Information

At Cisco Press, our goal is the creation of in-depth technical books of the highest quality and value. Each book is crafted with care and precision, undergoing rigorous development that involves the unique expertise of members from the professional technical community.

Readers' feedback is a natural continuation of this process. If you have any comments regarding how we could improve the quality of this book, or otherwise alter it to better suit your needs, you can contact us through email at feedback@ciscopress.com. Please be sure to include the book title and ISBN in your message.

We greatly appreciate your assistance.

Publisher: John Wait

Editor-in-Chief: John Kane

Production Manager: Patrick Kanouse

Development Editor: Betsey Henkels

Copy Editor: Paul Wilson

Editorial Assistant: Raina Han

Book and Cover Designer: Louisa Adair

Composition: Mark Shirar

Indexer: Tim Wright

Proofreader: Kayla Dugger

Cisco Representative: Anthony Wolfenden

Cisco Press Program Manager: Jeff Brady

Technical Editors: Mark Gallo, Stefano Testa, Maurice Traynor

CISCO SYSTEMS

Corporate Headquarters
Cisco Systems, Inc.
170 West Tasman Drive
San Jose, CA 95134-1706
USA
www.cisco.com
Tel: 408 526-4000
   800 553-NETS (6387)
Fax: 408 526-4100

European Headquarters
Cisco Systems International BV
Haarlerbergpark
Haarlerbergweg 13-19
1101 CH Amsterdam
The Netherlands
www-europe.cisco.com
Tel: 31 0 20 357 1000
Fax: 31 0 20 357 1100

Americas Headquarters
Cisco Systems, Inc.
170 West Tasman Drive
San Jose, CA 95134-1706
USA
www.cisco.com
Tel: 408 526-7660
Fax: 408 527-0883

Asia Pacific Headquarters
Cisco Systems, Inc.
Capital Tower
168 Robinson Road
#22-01 to #29-01
Singapore 068912
www.cisco.com
Tel: +65 6317 7777
Fax: +65 6317 7799

Cisco Systems has more than 200 offices in the following countries and regions. Addresses, phone numbers, and fax numbers are listed on the
Cisco.com Web site at www.cisco.com/go/offices.

Argentina • Australia • Austria • Belgium • Brazil • Bulgaria • Canada • Chile • China PRC • Colombia • Costa Rica • Croatia • Czech Republic
Denmark • Dubai, UAE • Finland • France • Germany • Greece • Hong Kong SAR • Hungary • India • Indonesia • Ireland • Israel • Italy
Japan • Korea • Luxembourg • Malaysia • Mexico • The Netherlands • New Zealand • Norway • Peru • Philippines • Poland • Portugal
Puerto Rico • Romania • Russia • Saudi Arabia • Scotland • Singapore • Slovakia • Slovenia • South Africa • Spain • Sweden
Switzerland • Taiwan • Thailand • Turkey • Ukraine • United Kingdom • United States • Venezuela • Vietnam • Zimbabwe

About the Author

Silvano Da Ros is currently a networking consultant in Toronto and has worked previously as a systems engineer for Cisco Systems. While at Cisco, he enjoyed working with enterprise organizations on emerging network solutions, including IP telephony, content networking, and security. Prior to joining Cisco, his computer science degree saw him as a software developer, developing client-server and web applications for numerous public and private sector agencies. Silvano holds a bachelor of computer science and a masters of engineering in internetworking from Dalhousie University in Halifax, Nova Scotia.

About the Technical Reviewers

Mark Gallo is a systems engineering manager at Cisco Systems within the Channels organization. He has led several engineering groups responsible for positioning and delivering Cisco end-to-end systems, as well as designing and implementing enterprise LANs and international IP networks. He has a BS in electrical engineering from the University of Pittsburgh and holds Cisco CCNP and CCDP certifications. Mark resides in northern Virginia with his wife Betsy and son Paul.

Stefano Testa joined Cisco in 1998, as part of the Catalyst 6500 software development team. Since moving to technical marketing in 2000, he's been focusing on technologies such as content switching, geographic load balancing, SSL acceleration, and integration with security products. He is currently managing a team of technical marketing engineers dedicated to Layers 4-7 application acceleration and security technologies. Stefano works closely with Cisco account teams to help customers design high-performance integrated data-centers and application-aware solutions. He also collaborates with several Cisco engineering teams on future software releases, network management, and platforms for Layers 4-7 services.

Maurice Traynor is a technical team lead (networks), for HP's (Hewlett-Packard—http://www.hp.com) Managed Services Group, where his team architects and builds networks for a large financial institution. He has worked in the networking arena for 14 years, with jobs in pre- and post-sales systems engineering, technical consulting, and teaching.

Dedications

This book is dedicated to my wife, Kimberley, and parents, Mario and Catherine. Thank you for your support and encouragement.

Acknowledgments

Writing a book is never a singular effort, and this one certainly required the help from a group of exceptionally qualified people. In particular, I'd like to give special recognition to my reviewers, Mark, Ted, Stephano, and Maurice, for their technical critique of this book. Thanks for your unique spin on many of the concepts in this book.

The Cisco Press editorial team, including John Kane, Raina Han, and Betsey Henkels, has also been a huge factor in the successful completion of this book. Thanks for your countless e-mails and phone calls during every stage of writing this book. It has been a pleasure and honor working on this project with Cisco Press.

Thanks to my friends at Cisco for help with ideas early on in the book's development; Haroon Khan for the CDM screenshots; and Tim Forehand, Jamund Ferguson, and Brooke Collins from RealNetworks for their time and effort spent on making the RealMedia portion of this book happen.

I and Cisco Press would also like to thank Niraj Jain and Ted Grevers for their contributions to the book.

This Book Is Safari Enabled

The Safari® Enabled icon on the cover of your favorite technology book means the book is available through Safari Bookshelf. When you buy this book, you get free access to the online edition for 45 days.

Safari Bookshelf is an electronic reference library that lets you easily search thousands of technical books, find code samples, download chapters, and access technical information whenever and wherever you need it.

To gain 45-day Safari Enabled access to this book:

- Go to http://www.ciscopress.com/safarienabled
- Complete the brief registration form
- Enter the coupon code RHAH-8AJC-THLR-HUC9-HXCP

If you have difficulty registering on Safari Bookshelf or accessing the online edition, please e-mail customer-service@safaribooksonline.com.

Contents at a Glance

x

Contents

Icons Used in This Book

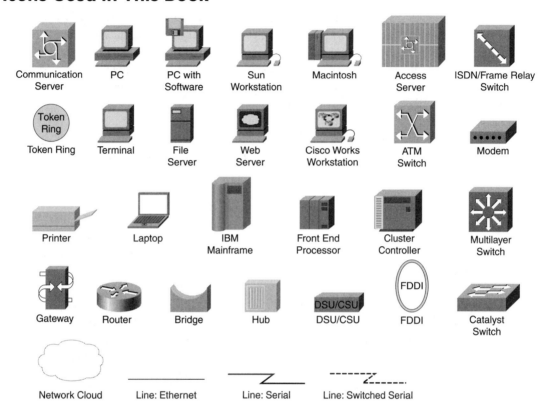

Command Syntax Conventions

The conventions used to present command syntax in this book are the same conventions used in the IOS Command Reference. The Command Reference describes these conventions as follows:

- **Boldface** indicates commands and keywords that are entered literally as shown. In actual configuration examples and output (not general command syntax), boldface indicates commands that are manually input by the user (such as a **show** command).

- *Italics* indicate arguments for which you supply actual values.

- Vertical bars | separate alternative, mutually exclusive elements.

- Square brackets [ ] indicate optional elements.

- Braces { } indicate a required choice.

- Braces within brackets [{ }] indicate a required choice within an optional element.

Introduction

Within Internetworking, there are numerous career fields, such as network security, IP telephony, and Storage Area Networking (SAN). Content networking is growing so much that it has become a discipline of its own. In the past, most organizations have given the content networking responsibility to the IT operations or network security staff, but these days the field has become so large and complex that organizations often require dedicated content networking professionals to design and operate their content networks.

The purpose of this book is to introduce content networking as an individual field of study, and explain how numerous application and networking concepts are married to make the discipline a whole.

Goals and Methods

This book will first introduce you to some basic underlying networking technologies, which have been around for quite a while but that content networking uses in new and unique ways to accelerate your applications.

Once you understand the underlying technologies, this book uses the divide-and-conquer approach to address the single broad topic of content networking. By further isolating and examining content networking's constituent technologies, you avoid the blurring and generalizing that tend to occur when discussing content networking. Covering each subtopic and its interdependencies in detail will give you valuable insight into the overall topic of content networking, without minimizing the importance of each subtechnology.

Who Should Read This Book?

This book is designed for any networking or application professional who requires an introduction to content networking. If you come to this book as an application professional, you will be able to obtain an introduction to the basic networking concepts from the first few chapters; this information may be superfluous to the network professional. On the other hand, networking professionals will be able to glean information about application concepts from the initial chapters to fully understand the content networking concepts discussed in this book.

Specifically, this book is an excellent resource for professionals who

- Design, implement, and maintain content networks
- Are preparing for the Cisco CCNP content networking exam
- Are responsible for technically justifying the purchase of content networking products to their management or purchasing departments

How This Book Is Organized

Although this book is designed to be read from cover-to-cover, it was also developed so that you can easily jump between its parts, chapters, and sections, enabling you to concentrate on only those topics that require your focused attention. As mentioned previously, both application and network-centric professionals will learn a great deal about their IT counterpart's native technologies. By allowing the reader to effectively concentrate on particular areas, this book benefits readers from diverse technical backgrounds.

Chapter 1 provides an introduction to content networking. Chapters 2 through 9 are framed as background chapters to content networking, giving a detailed examination of both the fundamentals of networks and applications. Chapters 10 through 14 are the core content networking chapters, with each chapter providing a detailed treatment of a particular subtechnology of content networking. If you intend to read all the chapters, the order in the book is an excellent sequence to use.

The chapters of this book cover the following topics:

- **Chapter 1, "Introducing Content Networking"**—This chapter offers general insight into the broad topic of content networking, including its purpose, goals, and subtechnologies.

- **Chapter 2, "Exploring the Network Layers"**—This chapter examines Layers 1 through 4 of the Open Systems Interconnection (OSI) reference model, giving approximately equal coverage on each layer. To glue the layers together, this chapter ends with an illustration of a sample application flow, showing how the layers interact with one another.

- **Chapter 3, "Introducing Switching, Routing, and Address Translation"**—This chapter introduces how frames are switched by Layer 2 switches, how packets are routed and switched by Layer 3 routers, and how the transport segment's IP addresses and port numbers are translated by Layer 4 content switches and firewalls.

- **Chapter 4, "Exploring Security Technologies and Network Infrastructure Designs"**—This chapter covers major topics for securing your applications and network, such as packet filtering, application inspection, and encryption, and provides design backdrops for common networking infrastructures, including WANs, campuses, and Internet Content Delivery Networks (ICDN).

- **Chapter 5, "IP Multicast Content Delivery"**—Streaming media and content distribution can consume a great deal of network bandwidth. To deal with this issue, Chapter 5 provides a way to minimize potential flooding using IP multicast.

- **Chapter 6, "Ensuring Content Delivery with Quality of Service"**—This chapter provides a way to minimize the impact of packet loss, delay, and jitter by enabling QoS features in your network.

- **Chapter 7, "Presenting and Transforming Content"**—This chapter covers how to use Extensible Markup Language (XML)-based markup laguages for describing, presenting, and transforming content.

- **Chapter 8, "Exploring the Application Layer"**—This chapter introduces the application layer and in particular the protocols that pertain to content networking concepts discussed throughout the book, including HTTP, Secure Sockets Layer (SSL), and FTP application layer protocols.

- **Chapter 9, "Introducing Streaming Media"**—This chapter covers streaming media concepts, including how video on demand (VoD), live, and rebroadcast events are delivered using Real-Time Transport Protocol (RTP), Real-Time Streaming Protocol (RTSP), and Motion Picture Expert Group (MPEG) protocols. This chapter also compares and contrasts Microsoft Windows, Apple QuickTime, and RealNetworks streaming technologies.

- **Chapter 10, "Exploring Server Load Balancing"**—This chapter shows how to design redundancy and high availability into your server farms by configuring load distribution algorithms, health checks, session persistence, and Layer 5–7 load balancing on your content switches.

- **Chapter 11, "Switching Secured Content"**—This chapter shows how to switch and offload encrypted content by importing, creating, and configuring certificates and keys in SSL termination devices, such as the Content Switching Module (CSM) with Secure Sockets Layer (SSL) daughter cards (CSM-S) and the Content Services Switch (CSS) SSL modules.

- **Chapter 12, "Exploring Global Server Load Balancing"**—This chapter shows how to design redundancy and high availability across your sites, using the Domain Name System (DNS), Distributed Director, proximity-based load balancing, and global sticky databases.

- **Chapter 13, "Delivering Cached and Streaming Media"**—This chapter examines how to configure your routers with Web Cache Control Protocol (WCCP) and content switches to switch requests to Content Engines (CE) for serving frequently requested objects. These frequently requested objects can include the following: HTTP and streaming media; standard caching services, such as web and reverse-proxy caching on your CEs using the Application and Content Networking System (ACNS); value-added services, such as content authentication and content preloading; and content freshness from CEs.

- **Chapter 14, "Distributing and Routing Managed Content"**—This chapter explores how to configure ACNS for content distribution and routing serivces, by configuring channels of CEs, forwarding content to those channels, and using content request routing technologies, such as simplified hybrid routing and dynamic proxy auto-configuration, to route client's requests for the distributed content.

Part I: Overview of Content Networking

Chapter Goals

This chapter provides a thorough overview of content networking to establish a general context for the more detailed topics covered in the remaining chapters. The chapter presents the overview by covering the following topics:

- **Definition of content networking** — Gives a general definition of the field.

- **The underlying technologies** — Defines content networking with respect to the Open System Interconnection (OSI) and TCP/IP protocol stacks.

- **Purpose and goals of content networking** — Informs the reader of the motivation behind content networking in terms of its purpose and goals.

- **Cisco content networking solutions** — Introduces Cisco content networking technologies in terms of supplying customers with end-to-end solutions for their business needs.

Introducing Content Networking

Since the early 1990s, web applications have grown considerably in scope. The web applications of the 1990s included only informational and advertising content, but by now they have become a robust suite of critical business functions. Cisco Systems, Inc., is a prime example of an organization that depends heavily on and promotes the web for most of its business functions, both internally and externally. Internally at Cisco, employees attend training seminars, book flights, fill out vacation requests, and reserve customer demonstration equipment online. Additionally, their phone system, corporate communications, remote access, and e-learning systems are run over the web. External customer-facing functions including ordering hardware, downloading software, requesting customer support, and receiving training are all completed over the web as well.

Not only have high-tech industries like Cisco been rapidly adopting web technologies, but seemingly old-fashioned brick-and-mortar companies are relying now more than ever on web-based portals for greater productivity gains, increased revenues, and cost savings. In turn, the increasing dependence of organizations on the use and growth of networked applications to ensure that success has grown to levels never seen before. This heavy reliance on web content has spurred organizations to achieve network cost savings and application acceleration to ensure continual growth and prosperity.

Defining Content Networking

Content networking involves elements from all aspects of network computing, from high-level applications to underlying network protocols. Understanding of the basics of both computer networking and applications developed for networks is a crucial prerequisite to obtaining a deeper understanding of content networking. Thus, this book covers the following three network entities to help you better understand this wide-reaching field:

■ **Originator**—The originator (or an origin server) provides content for requesting clients. The content can range from live video, software downloads, and file transfers to e-mail, static informational data, and dynamic fully-interactive multimedia. The applications may include e-learning, corporate communications, e-commerce, hosting services, and enterprise client/server applications, among many others.

■ **Network infrastructure**—The network infrastructure delivers the content. The network can be either a private or public network, composed of a number of underlying protocols and concepts, such as TCP/IP and Ethernet, plus the content networking services and intelligent network services discussed in this book.

■ **Recipient**—The recipient (or client) requests the content. The recipient can range from PC desktop client applications, such as web browsers and video players to cell phones, personal data assistants (PDAs), television sets, IP phones, and many more.

Figure 1-1 illustrates the relationships among these three entities. Related content networking concepts highlighted in the Figure 1-1 will be discussed in detail throughout this book.

Figure 1-1   *Relationship Between Recipient, Network, and Originator Content Network Entities*

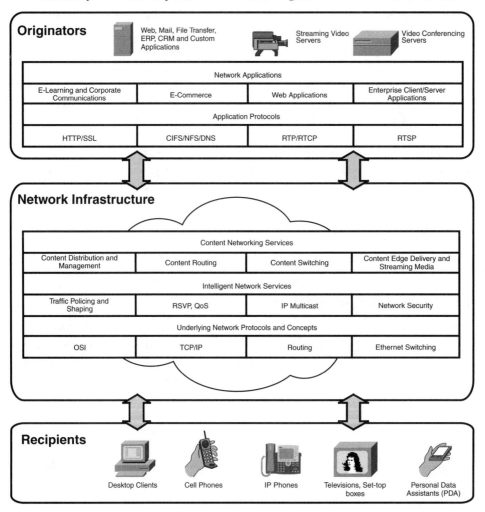

In the past few decades, TCP/IP has become the most common networking protocol, and its original intention has remained as valid today as when it was conceived in the late 1960s. That is, it remains a simple method to deliver a payload from one location to another. Indeed, in the recent past, the only service the network provided to an application was packet delivery, with either guaranteed or best-effort service levels. Moreover, clients were aware of only a few basic details concerning the origin server, such as name and services provided. The originators were completely unaware of details about their requesting clients, except those anticipated and hard-coded into the application by its developer. Neither knew much more about the network on which content was delivered and received than how to interface into it.

Until recently, the function of the network remained separate from the applications that ran on it. In the past few years, acknowledging the new and increasing demands for the network to add value to applications, the Cisco development team has pushed its networking software toward implementing content networking technologies. Slowly, existing network devices were extended with a few of the application protocols and intelligent network services shown in Figure 1-1. Eventually, however, a vast new suite of content-based products was created, resulting in the robust content networking solutions that exist today. As you will see throughout this book, content networking provides numerous services to accelerate content delivery and encompasses all aspects and protocols included within the three entities shown in Figure 1-1.

Content networking is a new paradigm of computing and communications. Concentration has shifted from both computers and networks, individually, toward the creation of a collective system called a content network, encompassing characteristics of both computers and networks. Thus, content networking can be broadly defined as content-awareness by not only the originator of the content but by all three basic network entities. As you may find, however, content networking is somewhat vague when defined generally. In the remainder of this chapter, you explore a more detailed definition of content networking in terms of the following three specific categories:

- Understanding the Underlying Technologies

- Purpose and Goals

- Cisco Content Networking Solutions

Understanding the Underlying Technologies

The need for the network to add value to applications is advanced by a growing thirst for more robust applications, which are able to respond instantaneously. Traditional networking software operated at intelligence levels too low to accelerate services, which were governed by these aggressive demands. However, a network installed with Cisco content networking software can be seamlessly enabled for content-awareness and thus easily fulfill such demands.

This book focuses on the content-aware Layers 4 through 7 of the OSI model. The OSI model is a standard reference for understanding networks and developing other standards. OSI is used most commonly as a detailed reference for which vendors develop networking protocol stacks, which in turn can themselves become standards.

Consider each layer of the OSI model to be a process responsible for a set of actions to be performed on an item of information on behalf of upper layers. When the item is processed at one layer, it is passed directly to the next layer for processing. Each layer also communicates indirectly with adjacent layers on other devices and specifies the addressing and identification details used among them.

Whereas devices connect physically to each neighbor at Layer 1, all layers above Layer 1 connect logically to the same layer on the communicating device. For Layers 2 and 3, the communicating devices are often switches and routers, respectively. For example, a workstation can connect logically at Layer 2 to another workstation through a Layer 2 switch. For Layer 4, the communicating device is often a firewall, or any network device capable of maintaining transport state information. In traditional networks, for Layers 5 through 7, the applications running on the client and origin server are in logical communication with one another over the network. Figure 1-2 illustrates the OSI model in traditional networks. The dotted lines represent inter-process communication between adjacent layers.

Figure 1-2   *The OSI Reference Model in Traditional Networks*

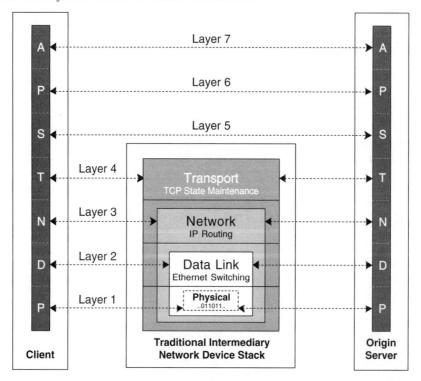

Before content networking, intermediary devices in the network would stop processing information at Layers 2, 3, and 4 in switches, routers, and firewalls, respectively. Within content networking devices, however, the processing continues up the protocol stack in order to add intelligence to the information exchanged between the communicating applications, as illustrated in Figure 1-3. Bear in mind that, although content networking devices are specialized for Layers 5 through 7 processing, they have numerous capabilities to process information at Layers 1 through 4.

Figure 1-3 *The OSI Reference Model in Content Networks*

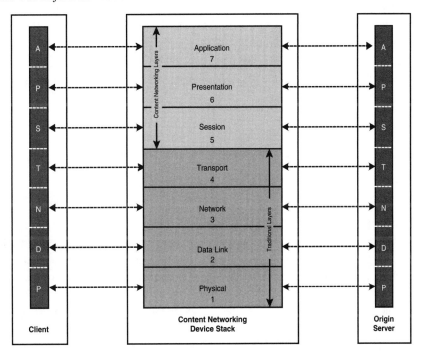

TCP/IP is the predominant network protocol suite of the Internet today. It is based on the OSI reference model, but its details are specific to the requirements of today's networks. This book focuses on characteristics of the OSI model as they pertain to TCP/IP. Chapter 2, "Exploring the Network Layers," will explain the lower four layers of the OSI model with respect to TCP/IP-based routing and switching and their related protocols. Although these lower layers are essential to understanding almost all content networking technologies, this book focuses more on subjects related to the upper-three OSI layers. These layers are rarely referenced separately in this book and are therefore combined and referred to collectively as "Layers 5 through 7," or simply "Layers 5–7."

> **TIP**   For an example trace of an actual application message passing through each layer of the TCP/IP protocol stack, see the "Putting It All Together with a Detailed Network Trace" section in Chapter 2.

Purpose and Goals

In most aspects of life, a need or problem often encourages creative efforts to meet the need or solve the problem. That is, necessity is often the mother of invention. This also pertains to network computing, where development is spurred by ever increasing end-user demands for richer content, more bandwidth, and increased reliability. To fulfill these demands, first you must address the following four areas:

- Scalability and Availability

- Bandwidth and Response Times

- Customization and Prioritization

- Security, Auditing, and Monitoring

Scalability and Availability

Different types of applications require increases to their performance levels. For example, a web application may require enhancements to its functionality and intelligence (that is, the computer programming code), and the current computer system does not have the resources to yield the same levels of performance as before. Another example might be with a corporate communication application, in which the number of participants has increased and been distributed over a large geographic region. These types of situations may require an increase in the scalability and availability of an application.

Scaling the Application

Content networking extends scalability services to the application by providing room for future growth without changing how the application works and with minimal changes to the network infrastructure. Scalability services include the following technologies, which will be discussed in detail throughout this book:

- **Content edge delivery**—Positioning application content away from the origin server, and in closer proximity to clients, scales the application by offloading requests to the content network.

■ **Enhanced content delivery with IP multicast, stream-splitting, and resource reservation**—IP multicast and stream-splitting scales the network by avoiding replication of identical flows over the same network link, thus minimizing end-to-end bandwidth consumption of content delivered to a large number of users. Resource reservation scales the application by manipulating network parameters to expedite application traffic delivery.

■ **Content transformation and prioritization**—Transformation provides conversion of content within the network without further burdening of origin servers. Prioritization enables custom network delivery of application traffic.

■ **Flash crowd protection**—Protection against sudden, but valid, traffic spikes directed toward an application is important to maintaining service levels to customers.

Increasing Application Availability

The general idea behind designing a system for availability is the addition of one or more components that are more or less identical to the first, without changing the overall structure of the existing individual components.

Availability services include the following, which will be discussed throughout this book:

■ **Content switching**—Increases availability by replicating origin server content across numerous identical systems, either within the same data center or across globally distributed data centers.

■ **Session redundancy**—Session redundancy provides failover from one network device, such as a firewall or load balancer, to an identical device without dropping existing TCP connections.

■ **Router redundancy**—Protocols, such as Hot Standby Router Protocol (HSRP) and Virtual Router Redundancy Protocol (VRRP), provide router gateway redundancy by having two routers or load balancers share a virtual IP (VIP) and MAC address for clients to use as their default gateway. If either fails, the other will take over within seconds.

■ **IP routing redundancy**—Dynamic IP routing protocols, such as OSPF, EIGRP, and IS-IS, provide availability within a routing domain by maintaining multiple paths to each network in the routing table.

■ **Layer 2 switching redundancy**—Spanning tree and Cisco Etherchannel provides Layer 2 redundancy in a switched environment.

Availability does not necessary follow scalability. For example, you can scale the disk drive capacity of a computer system by adding another hard drive, but if any one of those drives fails, loss of data is certain. Only when replication across the system occurs, such as with use of the

RAID protocol in this example, is availability possible. Router gateway redundancy has been around since the mid-1990s, with such protocols as HSRP and VRRP. However, application redundancy built directly into the network is a newer concept that follows the same basic premise. That is, it enables any individual component to fail without significantly affecting overall performance. In the same way that HSRP protects against network faults, application redundancy provides application and business continuity in the event of unexpected application failure.

Scheduled hitless application upgrades to replicated origin servers are possible with content networking availability services. By taking one server down at a time and allowing existing connections to complete prior to upgrading, the entire server farm remains available. Chapter 9, "Introducing Streaming Media," discusses Cisco's content networking availability services.

Looking at some simple probabilities, let us say that a single origin server is shown to be available 95.5 percent of the time, based on the empirical behavior data of the application. The 4.5 percent downtime in this example may account for scheduled server upgrades and unexpected system crashes. A simple formula to estimate the probability of an entire server farm failing is

$$P_{Serverfarm\_Failure} = 1 - P_{Individual\_Failure}{}^n = 1 - (1 - P_{Individual\_Success})^n$$

In this formula, n is the number of redundant servers and $P_{Individual\_Success}$ is the proportion of time that the original server is measured as available.

Replicating the system above and distributing load between two identical servers will provide $1 - (1 - 0.955)^2 = 0.99798$ or 99.937 percent availability. In order to achieve "five nines of availability," or 99.999 percent uptime, how many servers are needed? With three servers, we would have $1 - (1 - 0.955)^3 = 0.99990 = 99.998$ percent, and with four servers, $1 - (1 - 0.995)^4 = 0.99999 = 99.999$ percent. Therefore, with this simple formula, four redundant servers are required to provide 99.999 percent availability. But is this math a practical way to calculate availability? The answer is: it depends. Balancing the load across numerous identical servers is not necessarily transparent at the application level. Depending on the type of application, its logic may require modification in order to support a load balanced environment. As a result, the probability of failure may not decrease as steadily for certain applications as for others, when new nodes are added to the farm.

When designing a network application, there are many questions for you to consider in addition to those addressed by the simple math discussed previously:

■ What is the type of application?

■ Where should the content be located and is local high-availability sufficient or should cross-site availability be considered?

■ What are the security concerns and is encryption necessary?

Throughout this book, these questions and more like them will be answered when discussing concepts and configuring content network examples and scenarios.

Bandwidth and Response Times

In the 1990s, users accepted waiting upwards to 10 seconds for viewable content to download to browsers or for network file copies to complete. With the inexpensive increases in bandwidth availability to the desktop, which now reach gigabits per second, and through enhanced last-mile Internet access technologies, waiting more than a few seconds is no longer acceptable. However, within the network core, building additional infrastructure to increase bandwidth and decrease response times can be extremely expensive. Fortunately, in the past, various technologies have been used to make upgrades less expensive. Consider the following examples of using technology to increase capacity and add services without requiring modification to the existing infrastructure:

- Voice over IP (VoIP) for converging voice into existing IP networks makes it possible to avoid the need to maintain a separate analog voice network. Note that a significant investment in the existing IP network is essential before VoIP services are rolled out.

- Storage Area Networking (SAN) for transporting storage communication protocols, such as Small Computer System Interface (SCSI) and Fibre Channel over existing IP networks, uses existing high-availability networks for storage.

- For cross-continent satellite links, 500 millisecond round trip time (RTT) is common, which can cause issues for some delay-sensitive TCP-based applications. Applications can create multiple TCP streams that increase window sizes and other TCP-based solutions to circumvent these issues. The expensive alternative is to install cross-continent submarine fiber optics.

- Modem data compression methods increase the capacity of dedicated dialup lines.

- Emerging Internet last-mile technologies, such as aDSL, are used to better use available frequency on existing telephone lines to support data and analog voice simultaneously.

In a similar fashion, content networking makes better use of existing infrastructure by using technology instead of brute network upgrades. Content access is accelerated and bandwidth costs are saved by copying content in closer proximity to the requesting clients. Placing content surrogates toward the edge of the network and away from the central location decreases end-to-end packet latency. Furthermore, placing content at the edge eliminates the need to transit the WAN, enabling other types of traffic to use the WAN and possibly eliminate the need to upgrade WAN capacity.

Customization and Prioritization

As you will see throughout this book, inserting intelligence and decision-making capabilities into a network is central to the concept of content networking. Adding intelligence to the network while leaving the origin servers free to provide the services they were designed to perform is vital to the enhancement of application performance. In particular, customization and prioritization offers many benefits to applications that require increased efficiency.

Two forms of customization are available with content networking: request redirection and automatic content transformation.

- **Request redirection**—Clients requesting content can be redirected by the content network to various versions of an application, based on the following client criteria:

  — Spoken languages and geographic locations

  — Browser/media player types and cookies

  — Phone and PDA features, such as screen resolutions and operating systems

  Request redirection is beneficial because application developers need only create multiple versions of the same content and publish them to separate application servers. The customization is transparent to clients with different criteria. The various versions appear to be the same, because the name and IP address used to access the application are the same.

- **Automatic content transformation**—Content transformations by the network can be transparent to the clients and origin servers. A popular example of this is transformation of content from one markup language to another. The criteria for this example can be client browser or media player type.

To provide prioritization to application traffic, you can enable various QoS mechanisms within the network:

- **Packet Queuing and Scheduling**—Various content networking technologies can be used to classify applications into categories. Once applications are classified, the network can use these categories to sort applications into delivery priority and queue for transmission on the link.

- **Resource Reservation Protocol (RSVP)**—RSVP enables an application to allocate bandwidth on the network prior to sending data. When the data is sent, the network will send the traffic based on the promised bandwidth from the original reservation request.

- **Traffic Shaping and Policing**—The network can restrict available bandwidth for specific applications using shaping and policing. Shaping provides soft limits on bandwidth consumption and enables applications to rise above given thresholds. Traffic policing is strict and will thus drop traffic when thresholds are reached.

Please refer to Chapter 4, "Exploring Security Technologies and Network Infrastructure Designs," for information on these QoS technologies.

Security, Auditing, and Monitoring

Given the public nature of the Internet, secure communication is a high priority for organizations with publicly available services. For any organization investing resources in developing products and services protecting them from ending up in unwanted hands are critical steps in its network design.

However, securing a network is not a trivial task. A typical enterprise network may include e-mail, database transactions, web content, video, and instant messaging. The vast number of tools available for designing and implementing network security from different vendors makes the security design task even more difficult. To protect your network, Cisco offers numerous levels of security for deploying secure content networks.

Securing Content on the Network

Cisco SAFE Security Blueprint for Enterprises discusses Cisco's security solutions in terms of practical scenarios that apply to the majority of enterprise networks. The SAFE architecture highlights every basic security measure available for Cisco networks and recommends configuration options for deploying secure networks. These recommendations also pertain to designing and deploying content networks.

On all fronts of the design, successfully securing Cisco content networks requires security at all layers of the OSI model. To reduce the chance of security problems occurring and to help detect them when they do occur, you can use TCP/IP filtering and network security auditing.

TCP/IP Filtering

Access Control Lists (ACLs) in Cisco IOS are useful for permitting or denying requests to services that are available within the network. Because standard ACLs are stateless, TCP flows are not stored in memory, and every packet is applied to the ACL regardless of the TCP flow it is a part of. On the other hand, stateful ACLs provide various means to track TCP flows to ensure that packets belong to a valid flow before filtering traffic.

An important factor to consider when performing TCP/IP filtering is whether IP subnets are used to divide servers into groups. If not, and there are no plans to feasibly subnet the IP address space, firewalls operating transparently, at Layer 2 of the OSI model, can be used instead. Layer 2 firewalls are convenient for environments in which the IP addressing scheme is not subnetted, but servers are logically grouped according to the required security policies. The server groups can be cabled to different firewall ports and filtered according to appropriate security policies. This gives the ability to statefully secure groups from one another, even if they are on the same IP subnet.

To group servers based on IP subnets in a switched environment, use virtual LANs (VLAN). You can use VLANs within Cisco IOS ACLs or firewalls to either statelessly or statefully control traffic between logical groups of clients and origin servers. To further secure traffic *within* a VLAN, use private VLANs (PVLAN). PVLANs prevent malicious behavior between hosts on the same VLAN, by blocking all traffic between private switch ports, and enabling only traffic that originates from these ports to traverse configurable public ports.

Network Security Auditing

Various forms of network auditing are available to designers of Cisco networks:

- **Syslog and TCP/IP connection auditing**—When security issues arise, audit log entries can be extremely valuable in troubleshooting—either during or after an attack. Most firewalls can log invalid connection attempts, in addition to other known anomalous behaviors. For example, when specific ACL rules are violated, IP address and port information of the source and destination hosts at the time of violation can be configured to be logged to a Syslog server.

  Additionally, denial of service (DoS) attack awareness is crucial to any content network deployment. Whether they are low bandwidth or distributed, DoS attacks can bring network operations to a halt within minutes of their onset. In the event of an attack, influence can be minimized using various design techniques and disaster recovery methods, including:

  — Manually monitoring firewall connection levels or audit log entries or both

  — Using the Cisco Intrusion Prevention System (IPS) security appliances to monitor the incoming network for DoS traffic

  — Using Cisco Intrusion Detection Systems (IDS) to verify traffic against known DoS signatures

  — Using the Cisco Self-Defending Network architecture

- **Intrusion Detection Systems**—Firewalls and ACLs are excellent at filtering unwanted TCP/IP activity. They are not, however, able to detect network violations at the application layer. These types of upper-layer violations can be detected using IDSs. An IDS can be inserted in to a network to listen to incoming traffic for known malicious activity. Whereas criteria for allowing traffic in to a network with ACLs are established by user-defined rules at the TCP/IP layer, the IDS bases its criteria on signatures.

  Signatures are created by Cisco and can be enabled on the IDS. Depending on the applications in the environment, certain signatures may provide more value than others. They are frequently updated as new exploits are discovered and are made available for download on Cisco.com, sometimes within hours of the discovery of the vulnerability.

■ **Self-Defending Networks**—Instead of signature matching, analysis of the behavior of traffic avoids the need to maintain signature updates and thereby reduces operational costs and threats from unknown exploits. IDSs protect against known exploits but allow unknown attacks, referred to as *day-zero attacks*, to harm the network. Cisco's security prevention solutions provides day-zero protection with the expansion of its security product portfolio to include the technologies in the Cisco Self-Defending Network strategy. This strategy combines numerous security technologies together to form a hybrid security system that secures all layers of the OSI model.

Securing Client and Origin Server Content

Typically, securing network resources is only a first step in securing a content network. Intelligent systems for security vulnerability detection and counter-measuring on the client and origin server are becoming more important than ever. The origin servers must be secured from both physical and network intrusions. Physical security includes measures such as providing only key personnel with physical access to critical data center locations and limiting packet sniffing tools to specific users. Avoidance of switch monitor ports and the use of hubs, where possible, will also aid in protecting against unwanted sniffers in the network.

For server security, Cisco provides server agent software based on the Self-Defending Network architecture. This agent can identify malicious network behavior, thereby eliminating known and day-zero security risks and thus help to reduce operational costs. Cisco server agents combine multiple security functions to provide host intrusion prevention through behavior analysis, malicious mobile code protection, firewall capabilities, operating system integrity checks, and audit log consolidation.

The following additional security features are key in protecting Cisco content networks:

■ **Secure Sockets Layer (SSL)**—SSL is used to secure traffic over a public network. Numerous content networking devices are capable of performing SSL in either hardware or software, to offload the complex SSL processing from application servers.

■ **URL Filtering for Employee Internet Management (EIM)**—Content networking devices interact with third-party vendors to provide network-based URL filtering. With EIM, transaction logs track which users accessed which sites and can help monitor employee usage of the Internet.

■ **Virus Scanning**—Content networking devices also interact with third-party vendors to provide network-based virus scanning. You should consider employing a network-based virus scanner to ensure that viruses are detected and removed before entering your e-mail server or client systems.

■ **Authentication, Authorization, and Accounting (AAA)**—Methods for the authentication process when users request objects from a content network are varied. Insight in to which environments are most appropriate is a valued asset in designing secure content networks. Given security issues related to malicious user logins in a corporate environment, it is highly important to have HTTP and RTSP user authentication and URL filtering in a content networking deployment. You can also use accounting to help provide an audit trail for logins into a device, such as a router or switch, indicating what commands were issued and by whom.

Monitoring, Administration, and Reporting

Monitoring the health of the network and origin servers is important to ensure that application information is constantly being transported reliably. Various network and application monitoring tools that are available for use in monitoring a content network are described in the sections that follow.

Network Monitoring and Administration

Simple Network Management Protocol (SNMP), Syslog, and Network Time Protocol (NTP) are available for network monitoring.

SNMP is a standard messaging protocol for polling and receiving traps from network devices. SNMP managers can poll devices proactively for network information, such as bandwidth and CPU usage, to provide alerts in the event of receiving abnormal data. Historical archiving of polled data provides valuable information for administering and troubleshooting a network.

SNMP managers can also intelligently parse incoming traps from network devices and take action or recommend potential solutions. Programmatic interaction with SNMP managers is an invaluable means to provide intelligent automatic recovery in the event of failure. For example, most SNMP managers can run a program when an event is triggered from a trap received from a network device. The program can perform actions such as sending an e-mail to any individuals responsible for the network device, rebooting the device, or other actions that are pertinent to the event.

Syslog is a protocol used to capture events from network devices. Events such as ACL hits, network logins, packet loss, and interface and routing protocol transitions can be generated by network devices and sent to Syslog servers within the corporate LAN. These logs can then be used for post-mortem problem determination, to determine what failed, why it failed, and how the system can be designed to better prevent a catastrophic outage in the future. SNMP traps and Syslog are similar in that they both provide event-driven alarms when an error occurs in the network device.

NTP is necessary in secure environments to ensure that all time clocks in the network are synchronized. This way, log entries from different yet dependant devices can be traced precisely during the troubleshooting process.

Securing the administration of content networking devices is very important, both in-band and out-of-band.

■   If in-band management using Telnet or HTTP over a public network is available, cleartext passwords can potentially be read if intercepted. Secure Shell (SSH) can be used as an alternative to Telnet, and SSL in the place of HTTP, to provide encryption of the administration data that will traverse a public network. Additionally, the SNMP standard provides a means to secure the administrative passwords and the integrity of SNMP messages in version 3 of the protocol.

■   Out-of-band serial management is a secured network administrative tool. As long as the passwords are kept secret, they cannot be intercepted in transit over a private dial-up connection, or a direct console connection into the network device.

Application Monitoring and Administration

Application monitoring is performed separately from network monitoring. How closely monitoring is performed depends on the criticality, performance, and load of the server.

Most third-party application monitors have the ability to

■   Monitor availability and performance quality for applications, either in- or out-of-band.

■   Send alerts when application failures occur, or when thresholds are exceeded.

■   Recover failed applications automatically.

■   Provide historical reports to graph the behavioral trends of the applications.

In-band application monitors simulate valid requests to the server, check the responses, send alerts, and optionally perform actions to aid in remedying or troubleshooting the issue. The types of requests and responses depend on the applications being monitored. Possibly one of the most useful results of these tests is the measurement of latency. Because many applications are sensitive to latency, monitoring this parameter enables a Network Operations Center (NOC) to take action before clients perceive any latency issues associated with the particular application.

Out-of-band application monitoring is similar to network out-of-band monitoring in that it is used to monitor and recover servers over an interface other than the one providing the content to clients. The advantage is that, even when completely down, the origin server can still be monitored and recovered. The drawback is that often additional hardware is required.

Cisco Content Networking Solutions

Cisco offers complete solutions to meet customer's business needs, including IP telephony, security, optical, and storage solutions. Cisco also offers complete content networking solutions in order to achieve application acceleration.

The following networking environments are available for Cisco's content network solutions:

■ **Enterprise Campus**—Typically an environment that includes a main building to house central institutional or corporate resources. Smaller buildings are served by the main building and contain only client workstations.

■ **Enterprise Edge**—An Internet data center environment owned and maintained by the enterprise, normally residing in the main campus building.

■ **Branch Office**—Remote, or regional, office locations connect to the main campus or head-office location through WAN links.

■ **Internet Data Center**—Third-party data center environments for which enterprises may outsource facility, bandwidth, server hardware, and application hosting services.

Two or more of these types of data centers, connected over a geographically distributed network and enabled with the ACNS software, together make an Internet Content Delivery Network (ICDN). ICDNs require numerous content networking technologies to work together with unique content billing requirements. Content-based billing is necessary in an ICDN to generate revenue for customer bandwidth, content rule, and cache hit/miss usage as well as to apply various QoS policies based on different price plans. Numerous Cisco certified partners offer solutions that integrate with Cisco's content networking products for content billing.

The first three environments, when enabled with Cisco's content networking software, together form an Enterprise Content Delivery Network (ECDN).

The primary differences between ECDNs and ICDNs are the billing requirements, mentioned previously. That is, the software is the same in both, but in an ICDN scenario additional software for content billing is necessary. For details on each of these four environments see Chapter 4.

Content Switching

Content is switched in much the same way that frames are switched in Layer 2 Ethernet networks. With Ethernet, frames are forwarded to an appropriate switch port based on information in the frame header. That is, the switches provide Layer 2 intelligence to the routers in the network. In comparison, content switching provides Layers 5–7 intelligence to the origin servers and clients in the network. The content is inspected and forwarded to the most appropriate system based on information in the packet headers and payload. Content switching includes replication of a single system, formation of a group of systems of identical functionality, and distribution of client requests across them.

Content switching is used in the following scenarios:

■ Server and Cache Load Balancing (SLB)

■ Firewall Load Balancing (FWLB) and VPN Load Balancing

■ Global Server Load Balancing (GSLB)

Server Load Balancing (SLB)

SLB devices use health metrics, such as server response time and number of connections, as criteria for determining which origin server should receive a request for content. The health of the server is determined based on responses received from the servers in reply to health-check traffic generated by the content switch. Users are directed to the best origin server available at the moment of the request.

The challenges associated with balancing requests across multiple systems are addressed with the various content switching algorithms discussed in Chapter 10, "Exploring Server Load Balancing." You can also load balance caches using SLB devices and Web Cache Control Protocol (WCCP), as you will learn about in Chapter 13, "Delivering Cached and Streaming Media."

Firewall Load Balancing (FWLB) and VPN Load Balancing

Firewalls often contain built-in failover mechanisms for firewall availability services. For example, the Cisco PIX firewall uses a proprietary stateful failover mechanism for the standby firewall to know when to take over processing for the active firewall. Technically, you also can use FWLB to manage availability, but in most cases Cisco recommends using its proprietary mechanism for Cisco PIX failover. Furthermore, scaling the Cisco PIX firewalls by upgrading to a higher series firewall is often less costly in terms of financial investment in the hardware and resources required to manage the design. Load balancing numerous lower-end Cisco PIX firewalls with content switches requires much more overall hardware and resources to manage the solution. Unless many millions of concurrent connections and many gigabits per second of bandwidth are required, the highest series of Cisco PIX firewall should be able to handle the load. FWLB is more useful in the following circumstances:

■ Scalability and availability services when firewalls other than the Cisco PIX are used.

■ Migration from one firewall vendor to another.

■ Load balancing firewalls from multiple vendors in order to provide a diverse security scheme.

FWLB provides scalability and availability to firewalls in the same way that the SLB is used for origin servers, but with slightly more complexity and involved configurations. For example, FWLB does not support asynchronous routing. That is, the return traffic of a connection must be routed back through the originally selected firewall, in order for the firewall to reconcile traffic from like connections; otherwise, the firewall will drop the traffic. Additionally, "buddy" TCP connections from applications that originate connections in the reverse direction of the original connection, such as Active-FTP, must be sent through the originally selected firewall.

Cisco content switching also supports load balancing of signaling and data packets of VPN protocols, such as IPsec, Point-to-Point Protocol (PPTP), and Layer 2 Tunneling Protocol (L2TP) for scalability and redundancy of VPN devices.

Global Server Load Balancing

Although origin server redundancy within a single data center is achieved with SLB, global server load balancing (GSLB) is required when the following issues occur:

■ The entire infrastructure that houses the server farm goes down or the data center itself experiences a disastrous power outage or fire. The developers of ARPANET at the US Department of Defense (DoD) used this concept in developing IP in the 1960s. The idea was that, if one US communications hub was destroyed during war, another available hub would route information seamlessly in its place. The concepts of disaster recovery in GSLB follow the same basic principle as used by the US DoD but at Layers 5–7 of the OSI model.

■ Response times for content or DNS requests or both from clients in geographically dispersed locations cause perceived performance degradation. In the same manner that content edge delivery resolves response time issues by placing content closer to the clients, GSLB places the data centers themselves in closer proximity to clients.

■ The capacity of the current data center location has reached its bandwidth or physical limits and cannot handle an increase in load. Additional load can be relieved from the current data center to other data centers with GSLB, which enables the required growth.

Application and Content Networking System

The Application and Content Networking System (ACNS) provides customers an integrated system that consists of content edge delivery, content distribution, and content routing. The following solutions are available to a network installed with ACNS software:

■ **E-learning**—Providing educational material with an e-learning solution realizes major cost savings related to travel and accommodations for employees or students to attend in-person training.

- **Corporate communications**—Distribution of company events, messages, and news with ACNS enables employees to quickly adapt to changes in corporate initiative and structure.

- **Point-of-sale videos and web kiosks**—Retailers can use point-of-sale videos and web kiosks for customer-directed advertising or for employee product and procedural training.

- **File/software distribution and access**—Response times for resources from branch offices using ACNS and, in particular, the Cisco Wide Area File Services (WAFS) can be reduced. WAN bandwidth to the branches can be expedited with these features as well.

Content Edge Delivery

Most medium to large enterprises require regional office locations in closer proximity to areas of potential sales than the headquarters location. However, mission critical corporate applications, such as intranet web portals, Enterprise Resource Planning (ERP), Customer Relationship Management (CRM), and the database and file servers that store data for these applications, reside at the headquarters. Similarly, other applications, such as corporate Internet access, e-mail, and video streaming, are also normally located at the corporate headquarters. In most cases, installing these applications in the regional branches proves too costly for the majority of enterprises.

However, employees at these locations demand the level of service they would have if the applications were installed locally. Realizing that revenue will most definitely be affected by performance decreases and increases in bandwidth usage at the edges of the network, corporate executives also expect high availability and performance at these branch locations. With content edge delivery, content is served directly from the branch locations, in closer proximity to the employees.

There are two common content edge delivery technologies employed to solve issues surrounding bandwidth and latency issues in branch locations:

- Content Caching

- Streaming Media Delivery

Content Caching

Caching is by far the most commonly used feature in the short history of content networking topics. Generally speaking, the nature of content requests leans toward the popular 80/20 axiom in network computing: 80 percent of requests are for 20 percent of the content. To decrease server load, content is offloaded from an origin server to a device whose sole job is to deliver frequently requested content objects, in closer proximity to clients. Content is populated into the caches on-demand, as clients make the requests. How requests for content are handled by the local cache as opposed to the origin server itself is discussed in Chapter 13.

When users request an object from an edge delivery device, how can they be sure that it is identical to the content that resides on the origin server? Intelligent content freshness determination in globally and locally cached networks is essential to provide users with the most up-to-date version of the requested object. Therefore, any changes in the original content can be dynamically detected and uploaded by the edge caches, transparently to both client and server.

As with most aspects of network design, content edge delivery deployments also require attention to ensuring high availability and fast performance. As such, specific local content switching mechanisms are also applicable in designing availability into an edge deployment.

Streaming Media Delivery

Streaming media solves major issues with viewing video media on a network. Users no longer have to wait for downloads to complete before viewing video content online. Furthermore, the client video player displays video frames directly to the user as packets arrive on the network, which is similar to standard television broadcasting. As a result, live and scheduled video feeds are made possible with streaming media.

Streaming media benefits from content edge delivery by ensuring that only a single stream of video content traverses the network at any given time, resulting in bandwidth cost savings. Furthermore, streaming media can also benefit from caching, by storing the video feed locally for later viewing by clients.

Cisco's streaming media solution as supplied by ACNS within Content Engines, Cisco IP/TV, and industry partner streaming software, such as Real Networks, will be detailed in Chapter 13.

Content Distribution and Routing

Content distribution occurs in advance of client requests in order to position content into desirable locations within the network. In contrast, recall on-demand caching, in which content is populated to edge delivery devices as requests for content are fulfilled by the origin servers.

The act of distributing content throughout the network can be as taxing on networking resources as its delivery. Chapter 6, "Ensuring Content Delivery with Quality of Service," covers methods of minimizing network resource consumption during the distribution process, including IP Multicast, resource reservation, packet queuing, and scheduling.

Once the content network is populated with fresh content, requests for objects containing cached content are processed, in order to determine the best location of the requested content. In the same way that IP routers relay IP datagrams to their appropriate destination, content routers relay application messages. Content routers offer the best content to requesting clients based on factors such as geographic location, network load, and delay.

In the past, content has been a value-added service to customers. In this new millennium, content services are seen as a potential revenue generator. As such, third-party advertisement insertion, URL filtering, virus scanning, and e-mail spam filtering using various technologies can be performed on the content before delivery to the client. The section called "Enabling Transparent Value-Added Services on your CEs" of Chapter 13 discusses how these value-added services are performed.

Content Network Partnership Program

The Cisco Content Networking Partner Program enables third-party software companies to extend the Cisco ACNS infrastructure to provide complete end-to-end solutions to meet customers' business needs. The group of partner companies is known as an ecosystem, and each must fulfill certification criteria set by Cisco in order to become certified for membership. The main criterion is the use of standard interfaces to interoperate with Cisco's content networking products. The benefit of membership is the marketing program in place to promote partner software products coupled with Cisco's content networking infrastructure. In addition to this, customer solutions are guaranteed rigorous testing and verification before deployment.

End-to-end solutions offered by ecosystem partners may include e-learning, corporate communications, content filtering capabilities, and software and file distribution. These solutions can be offered to the customer as a managed service, located in the partner's data center, or installed as an enterprise server solution, requiring dedicated server hardware behind the customers' own firewall. Either way, Cisco's ACNS architecture is at the heart of the solution and provides the intelligence to ensure that the content is delivered reliably and efficiently to the end users.

Partners can offer solutions using any of the following content delivery categories:

- Content Management

- Content Distribution

- Content Providers

- E-Learning Applications

- Content Filtering and Scanning

Content Management

Content management partners offer applications and databases used for indexing, searching, and retrieving content. A typical customer may be a corporation that requires rapid distribution and retrieval of audio/video content for corporate communications and training.

Content Distribution

Content distribution partners provide efficient mechanisms to replicate content over low bandwidth and unreliable network links for delivery to Cisco content networks. These partners may have patent application protocols to improve efficiency and ensure security in distributing information to remote sites.

Content Providers

Content providers create content for training and corporate communications, such as video-on-demand, webcasts, or Macromedia Flash-based presentations. Providing packaged content for e-learning, corporate communications, product marketing, and sales support gives organizations the ability to concentrate on operational aspects of business rather than the production of content.

Producing educational material electronically and making it interactive and accessible for viewing anytime reduces training costs associated with instructor-led training and increases information retention rates among learners.

E-Learning Applications

An e-learning application is an enterprise-wide learning system containing tools for creating, delivering, and managing content, for live and on-demand training or information-exchange portals. The application may contain event administration, promotion, registration, and management functionality for company-wide collaborative events. Organizations may centrally prescribe personalized training to individuals or groups of employees on standard employee procedures, new-hire training, and mentoring. Organizations are also able to track employee competencies and certifications with an e-learning application.

Content Filtering and Scanning

Content filtering provides a means to control a user's online accessibility to content, increase employee productivity, and eliminate the organization's legal liability of inappropriate Internet access and instant messaging. These tools enable administration of access settings to enforce an organization's standards and ethics. Reporting on employee usage is also available.

Content scanning involves, as the name indicates, capabilities to scan content for anomalous items, such as viruses, before sending across the network.

Summary

This chapter introduces and justifies content networking in terms of various technologies used to enhance applications. Learning lessons from other various Internetworking technologies, such as SAN and IP telephony, content networking uses existing networking infrastructure to

- Reduce bandwidth and response times.

- Increase application scalability and availability.

- Manipulate network parameters to enhance application content delivery.

- Provide customization and prioritization using various technologies, such as QoS and traffic shaping.

Network security, auditing, and management are also important aspects of content networking. The Cisco SAFE architecture offers numerous solutions for securing and managing content networks.

Providing end-to-end networking solutions is a must for vendors competing in today's diverse networking climate. Cisco's content networking solution portfolio includes the Cisco ACNS architecture coupled with numerous certified ecosystem partners' software.

Review Questions

1. In which layers of the OSI model does content networking reside?

2. What are the four main purposes and goals of content networking?

3. Estimate how many servers are required to provide four nines of availability for an application known to fail 11.5 percent of the time?

4. What is the difference between application scalability and availability?

5. How are bandwidth and response times reduced in a content network?

6. What is the main difference between an ICDN and an ECDN?

7. Name four scenarios in which content can be switched.

8. Name four solutions that Cisco ACNS can provide.

Recommended Reading

SAFE blueprint: http://www.cisco.com/safe

ACNS architecture: http://www.cisco.com/go/content

Part II: Networking Fundamentals

Chapter Goals

This chapter will give you an overview of networking terms and concepts of the TCP/IP protocol suite against the backdrop of Layers 1–4 of the Open System Interconnection (OSI) model. The following topics are covered:

- **Physical Layer**—The physical layer covers the mechanical and electrical properties of the physical medium with respect to copper and fiber cabling specifications, binary signaling, and encoding technologies.

- **Data Link Layer**—The Ethernet data link layer is used predominantly in content networking implementations. Ethernet data link layer protocols, such as Ethernet II and 802.3, are discussed.

- **Network Layer**—The TCP/IP network layer is composed of IP, ARP, IGMP, and ICMP. These protocols are discussed in detail in this chapter.

- **Transport Layer**—Numerous TCP terms and concepts are illustrated with graphic real-world examples.

- **Putting It All Together with a Detailed Network Trace**—To glue the numerous terms and concepts discussed in this chapter together, a TCP/IP protocol stack trace is performed and described in detail.

CHAPTER 2

Exploring the Network Layers

In this chapter you will learn about the lower four layers of the TCP/IP protocol suite. Although content networks operate primarily at Layers 5–7, Layers 1–4 provide the foundation of content networking technologies. The TCP/IP protocols discussed in this chapter are related to the OSI model as outlined in Table 2-1.

Table 2-1 *TCP/IP Protocols in Relation to the OSI Reference Model*

OSI Model Layer	TCP/IP Protocols
Transport	**TCP**
	Three-Way Handshake
	Sliding Window
	Slow Start
	Congestion Avoidance
	Fast Retransmit and Fast Recovery
	Maximum Segment Size
	TCP over Satellite and Window Scale Option (WSOpt)
	Pragmatic General Multicast (PGM)
	User Datagram Protocol (UDP)
Data Link	**Ethernet Data Link**
	Ethernet II
	802.3 Media Access Control (MAC)
	802.2 Logical Link Control (LLC)
	Carrier Sensing Multiple Access/Collision Detection (CSMA/CD)
Network	**IP**
	Internet Control Management Protocol (ICMP)
	Internet Group Management Protocol (IGMP)
	Address Resolution Protocol (ARP)
	Protocol Independent Multicast (PIM)

continues

Table 2-1   *TCP/IP Protocols in Relation to the OSI Reference Model (Continued)*

OSI Model Layer	TCP/IP Protocols
Physical	**Ethernet Media**
	Unshielded Twisted Pair (UTP)
	Single Mode and Multimode Fiber
	Ethernet Signaling and Coding
	Manchester Encoded Signaling
	Multilevel Transition Level 3 (MLT-3) Signaling
	Non-Return to Zero (NRZ) Signaling
	NRZ-Inverted (NRZ-I) Signaling
	4B/5B Coding
	8B/10B Coding
	Pulse Amplitude Modulation Level 5 (PAM5)

Ethernet Physical and Data Link Layers

Most professional positions in the Internetworking industry require that individuals have a working knowledge of the physical layer. Often, network cable installation and maintenance is the responsibility of the network administrator or manager, in addition to specific responsibilities associated with the particular role. This is also the case with most content networking roles, because installing and maintaining content networking products also requires physical layer cable and network interface management.

Ethernet is the predominant protocol used in the content networking solutions. Figure 2-1 shows how the Ethernet layers coincide with the data link and physical layers of the OSI model.

Physical Layer

The first layer of the TCP/IP protocol suite includes the *mechanical* and *electrical* properties for sending and receiving information between Ethernet network devices.

Ethernet Mechanical Properties—The Media

The mechanical properties for Ethernet depend on the type of physical medium, with copper, fiber, and wireless media available. Although wireless is increasing in popularity for desktop connectivity, copper and fiber are the most popular physical layer media used for content network deployments.

Figure 2-1   *The Ethernet Protocols in Relation to the OSI Reference Model*

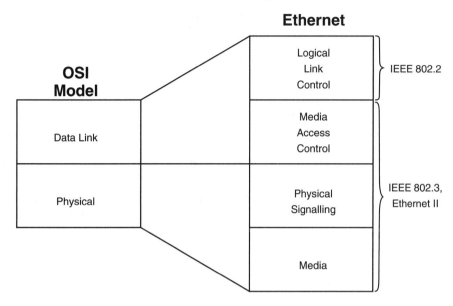

Ethernet over Copper

For Ethernet over copper, unshielded twisted pair (UTP) network cables are most common. UTP includes four twisted pairs of small copper wire, with an 8-pin RJ-45 connector at both ends to connect to network interfaces. For the 10 Mbps over UTP (10BASE-T) and 100 Mbps over UTP (100BASE-T) standards, only two pairs of the four are used, with one pair for transmitting and the other for receiving data. Alternatively, all four wire pairs are used for 1000 Mbps (1000BASE-T), with each pair capable of both sending and receiving data.

> **NOTE**   For Ethernet over copper, one wire of each pair is for transmitting a positive direct current (DC) voltage, and the other is for a negative DC voltage.

UTP cable pinouts refer to the position that the eight individual copper cables are inserted into the pins of an RJ-45 connector. The pinouts are the same for all Ethernet-over-copper protocols, and are given in Table 2-2.

Table 2-2   *Ethernet Pinouts for 10/100/1000 UTP Cables*

Pin	Color	Usage in 10/100BASE-T	Usage in 1000BASE-T
0	White with Orange stripe	Tx+	Bi0+
1	Orange	Tx-	Bi0-
2	White with Green stripe	Rx+	Bi1+

continues

Table 2-2 *Ethernet Pinouts for 10/100/1000 UTP Cables (Continued)*

Pin	Color	Usage in 10/100BASE-T	Usage in 1000BASE-T
3	Blue	Unused	Bi2+
4	White with Blue stripe	Unused	Bi2-
5	Green	Rx-	Bi1-
6	White with Brown Stripe	Unused	Bi3+
7	Brown	Unused	Bi3-

Figure 2-2 illustrates the groupings of the pairs within an RJ-45 connector. Although wires of the same color pairs (for example, [White with *Color-X* stripe, *Color-X*]) are twisted with each other within the cable itself, the two wires within the pair [White with Green stripe, Green] are separated and connected to pins two and five, respectively. The location of the receive (Rx), transmit (Tx), and bidirectional (Bi) signals are also given in Figure 2-2 for 10/100BASE-T and 1000BASE-T implementations.

Figure 2-2 *RJ-45 Connector Pinouts for Ethernet over Copper Using Standard UTP Cabling*

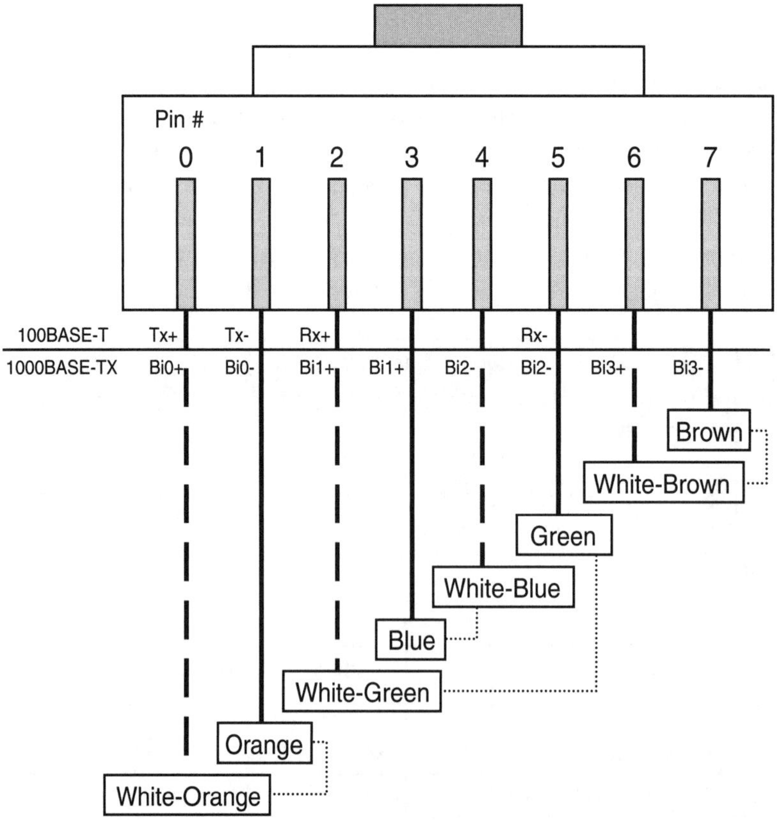

Ethernet over Fiber

Fiber-optic technologies allow rays of light to travel over hair-thin strands of glass. Light rays are guided down the core of the glass fiber. The core is surrounded by additional fiber called the cladding that traps the light within core. The technique for containing light waves completely within the fiber core is called "total internal reflection." That is, if light rays are emitted at particular angles in relation to the center of the core, they will not *refract* in to the cladding, but will rather *reflect* back in to the core fiber. Figure 2-3 shows the various components of a fiber-optic cable, and how total internal reflection compares to light refraction in to the fiber cladding.

Figure 2-3   *Fiber Cross-Section Showing Fiber Core, Cladding, Total Internal Reflection, and Light Dispersion*

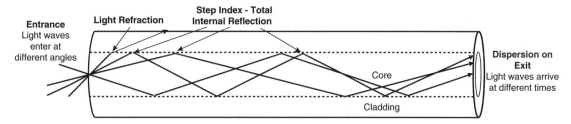

Ethernet over fiber commonly uses multimode (MM) and single mode (SM) fiber. MM fiber is designed to allow multiple light rays (called modes) through the core simultaneously. MM comes in two forms: *step index* and *graded index*. Step index fiber has the same fiber properties throughout core, resulting in a sudden refractive "step" into the cladding, as suggested previously by Figure 2-3. Rays entering at sharper angles will travel a further distance and, therefore, will arrive at the receiving end at a later point time than rays entering at duller angles. This difference in ray arrival times is known as dispersion. Step index is an older and slower technology than graded index, with the light source operating up to only 200 MHz, and is rarely used today because of dispersion.

With graded index, variations are imposed in the composition of the glass in the core, resulting in a gradual increase in refractive index toward the core. The refractive index is the degree to which the fiber will bend the light rays. This results in a gradual narrowing of rays toward the center of the fiber. Figure 2-4 shows how the rays are guided through the core of the graded index fiber.

Figure 2-4   *Graded Index MM Fiber Cross-Section*

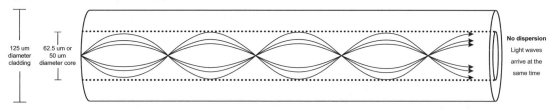

An important property of graded MM fiber optics is that rays travel more slowly and degrade faster toward the center of the core where the refractive index is highest. In Figure 2-4, although the outer light rays travel a longer distance than the inner rays, they are further away from the center and therefore travel faster than the inner rays. The result is that all light rays will arrive at the other end of the fiber at approximately the same time, thus overcoming the dispersion that occurs in step index fiber. Also notice that the rays no longer travel in straight lines but follow a more snake-like path that results from gradually being bent back toward the core. The bandwidth of graded index fiber is much higher than that of step index fiber, with source lasers capable of generating signals up to frequencies of 2 gigahertz (GHz).

Two sizes of MM fiber are available: 62.5 micrometer and 50 micrometer-diameter core fibers, both with 125 micrometers of cladding. However, with SM fiber the core is reduced to 9 micrometers in diameter as illustrated in Figure 2-5, which allows only a single ray of light through the core. Indeed, with such a small diameter, only a single ray is necessary to sufficiently light-up the core in order to send a signal. In comparison, MM fiber requires numerous rays to light up the core. Furthermore, the single ray follows a direct route through the fiber; therefore, SM supports much higher frequencies (100,000 GHz+), over greater distances than MM fiber.

Figure 2-5 *SM Fiber Cross-Section*

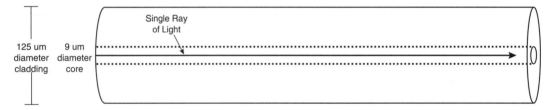

In comparison, if a single ray of light is sent straight down the center of a *graded index MM* fiber, it dissipates very quickly, because light degrades faster in the center of the MM core. In contrast, SM is able to sustain a single ray in the core because of the reduced core diameter, and the uniform fiber refractive index within the core. Additionally, dispersion is no longer an issue with SM fiber, because only a single light ray is used.

The speeds of SM fiber can exceed terabits per second (Tbps), and SM fiber supports multiple channels of bandwidth over the same fiber using dense wavelength division multiplexing (DWDM). With DWDM, multiple wavelengths of light traverse the same fiber without interfering with one another, thus providing one channel of bandwidth per wavelength.

NOTE   Comparing multiple light rays in MM fiber to multiple *wavelengths* in DWDM (over SM fiber), the different rays enter into MM fiber using the same wavelength, but at different *angles* with respect to the cladding of the fiber. However, with multiple *wavelengths* in DWDM, each wavelength is independent of other wavelengths, which allows multiple channels of bandwidth to travel straight down the center of the SM fiber core without interfering with one another.

MM fiber is used for shorter distances and lower bandwidths than SM fiber and is often used for server and desktop connectivity at 10, 100, and 1000 Mbps. MM fiber supports distances of 550 meters. SM fiber is typically used for connectivity at higher speeds and larger distances, upwards to 70 kms, between buildings or cities.

Because MM fiber has a much wider core, the area through which to emit light is much smaller, and therefore less expensive lasers are required to generate the light ray. The drawback is that numerous rays of light are required to light up the MM core in order to propagate the same signal that requires only a single ray in SM fiber.

Other important facts about fiber optics are

■ Both MM and SM fiber optical cables come in pairs, with one fiber for sending and the other for receiving.

■ The standard wavelengths for the light sources are between 850 nanometers (nm) and 1550 nm.

■ Rays are generated by either light emitting diodes (LEDs) or laser diodes (LDs). LDs are newer, more powerful, and more expensive than LEDs.

■ The connectors for fiber are SC, ST, and MTRJ connectors. Gigabit interface converters (GBICs) are used to connect these fiber connectors to Cisco hardware; standard GBICs and Small Formfactor Plugables (SFP) are available.

Ethernet Electrical Properties—The Signaling

The physical layer contains the electrical specifications and protocols that are responsible for encoding and transmitting data bits over physical wires. For Ethernet over copper, the bits are encoded and transmitted in terms of changes in direct current (DC) voltages. For Ethernet over fiber, changes in light intensity are used to convey binary data.

Most 10BASE-T implementations use Manchester encoding for signaling bit streams. This method uses transitions in the signal for encoding individual bits. Logic one is represented as an upward transition in voltage and logic zero as a downward transition. Figure 2-6 illustrates how the hexadecimal byte 0x9a (or binary byte 0b10011010) is sent using Manchester encoding.

Figure 2-6   *Sample of the Manchester Encoding Scheme Used in 10 Mbps Ethernet Data Encoding*

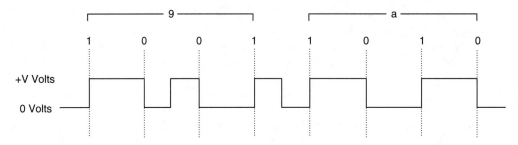

A benefit of Manchester encoding is that the speed of the clock is the same as the bandwidth transmission rate (that is, 10 Mbps is transferred using a 10 MHz clock). A drawback to Manchester encoding is that only a single bit is conveyed within a full signal wave.

To encode 100BASE-T, 4B/5B codes are used with Multi-Level Transition Level 3 (MLT-3) signaling. With MLT-3, three levels of voltage are used instead of two, as used in Manchester encoding. That is, MLT-3 cycles between –V to 0 to +V then back to –V, repeating indefinitely. Logic zero is encoded by stopping the cycle for one transition. Logic one is encoded by continuing the cycle. Before the byte is transferred with MLT-3, it is first encoded using 4B/5B encoding. With 4B/5B encoding, each hexadecimal 4-bit digit is encoded into an essentially uncorrelated 5-bit code, using the 4B/5B translation table in Table 2-3.

Table 2-3   *4B/5B Codes*

Hexadecimal Digit	4-Bit Data	5-Bit Code
0	0000	11110
1	0001	01001
2	0010	10100
3	0011	10101
4	0100	01010
5	0101	01011
6	0110	01110
7	0111	01111
8	1000	10010
9	1001	10011
a	1010	10110
b	1011	10111
c	1100	11010
d	1101	11011
e	1110	11100
f	1111	11101

The hexadecimal byte 0x9a is transferred using the codes 0b10011 and 0b10110 according to the transitions in Figure 2-7 and Figure 2-8. Figure 2-7 shows the first example with the voltage starting at 0 volts on the rise to +V volts. Figure 2-8 shows the second example with the voltage starting at –V volts. Although more bits are now being transferred (5/4ths more), the frequency of the clock is increased by the same proportion. For example, a 125 MHz clock transmits 100 Mbps of bandwidth. A benefit of 4B/5B with MLT-3 is that a full wave transmits two bits of data.

Figure 2-7 *4B/5B with the MLT-3 Encoding Scheme (Voltage Wave Starting at 0 V)*

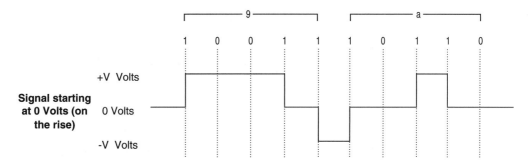

Figure 2-8 *4B/5B with the MLT-3 Encoding Scheme (Voltage Wave Starting at -V)*

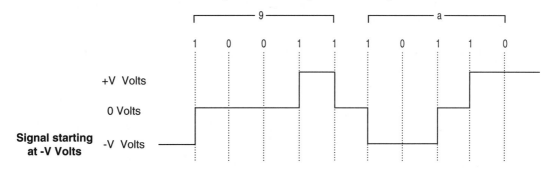

With Non-Return to Zero (NRZ) signaling, binary zero is represented as zero voltage and binary one as +V voltage. NRZ is the simplest form of bit encoding but causes problems with clock synchronization when long strings of zeros or ones are transmitted. With an uneven balance of zeros and ones, the signal generated by the source clock may become unsynchronized with the receiving clock, causing the receiver to improperly decode the bit stream. As with 4B/5B and MLT-4, for every full wave, two bits of data are sent. Figure 2-9 shows how the hexadecimal byte 0x01 is encoded with NRZ.

Figure 2-9   *NRZ Signaling with a Long String of Zeros Leading to Potential Clock Synchronization*

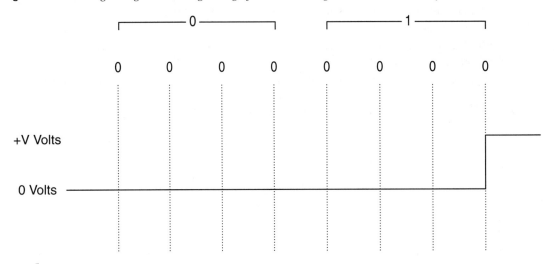

With NRZ-Inverted (NRZ-I), the binary zero is represented by no change in voltage, and binary one is represented by inverting the voltage from the previous level. NRZ-I is slightly beneficial over NRZ in cases where there are more ones than zeros in the bit stream, because more transitions are made than NRZ for long strings of ones. However, long strings of zeros still cause clock synchronization issues with NRZ-I. Figure 2-10 illustrates NRZ-I to transmit the hexadecimal byte 0xff (or 0b11111111).

Figure 2-10   *NRZ-I Encoding Resolves Clock Synchronization Issues for Long Strings of Ones*

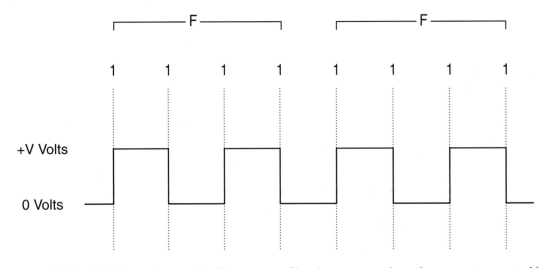

NRZ or NRZ-I must be used for Ethernet over fiber, because negative values are not supported in fiber transmission. That is, only two values are used for conveying the zeros and ones over fiber, by changing the light intensity within the fiber. For 100 Mbps over fiber (100BASE-FX), 4B/5B coding is used with NRZ-I signaling. For Gigabit Ethernet over fiber (1000BASE-SX/LX/ZX), 8B/10B coding is used with NRZ signaling. With 8B/10B, the code words are 10 bits long to convey 8 bits of data. Because the table now requires one code entry for each of the eight bit words, 2^8 (256) entries are required and therefore are not given here. The code words are formulated so that the number of zeros and ones are balanced, thus circumventing clock synchronization issues associated with NRZ.

For the hexadecimal byte 0x01, the 10-bit code is 0b0111010100 and will therefore require more transitions in the signal using 8B/10B, as illustrated in Figure 2-11, than with NRZ-I alone, as illustrated previously in Figure 2-10.

Figure 2-11 *NRZ with 8B/10B Encoding with Fewer Zeros, Thus Reducing the Risk of Clock Synchronization*

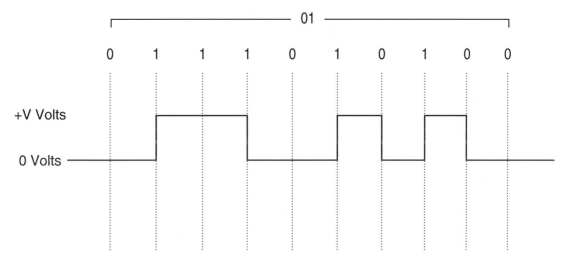

Clock synchronization is important for Gigabit Ethernet because the clock speeds are 10 times faster than that of Faster Ethernet and 100 times faster than 10 Mbps Ethernet.

Pulse Amplitude Modulation Level 5 (PAM5) signaling and coding is used for Gigabit Ethernet over copper (1000BASE-T) implementations. With PAM5, five voltage values (that is, $-2, -1, 0,$ $+1,$ and $+2$) are used to express the binary data. Using echo cancellation, PAM5 enables simultaneous transmission and reception on each wire pair. Consequently, each of the four pairs attains 250 Mbps throughput, thus achieving 1 Gbps aggregate throughput over the four pairs. In comparison to the other physical layer schemes in this chapter, the signaling and coding structure of PAM5 is very complex. Therefore, its details are left for further reading.

Organizations upgrading existing 100BASE-T networks to 1000BASE-T need not replace network UTP cables. Upgrading existing Network Interface Cards (NICs), leaving installed cabling in place, is sufficient to upgrade to 1000BASE-T.

Table 2-4 shows the physical layer specifications for prominent Ethernet standards.

Table 2-4 *Physical Layer Specifications for Ethernet*

Standard	IEEE release	Data Rate	Cable specifications	Max. Segment Length	Symbol Encoding	Data Encoding
10BASE-T	802.3i	10 Mbps	Two pairs Category 3 UTP	100 m	-	Manchester
100BASE-T	802.3u	100 Mbps	Two pairs Category 5 UTP	100 m	4B/5B	MLT-3
100BASE-FX	802.3u	100 Mbps	62.5 μm MM fiber	2 km	4B/5B	NRZ-I
1000BASE-SX	802.3z	1 Gbps	62.5 μm MM fiber	275 m	8B/10B	NRZ
			50 μm MM fiber	550m		
1000BASE-LX	802.3z	1 Gbps	62.5 μm MM fiber	550 m	8B/10B	NRZ
			50 μm MM fiber	550 m		
			9 μm SM fiber	10 km		
1000BASE-ZX	802.3z	1 Gbps	9 μm SM fiber	70 km	8B/10B	NRZ
1000BASE-T	802.3ab	1 Gbps	Four pairs Category 5 UTP	100 m	PAM5	PAM5

Data Link Layer

Whereas the physical layer is responsible for transferring raw bits into streams of data, the Ethernet data link layer is responsible for determining what the streams mean and when the streams should be sent. For a receiver on a segment, Ethernet frames are created from the raw binary data provided by the physical layer. Because the physical layer merely accepts and transmits streams of zeros and ones without any sense of the structure of the data, it is up to the data link layer to create and recognize frames. Figure 2-12 and Figure 2-13 include the fields of Ethernet II and IEEE 802.3 frames, respectively.

Figure 2-12 *Ethernet II Frame format*

Preamble 7 bytes	Destination MAC 6 bytes	Source MAC 6 bytes	Type 2 bytes	Data 46 to 1500 bytes	FCS 4 bytes

Figure 2-13 *Ethernet 802.3 Frame format*

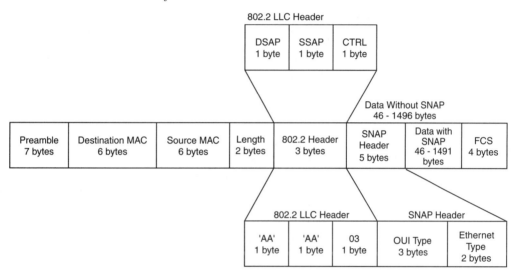

An Ethernet frame contains 14 bytes of header, 4 bytes of trailer, and between 46 and 1500 bytes of data. The various fields of the Ethernet frame formats from Figure 2-12 and Figure 2-13 are located in Table 2-5.

Table 2-5 *Fields in Ethernet II and IEEE 802.3 Frames*

Field	Description
Preamble	A pattern of alternating zeros and ones used to distinguish between frames. The preamble is not included when determining the length of the Ethernet frame.
Source Media Access Control address	48-bit hardware address of the sending host.
Destination Media Access Control address	48-bit hardware address of the receiving host.
Type/Length	This field contains a value in the range 0x0000–0x05DC to indicate that the frame is in 802.3 format. All values above 0x05DC (that is, 1518 bytes in length) are interpreted as Ethernet II type codes, because an Ethernet frame length cannot exceed 1518 bytes.

continues

Table 2-5   *Fields in Ethernet II and IEEE 802.3 Frames (Continued)*

Field	Description
Data	Frame data. The frame data must not be less than 46 bytes or more than 1500.
Frame Checksum (FCS)	A value calculated by the sender based on all fields (except the Preamble and FCS) and data. Upon reception, the receiver repeats the calculation and verifies it against the value in this field to ensure that the frame is not corrupt.
802.2 Logical Link Control (LLC) Fields	The logical link control layer enables different protocols, such as TCP/IP, IPX, and SNA, to communicate with one another directly over Ethernet. The SSAP and DSAP are the source and destination service access points in 802.2. These refer to the protocols of the sending and receiving hosts. For IP, the code is 0x06 in hexadecimal. A few others are 0x04 for IBM SNA, 0x80 for 3Com, and 0xE0 for Novel IPX. The control field is used for flow control. Alternatively, the LLC can be used to make up for the lack of type field in the 802.3 header. If the SAP values are both set to "AA," and the CTRL field to 0x03, then the Subnetwork Access Protocol (SNAP) header follows the 802.2 header within the first 5 bytes of the data field. As a result, the type is stored in a dedicated Ethernet type field. The Ethernet type for IP is 0x0800.
FCS	The checksum of the frame.

NOTE   Any frame that is less than 64 bytes is called a runt, and one that exceeds 1518 bytes is known as a giant. Some Cisco Catalyst series switches support the forwarding of frames exceeding the maximum frame size of 1518, because some vendor NICs generate large frames to increase overall application bandwidth. See your Catalyst switch configuration manual for support details.

Hosts on an Ethernet segment are configured to transmit in either full- or half-duplex mode. Hosts communicating with one another using half-duplex cannot transmit and receive data simultaneously. In half-duplex Ethernet environments, the LAN segment is shared among multiple hosts, resulting in the formation of a collision domain. When configured as half-duplex, network interfaces of Fast Ethernet speeds or higher support only two hosts on a segment, resulting in a collision domain containing two hosts. To send an Ethernet frame, and avoid a collision on the segment, the host must first determine if the carrier is in use by the other host. Ethernet provides contention resolution using Carrier Sensing Multiple Access/Collision Detection (CSMA/CD). This provides each station on the physical wire with a method to determine if the wire is in use and the ability to retransmit in the event of collision. If the wire is found to be in use, the station uses binary exponential back-off to retransmit the Ethernet frame. With this method, the station retransmits at a random time in the future, normally within a fraction of a second. If at that time the carrier is still in use, it doubles the previous time value and then attempts to retransmit. The method continues in this fashion until the carrier is free within the collision domain.

Hosts communicating with one another using full duplex may transmit and receive simultaneously. Therefore, in full-duplex environments, the collision domain is non-existent and thus CSMA/CD is not used. That is, a device at the end of a full-duplex Ethernet link does not have to listen for other transmissions before sending data.

Internet Protocol

IP corresponds to Layer 3 of the OSI reference model. IP is a mechanism to deliver application content over a network in the form of small packets of information.

IP will not guarantee that packets will arrive at the final destination as they were sent—they are transported with best-effort service only. IP checks for errors in the packet header but not for errors within the packet content. Furthermore, the TCP transport layer is responsible for retransmitting and reordering packets lost in transit or received out-of-order, respectively. Additionally, responsibility for packet content error checking is left to TCP. If an error is found in the packet header, IP simply drops the entire packet and assumes that the upper layers will detect a lost packet and, if necessary, retransmit it.

TCP was developed as the reliable transport layer mechanism used in the TCP/IP protocol suite. TCP determines if there are missing, out-of-order, or erroneous packets, as mentioned previously. User Datagram Protocol (UDP) uses IP's best-effort service, but checks for errors within the packet content, as opposed to performing header error checking only, as performed by IP. However, unlike TCP, UDP discards the packet if errors are found. Like IP, UDP assumes that the application layer will detect missing or out-of-sequence content and, if necessary, retransmit it. Figure 2-14 outlines the IP packet format.

Figure 2-14 *IP Packet Format*

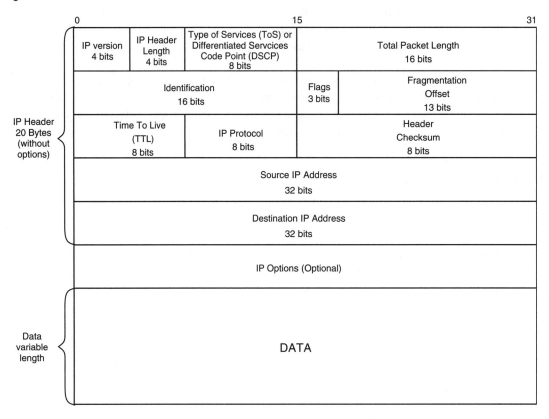

The various fields of the IP frame header are described in Table 2-6.

Table 2-6 *Fields in the IP Packet Header*

Field	Description
IP version	The version of IP used to encapsulate, address, and route this packet.
IP Header Length	The length of the packet header.
Type of Service (ToS) or Differentiated Services Code Point (DSCP)	This field is used to prioritize packets and, thus, to ensure that higher-priority packets are transmitted before lower-priority packets.
Total Packet Length	The length of the entire IP packet, including header and payload.
Identification	A unique identification number assigned to the current packet, for use during reassembly of fragmented packets.
Flags	Three bits of flags used for fragmentation control. If the first bit is set, the packet will not be fragmented. The second bit, if set, indicates that this is not the last fragment. The last bit is reserved for future use.

Table 2-6   *Fields in the IP Packet Header (Continued)*

Field	Description
Fragmentation Offset	Used for ordering fragmented packets, this offset indicates the position of the current packet in the original unfragmented packet.
Time To Live (TTL)	The maximum number of hops the packet will take throughout the network before being discarded by an intermediary router.
IP Protocol	Indicates the transport layer protocol within the packet. TCP is indicated by the hexadecimal number 0x06, and UDP is indicated by 0x11.
Header Checksum	The header checksum for detecting errors in the IP packet header.
Source IP Address	The IP address of the host that generated the packet.
Destination IP address	The IP address of the receiving host of the packet.
IP Options	32 options are available for such features as loose and strict source routing.
Data	The payload of the packet.

The 8-bit type of service (ToS) field includes IP precedence (3 bits), type of service (4 bits), and 2 unused bits. This field is used also for the Differentiated Services Code Point (DSCP) field definition.

This newer definition uses 6 bits for conveying DSCP, giving a total of 64 possible classes. The currently unused (CU) 2-bit field is now mapped to the Explicit Congestion Notification (ECN) field. If a router is congested, the ECN field is set by the router using Weighted Random Early Detection (WRED) to notify downstream network devices of the congestion.

NOTE   For more information on ECN and WRED, see the section "Configuring Weighted Random Early Detection" in Chapter 6, "Ensuring Content Delivery with Quality of Service."

Quality of service (QoS) in Cisco IOS uses either the IP precedence or DSCP for prioritizing traffic for delay-sensitive applications, such as voice and video. Figure 2-15 illustrates both the old ToS and new DSCP interpretations of this 8-bit field.

Figure 2-15   *The IP ToS and DSCP Service Field.*

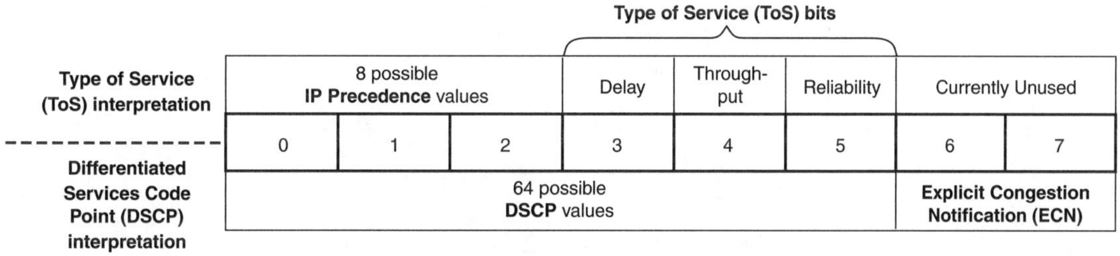

Content awareness at Layer 2 and Layer 3 is minimal, since little information about the content of the packet is available in the IP and Ethernet headers. However, content networking devices perform operations at this layer, based on content awareness at higher levels. For example, IP Multicast occurs at Layer 2 and Layer 3. Also, Network Address Translation (NAT) and application redirection is performed at Layer 3.

Although IP is used to transport the following protocols, they are most appropriately located at the same OSI layer as IP (Layer 3):

■ **Address Resolution Protocol**—The associations between MAC and IP address are resolved using ARP.

■ **Internet Control Management Protocol**—Control messages are transported to TCP/IP hosts using ICMP by applications requiring Layer 3 error reporting.

■ **Internet Group Management Protocol**—Members can join and leave multicast groups using IGMP. This protocol is discussed in detail in Chapter 5, "IP Multicast Content Delivery."

Address Resolution Protocol

A host uses Address Resolution Protocol (ARP) when it wants to communicate with another host or router in its broadcast domain and knows the IP address but does not know the MAC address of the host or router. To determine the MAC address, the sender creates an ARP packet and encapsulates it directly in to an Ethernet frame. The sender inserts a broadcast destination MAC address and its own MAC as the source into the Ethernet frame header. The ARP request is broadcast to all devices in the broadcast domain, and the station that bears the requested IP address will send the ARP response directly back to the sending device.

A broadcast domain is limited to a group of network devices that receive explicit broadcast requests originating from one another. This is normally limited to the IP subnet or Virtual LAN (VLAN) that the devices are located within, but will span multiple subnets if transparent bridging is used. You will learn topics on VLANs and bridging in Chapter 3, "Introducing Switching, Routing, and Address Translation."

Figure 2-16 illustrates the process ARP uses to determine the MAC address for a given IP address.

Figure 2-16 *The MAC Address Resolution Procedure*

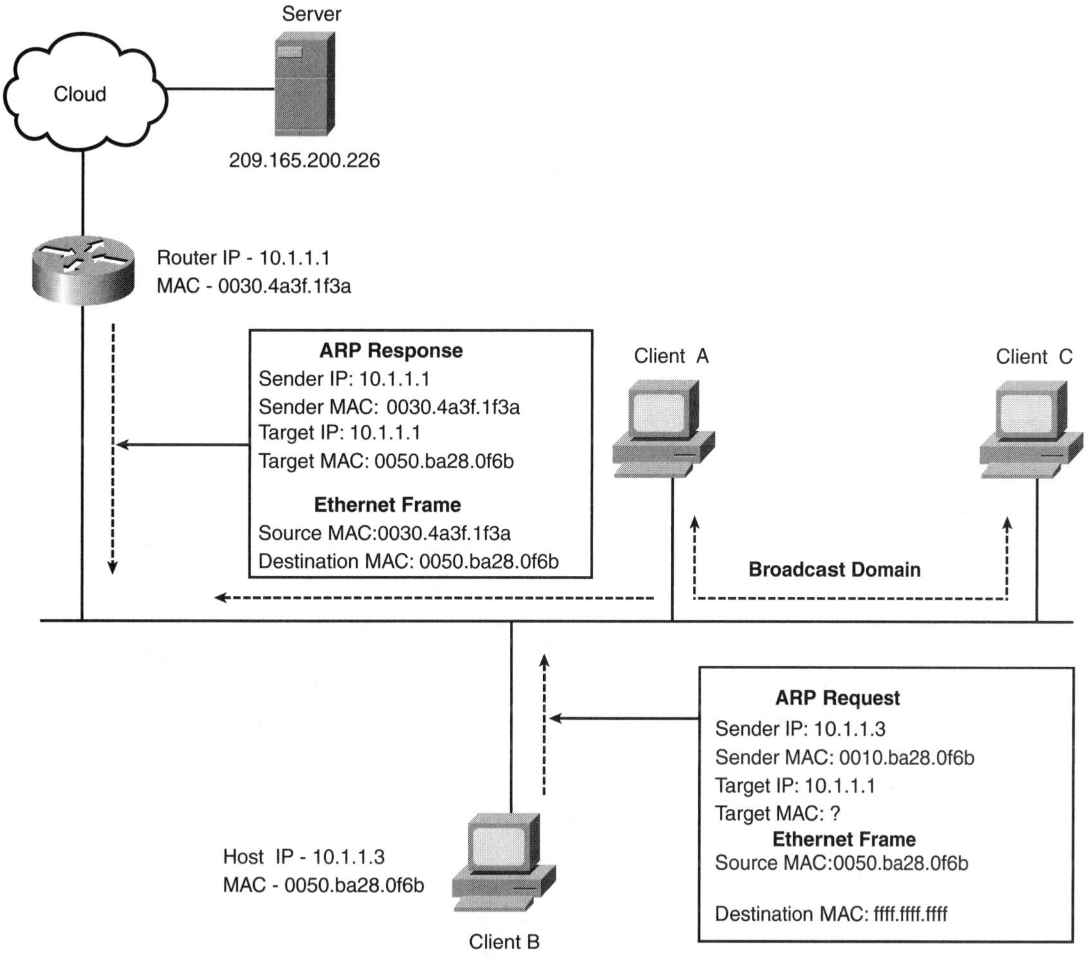

In Figure 2-16, Client B with IP address 10.1.1.3 generates an ARP request for its default gateway router address 10.1.1.1. The ARP request packet is then encapsulated in an Ethernet frame.

> **NOTE**   For more information on data encapsulation, see the section "Putting It All Together with a Detailed Network Trace," in this chapter.

The Ethernet frame is broadcast on to the local segment, and the router responds with an ARP response containing its MAC address that is associated with the requested IP in the ARP request. Clients A and C ignore the ARP request because they are not assigned the request IP address. Now that Client B in Figure 2-16 knows the router's MAC address, it will route all traffic destined to the Internet server 209.165.200.226 directly through the router.

Internet Control Message Protocol

ICMP provides management and error reporting between TCP/IP devices. ICMP has many facilities to aid network devices in packet delivery. A few of its mechanisms that pertain to content networking are

■ Layer 3 connectivity determination.

■ Reporting unavailable TCP/UDP Ports.

■ Announcing new default routers to clients/servers.

Layer 3 Connectivity Determination

ICMP provides a simple request-response facility to determine the status of a TCP/IP device and the roundtrip times between two hosts. ICMP Echo requests are sent to a destination device that will in turn send an ICMP Echo response back, if an ICMP process is available on the device to yield a response. Because ICMP is often implemented entirely within the operating system or TCP/IP driver of the end device, responses to ICMP Echo requests almost always determine that the host is at least powered on and available on the network. As a result, even if applications that a server is meant to serve are not available, the server may respond to ICMP echo requests.

A drawback to ICMP is that it runs at the IP layer and is therefore unreliable. This means that ICMP Echo requests or responses may get dropped along the path and cause additional problems during troubleshooting.

The Ping utility automates ICMP echo requests and responses. Ping is therefore normally the first test to perform in determining whether a remote host is available or not.

> **NOTE**   Because most Internet hosts and servers support ICMP, it is useful for calculating round trip times (RTT) between two devices. ICMP RTT is discussed in Chapter 12,"Exploring Global Server Load Balancing," for proximity determination in GSLB.

The IP header contains a Time To Live (TTL) field that is set by the sender to the maximum number of routers (or hops) that a packet will encounter on the way to its final destination. An intermediary router will send an ICMP "TTL exceeded" error message to the sender that indicates that the TTL has been reached and will drop the offending packet. TTL field is also useful to avoid infinite loops.

Unavailable Port Errors

ICMP sends error reports to clients in response to TCP or UCP requests for application layer services that are either not installed or currently unavailable. Because the application is unable to notify clients of the error at Layers 5–7, ICMP notifies clients on behalf of the application at Layer 3.

Announcement of New Default Routers

Hosts on an Ethernet LAN normally have only optimal TCP/IP configuration, including an IP address, a subnet mask, and a default gateway. When a LAN has multiple routers, a host's default router has the ability to direct hosts to another available router, if that router provides the more direct route to the ultimate destination. The default router updates the hosts routing table using ICMP redirect messages.

The ICMP redirect message includes the IP address of the requested destination and the IP address of the next hop router that can route to the requested destination. The requesting host creates a host route in its routing table by using the information in the ICMP redirect message. A host route is a route to an individual destination host that is masked with a full 32 bit subnet mask to match the entire host portion of an IP address. For example, say another router is placed in the broadcast domain in the Figure 2-16 and functions as a default router for Client A in order to route to other subnets in the private network. The new router is not directly connected to the Internet and therefore requires the routing of all traffic destined to the Internet through the original router in the broadcast domain. As a result, the new router sends an ICMP redirect message to Client A, instead of routing the traffic to the original router on behalf of Client A That is, a host route to destination server 209.165.200.226 via the original router (with an interface IP of 10.1.1.1) will be installed in the local routing table of Client A, which will enable Client A to route to the Internet host 209.165.200.226 directly.

Internet Group Management Protocol and Protocol Independent Multicast

Internet Group Management Protocol (IGMP) is used by clients to inform neighboring multicast routers of the multicast groups that the client is part of. These IGMP messages are used by multicast routers to track host memberships on each of its directly connected networks. By requesting to be a part of a multicast group, a host will receive all traffic destined to the group. A router on an Ethernet segment will forward traffic from the requested group directly to the client.

Protocol Independent Multicast (PIM) is a network layer multicast routing protocol used by Cisco routers. To route multicast traffic through the network, PIM uses your existing unicast routing protocol tables to determine the reverse path of the traffic (that is, the interface closest to the multicast source). Using Reverse Path Forwarding (RPF), PIM forwards the multicast traffic out all interfaces besides the reverse path interface. IGMP and PIM are described in detail in Chapter 5.

Transport Layer

Now that you have learned about the physical, data link, and network layers, you can tackle the intricacies of the transport layer. Whereas these lower layers deal with information within the network on a hop-by-hop basis, the transport layer works in an end-to-end fashion, between the communicating hosts. It provides the mechanism for ensuring that the content arrives in a fashion suitable to the particular application.

The following are the transport layer protocols used in the TCP/IP protocol suite.

■ **Transport Control Protocol**—TCP is reliable connection-oriented transport protocol used to transport application content between computers. Applications that require reliability should use TCP. An example of an application that uses TCP is HTTP, where data loss is not tolerated.

■ **User Datagram Protocol**—UDP is an unreliable connection-less transport protocol used to transport application content between computers. Applications that provide their own reliability or that do not require reliability should use UDP. Examples of UDP applications are streaming media and voice over IP, where some loss of data is acceptable. Retransmitting and reordering lost packets would disrupt the steady flow of real-time traffic, resulting in loss of perceived voice or video quality by the user.

■ **Pragmatic General Multicast**—PGM is a reliable multicast transport protocol. IP multicast was originally intended for real-time flows, such as live broadcasts and video conferencing, which do not require reliability. However, bulk file transfers can also benefit from multicast but because files transfers are not tolerant to packet loss, they require a reliable multicast transport. Refer to Chapter 5 for more detailed information on PGM.

Transmission Control Protocol

Applications that require reliability must first open a TCP connection for communication between the client and server application to commence. The beauty of the OSI layered model is that an application may deliver content over an underlying TCP connection and trust that the data will arrive as it was sent without worrying about the underlying transport details.

> **NOTE** The concept of an application session is different from that of a TCP connection in that a session may maintain multiple TCP connections simultaneously or open individual short-lived TCP connections to transmit the application content. Each application may use the controls of TCP differently within a session to ensure optimal delivery of the given content.

Application content is partitioned by TCP into smaller chunks of data that are transported in TCP segments. Figure 2-17 gives the TCP segment format.

Figure 2-17 *TCP Segment Format*

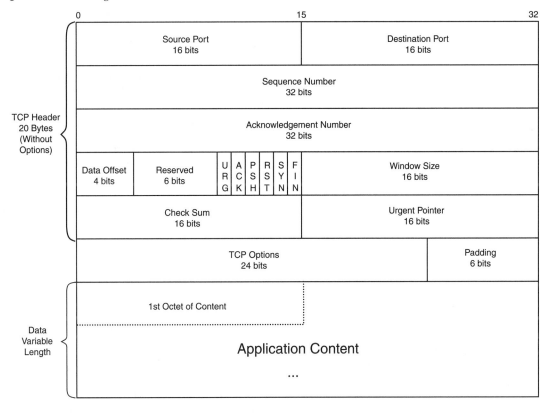

Table 2-6 outlines the TCP segment header fields in the TCP header.

Table 2-7 *Fields in the TCP Segment Header*

Field	Description
Source Port	A unique number for addressing the application on the requesting client.
	The Well Known Ports range from 0–1023. The Registered Ports range from 1024–49151. The Dynamic and/or Private Ports are those from 49152–65535.
Destination Port	A unique number for addressing the application on the origin server.
Sequence Number	Each TCP segment is assigned a sequence number to aid in ordering packets on reception.
Acknowledgement Number	The Sequence Number of the next expected packet by the receiver.

continues

Table 2-7 *Fields in the TCP Segment Header (Continued)*

Field	Description
Data Offset	The number of 32-bit words in the header, used to indicate where the data begins.
Reserved	Reserved for future use.
Control Bits	**ACK:** Used to acknowledge received TCP segments. **PSH:** Notifies TCP to not buffer the data in the window but to send it directly to the application layer. For example, numerous Telnet keystrokes that form a large TCP segment should not be stored by TCP. **URG:** The data is urgent but does not bypass the TCP window. Urgent Pointer is valid and is sent to the application pointing to the urgent content. For example, application interrupts are often implemented using the URG pointer. **RST:** Abruptly resets the connection. **SYN:** Used for synchronizing sequence numbers. **FIN:** Used during a graceful close. Indicates that there is no more data available from sender.
Window	The number of octets the receiver is willing to receive.
Checksum	A checksum on the TCP header and packet.
Urgent Pointer	This field is used in conjunction with the URG flag to point to the location of important data in the TCP payload. The URG pointer is considered the lowest level of content-awareness in the TCP/IP protocol stack.
Options	Application specific fields. Examples are the Maximum Segment Size option used to indicate the maximum size to avoid packet fragmentation (see section "TCP Maximum Segment Size" in this chapter) and the Window Scale Option (WSopt) discussed in the section "TCP over Satellite" of this chapter. Options are negotiated during the initial TCP three-way handshake.
Padding	Used to pad the TCP header length to a multiple of 32 bytes.

TCP Three-Way Handshake

To transport content reliably, TCP relies on sequence numbers to define the order in which segmented content must be assembled upon reception. Every data octet (or byte) in a TCP segment is logically assigned a sequence number. The sequence number in a TCP segment header references the first octet in the payload of the segment, residing directly after the TCP header, as illustrated previously in Figure 2-17.

Consider the following example in which a client requires information from a server. The client application generates a content request to send to the server. TCP segments the content request into chunks of data that are appropriately sized for an IP packet. Before sending the content request to the server, a TCP connection is established, as illustrated in Figure 2-18. TCP segments are sent in the direction of the arrows, with time proceeding downward.

Figure 2-18 *The TCP Three-Way Handshake*

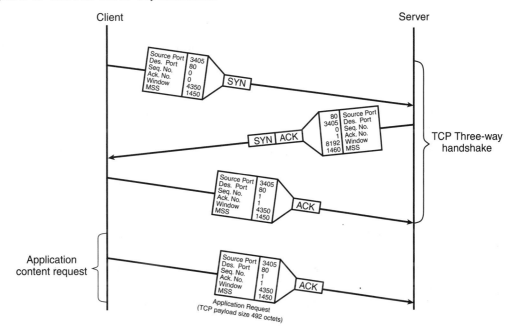

The TCP three-way handshake is used to synchronize TCP sequence numbers and exchange TCP options between TCP devices. In the example in Figure 2-18, the client generates a TCP SYN segment, with an initial sequence number, suggested receiver windows size, maximum segment size (MSS) TCP option, and the SYN flag set in the transport segment header.

The segment is then sent to the server. The server acknowledges the client's receiver window size and initial sequence number by sending a TCP SYN-ACK segment back to the client. The SYN-ACK contains the server's initial sequence number, suggested receiver window size, MSS TCP option, and both the SYN and ACK flags set in the TCP segment header. At this point of the handshake, the connection is half-opened. Not until the client further acknowledges the server's suggested values, by way of a TCP ACK segment, is the TCP three-way handshake completed. The TCP ACK segment simply contains the same information as the SYN segment except with both the sequence and acknowledgement numbers increased by one octet. Both the client and server are now aware of each other's sequence numbers and are thus synchronized.

> **NOTE** The acknowledgment number is the next anticipated byte number by the receiver. The acknowledgment mechanism is cumulative, so that an acknowledgment of octet YY indicates that all octets up to but not including YY have been received.

A TCP connection is fully established between the client and server, and the client may send the application request to the server. Actually, both ends may transmit and receive application requests or content or both through the open TCP connection, depending on how the application chooses to use it. Furthermore, with the window size agreed upon, the sender transmits enough segments to fill the allowable window, even if previously sent segments have not been acknowledged. This enables more efficient use of available bandwidth by using much less for the overhead that is associated with acknowledging every segment.

> **NOTE** In the example in Figure 2-18, the client connects to the well-known destination TCP port 80 for HTTP on the server. With HTTP, the client generates a random source port (3405) to distinguish between other TCP connections to the same server. With some applications, such as FTP, the source port is also a well-known TCP port (that is, port 21).

Either the client or server may initiate a graceful close of the TCP connection. To do so, the initiator of the close sends a FIN segment to indicate that it has no more data to send. The station on the other side of the close then sends a FIN-ACK segment to the initiator to acknowledge the close request. When the FIN-ACK is received, the connection is considered half-closed. The initiator of the close waits for the other station to finish sending its data and close its half of the connection. In the meantime, the initiator will not send data but must continue to receive data from the other station.

To abnormally abort a TCP connection, either side sends a TCP RST segment. After sending a RST, the TCP host need not await an ACK segment in response, nor continue to receive data from the other side. This reset method uses much less overhead to close a TCP connection. It is meant for use by one host that is signaling to another to close the connection during application layer errors or for use by a user who chooses to abandon the application session. For example, when a user closes a web browser, the browser sends a RST to the server to abruptly close the TCP connection.

Table 2-8 outlines the different variables thus far required by the client and server to send data over the TCP connection that results from the three-way handshake in Figure 2-18. Example values from Figure 2-18 are given in Table 2-8 as reference for the illustrations in subsequent sections in this chapter.

Table 2-8   *Example TCP Values for Variables When Sending and Receiving Data on a TCP Connection*

Host	Variable	Example Values
Server	Server Send Window Size	4350
	Server Sequence Number	0
	Maximum Segment Size	1450
Client	Client Send Window Size	8192
	Client Sequence Number (due to the application request of size 492)	493
	Maximum Segment Size	1460

For illustration purposes, both the client and server from the example in Figure 2-18 chose initial sequence numbers equal to zero. Under normal circumstances, however, the sequence number is chosen as a random number between 0 and $2^{32} - 1$ and is incremented as content is sent throughout the TCP connection. In Table 2-7, the client's initial sequence number increased to 493 from an application layer request shown at the bottom of the timeline in Figure 2-18.

TCP Sliding Window

TCP uses a sliding window approach to provide TCP congestion control. Windowing provides the ability to mitigate issues related to network congestion and faults, such as missing or out-of-sequence segments. Buffering segments in the window, before processing them at the application layer, enables the receiving host to reorder out-of-sequence segments and retransmit missing segments.

The scenario continues from the three-way TCP handshake shown previously in Figure 2-18, as the application server is now able to send data to the client, using the values in Table 2-8. In this example, the window size was chosen to fit three packets of length 1450 bytes. The application has eight of these equal-length packets to send to the client (11,600 bytes in total). Figure 2-19 illustrates how the TCP sliding window works in this environment.

Figure 2-19 *TCP Sliding Window Approach*

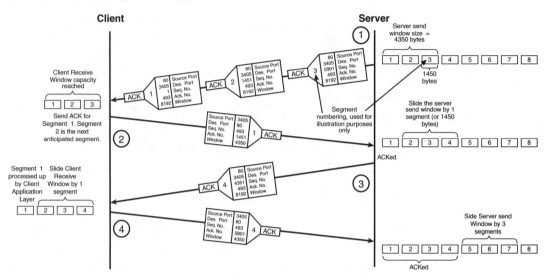

The following is the sequence of events that takes place during the first part of an application transaction, as illustrated in Figure 2-19.

Step 1   The server sends only the first three segments in accordance to the send window size.

Step 2   The client immediately acknowledges the first segment, upon its arrival. The first three segments are buffered within the client's receive window.

Step 3   Upon reception of the acknowledgement of the first segment, the server slides its send window by one segment. Then the server sends the fourth segment in accordance to the server send window.

Step 4   The client receives the fourth segment and allows the application to process the first, because the window size has been reached.

The server then sends the next three segments consecutively but causes the receiver to become congested, as illustrated in Figure 2-20. A receiver may run low on buffer space that results from receiving packets faster then it is capable of processing. If this happens, the receiver advertises a smaller window size to the sender. The new window size regulates the transmission rate according to the receiver's processing capabilities.

Figure 2-20 illustrates how the receiver must resize the window as a result of local congestion in its receive buffer.

Figure 2-20   *Window Resizing from Receiver Congestion*

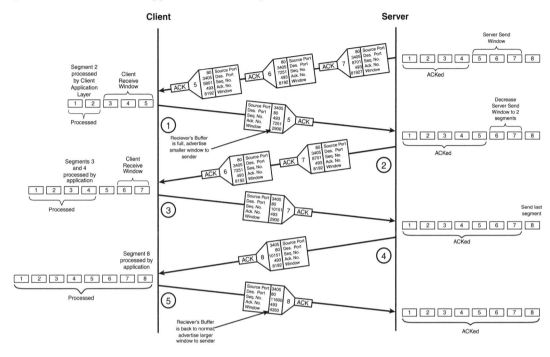

The following is the sequence of events that take place during the remainder of the transaction between client and server in Figure 2-20.

Step 1   The client receives and acknowledges segment 5 only, as the application is able to process only segment 2 from its receive window at that moment in time. As a result, the receiver advertises its window size as 2900 in order to throttle the sender's transmission rate.

Step 2   The receiver decreases its window size to 2 and sends segments 6 and 7.

Step 3   The client processes segments 3 and 4 from its buffer and is therefore able to handle receiving segments 6 and 7. The client then sends an acknowledgement for segment 7.

Step 4   The server receives the last acknowledgement and sends its last remaining segment to the client.

Step 5   The client application layer processes segment 8 and advertises a larger window size (4350 octets) within the acknowledgment for the segment.

TCP Slow Start

In addition to detecting and recovering from local buffer congestion, as illustrated previously in Figure 2-20, the TCP sliding window mechanism is also used for detecting congestion within the network. Network congestion is caused from router packet queues overloading, which forces packets to be dropped or to remain in the queue for excessive periods of time before transmission. During periods of network congestion, the sender will detect the anomaly by segment timeouts or by receiving duplicate ACKs from the receiver. TCP uses timers to detect packet loss. When each segment is sent, the sender starts an individual timer for that segment. If the ACK is not received within the timeout value, the segment is resent. Alternatively, if a duplicate ACK for a segment is received by the sender, the segment is deemed missing and is resent.

Figure 2-21 illustrates how congestion is detected by the server when a segment is lost in transmission and a duplicate ACK is sent by the receiver.

Figure 2-21 *Duplicate ACK Used to Detect Network Congestion*

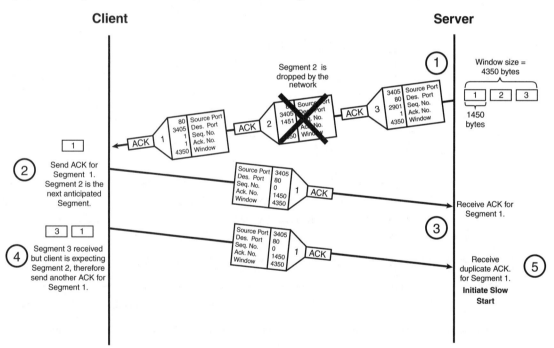

The following is the sequence of events that takes place when a packet is lost between client and server in Figure 2-21.

Step 1   The server sends three segments to the client.

Step 2   The client receives and acknowledges segment 1.

Step 3   The server receives the acknowledgement for segment 1.

Step 4   The client receives segment 3, but expects segment 2, and therefore sends another acknowledgment for segment 1.

Step 5   The server receives a duplicate acknowledgment, thus detecting that congestion is occurring in the network.

The server then initiates TCP slow start. With slow start, TCP assumes that the packet transmission rate is proportional to the rate of ACKs received by the sender. As individual ACKs are received, the sender's trust in the network increases. Specifically, when slow start is initiated, the sender creates a new variable called the congestion window (*cwnd*) and sets its value to 1. When the sender receives an ACK for the next TCP segment, it increases *cwnd* to 2 and sends two more segments. When the ACK arrives for the second segment in the window, the *cwnd* size is increased to 4, and four new segments are sent. When the ACK for the fourth segment arrives, *cwnd* is set to 8, and so on. The window increases in an exponential fashion until the precongestion window size is reached.

TCP slow start is often used in conjunction with TCP congestion avoidance during periods of network congestion.

TCP Congestion Avoidance

Traditionally, the TCP slow start exponential increase in *cwnd* would occur until the precongestion sender window size is reached. However, research has found that increasing *cwnd* in an exponential fashion until one half of the precongestion window size is reached proves to be much more practical in congested networks. Now when congestion occurs, *cwnd* is still set to 1, but a new variable, the slow start threshold (*ssthresh*), is set to half the precongestion window size. The *ssthresh* variable indicates when slow start ends and congestion avoidance begins. With congestion avoidance, TCP decreases the *cwnd* increase rate to a linear function from half to the full precongestion window size. As an example, Figure 2-22 illustrates the congestion avoidance mechanism using TCP slow start, with congestion occurring when the TCP window size reaches eight segments.

Figure 2-22   *Congestion Avoidance Using TCP Slow Start*

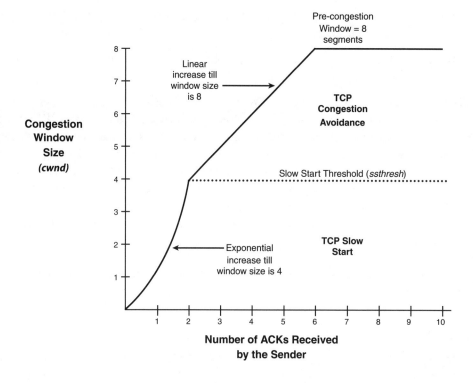

> **NOTE**   The TCP slow start and congestion avoidance causes problems if many users perform slow start at the same time. This global synchronization is resolved with Weighted Random Early Detection (WRED) discussed in Chapter 6.

In typical TCP implementations, slow start is employed for every new connection that is established, not just when congestion occurs. In contrast, congestion avoidance is employed in conjunction with slow start only when congestion is detected by the sender.

TCP Fast Retransmit

Recall that, when a segment is transmitted, the sender starts a transmit timer for the segment. If an acknowledgement is not received within a timeout value, the segment is deemed lost and is retransmitted by the sender. However, as you saw previously in Figure 2-21, the missing segment is detected by the sender receiving duplicate ACKs, not by the send timer reaching the timeout value. In most cases, a duplicate ACK is received for a missing segment before the timeout value is reached. This normally reduces the time with which segments are detected as missing, which results in faster transmission of missing segments and an overall improvement in performance of TCP. The feature for detecting missing segments using the duplicate ACKs instead of the transmit timer is called *TCP fast retransmit*.

Duplicate ACKs are also sent if out-of-sequence segments are received. To distinguish between out-of-sequence and missing segments, fast retransmit includes an increase in the number the ACKs (normally to three) that the sender must receive from the receiver before retransmitting the segment. Figure 2-23 illustrates how the TCP fast retransmit feature ensures that packets are actually missing, and not simply out-of-sequence.

Figure 2-23 *Duplicate ACKs from Out-of-Order Packets*

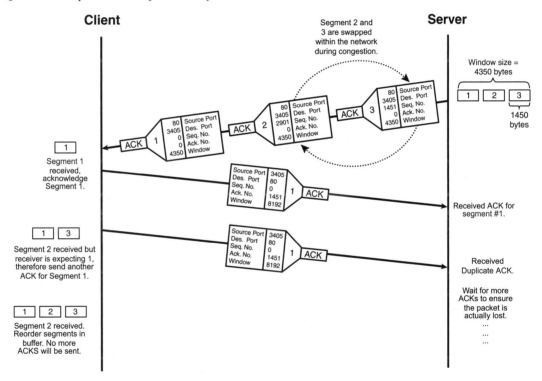

TCP Fast Recovery

Although duplicate ACKs detect network congestion, *some* segments are still being received by the receiver, which means that the network is only moderately congested. Recall that slow start reduces *cwnd* to one segment. This causes unnecessary bandwidth reduction during periods of only moderate congestion. Alternatively, when duplicate ACKs are detected by the sender, congestion avoidance is initiated instead. Congestion avoidance starts *cwnd* at half the precongestion window size, which results in a more conservative reduction in bandwidth during moderate congestion. This is called *TCP fast recovery*.

TCP timeouts occur at the sender when no packets are being received by the receiver, which implies that the network is under severe congestion. Only when TCP timeouts occur is slow start initiated by TCP in conjunction with congestion avoidance.

TCP Maximum Segment Size

Fragmentation occurs when an IP packet is too large for the Layer 2 medium. IP packets cannot exceed the Maximum Transmission Unit (MTU), which ranges from 512 bytes to 65,535 bytes but is most often 1500 bytes for Ethernet networks. Recall that the maximum frame length for Ethernet II and IEEE 802.3 is 1518 to account for up to 1500 bytes of payload and 18 bytes of frame header.

TCP has the ability to optionally negotiate a TCP option for setting the maximum TCP segment size, called the maximum segment size (MSS). MSS is used to ensure that the IP packet the segment resides in will not be fragmented.

In the case of Gigabit Ethernet, jumbo frames can optionally be configured on the device to increase the MTU from 1500 bytes to 65,535 bytes, which drastically reduces Ethernet framing overhead. Bear in mind though that, if IP packets generated for jumbo frames are routed to slower speed links with lower MTUs, they will inevitably require fragmentation.

NOTE Fragmentation is undesirable in content networking environments, because content switches direct packets based on Layers 5–7. Thus, if a packet spans multiple fragments, the content network device may have trouble enforcing its content policies. These issues are discussed in Chapter 10, "Exploring Server Load Balancing."

TCP over Satellite

The bandwidth for a single TCP connection is limited to the TCP window size divided by the end-to-end delay of the link. For example, for links with 750 ms delay, the bandwidth limitation imposed by a single TCP connection is approximately 85 kbps using the maximum TCP window size of 65,535 bytes. To overcome bandwidth limits caused by the maximum TCP window size, create an application session with multiple TCP connections and load share the content over the TCP connections. Load sharing over multiple TCP connections is often useful with high bandwidth satellite links, where the overhead associated with opening a connection is light enough to have a limited effect on the operation of the application.

Alternatively, the bandwidth of a *single* TCP connection can be scaled by increasing the maximum window size. This is possible with the use of the TCP option called the window scale option (WSopt), as defined in RFC 1323. WSopt is used to scale the existing TCP window field in the TCP segment header of 16 bits by up to 2^{256} times. However, these window sizes consume much more buffer memory on the TCP hosts.

TCP Variable Summary

Table 2-8 outlines the various TCP variables that are maintained on TCP hosts to communicate with one another, as discussed in this chapter.

Table 2-9   *Variables Required for Sending and Receiving Data on a TCP Connection.*

Variable	Description
Send Window Size	The size of buffer for sending data. It is maintained by the sender and advertised by the receiver across the network during the TCP three-way handshake.
Receive Window Size	The size of the buffer for receiving data. It is maintained by the receiver and advertised by the sender across the network during the TCP three-way handshake.
Sequence Number	A decimal value that references the first octet within the TCP segment payload.
Acknowledgement Number	A decimal value that acknowledges reception of data octets up to but not including this value. May also be considered the next expected data octet.
Congestion Window size	During periods of congestion, the sender uses this variable to manage the rate to which segments are sent to the receiver.
Slow Start Threshold	A threshold that indicates when slow start stops and congestion avoidance begins.
Retransmission timeout interval	When a segment timer reaches this retransmission timeout interval, the segment is retransmitted.
Maximum Segment Size	The maximum size of a segment supported by a receiver, which normally depends on the size of the MTU for the receiver. This is advertised by the receiver as a TCP option during the TCP three-way handshake.

NOTE   Content edge devices may tune the TCP parameters as discussed in Chapter 13, "Delivering Cached and Streaming Media."

User Datagram Protocol

User Datagram Protocol (UDP) provides segment delivery for applications that require efficient transport and tolerate loss of content. Unlike TCP, UDP does not:

■   Establish a connection before sending data.

■   Send acknowledgements for received segments.

■   Reorder out-of-sequence segments upon arrival.

The application using UDP is required to take responsibility for ensuring that the content is received intact. However, UDP ensures that segments arrive as they were sent by detecting errors in the UDP segment header and payload and will drop the packet if errors are found.

Additionally, UDP provides simple Internet Control Message Protocol (ICMP) error reporting if the destination port is not available at the server.

NOTE   The ICMP error messages are also available for other IP-based transport protocols, not only for UDP.

Figure 2-24 contains the UDP segment header fields.

Figure 2-24   *UDP Segment Header*

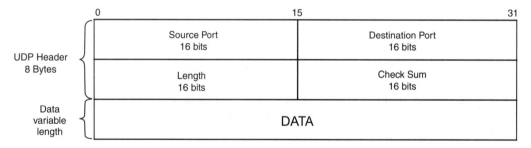

Putting It All Together with a Detailed Network Trace

You are now equipped to learn how content is prepared for sending over a TCP/IP network. As an example, say you enter **http://www.cisco.com** into a web browser URL field and press **Enter**. Your client and the Cisco.com origin server perform the following steps before the web page is sent to your browser.

Step 1   The hostname is resolved to an IP address using the Domain Name Service (DNS).

> **NOTE**   For more information on the operation of DNS, see Chapter 12.

Step 1   A TCP connection is opened from the client to the cisco.com origin server IP address using the TCP three-way handshake as illustrated previously in Figure 2-18.

Step 2   An HTTP GET request is written to TCP connection by the HTTP client application for the main page of the website. Figure 2-18 shows this GET request at the bottom of the timeline. This request is encapsulated and sent without any application data. The HTTP GET request resides in the header of the HTTP packet. Therefore, no application payload is necessary.

> **NOTE**   The HTTP protocol is discussed in detail in Chapter 8, "Exploring the Application Layer."

Step 3   The response from the server is encapsulated as illustrated in Figure 2-25.

In this example, the main page for Cisco.com is between 200 KB and 250 KB with approximately 30 files, including HTML, images, and dynamic content embedded within the page. The HTML for the main page is approximately 60 KB of text, which takes approximately 40 packets at 1500 bytes each. For simplicity, Figure 2-25 illustrates encapsulating the first packet of the HTML text sent to the browser from the web server hosting Cisco.com. Most web browsers load the HTML page first, and then, as the HTML hyperlinks to graphics and dynamic content are received within the HTML page, additional GET requests are sent and the process in Figure 2-25 is repeated.

Figure 2-25 *A Detailed Network Trace*

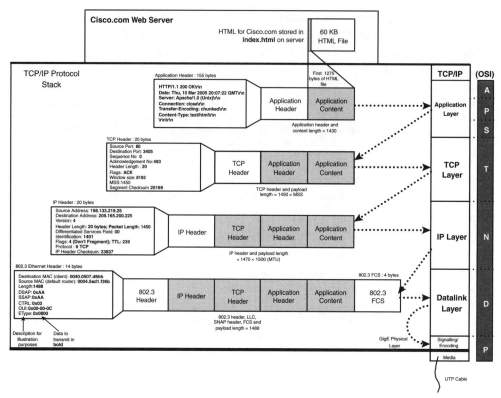

The following is the series of encapsulations that the content in Figure 2-25 goes through before being transmitted by the Ethernet physical layer.

Step 1 An HTTP header is added to the data chunk, with details such as the website URL, the HTTP method, and return code (the return code is "200 OK," in this case).

> **NOTE** Notice that the HTTP header is much larger than the TCP and IP headers. This is because the field names are included in the HTTP request, whereas, in TCP and IP, they are implied.

Step 2 An HTTP application segment is then encapsulated by adding a TCP header. The destination port used is the port generated by the client in the original TCP handshake. The ACK flag is set, and the acknowledgement number for the client's previous request is used.

Step 3   An IP header is then added to the TCP segment. The IP header includes Layer 3 information, such as source and destination IP address.

Step 4   An IEEE 802.3 frame header and footer is then added to the IP packet. The header includes the source and destination MAC addresses. When this packet is transmitted by the Cisco.com server, the source MAC is the server MAC, and the destination is the default gateway of the origin server.

Step 5   The Cisco.com origin server site is 1000BASE-T at the physical layer, in this example. The Ethernet frame is therefore transmitted over the UTP cable using PAM-5 to its default gateway router, ultimately destined to your web browser client.

Summary

This chapter introduces the lower four layers of the OSI reference model with respect to the TCP/IP protocol suite. The physical and data link layer protocols covered in this chapter are strictly Ethernet-based. The reason for not including other physical and data link layer protocols is that the Ethernet standards are the most commonly used protocols employed in modern-day Layer 1–2 networks.

The basics of IP are discussed in this chapter, as well as the IP-based protocol quartet that is directly transported over Layer 2: ARP, ICMP, PIM, and IGMP.

Understanding TCP is essential to the concepts detailed in later chapters. The basics of TCP operation including the TCP three-way handshake for TCP connection establishment are covered in this chapter. A more detailed examination of TCP is given through traffic control studies of the TCP sliding window and congestion control mechanisms.

Review Questions

1. How many wire pairs does 100BASE-T use of a UTP copper cable? How many does 1000BASE-T use?

2. What are the physical differences between step and graded index multimode fiber?

3. For 100BASE-FX, why is NRZ-I signaling used with 4B/5B encoding and not just straight NRZ?

4. What error checking is performed with IP, UDP, and TCP?

5. What is the purpose of the TCP three-way handshake?

6. How is packet loss detected by TCP senders?

7. Why is TCP bandwidth limited over satellite links? How can TCP bandwidth over satellite be accelerated?

8. What is the lowest level of content awareness in TCP/IP?

Recommended Reading

RFC 2001, *TCP Slow Start, Congestion Avoidance, Fast Retransmit, and Fast Recovery Algorithms*, W. Stevens, IETF, www.ietf.org/rfc/rfc2001.txt

RFC 1323, *TCP Extensions for High Performance, V. Jacobson, R. Braden, D. Borman, IETF,* www.ietf.org/rfc/rfc1323.txt

Charles E. Spurgeon, *Ethernet: The Definitive Guide*, O'Reilly, 2000

Chapter Goals

This chapter introduces the reader to TCP/IP routing and switching. The following topics are covered:

- **Layer 2 Switching**—Learn how Ethernet frames are switched by LAN switches.

- **Layer 3 Routing**—Learn how IP packets are routed by routers.

- **Layer 3 Switching**—Learn how IP packets are switched by routers.

- **Layer 3–4 Network Address Translation**—Learn how TCP segments and IP packets are translated by NAT-capable devices.

CHAPTER **3**

Introducing Switching, Routing, and Address Translation

In Chapter 2, "Exploring the Network Layers," you learned how TCP segments, IP packets, and Ethernet frames are generated, encapsulated, and transmitted onto a network by TCP/IP devices. In this chapter, you will learn how to design a network to efficiently translate, route, and switch the TCP segments, IP packets, and Ethernet frames that flow through your network. The following topics are discussed in this chapter:

■ **Frame Switching and Virtual LANs**—Switching TCP/IP involves forwarding Layer 2 Ethernet frames within VLANs.

■ **IP Routing**—Static and dynamic routing protocols define the path that traffic takes from one end system to the other.

■ **Packet Switching**—Packets are switched within routers using process switching, fast switching, or Cisco Express Forwarding (CEF)

■ **Network Address Translation**—Packets' IP address fields are rewritten to conserve IP addresses, and hide internal IP addressing schemes and load balancing requests across groups of servers.

Exploring Ethernet Frame Switching

LAN switches build tables of Media Access Control (MAC) addresses and associated switch ports assigned to TCP/IP devices within the network that are visible to the switch at Layer 2. The switches build their MAC tables by inspecting Address Resolution Protocol (ARP) requests that are traveling through the switch from TCP/IP devices, such as firewalls, routers, clients, and origin servers. Figure 3-1 illustrates the process of MAC learning in a small network, using the ARP request-response example discussed previously in Figure 2-16 from Chapter 2.

Figure 3-1 *Basic MAC Address Learning Using Transparent Switching*

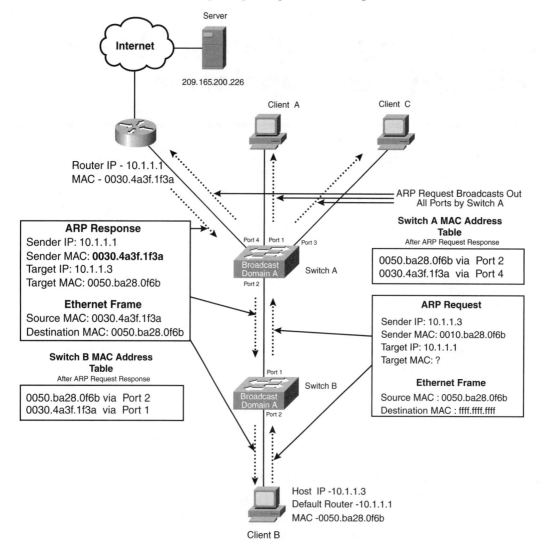

In Figure 3-1, Switch B receives the ARP frame at Layer 2 from Client B on Port 2 and creates the entry [0050.ba28.0f6b via Port 2] in its MAC table. The entry contains the MAC address of Client B, and the port number where the request was received. Because Switch B is unaware of the location of the router in the network, it broadcasts the frame, unmodified, to all ports (except the port the request was received on—Port 2). When the frame is received by Switch A from Switch B, the entry [0050.ba28.0f6b via Port 2] is created and stored in its MAC table. Switch A is unaware of the local port to which the router is connected and broadcasts the frame out all ports, except Port 2. The router receives the ARP request and responds with an ARP response, directly back to Client B. When Switch A receives the ARP response frame, it creates the entry [0030.4a3f.1f3a via Port 4] containing the router MAC and connected port. Switch A then sends the ARP response out Port 2, based on its existing entry for Client B.

Even though Client B is connected through an intermediary Layer 2 switch (Switch B), the router MAC entry is still located in Switch B's local MAC table [0050.ba28.0f6b via Port 2] and is pointing to the port connected to the "next-hop" switch (Port 2). The reason for this is that the switches are in the same broadcast domain and thus receive the ARP request-response Ethernet frames without modification from both the client and router.

With the MAC tables populated, Client B sends an application request to the Internet server with IP 209.165.200.226 via its default router 10.1.1.1. The switches transparently switch the frame according to the MAC entries for the router. Additionally, the return traffic from the Internet server is switched by the LAN switches using the MAC entries for Client B.

> **NOTE**   With some operating systems, workstations broadcast gratuitous ARP (GARP) frames to the LAN when it boots to advertise its IP-to-MAC association. Most Windows-based clients and servers use this facility to avoid duplicate IP addresses on the network. This facility is also beneficial for populating switch MAC forwarding tables.

Figure 3-1 illustrates a basic switched network; however, without fault-tolerance at Layer 2, if any single component fails, such as a switch or individual uplink, your entire network will be unusable. To provide resiliency to a Layer 2 network, you should consider enabling the following features in your switched network:

- **Spanning Tree Protocol**—When two or more switches are combined in a network, Layer 2 forwarding loops may occur. To deal with the negative impact of forwarding loops, enable the IEEE 802.1D Spanning Tree Protocol (STP) on your Layer 2 switches. STP provides path fault tolerance and redundancy within a segment, by taking advantage of backup paths created from Layer 2 forwarding loops. When more than one path is available, the STP selectively blocks some and leaves the others active, thereby avoiding potential loops and creating backups for the active paths.

- **EtherChannel or IEEE 802.3ad Link Aggregation**—Cisco EtherChannel load balances frames over multiple redundant Layer 2 links. One of the available links is selected for each frame by hashing the source and destination MAC addresses together. The result of the hash is the index of the preferred link for the frame. The concept of hashing will be discussed in Chapter 10, "Exploring Server Load Balancing."

Configuring Virtual LANs

Virtual LANs (VLANs) provide you a flexible means to logically separate devices that are physically attached to the same Layer 2 switch or across different switches. Broadcast traffic originating on a VLAN is not propagated to other VLANs. You need a Layer 3 device capable of inter-VLAN routing, such as a router or multilayer switch, to route traffic between VLANs.

With multilayer switches, such as the Catalyst 3550 and Catalyst 6500, a logical VLAN interface serves as the default gateway for all devices attached to the switch ports that are assigned to that particular VLAN. That is, the VLAN interface IP address is the default gateway for devices in the VLAN. Clients in different VLANs will have a different default gateway. For example, if three VLANs are configured on a Layer 3 switch, there will be three default gateways for your clients. Traffic destined to different VLANs is routed by the multilayer switching engine between VLAN interfaces.

Example 3-1 shows you how a VLAN interface and the switch ports that reside in the VLAN are configured on a Cisco Catalyst 3550 Layer 3 switch.

Example 3-1   *Configuring VLAN Interfaces and Switch Ports*

```
Router1#configure terminal
Router1(config)#interface vlan 100
Router1(config)#ip address 10.1.1.1 255.255.255.0
Router1(config)#no shut
Router1(config)#
Router1(config)#interface fastethernet 3/1
Router1(config)#switchport access vlan 100
Router1(config)#
Router1(config)#interface fastethernet 3/2
Router1(config)#switchport access vlan 100
Router1(config)#Ctrl-Z
Router1#
```

Configuring VLAN Trunking

VLAN trunking enables multiple VLANs to traverse a single link, thus providing multiple logical links. Either the Cisco-developed Inter-Switch Link (ISL) or the standard IEEE 802.1Q is available to you for configuring trunks. You can configure trunks between Cisco switches or, in order to perform inter-VLAN routing, between Cisco switches and routers. With both ISL and 802.1Q, an additional VLAN identification field is inserted into Ethernet frames, which indicates the VLAN that the frame belongs to. Figure 3-2 shows where the 802.1Q VLAN tag is added to the 802.3 frame.

Figure 3-2 *802.3 Frame Format with 802.1Q Tagging*

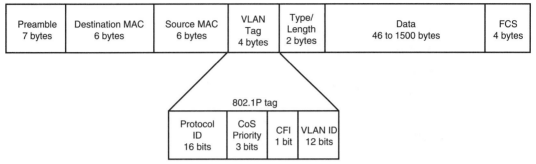

Table 3-1 defines the fields in the 802.1Q tag field.

Table 3-1   *Fields in 802.1Q Tag Field*

Field	Description
Protocol Identifier	The tagging protocol used. This field is set to a value of 0x8100 to identify the frame as an IEEE 802.1Q tagged frame.
802.1P Priority	The priority field used for class of service (CoS) priority assignments.
Canonical Format Indicator (CFI)	Indicates the canonical form of the MAC address in the frame. If the value is zero, the MAC address is stored in canonical format. If the value of this field is one, the MAC address is in non-canonical format.
VLAN ID	The VLAN number.

Example 3-2 shows how a switch port is configured with an 802.1Q trunk on a Cisco Catalyst 3550 switch.

Example 3-2   *Configuring an ISL Trunk on a Port*

```
Router1#configure terminal
Router1(config)#interface GigabitEthernet 4/1
Router1(config)#switchport mode trunk
Router1(config)#switchport trunk encapsulation dot1q
Router1(config)#switchport trunk vlan add 100
Router1(config)#switchport trunk vlan add 200
Router1(config)#Ctrl-Z
Router1#
```

Exploring MAC Learning with Multiple VLANs

Figure 3-3 illustrates how MAC learning is performed after segmenting the network from Figure 3-1 into two different VLANs.

Figure 3-3 *MAC Learning with Two VLANs and Inter-VLAN Routing*

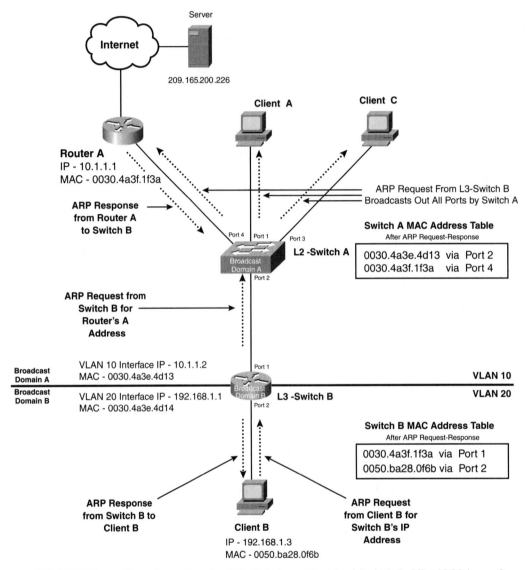

VLAN 10 is configured on all ports of Switch A and Port 1 of Switch B. VLAN 20 is configured on Port 2 Switch B. Switch B is configured with a VLAN interface for VLAN 10 and another for VLAN 20 in order to route between the two VLANs.

NOTE   For more information on IP routing, see the section "Understanding IP Routing" later in this chapter.

Because Switch B is a Layer 3 switch, it maintains its own ARP cache in addition to a Layer 2 MAC table and serves as the default gateway for Client B. For example, Client B sends an ARP request for Switch B's IP address, instead of Router A's IP address as shown previously in Figure 3-1. Therefore, Switch B originates an ARP request for the IP address of router A in order to determine where to route the client's upcoming application request to the Internet. Notice how the resulting MAC table for Switch A is slightly adjusted in Figure 3-3 from Figure 3-1. Switch A no longer has an entry for Client B but instead has the entry [0030.4a3e.4d13 via Port 2] for the VLAN 10 interface of Switch B.

VLAN Trunking Protocol

VLAN trunking protocol (VTP) is used to manage the creation, removal, and availability of VLANs in a switched network. You can configure your switches with VTP by assigning them as servers, clients, or transparent. You can create, change, and delete VLAN information on a VTP server, including the VLAN number and name. The VLAN information is permanently stored in a VTP database within non-volatile RAM (NVRAM) of the VTP server. VLANs are not created on VTP clients — VTP servers advertise the VLAN information to the VTP clients over trunk links, in the form of VTP messages. The VTP clients store the information dynamically in RAM and in turn forward the VTP message out all VLAN trunks, except the trunk that the VTP message was received on.

You must add VLANs to the VTP server before assigning the VLANs to ports on either VTP servers or clients. However, switches assigned as VTP transparent do not participate in VTP but will relay the VTP updates to other switches in the domain. You must create and remove VLANs locally on transparent switches. The VLANs are stored in NVRAM on the VTP transparent switch, but they are not advertised to the VTP domain. Figure 3-4 illustrates how VLAN information is advertised over VLAN trunks using VTP.

In this example, a new VLAN is added to the VTP server for the human resources department. The update is sent out on all VLAN trunk ports, to all switches in the domain. The transparent switch simply forwards the update to its downstream neighbor.

Figure 3-4 *A Simple VTP Domain with a VTP Server Sending Updates to VTP Clients*

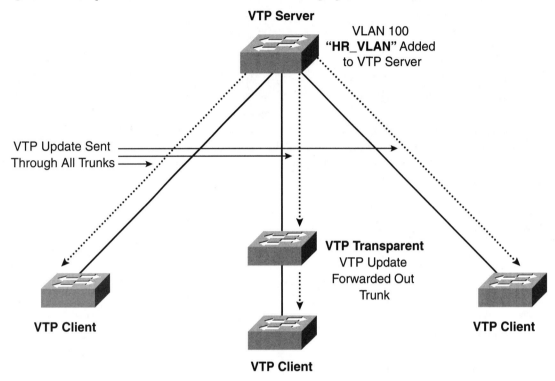

Important facts that you should know about VTP are

- **VTP Administration**—VTP is a VLAN administration protocol for ensuring VLAN configuration consistency across switches in your network. Additionally, VTP saves configuration time in large networks because VLANs need not be added to every switch in the network.

- **VLAN Flood Prevention**—VTP pruning prevents broadcast and multicast traffic from being flooded over trunks to switches that do not have any ports assigned to the VLAN.

- **Decrease NVRAM**—NVRAM space is better used in large networks, as only a single copy of the VTP database is stored centrally in the NVRAM of the VTP server, not in every switch in the network.

- **Human Readable VLAN Names**—VTP is useful for providing human readable names for VLANs.

- **CLI and SNMP Configuration Support**—You can administer VTP on your switches using both the command-line interface (CLI) and Simple Network Management Protocol (SNMP).

Understanding IP Routing

So far you've learned how frames are forwarded within and across broadcast domains. Forwarding Ethernet frames within a broadcast domain is a Layer 2 decision and therefore requires a Layer 2 switch. In contrast, forwarding frames across different broadcast domains requires a router in order to move Layer 3 packets from one end-system to another. Routers use IP routing to determine the path between end-systems by manually defined static routes or dynamic routing protocols or both. Figure 3-5 gives a simple IP routing network with three Cisco routers.

Figure 3-5   *A Simple IP Routing Environment*

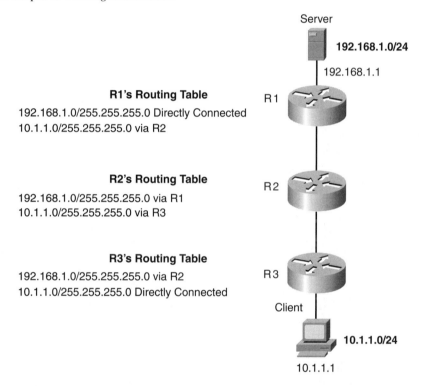

R1's Routing Table
192.168.1.0/255.255.255.0 Directly Connected
10.1.1.0/255.255.255.0 via R2

R2's Routing Table
192.168.1.0/255.255.255.0 via R1
10.1.1.0/255.255.255.0 via R3

R3's Routing Table
192.168.1.0/255.255.255.0 via R2
10.1.1.0/255.255.255.0 Directly Connected

Server
192.168.1.0/24
192.168.1.1
R1

R2

R3
Client
10.1.1.0/24
10.1.1.1

Assume in this example that each of the router's routing tables are inclusive of entries for both the client and server subnets. Each entry contains the IP subnet and next-hop address pointing to the adjacent router in the direction of the destination subnet. In order to forward frames to adjacent routers, each next-hop IP address from the routing table and its associated MAC address must reside in the ARP table on the router. Also assume in this example that ARP entries for neighboring routers have been created on the three routers, the client, and the server.

The client requesting content from the server across the network first sends the request for IP 192.168.1.1 to its default gateway router, R3. Router R3 then performs a route lookup in its routing table using the requested IP as the key to determine the closest matching routing entry. The result of the lookup is the following route for the server's subnet:

> 192.168.1.0/255.255.255.0 via R2

In this route, the subnet is 192.168.1.0, and the mask is 255.255.255.0. The next-hop is via R2, meaning that R1 should route the packets to the neighboring interface of R2. Using this route, router R3 routes the packet to the next-hop R2. When R2 receives the packet, it too performs a routing table lookup resulting in the entry [192.168.1.0/255.255.255.0 via R1], and in turn routes the packet to R1. R1 receives the packet, performs a route lookup, and determines that the subnet 192.168.1.0 is directly connected. R1 performs an ARP lookup for the server IP 192.168.1.1 and sends the packet to the server with the resulting MAC address.

> **NOTE**   Subnet masking involves performing a bit-wise AND operation between the mask and the IP address used as the key for the routing table lookup. The closest match route is the route with the longest subnet mask that, when masked to the requested IP, results in the subnet address of the associated routing entry. For example, when R2 uses the server IP 192.168.1.1 as key and applies the mask 255.255.255.0 associated to the entry [192.168.1.0/255.255.255.0 via R1], the result is 192.168.1.0. This matches the subnet in the routing entry; therefore, the router chooses this route for the request. If the subnet did not match, the router tries the other entries in its routing table until a match is found. If there happened to be other entries that also matched, the router would choose the entry with the longest subnet mask.

You can configure routers to populate their routing tables either by configuring static routing entries or by enabling dynamic routing protocols to automatically learn the different routes in the network.

Configuring Static Routing

To manually add routes to routing tables, use static routing. In Figure 3-6, router R1 requires knowledge of subnets 192.168.1.0/24, 192.168.2.0/24, and 192.168.3.0/24. To add these three routes to the routing table of R1, use the following static routes.

> **ip route 192.168.1.0 255.255.255.0 10.1.3.1**
> **ip route 192.168.2.0 255.255.255.0 10.1.3.1**
> **ip route 192.168.3.0 255.255.255.0 10.1.3.1**

Alternatively, you can summarize these three static routes using the single static route:

> **ip route 192.168.0.0 255.255.0.0 10.1.3.1**

Example 3-3 illustrates how to add this static route to R1.

Example 3-3 *Configuring a Summary Static Route on a Router*

```
Router1#configure terminal
Router1(config)#ip route 192.168.0.0 255.255.0.0 10.1.3.2
Router1(config)#
```

Router R3 requires knowledge of the three subnets in the network 10.1.0.0/16. To add these three routes to the routing table of R1, use the following static routes.

> **ip route 10.1.1.0 255.255.255.0 192.168.3.1**
> **ip route 10.1.2.0 255.255.255.0 192.168.3.1**
> **ip route 10.1.3.0 255.255.255.0 192.168.3.1**

Alternatively, you can summarize these three routes using the single static route:

> **ip route 10.1.0.0 255.255.0.0 192.168.3.1**

Router R2 has directly connected interfaces in 10.1.3.0/24 and 192.168.3.0/24 but is not aware of any of the other subnets on R1 and R3. Therefore, you can add the following two summary routes to the routing table of R2 in order for it to know how to route to these subnets.

Figure 3-6 *A Static Routing Environment with Manual Summary Routes*

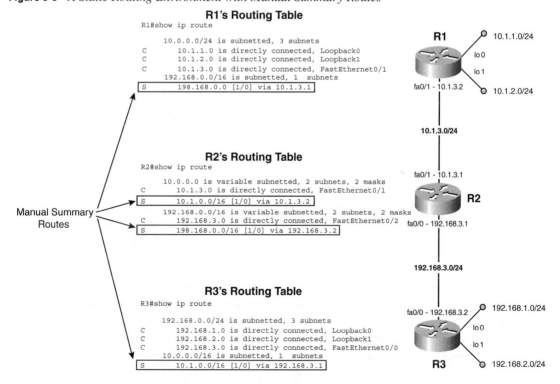

Understanding Dynamic Routing

To enable a router to automatically determine optimal paths to the subnets in a network, use dynamic routing protocols. Dynamic routing protocols can be:

- Distance-vector, such as Routing Information Protocol (RIP), and Interior Gateway Routing Protocol (IGRP)

- Link-state, such as Open Shortest Path First (OSPF) and (Intermediate System-to-Intermediate System) IS-IS

- Distance-vector/link-state hybrid called Enhanced Interior Gateway Routing Protocol (EIGRP)

These protocols exchange information between routers in order to discover network topology. If similar routes are learned by a protocol, then the route with the longest subnet mask is selected. Otherwise, the protocol's metric is used to break the tie. Dynamic protocol metrics are numeric values that specify which route should be preferred to reach the destination network.

Distance-vector metrics are calculated based on the number of router hops between end-systems. All hops are considered equal, regardless of the attributes of the links between routers. In contrast, link-state protocols intelligently calculate metrics based on the "state" of the links between routers. The metrics are based on link attributes, such as bandwidth, delay, reliability, load, and MTU. As a result, link-state metric calculations are far more processor- and memory-intensive than distance-vector metric calculations.

Distance-vector and link-state algorithms differ also in the way in which network information is discovered. With distance-vector algorithms, all or a portion of the routes from the routing table are sent to neighboring routers periodically (normally every 30 seconds), even if no changes in the network occur. When a neighboring router receives an update packet, it calculates the metric (or *distance*) and direction (or *vector*), updates its routing table, and in turn sends the update to its neighbors (except to the neighbor it came from). You can configure distance-vector protocols to filter routes before receiving and sending updates in order to prevent knowledge of certain routes from being known by particular routers in the network. Route filtering provides you with the ability to fine-tune your network routing policies.

Link-state protocols differ from distance-vector protocols in that they send updates when changes in the network occur, such as the failure of a network link or the addition of new links to the network. If no changes occur, link-state protocols send out periodic updates but less frequently than distance-vector algorithms, normally every 30 minutes.

Link-state algorithms store routes locally in a separate database before updating the main routing table. This database is called a routing information base (RIB). Each router sends its entire forwarding information base (FIB) database to its neighbors, within link-state advertisements (LSA), which in turn propagate the LSAs to neighbors, until the LSAs are received by all routers in the network. The main routing tables are not updated until all routers are aware of the LSAs from all other routers in the network. This network-wide awareness prevents those routing loops that often occur in distance-vector protocols and result from routers immediately updating routing tables directly upon reception of routing entries from their neighbors. Link-state protocols are not capable of filtering network updates in order to ensure that all routers receive the LSAs of all other routers in the network. Routing loops cannot form if routers are aware of the entire network before updating their routing tables

Hybrid protocols incorporate the efficiency of distance-vector algorithms and intelligent metric calculation of link-state algorithms. Use EIGRP to enable routers to automatically learn necessary routing information, as illustrated in Figure 3-7. Notice that EIGRP automatically summarizes the routes from the RIB for the subnets within 10.0.0.0/24 into the routing table. However, because the 192.168.x.0 networks are classful networks, EIGRP will not summarize these routes any further.

Figure 3-7   *A Dynamic Routing Environment with EIGRP-Learned Routes*

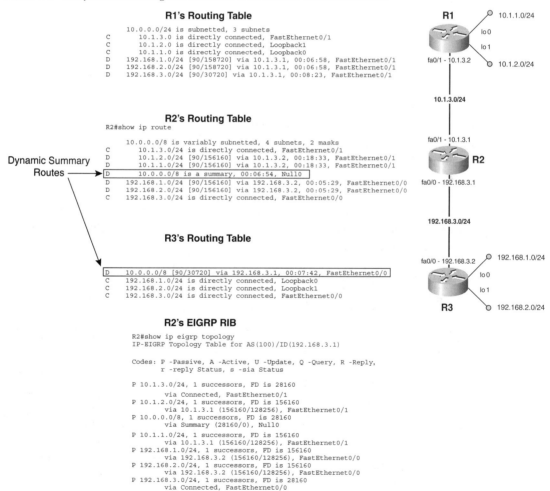

The routes 10.1.3.0/24 and 10.1.0.0/16 are both available in R2's routing table but have different subnet mask lengths. The first is more specific, so it will be selected as best for all traffic destined to that subnet. Figure 3-7 uses the EIGRP configurations on R1, R2, and R3 in Example 3-4.

Example 3-4   *Sample EIGRP Routing Configuration*

```
R1
router eigrp 100
 network 10.0.0.0
 network 192.168.3.0

R2
router eigrp 100
 network k 10.0.0.0
 network 192.168.3.0

R3
router eigrp 100
 network 192.168.1.0
 network 192.168.2.0
 network 192.168.3.0
```

As with static routing, each dynamic routing entry in the routing table contains the destination network, mask, next-hop to the destination, and the routing protocol used to determine the route. The metric and administrative distances are also included in the routing table entry for both static and dynamic routing entries. Metrics and administrative distances are used to determine the optimal path if more than one entry is available for the same subnet.

Each routing method has an administrative distance, which assigns a priority to the protocol to help in determining the optimal path for individual routing entries. Table 3-2 gives the administrative distances for each method.

Table 3-2   *Administrative Distances for All Available Routing Methods*

Routing Method	Distance
Connected interface	0
Static route	1
Enhanced Interior Gateway Routing Protocol (EIGRP) summary route	5
External Border Gateway Protocol (BGP)	20
Internal EIGRP	90
IGRP	100
OSPF	110
Intermediate System-to-Intermediate System (IS-IS)	115

Table 3-2   *Administrative Distances for All Available Routing Methods (Continued)*

Routing Method	Distance
Routing Information Protocol (RIP)	120
Exterior Gateway Protocol (EGP)	140
On Demand Routing (ODR)	160
External EIGRP	170
Internal BGP	200
Unknown	255

Most routers are capable of running numerous routing protocols as routing processes. Each process stores learned network information in a separate RIB, which is used to update the router's main routing table. If routes to the same destination network are installed from different processes into the routing table, the one with the longest subnet mask is selected as the best route. If routes with the same subnet mask length are installed, the administrative distances listed in Table 3-1 are used to break the tie. All inferior routes are stored in the RIBs, for later use in the case of topology change or route recalculations, if necessary.

NOTE   Besides determining optimal routes, metrics and administrative distances are also used for multicast reverse path forwarding (RPF) lookups, which will be covered in Chapter 6, "Ensuring Content Delivery with Quality of Service".

Internal gateway protocols (IGPs) are used to learn subnets within an autonomous system (AS). An AS is a network or group of networks administered by the same entity, such as an organization or university. Examples of IGPs are EIGRP, OSPF, and RIP. Alternatively, external gateway protocols (EGPs) are used to route information between autonomous systems, through autonomous system border routers (ASBRs). Each AS is given a globally unique identifier, referred to as an AS number. The AS number is used for peering relationships and routing loop detection across autonomous systems.

Packet Switching

IP switching is similar in concept to frame switching. The difference is that routers use Layer 3 IP addresses for switching criteria whereas frame switching uses Layer 2 MAC addresses.

Switching packets within a router adds delay to applications that require real-time responses. To switch a packet, a router uses the following steps, each of which adds to the end-to-end delay of a packet through a network.

Step 1   Determine if the destination in the IP packet header is reachable.

> **Step 2**   Determine the MAC address and interface of the next-hop toward the final destination.
>
> **Step 3**   Rewrite the MAC address of the Ethernet frame and forward the packet out the next-hop interface.

A packet may take one of three switching paths through a router. These paths are ordered by efficiency and, depending on the path packets take through a router, can affect the perceived delay of your application.

1. Process switching path

2. Fast switching path

3. Cisco Express Forwarding (CEF) switching path

Process Switching Path

With process switching, each packet's destination is deemed reachable by looking directly in the routing table. If the entry is available, the IP address of the next-hop is retrieved from the entry. Additionally, the MAC of the next-hop is retrieved directly from the ARP table. Figure 3-8 illustrates how packets are switched using the process switching path.

Figure 3-8   *The Process Switching Path*

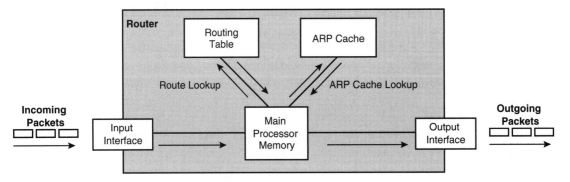

Per-packet load sharing is available in the process switching path, for subnets with more than one routing table entry to the final destination. Each packet within an individual flow will take a different route. Unfortunately, per-packet load sharing may introduce TCP reordering, because packets take different paths toward the destination and may end up at the receiving host at different times. As you learned in Chapter 2, TCP-based applications are not affected by out-of-sequence packets. However, for UDP-based real-time applications, such as IP telephony and streaming media, out-of-sequence packets pose major quality issues.

Performing lookups into both the routing and ARP tables for each packet is a relatively expensive task. To avoid routing table and ARP cache lookups for each packet in a flow, use the fast switching or Cisco Express Forwarding (CEF) path.

Fast Switching Path

With fast switching, to avoid both routing table and ARP cache lookups for every packet in a flow, the router gradually builds a flow cache from traffic received by the router. The flow cache is built by process switching the initial packet of each flow through the process switching path. Necessary forwarding information, such as next-hop interface, next-hop MAC address, and IP subnet, is retrieved from the ARP cache and routing table and stored in another table called the FIB. Subsequent packets of the flow are switched using the FIB.

The premise behind fast switching is that, if a specific destination IP address is required once, more than likely it will be required in the near future. FIBs contain less information than available in both the routing tables and ARP caches, making them much more efficient for destination IP lookups.

Figure 3-9 illustrates how fast switching operates.

Figure 3-9 *The Fast Switching Path*

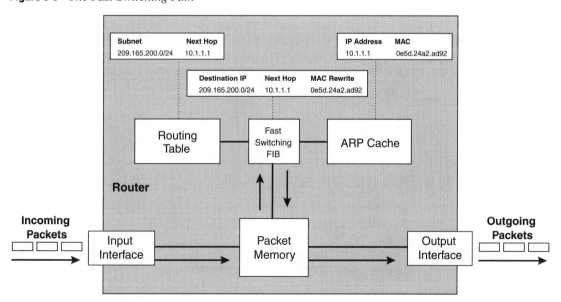

As shown in Figure 3-9, the router receives a packet with destination IP 209.165.200.255. In its routing table it has a single entry [209.165.200.0/24 via 10.1.1.1] for this destination IP.

Additionally, its ARP table contains the entry [10.1.1.1, 0e5d.24a2.ad92] for the next-hop of the routing table entry. The resultant FIB entry contains the IP subnet, with the MAC and IP address of the next-hop router.

Per-destination load sharing is available in the fast switching path for subnets with more than one routing table entry to the final destination. That is, flows with the same destination IP address take the same route to that destination.

Most routes in large ISP networks are learned from BGP where the next-hop in the routing table entry is not a directly connected neighbor of the router. Instead the next-hop entry is for a remote BGP route, located at the border of the AS. In these instances, the next-hop field in the fast switching FIB entry for the remote BGP router is determined by performing an ARP cache lookup of the neighbor router IP that the BGP route was learned from. This additional lookup occurs while process switching the first packet of the flow and is referred to as a *recursive lookup*. For example, in Figure 3-10, the next-hop for the route to 209.165.200.0/24 is 10.1.2.2. The first packet of a flow arriving for the server 209.165.200.0 is process switched. The router notices that the next-hop is not directly connected and performs another routing table look up for 10.1.2.2. The result is the directly connected next-hop 10.1.1.2, the router that the BGP update was learned from. The router then looks into its ARP cache for 10.1.1.2 and populates the FIB entry with the result.

Figure 3-10 *Handling Nonadjacent Next-Hop Routing Table Entries*

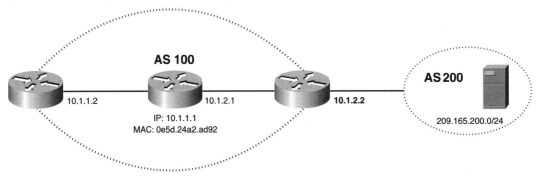

The router automatically refreshes the fast switching FIB periodically by randomly invalidating 1/20th of the cache entries every minute; otherwise, the FIB could grow extremely large in a short time. Changes to the routing table also cause invalidation of cache entries, resulting in a cache refresh. Routers with high route churn cause the fast switching FIB to be frequently refreshed. To avoid issues related to cache invalidation, refreshing, and recursive lookups, you should enable the CEF switching path in your network.

Cisco Express Forwarding

With CEF switching, every entry in the routing table has an associated entry in the CEF FIB. Additionally, every entry in the ARP table has an associated entry in a separate adjacency table, thus separating the reachability information from forwarding information in the CEF path. A benefit of this separation is that the process switching path is not required to build the CEF entries—the router builds the CEF tables in parallel to the routing table.

The data structure of CEF is called a *trie* with its leaves pointing to individual entries in the adjacency table instead of containing the forwarding information themselves. A trie has the benefit of providing per-flow load sharing by inserting a load sharing hash bucket table between the FIB and adjacency table to determine which of multiple paths each packet should take, if more than one is available.

> **NOTE**   The CEF trie is not built on-demand, as is the fast switching cache and therefore does not require refreshing.

Hash tables provide rapid access to data items that are distinguishable by a key. Each data item to be stored is associated with a key, such as IP address. A hash function is applied to the key, and the resulting hash value is used as an index to select one of a number of "hash buckets" in a hash table.

> **NOTE**   Hash buckets that are used for content distribution in caching environments will be discussed further in Chapter 12, "Exploring Global Server Load Balancing."

The buckets contain pointers to the original items. In the case of CEF, the pointers point to the CEF adjacency table entries. The Cisco IOS maintains a hash table with 16 buckets. That is, the maximum number of active paths that are load shared is 16. If 16 is not evenly divisible by the number of active paths, the last few remain unused. Per-flow load sharing is achieved because a source-destination hash provides the same hash bucket entry each time, so the same interface is chosen for every packet in the flow. To enable per-flow load sharing, use the interface configuration command **ip load-sharing per-destination**.

> **NOTE** Although the **ip load-sharing** parameter is "**per-destination**," both the source and destination are hashed together to provide per-flow load sharing. TCP ports are not hashed; therefore, a CEF flow is not a Layer 4 transport connection. Rather, a flow is the traffic generated between a source-destination IP pair at Layer 3.

Table 3-3 provides an example hash bucket table for a router with three serial interfaces available for CEF load sharing.

Table 3-3 *A Sample CEF Per-Flow Load Sharing Table*

Bucket Number	Path
1	Serial1
2	Serial2
3	Serial3
4	Serial1
5	Serial2
6	Serial3
7	Serial1
8	Serial2
9	Serial3
10	Serial1
11	Serial2
12	Serial3
13	Serial1
14	Serial2
15	Serial3
16	unused

After the FIB lookup, the source and destination IP address are hashed to determine which adjacency to use in the adjacency table—that is, which interface to forward the flow to.

If most traffic is coming from a single source-destination pair, one of the paths may be overloaded. In this case, you should consider enabling CEF per-packet load balancing instead, using the **ip load-sharing per-packet** interface configuration command.

Figure 3-11 illustrates the CEF switching path.

Figure 3-11   *The CEF Switching Path*

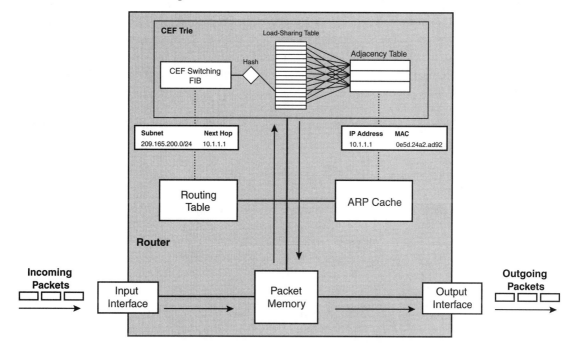

> **NOTE**   Even with CEF switching, each packet is sent to main packet memory. To bypass main packet memory, use distributed CEF switching (dCEF). dCEF stores copies of CEF trie on supported Cisco router line-cards. Incoming packets destined to next-hop routers reachable from the local line-card are switched by the local trie to the next hop interface and not to main packet memory.

To allow failover to the next less efficient path, most routers support running all three switching paths (each with its own FIB structure) in tandem. As new features are released by Cisco, such as QoS features, they normally start in the process switching path until they are well-tested; only then can they be promoted to a more efficient switching path.

Netflow is the intermediary switching technology to CEF switching, but it has been superseded as a switching path by CEF. However, Netflow accounting and flow-acceleration remain as powerful IP switching features for content networking and work in conjunction with the previously described switching paths. Netflow accounting exports real-time flow information for billing purposes.

Transparent Bridging

Transparent bridging is similar to Layer 2 frame switching but is performed on Layer 3 routers to bridge between different VLANs that are on the same IP subnet. Bridging is useful for migration from one VLAN number to a new VLAN number, while keeping the same IP subnet. For example, if you require changing the number of a VLAN in your network, first configure your router to bridge between the old and new VLANs. Then create a new VLAN and reassign switch ports to the new VLAN one port at a time. Your router will bridge between the existing VLAN and new VLAN during the migration period.

Figure 3-12 illustrates how bridging is performed by Cisco IOS routers in a simple transparent bridging configuration.

Figure 3-12 *Transparent Bridging*

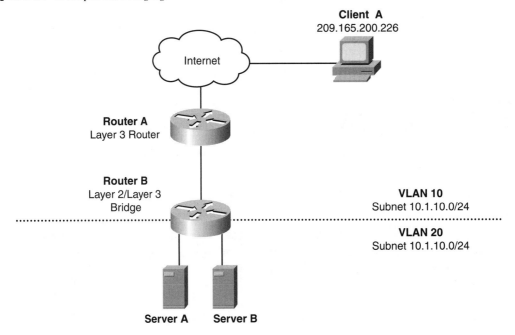

In Figure 3-12, for the client to access Server A or B on VLAN 20, Router A first routes the packets to Router B. Router B then bridges packets between VLAN 10 and VLAN 20 at Layer 3 to the individual servers. For the servers to access one another, packets are switched at Layer 2 within VLAN 20 on Router B.

> **NOTE**   Server load balancing (SLB) devices bridge between client-facing VLANs and server farm VLANS in the same way as Router B bridges in Figure 3-12. More information on bridging will be discussed in Chapter 10.

Like most of the examples throughout this book, the servers in Figure 3-12 are assigned private addresses for illustration purposes only. In your network, publicly addressed servers may be beneficial. In order for the privately addressed servers in Figure 3-12 to communicate with the publicly addressed client at Layer 3, Network Address Translation (NAT) is required.

Exploring Network Address Translation

NAT involves rewriting IP addresses in the IP packet header to a different IP address before routing the packet to its final destination. You can use the following two forms of NAT in your network to translate IP addresses:

- Source Network Address Translation

- Destination Network Address Translation

Source Network Address Translation

In order to protect internal resources in your network, you should assign private addresses to corporate computers that do not serve content to Internet clients. By privately addressing these computers, you hide them from the view of the public Internet. In contrast, you should assign publicly available server registered addresses and locate them on a secure segment of the network. By assigning your private corporate servers with private addresses, you conserve registered IP addresses for use on the publicly available servers.

> **NOTE**   Network security and firewalls are discussed in Chapter 4, "Exploring Security Technologies and Network Infrastructure Design."

To achieve registered address conservation and computer hiding, first assign private addresses to corporate computers within your corporate network, such as workstations or internal servers. Then apply one or more of the following policies on a NAT-capable device, such as a router or firewall:

- Static Network Address Translation

- Dynamic Network Address Translation

- Port Address Translation

> **NOTE**   The following ranges are designated as private IP addresses for their respective classes:
>
> - Class A : 10.0.0.0 – 10.255.255.255
> - Class B : 172.16.0.0 – 172.31.255.255
> - Class C : 192.168.0.0 – 192.168.255.255

Static Network Address Translation

With static NAT, publicly registered IP addresses are mapped one-to-one to privately addressed workstations and servers located on the inside of the firewall. When a privately addressed computer attempts to access an IP address on the Internet, the NAT device first rewrites the source IP of the packet before routing the packet to the outside network. Return packets are subsequently rewritten with the private IP address and the packets are routed to the appropriate internal computer.

In Figure 3-13, the following static NAT entries are configured on the NAT device in order for the three inside clients to access outside services:

1.   Inside source 10.1.1.5 translates to 209.165.200.225

2.   Inside source 10.1.1.6 translates to 209.165.200.226

3.   Inside source 10.1.1.7 translates to 209.165.200.227

In Figure 3-13, a group of three users access an HTTP server with IP address 209.165.200.1. The NAT translation table on the right shows the NAT entries accumulating as the connections are translated on the NAT device. In the first two entries, the user with IP address 10.1.1.6 connects to the HTTP server twice by opening two browser windows to the site. The same registered source IP of 209.165.200.226 is used for both TCP connections. The two NAT entries are distinguished by source port numbers 5234 and 5235. The second two entries are from the other two users also connecting to the HTTP server at 209.165.200.1.

Static NAT is useful in environments where tracking rewritten IP addresses is necessary. The mappings are permanent or at least available as long as the firewall configuration remains unchanged. Conversely, dynamic NAT mappings are short lived and therefore difficult to track.

Figure 3-13 *A Static NAT Example*

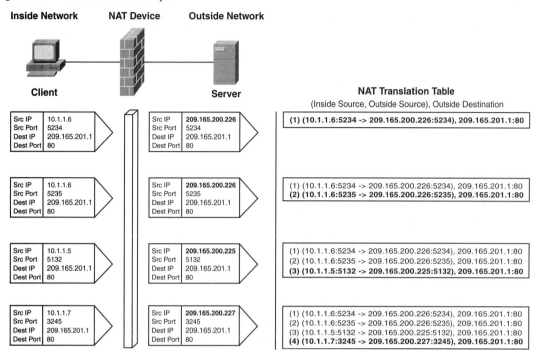

Dynamic NAT

As with static NAT, dynamic NAT rewrites each private source IP address with a dedicated registered IP address, but the IP is dynamically chosen from a pool of addresses that you configure for NAT. Once all addresses from the pool have been assigned, the pool is considered empty and no other computers are granted access to the outside network.

Figure 3-14 illustrates the IP address translations that occur using the following pool of outside addresses:

1. Outside address A: 209.165.200.225

2. Outside address B: 209.165.200.226

3. Outside address C: 209.165.200.227

Using the example in Figure 3-13, which was discussed previously, the same sequence of events occurs but results in different translations because IP addresses are allocated in sequence from the pool.

Figure 3-14   *A Dynamic NAT Example*

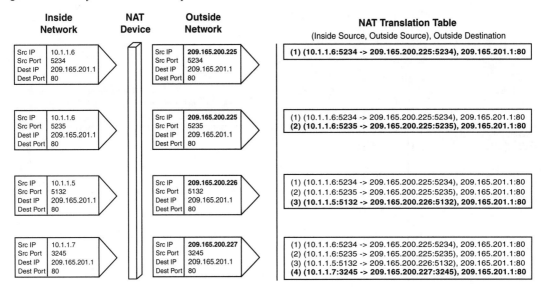

Port Address Translation (PAT)

Besides using static or dynamic source IP address NAT to conserve registered IP addresses and hide internal resources, you can also use Port Address Translation (PAT). However, with PAT a single IP address serves multiple source IP addresses. Additionally, neither static nor dynamic source NAT rewrites the source port of the source TCP segments. In contrast, PAT rewrites the source transport port of the TCP or UDP segments in order to distinguish between NAT entries in the translation table. Figure 3-15 illustrates how the single IP 209.165.200.225 is used by three privately addressed computers to access an HTTP server on the outside network at 209.165.201.1. The source ports 6001, 6002, and 6003 are used by the NAT device in this example to distinguish the PAT entries in the translation table. In practice, the source port numbers chosen by a NAT device are generated randomly.

Figure 3-15 *A Port Address Translation Example*

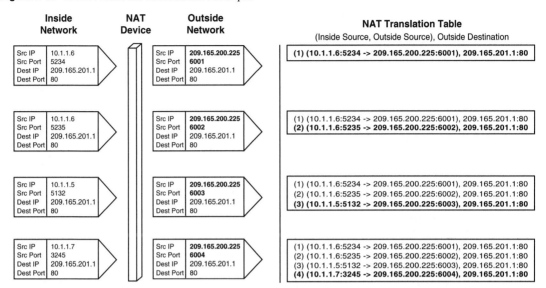

Destination Translation

A less common form of NAT is destination NAT, which is used primarily by content switches to perform server and cache load balancing. With SLB, server farms containing real servers that are each assigned individual IP addresses share the incoming connections. The content switch rewrites the destination IP of a packet to one of the real server IPs and forwards the packet to the real server that is allocated that IP. In Figure 3-16, three sources from the public Internet (that is, the outside network) access an inside HTTP server using the virtual IP (VIP) 209.165.201.1. The three clients are addressed as follows:

1. Client A: 209.165.202.129

2. Client B: 209.165.202.130

3. Client C: 209.165.202.131

The four individual inside real servers that are accessed using the VIP 209.165.201.1 are addressed as follows:

1. Real server A: 209.165.200.225

2. Real server B: 209.165.200.226

3. Real server C: 209.165.200.227

4. Real server D: 209.165.200.228

Figure 3-16 illustrates the translations that take place when the three clients access the virtual IP.

Figure 3-16 *A Destination NAT Example*

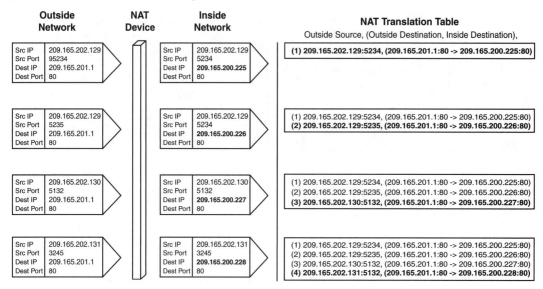

In the first two entries, the same user with IP address 209.165.202.129 accesses the HTTP server by opening two browsers to the main page, as in previous examples. But NAT now occurs on the destination address of the HTTP server. The NAT device allocates the next available IP in the pool, rewrites the destination IP address in the packet, and forwards the packet to the real server.

> **NOTE** Much more memory is required for destination NAT, because the sources are from the Internet and are not limited to the number of clients in your organization.

Summary

This chapter introduces the reader to many Layer 2–4 services available in Cisco routers, switches, firewalls, and content switches:

- **Layer 2 frame services**—Cisco Layer 2 switches perform MAC address learning in order to transparently switch MAC frames at Layer 2.

- **Layer 3 packet services**—Cisco IOS routers determine the path that packets take throughout a network using static or dynamic routing. Within the router, packets forwarded using process, fast, and CEF switching.

- **Layer 4 segment services**—Cisco IOS routers and firewalls perform network address translation to conserve registered IP addresses and hide internal IP addressing schemes. Cisco content switches perform destination address translation to distribute requests across identical servers in a server farm.

Review Questions

1. How are MAC address tables built in Layer 2 switches?

2. Do Layer 3 switches maintain an ARP cache or a MAC address table?

3. What is the purpose of VTP?

4. What is the difference between distance-vector and link-state dynamic routing protocols?

5. What is an RIB? Give a few examples of protocols that use RIBs.

6. What is an FIB? Give a few examples of switching paths that use FIBs.

7. What form of NAT do content switches use to load balancing requests across server farms?

Recommended Reading

Doyle, Jeff. *Routing TCP/IP*, Volume I, Second Edition. Cisco Press, 2005.
Clark, Kennedy, and Kevin Hamilton. *Cisco LAN Switching Fundamentals*. Cisco Press, 1999.

Chapter Goals

By covering the following topics in this chapter, you will learn how to design and secure content network infrastructures:

- **Securing Your Network**—You secure applications on your network with packet filtering and application inspection technologies.

- **Designing Enterprise Campuses**—Campus networks use routing and switching technologies to transport enterprise applications for corporate users.

- **Designing Enterprise Edge (or Data Center) Networks**—The data center for your organization contains the demarcation between the public and private network domains.

- **Designing Headquarters with Remote Office Networks**—Remote office users access corporate resources, the Internet, and other satellite offices through the corporate headquarters.

- **Designing Internet Content Delivery Networks**—Third-party content delivery networks provide edge content replication services for enterprises.

CHAPTER 4

Exploring Security Technologies and Network Infrastructure Designs

Information security is a major concern for organizations with any amount of critical business content in their networks. Within the context of content networking, four fundamental techniques are available for you to use for securing content:

- Application Layer Encryption

- Packet Filtering

- TCP enhancements

- Application Layer Inspection

You will learn content encryption using the public key infrastructure (PKI) in Chapter 8, "Exploring the Application Layer," along with PKI offloading technologies.

Filtering Packets with Access Control Lists

You can use access control lists (ACL) to permit or deny requests to services that are available within your network. You can apply ACLs to packets entering or leaving a firewall interface. Two forms of filters exist: stateless and stateful session ACLs. Firewalls that you enable with stateless ACLs treat each packet as an individual entity. Because stateless ACLs do not track transport connection information, routers apply the ACL to every packet regardless of the transport flow the packet is part of. Conversely, stateful session ACLs track flows to ensure that packets belong to a valid flow before filtering takes place.

> **NOTE** Firewalls can track TCP flows by inspecting the TCP flags and sequence numbers in the TCP segment header. Although UDP is connectionless, firewalls approximate UDP "connections" by examining the IP addresses and ports in the UDP segment and matching packets with the same UDP packet information. The firewall or router considers packets to be part of the same UDP connection if it receives UDP packets with the same IP addresses and UDP ports within the same approximate timeframe.

Stateful session ACLs are useful for filtering that is based on TCP/IP when you need to know the direction that the connection originates from. For example, your internal users may require access to an FTP site on the Internet, but you should block incoming FTP access to your internal network from the Internet. You cannot achieve this type of access control using stateless ACLs. Instead, you can use basic ACLs, reflexive ACLs, context-based access control (CBAC), or Cisco PIX firewalls, because these protocols use stateful inspection.

With stateful inspection, when your workstation sends an *outgoing* TCP SYN segment to an external resource, the firewall creates a temporary *incoming* ACL entry for your return traffic. The entry contains the same IP addresses and TCP port numbers as your outgoing request but with the source and destination values swapped. Figure 4-1 illustrates how firewalls implement stateful ACLs. In this example, the firewall is performing static source Network Address Translation (NAT), translating your client private IP 10.1.1.5 to the registered IP 209.165.200.225. When the server responds to your TCP SYN segment, it uses the registered IP in its TCP SYN-ACK response. This example configures the firewall to block all incoming traffic on interface Ethernet 0. However, the outgoing connection in this example creates a temporary incoming rule to permit return traffic to the inside user.

> **NOTE** Temporary ACLs approximate stateful inspection using a temporary incoming ACL entry. To perform true stateful inspection, Cisco devices maintain entries for individual flows in state tables. You will learn about state maintenance with session filtering later in this section.

Figure 4-1 *Stateful ACL Operation*

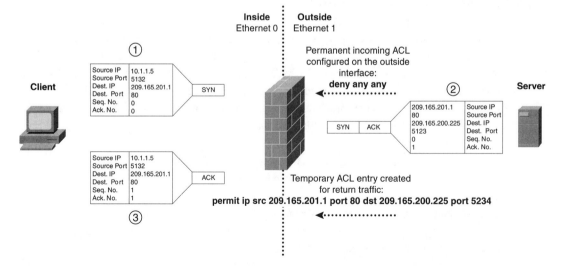

Cisco supports three types of stateful ACLs:

- **Basic Access Lists**—Basic ACLs do not automatically create temporary incoming entries for your return traffic. You must manually configure basic ACLs on your Cisco IOS firewall to approximate stateful session filtering by using the **established** keyword within **permit** ACL entries. The **established** keyword permits incoming TCP segments with their ACK or RST flag set—segments with these flags set indicate that they are not the first packet in the session. For example, the extended ACL entry **access-list 101 permit 10.1.1.0 0.0.0.255 any established**, when applied to incoming packets on the outside interface of the firewall in Figure 4-1, permits return packets of established TCP connections to your inside network in the subnet 10.1.1.0/24.

- **IP Session Filtering (Reflexive ACLs)**—IP session filters create temporary ACL entries for incoming TCP traffic. Example 4-1 illustrates how you can configure IP session filters. The outgoing named ACL **outsession** defines the entry to trigger the temporary incoming rule. You must give a name to your reflexive ACL entry; this example calls it **tcpreflect.** The incoming rule **insession** defines the ACL that denies all incoming traffic in this example. You can add specific entries to this rule if you would like to permit other types of traffic into your network (for example, you may want to allow incoming FTP access to your network). Use the **evaluate** statement to permit return traffic from established connections into your network. Use the command **ip reflexive-list timeout** to set the amount of time during which temporary entries will remain active without any traffic activity from the TCP session.

Example 4-1 *Configuring IP Session Filters*

```
interface FastEthernet 0/1
 ip access-group insession in
 ip access-group outsession out
!
ip reflexive-list timeout 120
!
ip access-list extended outsession
 permit tcp any any reflect tcpreflect
!
ip access-list extended insession
 deny ip any any
 evaluate tcpreflect
```

Temporary ACL entries store 5-Tuples (that is, protocol, source port, source IP address, destination port, and destination IP address) in RAM but do not store TCP connection state information including TCP flags and sequence numbers in RAM. Use the Cisco IOS Context Based Access Control (CBAC) firewall feature or PIX Firewall ACLs if you need your sessions stored in RAM.

■ **Cisco IOS Context Based Access Control (CBAC) firewall feature and PIX Firewall ACLs**—You can use CBAC or PIX firewalls to perform true stateful session filtering. When your users initiate new connections from the inside, the firewall first creates a session entry in its state table. The router then creates a temporary entry for return traffic. The benefit of maintaining the connection state in RAM is that the firewall is able to look further into the content within the connection using application layer inspection. The drawback is that your firewalls require much more memory to store the state table.

> **NOTE**   Firewall load balancing is available to you as a content networking security service. See Chapter 11, "Switching Secured Content," for more information on firewall load balancing.

Application Layer Inspection

Interesting TCP enhancements that fall "in between" packet filtering and application inspection are TCP normalization and SYN-cookies. Cisco Security Appliances use TCP normalization to drop packets that do not appear normal. Additionally, SYN cookies are initial TCP sequence numbers that encode a sender's IP address to enable the receiver to know which packets are from valid senders during a SYN-flood. These TCP enhancements prove to be beneficial for securing most applications. SYN-cookies are discussed in Chapter 11.

Application layer inspection is available with the Cisco PIX Firewall, Cisco Security Appliance, and the CBAC IOS firewall feature. In order to ensure the correct behavior of known applications, Cisco PIX Firewall and the CBAC IOS firewall feature store application layer session information along with the transport layer connection information in the state table. The firewall will drop the application layer session if behavior of the application is not RFC-compliant, even when the application session spans multiple TCP connections. Examples of RFC-compliance are

■ Users attempt valid application commands over the connection.

■ Commands occur in the correct sequence during the connection. For example, an HTTP response without an HTTP request violates the RFC 2626 definition of the HTTP request-response sequence.

To enable application inspection on the PIX firewall, use the **ip protocol fixup** command for each of the protocols that you would like to inspect. The PIX firewall will ensure that the protocol you configure obeys the common operation of the application protocol.

> **NOTE**   The PIX firewall also supports HTTP method and URL filtering. Additionally, the Cisco Application Velocity System (AVS) platform supports HTTP-specific application security features, such as cookie encryption, resource cloaking, and filtering based on HTTP encoding types.

To configure CBAC, you configure the applications you want to inspect using the **ip inspect** global configuration command. In Example 4-2, the CBAC list "inspectapps" gives the applications that the IOS firewall will inspect.

Example 4-2 *Configuring CBAC*

```
ip inspect name inspectapps rtsp timeout 30
ip inspect name inspectapps ftp timeout 30
ip inspect name inspectapps realaudio timeout 30

interface FastEthernet 0/1
 ip access-group insession in
 ip inspect inspectapps out
!
ip access-list extended insession
 deny ip any any
```

Common applications that you can inspect using CBAC or the PIX firewall are:

■ HTTP

■ Real-Time Session Protocol (RTSP)

■ H.323

■ FTP

■ Internet Control Management Protocol (ICMP)

■ Simple Mail Transfer Protocol (SMTP)

■ TFTP

NOTE   Network Based Application Recognition (NBAR) also inspects application traffic to classify packets for QoS policies. To learn more about NBAR, see Chapter 6, "Ensuring Content Delivery with Quality of Service."

Although CBAC and the PIX provide application layer inspection in addition to packet filtering capabilities, intrusion prevention systems (IPS) were developed by Cisco specifically to provide application layer inspection. IPSs are standalone appliances that protect your network by detecting, classifying, and blocking spyware, worms, adware, network viruses, and application abuse by inspecting information at Layers 2–7. IPSs evolved from the intrusion detection systems (IDS) to include a more robust set of threat identification methods to minimize false-positive alerts, such as:

- **Pattern recognition**—Detects code vulnerabilities by matching against text patterns (or "signatures") in the application payload, and thereby protects against Internet worms such as Code Red and Nimbda.

- **Protocol analysis**—Inspects known applications for deviations from RFC-compliant behavior.

- **Traffic-level anomaly detection**—Notices abnormal changes in application traffic levels. For example, an IPS detects ICMP floods if the number of ICMP packets exceeds a threshold over a given amount of time.

> **NOTE** The Cisco Traffic Anomaly Detector device is also available for distributed denial of service (DDoS) anomaly detection (via technology obtained from the Riverhead acquisition).

Designing Enterprise Campuses

In typical campus designs, individual buildings connect to a central building by way of physical layer uplinks. You can create uplinks using optical wavelengths, where numerous wavelengths of light create separate logical channels on single mode fiber. Optical technologies including dense wavelength division multiplexing (DWDM) and Cisco coarse wavelength division multiplexing (CWDM) have major bandwidth benefits between buildings but at a much higher cost than more traditional campus cabling designs. A possible reason for the higher cost of using DWDM or CWDM is that you require dedicated physical layer optical networking gear to multiplex the wavelengths onto the single mode fiber. Traditional physical layer uplinks include dark fiber, copper cabling, or wireless connectivity between the buildings.

You should centralize your user's access to corporate services, WAN connectivity to branch offices, and Internet access in the main campus building. Your users can connect through access switches at Layer 2 or 3 by routing or switching traffic to the central building through distribution switches located in the individual campus buildings. To provide resiliency for user access to centralized corporate resources, you can use Spanning Tree Protocol (STP), Etherchannel, or redundant routed links between the campus backbone and distribution switches. Figure 4-2 gives a fully redundant campus network design.

Figure 4-2 *A Typical Core/Distribution/Access Layer Campus Network Design*

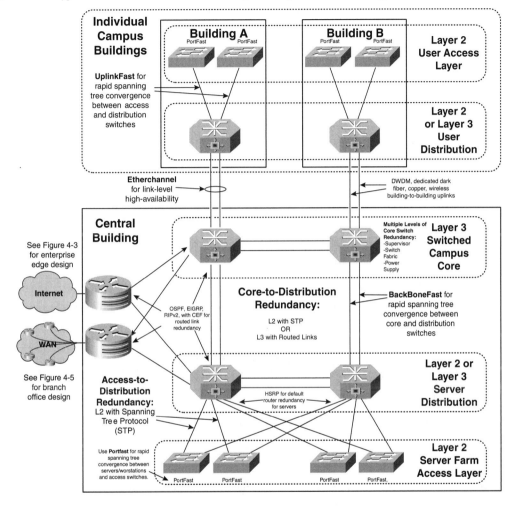

The central building contains the enterprise edge for incoming connections from the Internet and serves as the headquarters for satellite offices. You will learn about designs for enterprise edge and branch office networking in subsequent sections.

To provide high availability in the campus backbone, the core and distribution layers contain multiple levels of redundancy as follows:

■ **Supervisor module redundancy**—Core Catalyst 6500/7600 switches are often used as distribution and core campus switches. These high port-density switches have the capacity for both supervisor module and switch-fabric module redundancy. You can achieve supervisor module redundancy within a single chassis by adding a second supervisor. You can also use two chassis with a single supervisor in each to achieve supervisor module redundancy. When you have multiple supervisors, if any single component of one of the supervisors fails, such as DRAM memory or embedded switch fabric, the other will automatically take over processing in a stateless fashion, normally within 3 seconds. The standby supervisor maintains identical configuration, routing tables, ARP caches, Routing Information Bases (RIB), and Forwarding Information Bases (FIB) as the primary supervisor, thereby enabling fail-over in the event of primary supervisor failure.

NOTE Lower-end distribution switches, such as Cisco 4500 and Catalyst 3750 series switches, do not provide supervisor or switch fabric redundancy.

■ **Switch fabric redundancy**—In older versions of Catalyst 6500 switches, the switch fabric was built directly in to the chassis backplane (known as an active backplane) or was available as a separate line-card module, called a switch fabric module (SFM). To provide switch fabric redundancy to an active backplane, a dual chassis configuration is necessary. For SFM redundancy, you can install two SFMs in a single chassis for redundancy.

In more recent versions of the Catalyst 6500/7600 supervisor (that is, the Sup 720), the switch fabric is integrated into the supervisor module. With either the embedded supervisor switch fabric or a SFM line-card, redundancy is achieved within a single chassis.

NOTE The **switch fabric** is where intelligent switching occurs between the individual line-card modules and supervisor module(s). In contrast, the **backplane** is the physical circuit board where the individual modules attach. If you have an SFM in a Sup II or integrated switch fabric in a Sup 720, the switch fabric and backplane are physically separate entities. To use the switch fabric, make sure that you install fabric-enabled line cards.

■ **Layer 3 Routing redundancy**—Routing next-hop redundancy is performed using any dynamic routing protocol in Cisco IOS, such as IS-IS, EIGRP, or OSPF. Routers install multiple routes from the routing protocol FIBs and load balance between the routes using CEF per-destination or per-flow load balancing. You can achieve router default gateway redundancy for hosts using Hot Standby Router Protocol (HSRP).

■ **Layer 2 switching and link-level redundancy**—You can achieve uplink redundancy between access, distribution, and core switches using Etherchannel or STP. The Cisco Etherchannel supports link-level redundancy within the same switch module or across two or more different Ethernet modules.

For rapid spanning tree convergence between users/servers and access switches, enable Cisco PortFast on the appropriate switch ports; between access and distribution switches, enable Cisco UplinkFast; and between core and distribution switches, enable BackboneFast. These protocols reduce spanning tree convergence time by bypassing particular states in the spanning tree's finite state machine.

- **Power Supply redundancy**—The Cisco 6500/7600 provides space for dual power supplies within a single chassis. Alternately, two chassis with a single power supply in each achieves the same result.

Designing Enterprise Edge Networks

Within a corporate headquarters location, you can design a data center to house internal corporate servers and public servers accessible from the Internet. The corporate data center consists of the Internet access demarcation point to the Internet service provider (ISP). You will require a router in order to peer with the ISP router to share Internet routing information. To secure the network, use a firewall to provide stateful flow inspection of incoming traffic destined to your groups of servers. Your server groups may include

- **Public Internet Servers**—Public servers are available to anyone on the Internet. Your public servers may require initiating connections to the Internet for downloading software updates. They may also require connecting to internal resources, such as databases, e-mail, and storage servers.

- **Extranet Servers**—Semi-private servers contain sites dedicated to providing services to partners or customers that require network segmentation from other less-secure server groups. Like the public servers, the extranet servers may require the initiation of connections to the Internet and to certain internal resources.

- **Intranet Servers**—Private servers available only to internal corporate applications. Your public or extranet applications may require access to specific applications running on the intranet servers. In that case, you should locate the public databases, e-mail, storage, and file servers here for the public and extranet servers to access. Also, some of the private servers may require initiating connections to the Internet.

- **Corporate Network Workstations and Servers**—You should locate corporate clients and servers that are not publicly accessible from the Internet on a separate segment. These segments require firewall filtering from the public servers as well as from the Internet. A second firewall is beneficial for this purpose, as illustrated in Figure 4-3. Workstations and servers in the corporate network must be able to initiate connections to the Internet and to all server groups discussed previously.

Figure 4-3 *A Typical Enterprise Data Center Design*

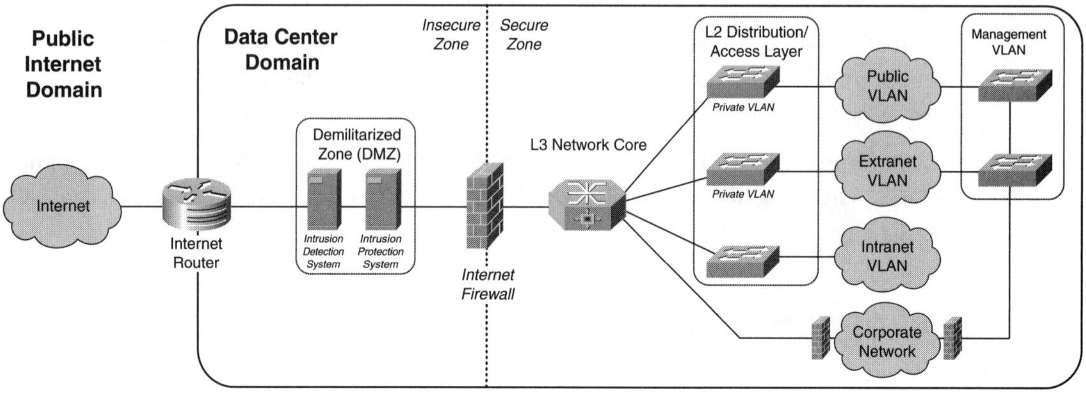

> **NOTE** For simplicity, the data center core is illustrated with only a single switch in Figure 4-3, but instead of using a single switch, you can use the highly available network core as illustrated in Figure 4-2. As such, you may enable most features in Figure 4-2 in this environment.

Figure 4-3 uses a Layer 3 core switch to provide VLAN capabilities in order to logically segment the groups of servers into VLANs. If you have a Firewall Service Modules (FWSM) in a Catalyst 6500 series core switch, you can apply filtering rules directly to the VLANs within the switch. Alternatively, you can trunk the VLANs from the Catalyst 6500 switch to the PIX firewall, where you can apply stateful filtering. The last option is to filter VLANs in the Catalyst 6500/7600 IOS using stateless ACLs, basic ACLs, reflexive ACLs, or CBAC as discussed previously. Other Layer 3 switches such as the Cisco 4500 and 3550 series switches that are smaller than the Catalyst 6500 are available for you to use in the data center core to provide similar VLAN routing and security capabilities within IOS.

> **NOTE** Enabling the IOS firewall feature set substantially increases the switch-processing load. Carefully evaluate whether your switch has the capacity to handle the traffic load before enabling any IOS firewall features.

You can also connect individual switches directly to the firewall on dedicated ports to achieve the same logical security design as illustrated previously in Figure 4-3. However, dedicated firewall ports are more expensive than using VLANs. Figure 4-4 illustrates how to connect the VLANs to the firewall directly.

Figure 4-4 *Using Dedicated Firewall Ports to Secure VLANs*

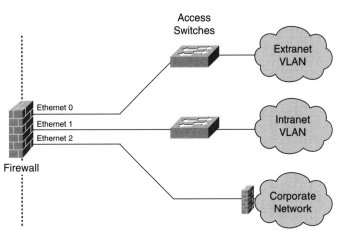

Your organization's corporate clients and servers should reside within a corporate network segment. As Figures 4-3 and 4-4 suggest, a separate firewall for the corporate network is beneficial for providing additional security to the internal network. To manage the public servers, use a second management VLAN, with a direct link into the corporate network. Each server in the public and extranet VLANs requires a separate network interface with only limited management protocols enabled, such as SNMP and remote console services.

The Demilitarized Zone (DMZ) segment is available for transparent IPSs and IDSs. These devices should receive and process traffic before it is filtered on the firewall. IPSs and IDSs must receive non-filtered traffic in order to accurately inspect application traffic and block offending traffic. Traffic is blocked by the IPS or IDS appliances by configuring it to apply policy rules to firewalls, adjusting routing metrics advertised to the ISP, or actively spoofing and resetting incoming TCP connections directly. You must configure the public facing network interface of the IPS or IDS as a monitoring port and configure port mirroring on your DMZ switch. To manage these servers, you can install and configure another network port and attach it to an internal segment.

Sandwiching public servers between two different firewalls has the benefit of using firewalls from multiple vendors to secure internal resources. Because firewalls from different vendors rarely share the same security vulnerabilities, if an attacker compromises the first firewall, the second will protect the internal network from attacks. Figure 4-5 illustrates the public VLAN that is between two firewalls, instead of hanging off a single firewall with the rest of the VLANs in your network.

Figure 4-5 *Using Two Firewalls to Secure a Public VLAN*

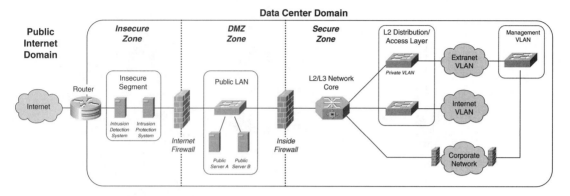

You can design a shared or dedicated web hosting data center in a similar fashion to the enterprise data center illustrated previously in Figure 4-3. However, in some dedicated hosting environments, you would want to give your customers full administrative access to the servers they lease. The fact that you would have numerous untrusted clients administering servers within your network introduces further security concerns. Although enterprise data center servers are publicly accessible, users often have access only to specific services such as HTTP on port 80, not full administrative rights of the server unless compromised by a hacker. For these types of insecure segments, you should use private VLANs to ensure that one computer cannot access another in the Layer 2 broadcast domain. Private VLANs enables server traffic to reach router ports only and block traffic originating from server ports destined to other server ports. For example, switches with private VLANs enabled do not broadcast an Address Resolution Protocol (ARP) request from one server to all other servers on the same broadcast domain (or VLAN, in this case). The switch forwards the ARP request only to switch ports you configure as promiscuous. Promiscuous ports receive the traffic from all the private ports. You should configure switch ports with routers connected as promiscuous.

Designing Headquarters with Remote Office Networks

If your enterprise extends across cities, countries, or continents, you can have three possible network topologies: hub and spoke, partial mesh, and in some cases, full mesh. With a hub and spoke topology, your branch office users have a single connection to the corporate headquarters. If they require access to the other branches, their branch router routes their traffic indirectly to the other branches by way of the headquarters router. In a fully meshed configuration, all locations have a single connection to every other location, enabling direct access to one another. A less extreme version of this is a partial mesh topology. As the name indicates, each branch maintains only a few connections to the other locations. Figure 4-6 illustrates the three branch office to central office access topologies.

Figure 4-6 *Typical Branch Office Network Designs*

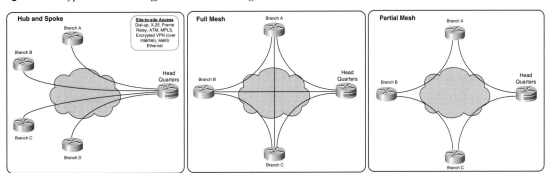

You can use various site-to-site WAN technologies to connect branch office buildings to the headquarters location. More traditional WAN access includes circuit-switched connectivity, such as Public Switched Telephone Network (PSTN) dialup links. Circuit-switched technology provides dedicated connectivity between end points.

Slightly less traditional access technologies include various private packet-switched network types, such as ISDN, X.25, Frame Relay, and ATM. These technologies provide a *logical* dedicated link between offices but use a shared non-IP-based packet-switched core. They are therefore much less expensive than circuit-switched networks. Packet-switched networks enable network service providers to provision for customers who have fluctuating traffic levels, which is the case with the majority of organizations. That is, a customer's traffic may burst above the agreed bandwidth on occasion and not affect other subscribers in the shared network. Under these circumstances, the provider may not charge the customer with a violation in the agreed bandwidth contract.

You can also use IP-based private and public packet-switched networks to create tunnels to form a VPN between locations. MPLS VPNs and encrypted Internet VPNs are available to you, at a major cost savings over traditional site-to-site technologies. Additionally, the underlying Layer 1 and 2 technologies are often much less expensive for IP-based networks than their traditional counterparts, making them very attractive to today's emerging organizations.

You can easily insert QoS into traditional access technologies to provide delay-sensitive applications, such as video and voice, with guaranteed delivery across the network. Additionally, you can achieve QoS inherently within the MPLS protocol. However, because the Internet is uncontrolled by nature, traffic prioritization is impossible for most Internet VPNs. You will learn about QoS in detail in Chapter 6.

You will also learn how branch topologies benefit from edge content caching, distribution, and routing in Chapter 13, "Delivering Cached and Streaming Media," and Chapter 14, "Distributing and Routing Managed Content," respectively.

Employing Internet Content Delivery Networks

If you are an organization with clients located across the globe, it would be beneficial to position your content in closer proximity to your clients. To do so, you can build your own Internet Content Delivery Network (ICDN). With an ICDN, you require two or more distributed data center locations, such as those illustrated in the Figure 4-3 and Figure 4-5, to share the traffic load from clients. For example, if your main data center is located in California but you have determined that 30 percent of your clients actually originate from Europe, it may be beneficial to replicate some critical services and deploy another data center somewhere in Europe. Figure 4-7 shows a simple ICDN.

Figure 4-7 *An ICDN Network Topology*

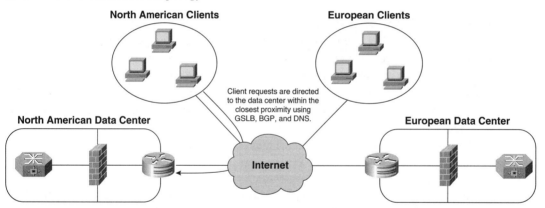

Alternatively, if you are a service provider, such as a web or application hosting provider, your clients may benefit from an ICDN. If so, you can develop an ICDN to replicate your *client's* content across geographic locations, not just your own content.

To achieve a distributed data center environment, you will learn content networking technologies such as Domain Name Service (DNS), Border Gateway Protocol (BGP), and Global Server Load Balancing (GSLB) in Chapter 12, "Exploring Global Server Load Balancing."

> **NOTE**   With ICDN, requesting clients perceive lower response times and cross-site redundancy is achieved in the event of the primary data center failing.

Numerous third-party ICDNs exist today to provide dedicated global ICDN services, such as Akamai and Digital Island. These companies have thousands of data centers worldwide, which are available to house surrogates of your content content. These ICDNs offer replication of static and even dynamic content. The benefit of outsourced ICDN services is that you do not require the initial capital expenditure and ongoing data center management costs to set up and manage your own global Internet CDN.

Summary

This chapter discusses several infrastructures common to content networking deployments:

- **Campus Networks**—Learning campus network designs helps put in perspective the fundamental routing and switching concepts you learned in earlier chapters. Campus networking benefits from content networking technologies such as video streaming with IP multicast.

- **Campus Edge**—Understanding how edge networks are built will help you when you learn about topics on content switching in later chapters. Being able to apply packet filtration and application inspection to content is crucial in securing your data center environment.

- **Branch Office Networks**—Branch office networks are designed such that remote user productivity is not affected by the connectivity to the headquarters. Content routing and delivery solutions are deployed to branch offices over remote links in order to achieve transparent resource access by remote users.

Review Questions

1. What is the difference between stateful and stateless ACLs?

2. How do stateful ACLs track transport state information?

3. How can you approximate UDP connections?

4. How can you achieve supervisor redundancy?

5. How can you achieve switch fabric redundancy?

6. What is one benefit of sandwiching public servers between two firewalls?

7. What content networking solutions do remote branch users benefit from?

Recommended Reading

Mauricio Arregoces, Maurizio Portolani, *Data Center Fundamentals*, Cisco Press, 2003

Gert DeLaet, Gert Schauwers, *Network Security Fundamentals*, Cisco Press, 2004

Ronald W. McCarthy, *Cisco WAN QuickStart,* Cisco Press, 2000

Part III: Intelligent Network Services for Content Delivery

Chapter Goals

In this chapter, you will learn how to design and configure two of the main types of IP Multicast networks:

- **Internet Standard Multicast (ISM)**— With ISM Multicast networks, the network discovers and distributes sources, creating additional load on network devices.

- **Source Specific Multicast (SSM)**— With SSM multicast networks, the sources are known by the receivers, thereby offloading source maintenance from the network to the receivers.

IP Multicast Content Delivery

To stop floodwaters from entering roads, property, and tributaries, people build dams and place sandbags at appropriate physical locations. IP Multicast is the Internetworking equivalent that prevents broadcast-based applications from flooding your entire network. This chapter introduces you to the Layers 2–4 protocols that Cisco routers and switches use for making upper-layer content networking applications more efficient.

IP Multicast technologies transport applications, such as live and on-demand audio–video feeds, video conferencing, and file transfers between participants. In the past, if multiple receivers required the same content from a single source, the sender generated a copy for each receiver. Multicast enables you to send traffic from a single source to multiple receivers, without replicating the information at the source. Your network forwards the traffic only to segments that contain hosts interested in receiving the traffic. At any given point in your network, there is never more than a single flow of the content on the same link. The result is an efficient use of bandwidth for disseminating your content.

> **NOTE**   For more information on applications and protocols that benefit from IP Multicast, see Chapter 9, "Introducing Streaming Media."

Introducing IP Multicast

With IP Multicast, an application source (S) sends traffic to a group (G) of receivers across your network. You assign the source with a unicast IP address and each group with a single multicast IP address within the registered multicast class D IP address range. When receiving hosts want to receive traffic from a multicast flow G, it is their responsibility to join the group themselves by using Internet Group Management Protocol (IGMP). Multicast routers do not track the IP addresses of the receivers, only whether or not there are any on the local LAN that want to receive the multicast traffic. That is, only those receivers that explicitly join a group receive traffic for that group.

You can configure your network for multicast using one of the following technologies.

- **Internet Standard Multicast (ISM)**—Any number of sources deliver ISM Multicast streams to a group of receivers. The receivers subscribe to groups, and the routers track the sources sending the multicast traffic in (S, G) state table entries. The receivers do not need to be source-aware and use IGMPv1 or IGMPv2 to join (*, G) host groups. Bidirectional streams are also available with ISM.

> **NOTE**   The notation (S, G) indicates that the individual source S is actively sending traffic to group G. In contrast, the (*, G) notation refers to any source * sending to group G.

- **Source Specific Multicast (SSM)**—With SSM Multicast, the network delivers a stream from one sender to a group of receivers. The receivers are source-aware and explicitly request multicast traffic from individual senders of a desired group in (S, G) IGMPv3 Include/ Exclude Join messages. The routers do not need to track the sources of the multicast groups and store only (*, G) state in their multicast routing tables. Therefore, SSM greatly reduces the complexity of the networks that are required to deliver multicast streams by offloading the source state to the receivers.

> **NOTE**   The sources do not signal any information to the network in either ISM or SSM; they simply start sending their traffic to the network when you schedule them to send.

Multicast IP addresses fall within the registered class D multicast range 224.0.0.0– 239.255.255.255. This range conveyed in binary, with the first half octet (4 bits) set to 1110, is

11100000.00000000.00000000.00000000 to

11101111.11111111.11111111.11111111

This range gives you 28 total bits of available multicast IP addresses. Table 5-1 gives the uses for the reserved multicast address ranges that pertain to multicast content delivery. Note that many network protocols, such as Open Shortest Path First (OSPF), also rely on multicast addresses to function (for example, 224.0.0.5 and 224.0.0.6) but are not included in Table 5-1.

Table 5-1   *IP Multicast Address Usage*

Address(es)	Usage
Link Local Scope	
224.0.0.1	All systems on this subnet
224.0.0.2	All routers on this subnet
224.0.0.13	All PIM routers address group

Table 5-1   *IP Multicast Address Usage (Continued)*

Address(es)	Usage
Global Scope	
224.0.1.0 to 238.255.255.255	Allocated for multicasting traffic across the Internet. SSM reserves the range 232.0.0.0/8. The addresses 224.0.1.39 and 224.0.1.40 are used for Auto-RP negotiation. You can assign the remaining IP address to your ISM applications.
Administrative Scope (AS)	
239.0.0.0/8	Allocated for organizations that own an AS number to multicast across the Internet. The AS number of the organization is embedded in the 2nd and 3rd octets of the multicast IP address. For example, the AS 64501 is FBF5 in hexadecimal, with FB and F5 (or 251 and 245 in decimal) representing the 2nd and 3rd octets of the IP address, respectively. The resulting subnet 233.251.245.0 is globally reserved for AS 64201 to use. These addresses are called GLOP addresses.

The multicast IP addresses in Table 5-1 map to the Ethernet MAC addresses that range from 0100.5e00.0000 to 0100.5e7f.ffff. These addresses are owned by the Internet Assigned Numbers Authority (IANA). This range allocates 23 bits of the MAC for a direct copy of the last 23 bits of multicast IP address. For example, in Figure 5-1, the multicast IP 224.1.16.33 maps to 0x0100.5e01.1021.

Figure 5-1   *A Sample Multicast MAC to Multicast IP Address Mapping*

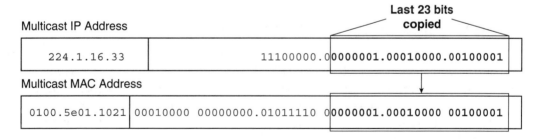

Recall that multicast IP addresses use 28 bits of IP address, resulting in the first 5 bits of multicast IP address being lost during the address copy. As a result, you can see in Figure 5-2 that 224.129.16.33 also maps to the MAC address 0x0100.5e01.1021.

Figure 5-2   *An Illustration of MAC-to-IP Address Overlapping*

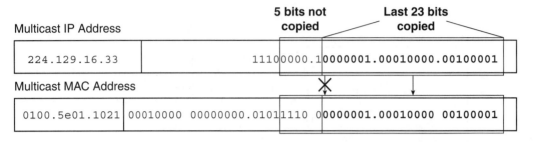

Figure 5-3 shows the 32 multicast IP addresses that map to the MAC address 0x0100.5e01.1020.

Figure 5-3   *Each Multicast MAC Has 32 Corresponding Multicast IP Addresses*

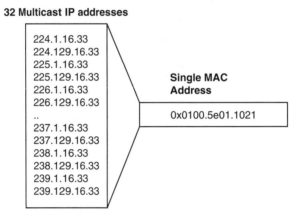

Internet Group Management Protocol

Receivers use IGMP to inform last-hop routers of the groups they would like to become members of. The last-hop multicast routers use the IGMP messages to track group memberships on each of its directly connected LAN segments. The router forwards traffic from the requested group to the LAN segment that contains members of the group. If there are any intermediary switches between the client workstation and router, you can configure Cisco Group Multicast Protocol (CGMP) or IGMP snooping to avoid duplicating the multicast group across Layer 2 networks. There are currently three versions of IGMP: IGMPv1, IGMPv2, and IGMPv3.

Internet Group Management Protocol, Version 1

With IGMPv1, there are only two messages: IGMP Membership Queries and IGMP Membership Reports. Hosts can join multicast groups, using Membership Reports, but cannot explicitly leave the groups that they are members of. To determine if there are any receivers available for a group, routers send IGMP Membership Queries for the group in question to the all-hosts group 224.0.0.1 on its local LAN segments every 60 seconds. If the router does not receive an IGMP Membership Report for three consecutive queries (3 minutes), it stops forwarding traffic to that local LAN segment.

In Figure 5-4, the router first sends a general query to the all-hosts group. When the hosts receive the query from the router, they each start a local countdown timer. The countdown timer is a random time value between the range of 0 and 10 seconds for IGMPv1. When its countdown timer expires, the host sends a membership report to the all-hosts group with a Time To Live (TTL) of 1. If a host receives a report for the desired group within its countdown timer, it suppresses its own report because the router requires only one report per LAN segment.

NOTE   Hosts set the TTL in the IP header to 1 to contain the IGMP report to the local LAN segment. Recall that, when a router receives a packet with a TTL of 1, it processes and then discards the packet.

In Figure 5-4, Client B is the first to send a report, and the others therefore suppress their respective reports. The router sends periodic queries to the all-hosts group to ensure that there are still receivers on the LAN, and the process described previously is repeated.

Figure 5-4 *IGMPv1 Operation*

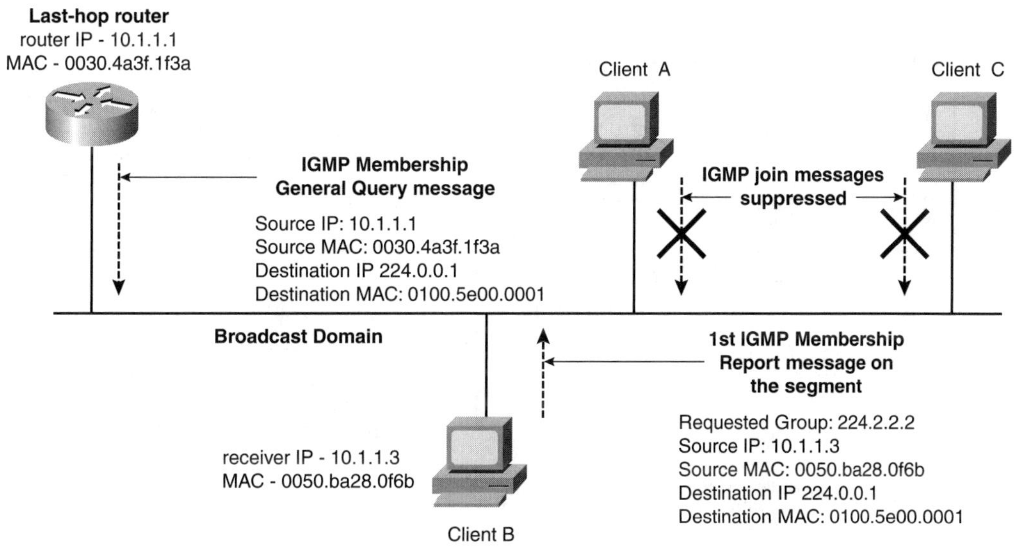

To enable IGMPv1 on last-hop routers, use the interface configuration command **ip igmp version 1**.

Internet Group Management Protocol, Version 2

IGMPv2, adds Leave messages for receivers to terminate group membership in a timely fashion. The timeout-based group membership termination method described previously for IGMPv1 proves inefficient for groups whose membership is volatile. High-bandwidth groups also suffer from this method because bandwidth continues streaming to LANs with no receivers until the timeout period expires.

With IGMPv2, when a host wants to leave a group, it sends an IGMP Leave message to the all-routers group 224.0.0.2. When the router receives the Leave message, it sends a group-specific query to make sure that there are no other members of the group on the LAN before terminating the stream. You can configure the number of queries the router sends before terminating the stream by using the interface configuration command **ip igmp last-member-query-count**. You can also configure the time between group-specific queries using the interface configuration command **ip igmp last-member-query-interval.**

In Figure 5-5, Client B sends an IGMPv2 Leave message, but hosts A and C still require the multicast traffic group for group 224.2.2.2. Therefore, they send group membership reports in response to the router's query.

Figure 5-5 *IGMPv2 Operation*

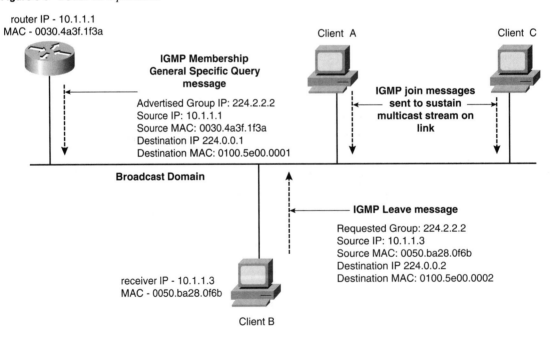

> **NOTE**   IGMPv2 is backward compatible to IGMPv1.

To enable IGMPv2 on the last-hop router, use the interface configuration command **ip igmp version 2**.

Internet Group Management Protocol, Version 3

IGMPv3 adds source-filtering capabilities to the IGMP protocol. Source filtering enables receivers to specify the list of senders from which they want to receive multicast traffic.

> **NOTE**   IGMPv3 is backward compatible to IGMPv1 and IGMPv2 and is necessary for SSM, which will be discussed later in this chapter.

You can configure IGMPv3 on receivers and last-hop routers in your network by using one of the following host signaling mechanisms:

- **IGMPv3 Host Signaling**—IGMP receivers announce membership into multicast groups using either of the following two membership report messages:

  — **INCLUDE messages**—Specifies which multicast groups and sources the host wants to receive.

  — **EXCLUDE messages**—Specifies which multicast groups and sources the host does not want to receive.

  Figure 5-6 specifies the IGMPv3 operation. The last-hop router sends a general query to its LAN segment, and Clients A and B respond for (S, G) groups that they want to receive data from. IGMPv3 is backwards-compatible with IGMPv2 and therefore allows receivers to use IGMP Leave messages.

  Enable IGMPv3 on the last-hop router with the interface configuration command **ip igmp version 3.**

Figure 5-6   *IGMPv3 Operation*

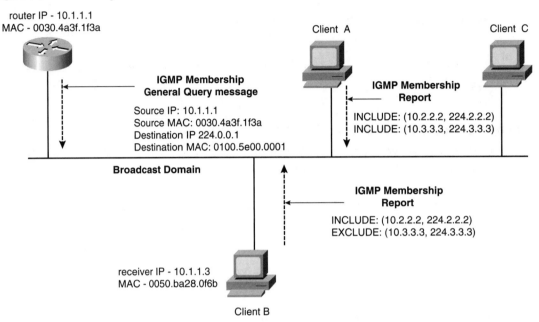

- **IGMP v3lite Hosting Signaling**—This is a Cisco-developed protocol used to transition from ISM to SSM applications. IGMP v3lite enables receiving hosts that do not yet support IGMPv3 in their operating systems to signal last-hop routers of their interest in (S, G) multicast traffic. The IGMP v3lite software is available as an extension to the receiving host's operating system with the Host Side IGMP Library (HSIL). This software supplies applications with a subset of the IGMPv3 application programming interface (API) that is required to write IGMPv3 applications.

  You can enable IGMP v3lite on the last-hop router with the interface configuration command **ip igmp v3lite**.

- **URL Rendezvous Directory (URD)**—Besides IGMP v3lite, you can also use the URD protocol to enable non-IGMPv3 supporting receivers with IGMPv3 capabilities. You need to enable only URD on the last hop router with the command **ip urd**. To specify the group and sources to the last-hop router, you need to open a web browser with the IP address of the last-hop router, TCP port 465, group multicast IP address, and desired sources of the multicast. For example, you should enter the following URL in the URL field of your browser to receive multicast traffic of group 232.1.1.1 from sources 10.2.2.2, 10.3.3.3, and 10.4.4.4, if your last-hop router is 10.1.1.1.

```
http://10.1.1.1:465/
path?group=232.1.1.1&source=10.2.2.2&source=10.3.3.3&source=10.3.3.3
```

The router will inspect the URL and remember the group and sources requested when the receiver application sends the IGMPv1 or IGMPv2 (*, G) Join message to the router. After the router receives the HTTP request from your browser, either of these Join messages will trigger the router to send PIM (S, G) Joins to each source your specify in the URL.

You can enable URD on the last-hop router with the interface configuration command **ip urd**.

Internet Standard Multicast

ISM uses the following protocols to control broadcasts in your network:

- Distribution trees

- Protocol Independent Multicast (PIM)

- Reverse Path Forwarding (RPF)

- Router Group Management Protocol (RGMP)

- Bidirectional PIM (Bidir-PIM)

- Pragmatic General Multicast (PGM)

Distribution Trees

From a Layer 3 perspective, multicast information is propagated through a network with the use of distribution trees created by Layer 3 routers. Routers create source trees with the source of the multicast traffic at the root of the tree. Source trees provide the shortest path to each destination and are therefore called shortest path trees (SPT). The drawback to source trees is that routers in the network must track all sources by maintaining state information for each source. That is, each router in the network has an entry in its multicast state table for every source.

> **NOTE**   For source trees, routers maintain state table entries in the form (S, G), where S is the source's IP address and G is the multicast group address.

With shared trees, however, routers are at the root; therefore, routers do not maintain individual sources in their state tables. The root of a shared tree is called a Rendezvous Point (RP). RPs establish multicast sessions between sources and receivers. Sources register with and forward all multicast traffic to the RP. The RP in turn forwards the traffic to receivers on behalf of sources.

NOTE   For shared trees, the group has a single entry stored as (*.G) in multicast state tables.

Although shared trees do not provide the shortest path to the receivers, the tradeoff is that routers need not track the state of all multicast sources. A large network with thousands of sources would have a significant performance impact on multicast routers.

Protocol Independent Multicast

PIM is a protocol to forward multicast traffic through a network. Instead of building its own routing tables, PIM uses the IGP routing protocol that populates the routing tables on the router. PIM uses RPF to ensure that multicast traffic is correctly distributed down a distribution tree. If the multicast traffic source is reachable through the interface that it was received on, the packet is forwarded out of the router's outgoing interface (OIF) list. The OIF list contains all interfaces enabled with multicast that are downstream from the source of the multicast data.

With RPF, if the multicast traffic source is not reachable through the interface the router received it on, then the router drops the packet. In other words, before forwarding multicast traffic, when the router receives a multicast packet it first looks up the source of the packet in its routing table. If the routing entry's next hop address is not via the same interface that the router received the packet from, then there may be a multicast forwarding loop. Therefore, the router drops the packet to avoid any loops in the distribution tree.

In Figure 5-7, Router B inadvertently forwards traffic to Router C instead of Router A. The RPF checks will pass on Routers B, C, and D. However, when Router A receives the packet from Router D and performs the RPF check, the router drops the packet, because the next hop of the routing entry for the source is via Router B, not Router D.

Figure 5-7 *RPF Operation*

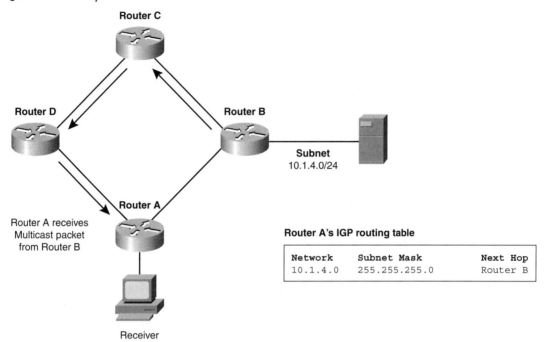

Router C

Router D

Router B

Subnet
10.1.4.0/24

Router A

Router A receives
Multicast packet
from Router B

Router A's IGP routing table

Network	Subnet Mask	Next Hop
10.1.4.0	255.255.255.0	Router B

Receiver

> **NOTE** With shared trees, the PIM slightly modifies its RPF check to see if the packet came from the interface that the router uses to reach the *RP*, not the source.

Table 5-2 gives the available PIM messages. This chapter explains the function of each of these messages.

Table 5-2 *PIM Messages*

Type	Description
0	Hello
1	Register
2	Register-Stop
3	Join/Prune
4	Bootstrap
5	Assert
6	Graft (used in PIM-DM only)
7	Graft-Ack (used in PIM-DM only)
8	Candidate-RP-Advertisement

The three PIM modes are

- PIM Dense Mode

- PIM Sparse Mode

- Bidirectional PIM Mode

> **NOTE** PIM routers periodically send PIM Hello messages to the all-PIM-routers group
> 224.0.0.13, out all their interfaces, to discover neighboring PIM routers.

PIM Dense Mode

In PIM dense mode, the multicast traffic is initially flooded throughout the network. Last-hop
routers that do not contain active receivers of the multicast traffic on their directly connected LANs
send PIM Prune messages in the reverse direction. To enable PIM dense mode on your network,
use the interface command **ip pim dense-mode.**

During the flood-prune period, routers store (S, G) group information along with an associated
OIF list for each (S, G) entry. Initially, the OIF list contains all interfaces except the RPF interface.
However, when upstream routers receive Prune messages on an OIF interface, they remove that
interface from the OIF list.

In Figure 5-8, the receiver joins the multicast group by sending an IGMP join message to Router
A, before the sender starts sending data. When the multicast information is propagated toward the
last-hop routers, all routers but Router A send prune messages toward the sender.

After the sender commences sending data, receivers may join the multicast session by sending
IGMP joins to their last-hop routers. For example, in Figure 5-8, imagine that a new receiver on
the LAN segment attached to Router B decides to join the session. To elicit the multicast session,
Router B sends a PIM Graft message up the distribution tree. The router uses a Graft message to
indicate to Router E that it should start sending the multicast traffic down the tree. Router E in
response sends a PIM Graft-Ack message to Router B, before sending the multicast data.

The result of this flood-prune mechanism is a SPT with the sender at the root of the tree, free of
unnecessary flood traffic (once the PIM routers complete the prune process). However, because
the flood process repeats every 3 minutes, dense mode may prove inefficient if your application
does not have receivers on the majority of your LAN segments. Your network may experience
unnecessary congestion during these periods. However, with the PIM dense mode state-refresh
feature, you can configure your PIM routers to send periodic PIM control messages down the
source distribution tree to prevent the state of the tree from timing out every three minutes. The
control messages simulate flood traffic to check to see if downstream routers have members of the
group. If the downstream routers have members, they do not respond to the control messages with

PIM Prune messages. As a result, the upstream router adds the interface to its OIF list and starts forwarding the traffic downstream. If the downstream routers do not have members of the requested group, they send a PIM Prune message upstream. To enable the state refresh feature, use the interface configuration command **ip pim state-refresh origination-interval**.

Figure 5-8   *Dense Mode Operation*

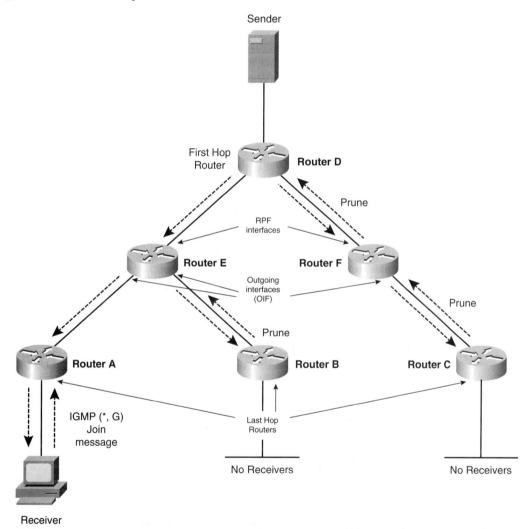

PIM Sparse Mode

PIM Sparse mode uses a pull method to send multicast traffic only to last-hop routers that have LAN segments that contain active receivers. The receivers solicit group traffic for group (G) using IGMP join messages. The IGMP Join triggers the last-hop router to send a PIM Join message toward the RP. Routers send the PIM Join message to the all-PIM-routers address 224.0.0.13 with a TTL of 1, out its RPF interface. Each router updates the PIM state tables with an (*, G) entry for the desired group and forwards the Join hop-by-hop along the path to the RP. Additionally, the interface the PIM Join was received on is added to the outgoing interface (OIF) list for the (*, G) entry. Figure 5-9 illustrates how PIM-SM creates a shared tree.

Figure 5-9 *Creating the PIM-SM Shared Tree*

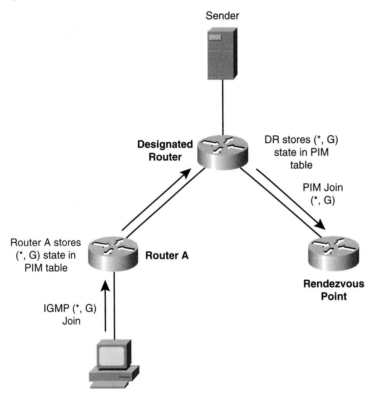

> **NOTE** To enable PIM sparse mode on your network, use the interface command **ip pim sparse-mode.**

When a source has multicast traffic to send to a multicast group, it simply starts sending. In Figure 5-10, the multicast data triggers the first-hop designated router (DR) to create a (S, G) state entry in its PIM table and register the group with the RP on behalf of the source. To register with the RP, the DR encapsulates the multicast UDP packets from the source into unicast PIM Register messages. The PIM Register messages are routed with the unicast IGP routing table to the RP.

NOTE   You can configure a leaf router with the RP IP address using the global configuration command **ip pim rp-address** or by using Auto-RP, as discussed later in this chapter.

Figure 5-10 illustrates how the RP receives and forwards the multicast data down the shared tree.

Figure 5-10   *Registering a Multicast Group with the RP*

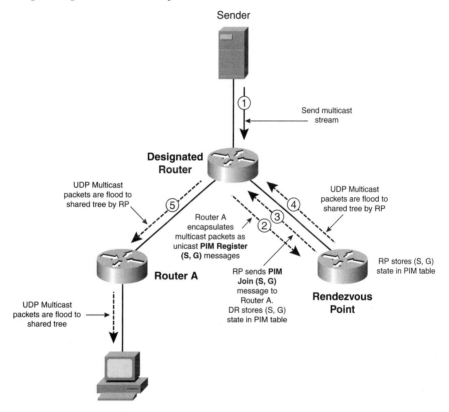

Because the RP is aware of receivers interested in the group, it decapsulates the PIM Register messages and forwards the multicast data down the shared tree. The shared tree consists of the RP, DR, and Router A, in that order. The RP then responds to the DR's PIM Register with a PIM Join message, to join the SPT to the receiver, rooted at the source. The SPT consists of the DR, RP, DR, and Router A, in that order (notice that the DR is in the tree twice). When the DR receives the Join message, it sends the raw UDP multicast traffic stream to the RP, thus duplicating the UDP stream.

Not until the RP sends a PIM Register Stop message to DR will the DR discontinue sending the multicast stream encapsulated within PIM Register messages.

> **NOTE**   It is preferable for the RP to receive native multicast data, because decapsulation of PIM headers takes unnecessary router memory and processing cycles.

Once this registration is completed, the DR sends dataless periodic PIM Register messages (approximately every 2 minutes, by default) to the RP in order to maintain (S, G) state on the DR and RP.

In Figure 5-10, you can see that the multicast traffic does not take the most efficient route to the receiver. Indeed, the SPT is not the "shortest path," because the shared tree consists of the DR, followed by the RP, the DR again, and then Router A. Therefore, when the edge Router A receives the multicast traffic, it attempts to optimize the connectivity to the source by switching over to a source distribution tree. Figure 5-11 illustrates the switchover to a source tree by sending a PIM (S, G) Join message not to the RP, but to the source of the multicast.

> **NOTE**   Because PIM Join messages travel upstream, in the opposite direction of downstream multicast data, the RPF algorithm fails because the source of the packet is not reachable from the interface that the router uses to reach the RP. Instead of checking to see if the source of the packet (the last hop router, in this case) is reachable from the RP interface, the router checks its OIF list. If the router received the packet from an interface in its OIF list, it forwards the packet out its RPF interface; otherwise, the router drops the packet to avoid multicast loops.

To switch to a source distribution tree, each router compares the IGP routing metrics of the RP and source of the multicast. If the RP metric is better, the router forwards the PIM Join toward the RP, based on the PIM forwarding table; otherwise, the router forwards the PIM Join toward the source. Router B then sends a PIM Prune message, with the RP-bit flag in the PIM header set to 1, to the RP to indicate that the shared tree traffic is no longer necessary. The result is now truly the SPT, consisting of only the DR followed by Router A.

Figure 5-11 *Switchover to a PIM-SM Source Tree*

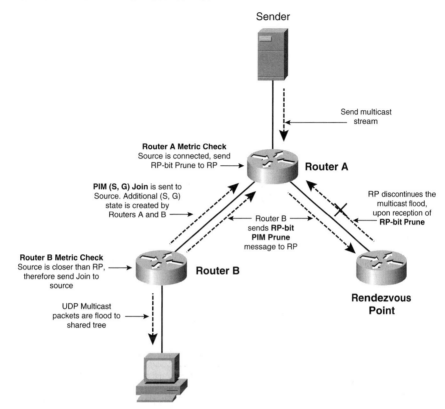

By default, last-hop routers immediately switch over to a source distribution tree. However, you can configure the bandwidth threshold that the router must reach before switching to SPT by using the **ip pim spt-threshold** global configuration command.

PIM routers detect LAN loops when multicast traffic is received on an OIF. The routers on the LAN elect a designated router by sending PIM Assert messages to one another. The routers then compare routing metric values to the RP. The one with the best route to the RP is elected as the DR for the LAN. Figure 5-12 shows how routers elect the DR upon reception of multicast traffic on an OIF.

Figure 5-12 *Designated Router Election*

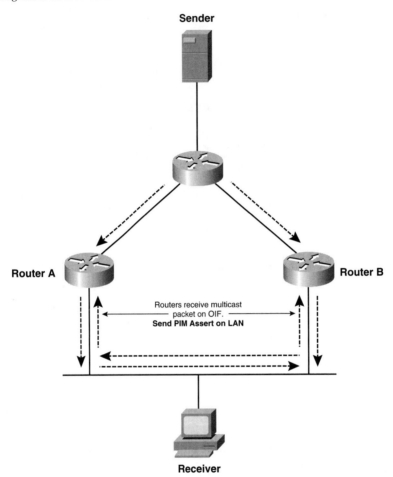

PIM Sparse-Dense Mode

Instead of designating every group in a network to either sparse or dense mode, sparse-dense mode enables different groups to run in different modes. This enables easy migration from one mode to the other. If a group contains an RP, the router is in sparse-mode for the group; otherwise, the group is considered dense. To enable sparse-dense mode, use the interface configuration command **ip pim sparse-dense-mode.**

Bidirectional PIM

PIM-SM allows routers to forward multicast traffic down only the shared tree. PIM-SM is beneficial for applications such as corporate communications, in which a single user, such as the CEO, must convey a message to many employees. However, many-to-many applications, such as video conferencing, require a bidirectional infrastructure to enable any participant to both send and receive data up and down the tree during the communication. Bidir-PIM extends PIM-SM to enable any number of sources to send multicast traffic over a shared tree in both directions.

Recall with PIM-SM that data traveling up the distribution tree requires a modified forwarding mechanism, such as described previously for PIM Join messages. Also, recall that source multicast traffic is encapsulated into PIM Register messages and sent to the RP. The RP then joins the SPT with the source as the root of the shared tree, and forwards the multicast traffic to the receivers in the shared tree.

Bidir-PM uses shared trees with the RP permanently remaining at the root—last-hop routers can no longer switch over to source distribution trees. In order to enable senders to forward loop-free multicast traffic upstream, Bidir-PIM requires every network segment (including point-to-point links and LAN segments) to elect a designated forwarder (DF) for the segment. Now, if routers receive multicast traffic on an upstream interface, the DF for the segment forwards multicast traffic toward the RP. Downstream traffic still uses the RPF mechanism.

Routers elect the DF in the same manner as they elect DRs for LAN segments with PIM-SM. Using PIM Assert messages, the routers select the router with the best unicast routing metrics to the RP as the DF. Routers with identical metrics break the tie using the router with the lower IP address. In Figure 5-13, the sender forwards traffic upstream through Router A and Router E to the RP. Router B is not elected as DF for traffic originating from the sender because its unicast routing metrics to the RP are not better than those for its directly connected neighbors.

NOTE   No source state is maintained through (S, G) entries in the Bidir-PIM tables.

Figure 5-13   *Illustrating Bidirectional PIM*

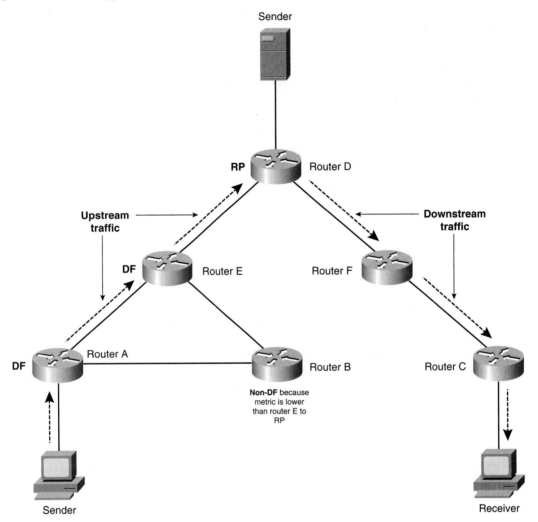

To configure Bidir-PIM, use the global interface configuration command **ip pim bidir-enable**.

So far, you've learned the basics of how IP multicast networks function and the basic commands for enabling IP multicast. The remainder of the "Internet Standard Multicast" section will show you how to fine-tune your ISM network, by teaching you how to configure:

■   Redundant RPs

■   Inter-domain Multicast

- Any-cast RP

- Cisco Group Management Protocol (CGMP) and IGMP Snooping

Configuring Rendezvous Point and Multicast Group Selection

You learned previously that RPs establish multicast connectivity between senders and receivers. DRs send PIM Register messages to RPs on behalf of hosts sending traffic to a multicast group. Additionally, last-hop routers send PIM Join messages to RPs, on behalf of receivers of the group, to inform of group membership. You can assign routers as RPs based on the location of the senders and receivers of the group traffic. For example, if your application restricts the senders and receivers of a particular range of multicast addresses to a portion of your network, then allocate the multicast group address ranges to an RP in close proximity to the participants. If the application's participants are located throughout your network, then assign a router in a central network location as the RP.

> **NOTE**   Because routers use only the RP to connect sources to receivers, once the participants establish a multicast session, failure of the RP has no effect on the session. RP failures affect only new sessions.

The routers in your PIM network must be aware of the IP addresses of the RPs and the multicast address ranges they serve. To configure the PIM routers in your network to obtain RP-to-group mappings, you have three options:

- Static RP

- Auto-RP

- Bootstrap Routers (BSR)

To configure static RP addresses, you must use the **ip pim rp-address** command on each router in your network. Because static RP does not provide redundancy and is not scaleable, you should use it for small multicast deployments only.

For large multicast environments, use either Auto-RP or BSR. These two protocols provide scalability and redundancy of RP-to-group assignments. They can scale your PIM-SM domain by automatically distributing RP-to-group mappings throughout your network. Automatic distribution ensures that the mappings are consistent throughout the network—static RP configuration may lead to inconsistencies in large networks. They also enable you to configure load sharing and backup of multicast groups across RPs.

The advantage of using Auto-RP or BSR or both is that, if you decide to change the RPs, you need make changes only on the candidate RPs, not on every router in your network.

Auto-RP

Auto-RP is a Cisco proprietary protocol for automatically advertising RP-to-group mappings to routers in your PIM network. It is an extension of PIM version 1 that provides automatic RP-to-group mapping distribution, load sharing, and backup of RPs.

Auto-RP mapping agents elect RPs from available candidate RPs and advertise the RP-to-group mappings to the other routers in your network. You need to configure at least one router as a candidate RP and at least one router as a candidate mapping agent for Auto-RP to work. However, you can configure more than one of each to provide fault tolerance between mapping agents and between RPs.

To assign a router as a candidate RP, use the global configuration command **ip pim send-rp-announce**. To assign a router as a mapping agent, use the global configuration command **ip pim send-rp-discovery**.

When you configure more than one router as a mapping agent, no election process takes place—all configured mapping agents are active at once. The RP candidates advertise their groups to the mapping agents by sending PIM Candidate-RP-Advertisement messages to the reserved address 224.0.1.39 using PIM dense-mode multicast. Once the mapping agents select the RPs and groups from these advertisements, they in turn advertise the mappings to the PIM routers in the network by sending PIM Candidate-RP-Advertisement messages to the address 224.0.1.40 using PIM dense-mode multicast. The mapping agents select the candidate with the highest IP address as the RP for the group.

The PIM first-hop routers use the mappings to send PIM Register messages to the correct RP for the desired group. Additionally, the last-hop routers use the mappings to send PIM joins to the correct RP for the desired group.

> **NOTE**   To configure Auto-RP, your PIM network must be in sparse-dense mode. The network must be able to perform dense-mode multicast to flood RP-to-group mapping information through the network. BSR does not use dense-mode to flood candidacy information. Therefore, you can configure BSR in sparse-mode only.

Figure 5-14 designates the two core routers both as RP candidates and mapping agents.

Figure 5-14 *Auto-RP and Mapping Agent Fault-Tolerance*

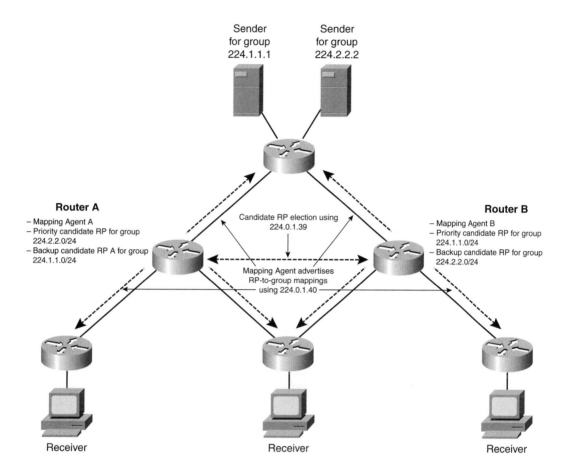

In Example 5-1, both Routers A and B are active mapping agents. Router A is the RP for group 224.2.2.2, and Router B is the RP for group 224.1.1.1, thus providing load sharing of the two multicast groups between the RPs. Because Router A's Loopback 1 interface has a higher-value IP address for group 224.2.2.2 than Router B's Loopback 0 interface, Router A is elected RP for group 224.2.2.2. Additionally, because Router B's Loopback 0 interface has a higher-value IP address for group 224.1.1.1 than Router A's Loopback 0 interface, Router B is elected RP for group 224.1.1.1.

This configuration also provides redundancy between the mapping agents and RPs because, if one of the routers fails, the other takes over group and mapping-agent responsibilities.

Example 5-1 *Configuring Auto-RP and Mapping Agent Fault-Tolerance*

```
Router A
ip multicast-routing
access-list 1 224.1.1.0 255.255.255.0
access-list 2 224.2.2.0 255.255.255.0

interface loopback 0
 ip address 10.1.1.1 255.255.255.0
 ip pim sparse-dense-mode
interface loopback 1
 ip address 10.3.3.3 255.255.255.0
 ip pim sparse-dense-mode

ip pim send-rp-announce interface loopback 0 group-list 1
ip pim send-rp-announce interface loopback 1 group-list 2
ip pim send-rp-discovery interface loopback 0
Router B
ip multicast-routing
access-list 1 224.1.1.0 255.255.255.0
access-list 1 224.2.2.0 255.255.255.0

interface loopback 0
 ip address 10.2.2.2 255.255.255.0
 ip pim sparse-dense-mode

ip pim send-rp-announce interface loopback 0 group-list 1
ip pim send-rp-discovery interface loopback 0
```

Bootstrap Routers

PIM version 2 introduces a standards-based mechanism for RP fault tolerance and scalability. With PIMv2, BSRs provide automatic discovery and distribution of RP-to-group mappings. Use Auto-RP if you have only Cisco routers in your network. Otherwise, use BSR if you have any non-Cisco routers and require RP fault tolerance and scalability.

BSR candidates are the mapping agents and announce themselves to PIM routers by sending PIM Bootstrap messages to the all-PIM-routers group address 224.0.0.13. Routers do not distribute messages sent to this address using dense-mode multicast. Rather, when PIMv2 routers receive PIM Bootstrap messages on a local interface to this address, they forward the message out all interfaces except the originating interface. This hop-by-hop forwarding avoids having to multicast the candidacy information throughout the network by using dense-mode flooding.

> **NOTE**   An advantage of BSR over Auto-RP is that you can configure interfaces to operate only in sparse mode by issuing the **ip pim sparse-mode** command. This is because BSR messages are flooded hop-by-hop and not by using dense-mode flooding.

All routers in the PIM domain (including the RP candidates) receive the PIM Bootstrap messages and choose the BSR themselves based on the candidate with the lowest configured priority value. Because candidate RPs are aware of the IP address of the BSR, they unicast the groups they serve to the BSR directly. In turn, the BSRs forward the RPs-to-group mappings to the PIM routers hop-by-hop. The PIM routers choose the best RP-to-group mappings themselves using the priority values you configure for the RP candidates. In contrast, the Auto-RP mapping agents elect the appropriate RP-to-group mappings before advertising the mappings to the network

You can assign one or more routers as a BSR using the global configuration command **ip pim bsr-candidate**. To assign one or more routers as RP candidates, use the global configuration command **ip pim rp-candidate.** If you configure multiple RPs to serve the same group, PIMv2 will load-share requests across them. When last-hop PIM routers receive the sender's multicast data, to choose which RP to select for the group traffic, they perform a hash on the sending source and group address. The router uses the result of the hash function as the index into a table of candidate RPs for the group. The hash function is deterministic in that all PIM routes hash to the same RP for a particular group. As with Auto-RP, only one RP per group is in use at any time. You can set an RP to take priority over another by specifying a priority level in the **ip pim rp-candidate** command. The router selects the RP with the *lowest* configured priority value. If the priority values are the same, the router chooses the RP by the hash value. If both the priority and hash values are the same, then the PIM routers choose the RP with the lowest IP address.

In Example 5-2, Router B is the BSR, because it has a higher priority (200) configured than Router B (100). Based on the priority values, Router A is the RP for groups within 224.1.1.0/24, and Router B is the RP for groups within 224.2.2.0/24. Because Router A has a higher priority value (200) for group 224.2.2.2 than Router B (150), Router A is elected RP for group 224.2.2.2. Additionally, because Router B has a higher priority value (150) for group 224.1.1.1 than Router A (100), Router B is elected RP for group 224.1.1.1. Note that the Loopback IP addresses in Example 5-2 are used by the last-hop PIM routers to reach the RPs, not to select which RP to send the PIM Join message to.

Example 5-2 *Configuring PIM Version 2 BSR and RP Fault-Tolerance*

```
Router A
ip multicast-routing
access-list 1 224.1.1.0 255.255.255.0
access-list 2 224.2.2.0 255.255.255.0

interface loopback 0
 ip address 10.1.1.1 255.255.255.0
 ip pim sparse-mode

ip pim bsr-candidate loopback 0 24 100
ip pim rp-candidate loopback 0 group-list 1 priority 100
ip pim rp-candidate loopback 0 group-list 2 priority 200
```

continues

Example 5-2   *Configuring PIM Version 2 BSR and RP Fault-Tolerance (Continued)*

```
Router B
ip multicast-routing
access-list 1 224.1.1.0 255.255.255.0
access-list 1 224.2.2.0 255.255.255.0

interface loopback 0
 ip address 10.2.2.2 255.255.255.0
 ip pim sparse-dense-mode

ip pim bsr-candidate loopback 0 24 200
ip pim rp-candidate loopback 0 group-list 1 priority 150
```

Although you can configure multiple RPs per group with Auto-RP and BSR, only one is active at any given time. Only when the active RP fails will the other RP for the group take over. This provides load sharing and not load balancing. Load sharing means that RPs serve different groups but share the *overall* multicast traffic load. For example, Router A serving 224.2.2.2 and Router B serving 224.1.1.1 provide load sharing of the total load of the two groups. Load balancing would have both routers serving 224.2.2.2, with the PIM routers distributing requests for the group between the two RPs. Unfortunately, neither Auto-RP nor BSR supports load balancing across multiple RPs for the same group. To provide true RP load balancing, you can use Anycast RP with the Multicast Source Discovery Protocol (MSDP).

Configuring Inter-Domain Multicast with Multicast Source Discovery Protocol

You can use MSDP to advertise sources between PIM-SM domains. Recall that, with PIM-SM, a source multicast stream is encapsulated in PIM Register messages by the first-hop DR and sent to the RP for the domain. The RP decapsulates the traffic and forwards the multicast data down the local shared tree. With MSDP, RPs of different domains maintain TCP connections between one another to advertise their sources across domains.

Figure 5-15 illustrates how RPs communicate source traffic across three domains.

Figure 5-15   *Multicast Delivery Across PIM Domains Using MSDP*

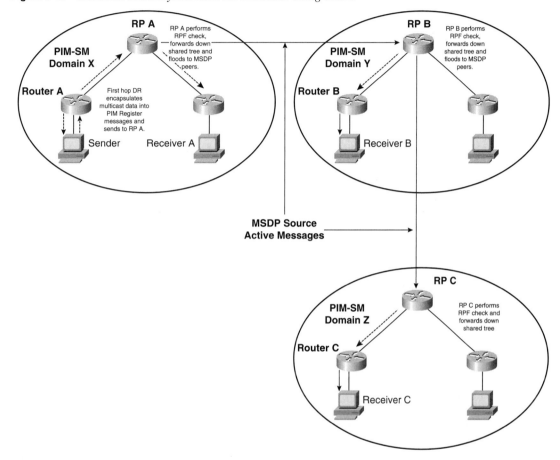

In Figure 5-15, when RP A receives the source multicast PIM Register messages, it determines that it has a (*, G) entry in its PIM table for the group, decapsulates the traffic, and forwards it down the shared tree for the Receiver A. RP A then reencapsulates the first data packet into MSDP Source Active (SA) messages and forwards it to remote RP B. When the RP B receives the traffic, it first verifies the peer using a modified version of RPF. The modified RPF includes RP B performing a lookup into its BGP RIB table or MBGP table to determine the next-hop peer (RPF peer) for the domain that the MSDP SA message originated from. If the RPF peer is not in the direction of the originating MSDP peer, RP B drops the SA message to avoid loops. Otherwise, RP B decapsulates the packets, forwards them down the local shared tree to Receiver B, and joins the SPT to the source. When Receiver B receives the traffic, it too joins the SPT to the source and sends a RP-bit PIM Prune message to RP B to remove RP B from the SPT.

RP B then floods the MSDP SA message using peer-RPF flooding. With peer-RPF flooding, RP B floods the MSDP SA messages to all MSDP peers except to the peer that it originated from. That is, in this example, RP B floods the MSDP SA message to RP C. In turn, RP C performs the RPF check to verify the message received from RP B and then decapsulates the data and forwards the traffic to members of the group (Receiver C).

Anycast RP

BSR and Auto-RP allow only a single active RP per group. All other candidate RPs are backups to the active RP. To load balance requests for RP serving the same group, you can use Anycast RP.

With Anycast RP, you configure your RP candidates with the same IP address. When the first- and last-hop PIM routers send registers and joins to the shared RP IP address, they use the underlying IGP to route the packets to the candidate RP closest to the originating PIM router. The router selects the route with the best metrics. In case your routers have equal-cost routes to the RP, you should enable CEF per-flow load balancing. Most PIM messages do not span multiple packets, but if they did, per-packet load balancing would distribute the multipacket message to both RPs, causing both RPs to drop the request.

To enable Anycast RP, you must first configure MSDP to connect the candidate RPs together. The candidate RPs must be aware of all the groups that the other RPs serve. Otherwise, if the IGP forwards the PIM Join message of a group to a different RP than it sends the PIM Register messages to, the session is not established. Figure 5-16 illustrates the MSDP requirement for Anycast RP.

In Figure 5-16, when RP A receives the PIM Register messages from the sender, it determines that it does not have an entry (*, G) in its PIM tables (that is, it has not received any PIM Join messages from interested receivers). As a result, RP A peer-RPF floods the register as an MSDP SA message to RP B. Because RP B has an entry for (*, G), it decapsulates the MSDP SA message, forwards the traffic down its shared tree to the receiver, and joins the SPT to the source. When the last-hop router receives the traffic, it joins the SPT to the source and forwards a PIM RP-bit Prune to RP B to remove RP B from the SPT.

> **NOTE**   Global Server Load Balancing also uses the IGP Anycast for global site selection, as described in Chapter 12, "Exploring Global Server Load Balancing."

Figure 5-16   *Using Anycast RP to Provide Per-Group Load Balancing Across Multiple RPs*

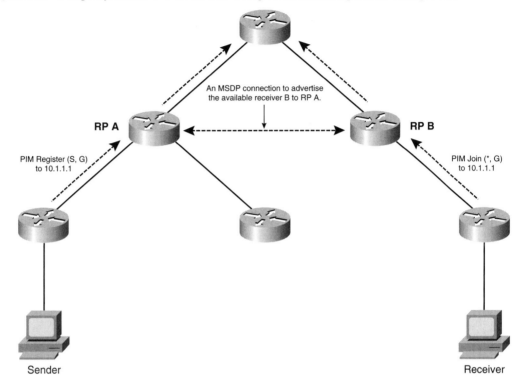

Layer 2 Multicast Protocols

For switched environments, to avoid duplicating multicast traffic on LAN switch ports, you can use either Cisco Group Management Protocol (CGMP) or IGMP Snooping.

Cisco Group Management Protocol (CGMP)

To reduce multicast traffic at Layer 2, you can configure CGMP between routers and switches (that is, you do not configure CGMP between hosts and routers). When a router receives an IGMP join message from a receiver, it sends a CGMP Join message to the switch. The CGMP Join message includes two MAC addresses: one for the receiver and the other for the multicast group. The switch then looks up the receiver MAC (from the CGMP join packet) in its MAC address table to deduce the switch port number that the receiver is located on. The switch then adds an entry in its MAC forwarding table for the multicast group MAC and receiver switch port. Figure 5-17 illustrates the CGMP process of learning the multicast MAC address and receiving switch ports.

Figure 5-17 *CGMP Operation*

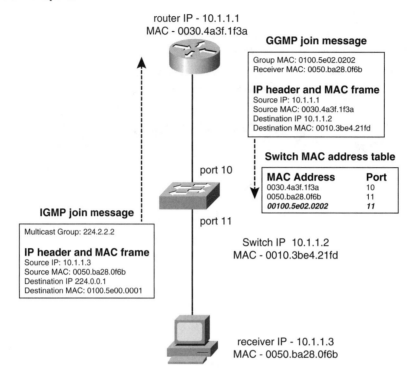

In Figure 5-17, the receiver with MAC 0050.ba28.0f6b on port 11 of the switch sends an IGMP join for group 224.2.2.2 with group MAC address 0100.5e02.0202. The switch then generates the entry [0010.3be4.21fd, port 11] for the receiver. When the router receives the IGMP Join, it sends a CGMP Join to the switch. The switch then generates the entry [0100.5e02.0202, port 11] based on the CGMP join that it receives from the router.

IGMP Snooping

For IGMP Snooping, the switch inspects Layer 3 information of the IGMP packet directly and builds the MAC entries for multicast groups based on information that it inspects. You should enable IGMP Snooping on high-end switches only, such as the Catalyst 4000 and 6000-series switches, because they have dedicated ASICS for multicast inspection. IGMP Snooping also inspects CGMP join messages generated by routers, thereby allowing you to enable both CGMP capabilities in conjunction with standard IGMP snooping.

Router-Port Group Management Protocol

CGMP and IGMP Snooping are appropriate for networks where Layer 3 routers are at the core/ distribution layer and Layer 2 switches are at the access layer. However, if Layer 2 switches are located in the core of your network and routers are at the access layer, you should use Router-Port Group Management Protocol (RGMP) to limit multicast traffic to the necessary switch ports in the core. Neither IGMP snooping nor CGMP are useful in the network illustrated in Figure 5-18 because both work by using IGMP Join messages. You can configure your router with RGMP to indicate to the core switch that it wants to receive traffic from a particular multicast group. When a receiver sends an IGMP Join to the router, the router generates and sends an RGMP join to the switch, in addition to forwarding the PIM join from the receiver destined to the RP. In Figure 5-18, the switch populates its forwarding tables using the RGMP join.

Figure 5-18 *RGMP Operation*

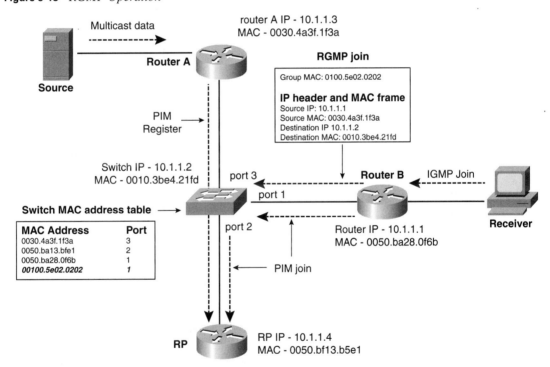

Source Specific Multicast (SSM)

Recall that networks enabled with multicast protocols from the Internet Standard Multicast (ISM) model must maintain knowledge of both sources and groups (S, G) to enable the receiver to subscribe to (*, G) groups without any knowledge of what senders they are receiving the multicast traffic from. With the SSM model however, the receivers must explicitly subscribe and unsubscribe to the (S, G) multicast channels from which they want to receive traffic. Your receivers must specify both the source unicast IP address that the stream is originating from and the multicast group address that the stream is destined to. Receivers must learn of the sources by a method external to the SSM model, such as through a user selection from a list of sources on a webpage. Internet-based multicast applications, such as audio, video, and stock quote streaming, fit the one-to-many SSM model.

Benefits of SSM over ISM are

- **Reduced source address state maintenance by routers**—SSM enables routers to maintain only the group IP address in their routing tables and not both source and group IP addresses, greatly reducing the amount of memory and processing that your routers require to distribute multicast traffic. SSM no longer requires the source discovery and distribution protocols ISM uses, including PIM-SM, Auto-RP, BSR, and MSRP.

- **Denial of service protection**—The SSM network only forwards traffic if last-hop routers explicitly receive IGMPv3 (S, G) join messages. In contrast, ISM forwards multicast traffic from any active source to all receivers requesting traffic from group G's.

- **Reduced group address management**—Because SSM indexes streams by unicast source IP address in addition to the group IP address, you can configure sources of different applications to use the same group address without the receivers worrying about receiving traffic from both sources. Traffic from each source is forwarded through the network independently of one another. As a result, you do not have to manage your multicast address allocation to avoid group IP address overlap as you must with ISM multicast.

The drawbacks to SSM are

- **SSM state maintenance**—As long as receivers send IGMPv3 joins for a source, the routers within the SSM network maintain (*, G) state for the source of the multicast, even if the source is no longer sending data. In contrast, ISM routers detect sources that discontinue sending data and tear down the (S, G) state.

- **IGMP snooping and CGMP support**—IGMP Snooping and CGMP may not recognize IGMPv3 Include/Exclude messages. Ensure that the version of Cisco IOS you are running supports compatibility between these protocols before deploying multicast in your network.

Recall that IGMPv3, IGMP v3lite, and URD enable receivers to send join messages that contain the sources and group (S, G) pairs they want to join. Once first-hop routers join the RP shared tree, they switch over to the SPT by sending PIM (S, G) joins directly to the source, creating a SPT from the source to the receivers. The source multicast stream is then forwarded through the SPT from the source directly to the receivers using the PIM (S, G) state tables and RPF.

The PIM-SSM multicast protocol is derived from PIM-SM and includes only the generation and sending of PIM join (S, G) messages destined to sources. PIM (S, G) and (*, G) join messages are no longer generated and sent to RPs by PIM-SSM last-hop routers. First-hop routers no longer generate PIM-SM register messages. Furthermore, routers enabled with PIM-SSM ignore all Auto-RP, BSR, and MSDP-related messages.

You can run PIM-SSM concurrently with PIM-SM in your network. To enable SSM in a network already enabled for PIM-SM, you need only enable the last-hop routers with the SSM **ip pim ssm** interface configuration command on select interfaces. The last-hop routers process PIM messages for groups within the SSM IP address range with PIM-SSM functionality. PIM routers treat all PIM messages for groups outside the SSM range with PIM-SM functionality.

To enable PIM-SSM alone in your network, use the **ip pim ssm** command on all router interfaces.

Ensuring Multicast Delivery With Pragmatic General Multicast

IP Multicast uses UDP for transporting multicast packets. You learned that UDP is an unreliable transport in Chapter 2, "Exploring the Network Layers." Multicast applications, such as video conferencing and corporate communications, do not require reliable delivery. However, for applications that require reliable delivery, such as bulk file and software distribution, you can use Pragmatic General Multicast (PGM).

> **NOTE**   To learn how to enable PGM on your content engines to distribute content reliably to receiving applications, refer to Chapter 14, "Distributing and Routing Managed Content."

PGM uses transport session identifiers (TSI), similar to TCP port numbers, to identify multicast transport sessions. PGM hosts assign sequence numbers to detect missing packets and reorder out-of-sequence packets. Based on the sequence numbers, PGM hosts maintain transmit and receive windows to manage the flow of multicast traffic. Recall that TCP hosts use positive acknowledgements (ACK) to acknowledge data they receive. Unlike TCP, in multicast environments, lost packets affect large numbers of receivers, not just a single host. As such, the PGM flow control mechanism must not overburden the source with positive acknowledgement traffic. Therefore, multicast receivers send selective negative acknowledgements (NAK) instead. PGM receivers selectively send NAKs to PGM senders only when packets are missing. Therefore, in practice, NAKs are far more scalable than positive ACKs for multicast environments.

PGM senders periodically send source path messages (SPM) with the original data (ODATA) for PGM-enabled routers to maintain the route with which the multicast session packets traverse the distribution tree downstream. PGM routers do not use this state information to route the downstream multicast packets—PGM routers save this state to route upcoming NAKs from receivers back up the distribution tree.

NOTE   PGM is a Layer 4 transport layer protocol and relies on PIM multicast routing at Layer 3 to route downstream multicast traffic downstream.

PGM receivers detect missing packets by inspecting the sequence numbers of incoming packets. A PGM host detects packet loss if it receives packets with higher-sequence numbers than the expected packet. To ensure that the packet is not simply out of order, PGM hosts wait for numerous packets of higher-sequence numbers before generating a NAK for the missing packet. To detect whether the last packet of a stream is actually missing, PGM hosts use timers.

A receiver sends the NAK upstream to the sender. The sender in turn responds with a NAK confirmation (NCF) and repair data (RDATA) downstream to the multicast group receivers.

NAKs are unicast by PGM receivers to the last-hop routers. Before sending the NAK to the last-hop PGM host, the receiver backs off for a random amount of time, in case other receivers on the segment also need to send a NAK. The PGM router configured with the PGM router-assist feature responds to the receiver by sending an NCF message to the multicast group out the originating interface. If a receiver receives an NCF before its back-off timer expires, it does not send its NAK. The router then forwards the NAK upstream to the sender using the source state information created previously, but suppresses duplicate NAKs received on a network segment by multiple receivers. The overall result of both the random back-off by the receiver and the router NAK suppression feature is that the source receives only one or a few NAKs, and not one from every receiver that requires the missing data. Furthermore, when the upstream PGM routers receive the NAK message, they create a repair data state to know how to send the sender's upcoming NCF and RDATA downstream. With this repair state, PGM routers send only NCFs and RDATA to the segments that contain receivers that are missing the requested data.

When the source eventually receives the NAK, it too multicasts an NCF message to the group along with the requested RDATA. The downstream PGM routers, if necessary, suppress the NCFs on interfaces that do not have active receivers. Figure 5-19 shows how receivers send NAKs and receive RDATA for missing packets.

Figure 5-19 *PGM Receivers Soliciting Missing Data*

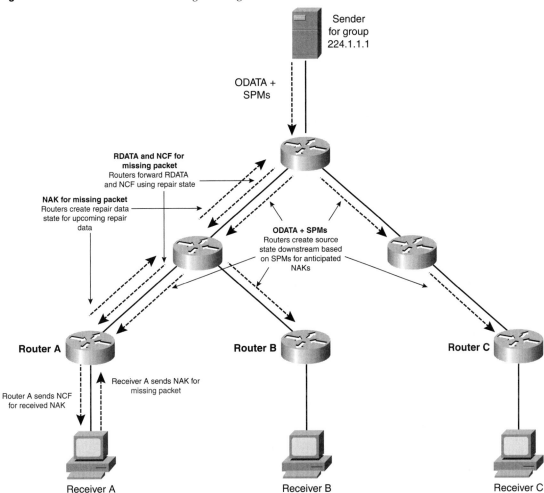

You must enable PGM on at least the sending and receiving hosts of multicast traffic in your network to benefit from the reliable transport mechanism of PGM defined in RFC 3208. This RFC also defines the PGM functions for routers to assist in the reliable transport of multicast traffic over a network. To enable the PGM Router-Assist feature on your routers, enter the global configuration command **ip pgm router**. This command enables the routers to create source and repair state, and efficiently forward NCFs and RDATA to receivers.

Summary

In this chapter, you learned how to design and configure IP Multicast networks using the following multicast infrastructures:

- **Internet Standard Multicast (ISM)**—The ISM model includes protocols for maintaining source state within your network. ISM uses Rendezvous Points to connect receivers to sources. Senders must register with and receivers must join desired groups through the RP. To provide RP redundancy and fault tolerance, you can use the Cisco-developed Auto-RP protocol or the PIMv2 BSR standard protocol. To provide per-group load balancing between RPs, you can enable Anycast RP. With Multicast networks, the network discovers and distributes sources, creating additional load on network devices. For cross-domain source distribution, use MSDP.

- **Source Specific Multicast (SSM)**—With SSM multicast networks, source maintenance is offloaded from the network to the receivers. Last-hop routers join the SPT directly upon receiving IGMPv3 Joins from receivers.

- **Reliable Multicast**—IP Multicast uses UDP as its underlying transport. To provide reliable multicast delivery, you learned how to configure the Cisco IOS PGM Router-Assist feature. This feature provides a guaranteed datagram delivery service to IP Multicast networks by using parallel concepts to TCP, such as datagram sequencing and send-receive windowing. Negative ACKs provide the receiver with a means to request missing datagrams.

Review Questions

1. What is the difference between the ISM and SSM multicast models?

2. How many possible globally scoped multicast addresses are available for ISM? For SSM?

3. What is the difference between source and shared distribution trees?

4. How does dense-mode multicast differ from sparse-mode multicast?

5. How do multicast routers route multicast packets downstream?

6. How do multicast routers route multicast packets upstream?

7. What is the difference between Auto-RP and BSR?

8. What are the differences between Auto-RP, BSR, and Anycast RP?

9. What are the differences between CGMP and IGMP snooping?

Recommended Reading

Beau Williamson, *Developing IP Multicast Networks, Volume I*, Cisco Press, 1999

Cisco Systems, Inc., *Interdomain Multicast Solutions Guide*, Cisco Press, 2002

RFC 3208, *PGM Reliable Transport Protocol Specification,* IETF, http://www.ietf.org/rfc/rfc3208.txt, 2001

RFC 2362, *Protocol Independent Multicast-Sparse Mode (PIM-SM): Protocol Specification*, IETF, http://www.ietf.org/rfc/rfc2362.txt, 1998

RFC 2365, *Administratively Scoped IP Multicast*, IETF, http://www.ietf.org/rfc/rfc2365.txt, 1998

Chapter Goals

This chapter discusses how you can guarantee content delivery by using the following Quality of Service (QoS) technologies:

- **Classification and Marking**—You can classify and assign different priorities to your applications.

- **Congestion Management**—Based on the different priorities you assign to your applications, routers can switch packets with a queuing mechanism and apply shaping or policing.

- **Congestion Avoidance**—You can configure your routers to randomly drop packets periodically based on priority before congestion occurs. Signaling allocates bandwidth and QoS for traffic flows before sending the application traffic.

Ensuring Content Delivery with Quality of Service

Cisco Quality of Service (QoS) ensures that routers give appropriate network services to real-time applications that are sensitive to delay, jitter, packet loss, and bandwidth. Your applications may be sensitive to any one of the following network-related constraints:

- **Packet Delay**—Congestion causes delay due to an overload of traffic on the network. Routers that store packets in queues for excess durations prior to forwarding them to the network may cause packets to delay.

- **Jitter**—Jitter refers to a variation in packet delay, resulting in differing packet inter-arrival times or out-of-sequence packets or both.

- **Packet Loss**—Packet loss results from network errors due to congestion or other faults. You learned in Chapter 2, "Exploring the Network Layers," how TCP hosts automatically detect and retransmit lost packets.

> **NOTE** Delay and jitter may cause out-of-sequence packets, which are a major problem when UDP is used as the transport. Applications that rely on TCP for transport deal with out-of-order packet delivery by buffering and reordering TCP segments as they arrive. TCP also can deal with packet loss by resending missing packets.

- **Bandwidth**—Applications often require fixed bandwidth in order to deliver content, such as streaming audio-video.

The quality of real-time applications invariably suffers from delay, jitter, packet loss, and insufficient bandwidth. The basis for QoS stems from the need to address these common network issues. QoS is divided into the following components:

- **Classification and Marking**—Packet forwarding priorities for different groups of applications.

- **Congestion Management**—Based on packet forwarding priorities, switch packets with various queuing mechanism and apply shaping or policing. Congestion management also dictates the type of traffic that can be delayed. This traffic can either withstand some delay or is the least important type of traffic, making it acceptable for dropping.

■   **Congestion Avoidance**—Based on class, you can configure the router to randomly drop TCP segments periodically before congestion occurs. You can also configure bandwidth shaping and policing to ensure that your bulky applications do not flood your links. Additionally, Policy Signaling can be used to allocate bandwidth and QoS for traffic flows prior to sending the application traffic.

Classification and Marking

Classification involves differentiating services at the edge of your network. When you classify applications, the router marks individual packets according to the type of application they belong to. When configuring marking, you should consider an application's overall priority as compared to other applications in your network. An application's overall priority typically depends on the business criticality or time sensitivity of the application for minimal and consistent latency and jitter. You can assign each application in your network to a different priority value, or, depending on the number of applications running in your network, you can group applications into classes of traffic. Once the router marks a packet, you can configure downstream routers to apply congestion management and congestion avoidance techniques to it.

You can use the following technologies to classify and mark your applications in your network:

■   **Class-Based Packet Marking**—Class-based packet marking is an enhanced classification mechanism. You can use it to mark a packet's IP Precedence, Differentiated Services Code Point (DSCP), Layer 2 Class of Service (CoS), or QoS group values in order to differentiate your applications.

■   **Network-Based Application Recognition (NBAR)**—You can use NBAR to classify traffic at the application layer. NBAR classifies based on traffic behavior to determine applications that use dynamic ports.

■   **Policy-Based Routing (PBR)**—PBR is traditionally a feature for extending normal routing features. You can use PBR in your network to specify custom routing paths for traffic flows, using criteria such as IP address, TCP/UDP ports, MAC addresses, and packet size. However, you can also use PBR to mark a packet's IP Precedence value.

■   **Class-Based Policing and Committed Access Rate (CAR)**—Both class-based policing and CAR are policing features that you can use to rate-limit traffic entering your network. You also can use them to classify packets when bandwidth levels exceed configured thresholds. Routers within your network apply congestion management and avoidance QoS features to the marked packets. You will learn about policing later in this chapter.

■   **QoS Policy Propagation via BGP**—With this feature, you can classify traffic based on criteria, including BGP communities, AS paths, and access lists, in your routing domains. For example, a BGP router may advertise three routes assigned to three different communities.

When its peers receive the three BGP routes, they translate the community values into three levels of IP Precedence. When its peers receive packets destined to the BGP routes, they assign the respective IP Precedence before routing the packet.

■ **QoS for Virtual Private Networks (VPN)** — QoS for VPNs classify packets before they enter VPN tunnels to allow for tunnel routers to apply QoS policies.

Marking Packets at Layer 3

The three values that you can use to mark packets at Layer 3 are

■ IP Precedence

■ IP DSCP

■ QoS group value

Marking a Packet's IP Precedence Value

As you learned in Chapter 2 the IP Precedence uses three bits of the 8-bit type of service (ToS) field in the IP packet header, as defined in the Internet Protocol RFC (RFC 791). The eight possible values of IP Precedence are given names in RFC 791, but you can use these values to differentiate whatever classes of traffic you have in your network. IP Precedence values 6 and 7 are reserved for network control information, such as routing updates and link keep-alives, leaving six values from 0 to 5 for use in your network. Table 6-1 gives these IP Precedence values and their respective names as specified in RFC 791.

Table 6-1   *IP Precedence Values*

IP Precedence Value	Name
0	routine
1	priority
2	immediate
3	flash
4	flash-override
5	critical
6	internet
7	network

For example, you should use IP Precedence 0 for applications that do not require QoS guarantees, and IP Precedence 5 for the most critical applications in your network. You can mark packets with IP Precedence using any of the following marking tools in Cisco IOS:

- Policy-Based Routing

- QoS Policy Propagation via Border Gateway Protocol

- Committed Access Rate and Class-Based Policing

- Network-Based Application Recognition

- Class-Based Packet Marking

Example 6-1 gives a Layer 3 marking configuration to mark packets entering a network from a high-priority source subnet 10.1.1.0/24 with IP Precedence 5, using policy-based routing (PBR). Packets from the less critical subnet 10.1.2.0/24 are marked with IP Precedence 0.

Example 6-1 *Configuring Layer 3 Packet Marking Using Policy-Based Routing*

```
ip cef
access-list 1 permit 10.1.1.0 255.255.255.0
access-list 2 permit 10.1.2.0 255.255.255.0

interface fastethernet 0/1
 ip policy route-map markprec
!
route-map markprec permit 10
 match ip address 1
 set ip precedence 5

route-map markprec permit 20
 match ip address 2
 set ip precedence 0
```

NOTE By default, routers switch packets treated with PBR by using CEF switching when you enable CEF on your router. However, you also can switch PBR with the process or fast switching path.

Marking a Packet's IP Differentiated Services Code Field

To mark packets using the IP DSCP definition, you must use class-based packet marking. As you learned in Chapter 2, there are six available bits to classify traffic, giving 64 possible traffic classes. Table 6-2 lists the supported IP DSCP values.

Table 6-2   *IP DSCP Values*

DSCP Value	Service Name	IETF Description/Cisco IOS "set" Command Code
0	Best effort	Best effort (default)
8	Class 1	Class 1 (CS1)
10	Class 1, gold	AF11
12	Class 1, silver	AF12
14	Class 1, bronze	AF13
16	Class 2	Class 2 (CS2)
18	Class 2, gold	AF21
20	Class 2, silver	AF22
22	Class 2, bronze	AF23
24	Class 3	Class 3 (CS3)
26	Class 3, gold	AF31
28	Class 3, silver	AF32
30	Class 3, bronze	AF33
32	Class 4	Class 4 (CS4)
34	Class 4, gold	AF41
36	Class 4, silver	AF42
38	Class 4, bronze	AF43
40	Express forwarding	Express forwarding (CS5)
46	Expedited forwarding	Expedited forwarding (EF)
48	Control	Control (CS6)
56	Control	Control (CS7)

Table 6-3 maps the IP Precedence values to the supported IP DSCP values.

Table 6-3   *IP DSCP-to-Precedence Mappings*

DSCP Value	IP Precedence	Purpose
0	0	Best effort
0	1	Class 1
8,10	2	Class 2

continues

Table 6-3   *IP DSCP-to-Precedence Mappings (Continued)*

DSCP Value	IP Precedence	Purpose
16, 18	3	Class 3
24, 36	4	Class 4
32, 34	5	Express forwarding
48	6	Control
56	7	Control

Example 6-2 gives a Layer 3 marking configuration to mark packets entering a network from the high-priority source subnet 10.1.1.0/24 with IP DCSP 40 (CS5) and from a less critical source subnet 10.1.2.0/24 with IP Precedence 0 (default). You can perform this example using class-based packet marking, configurable within the Cisco Modular QoS CLI (MQC).

> **NOTE**   The MQC enables you to create traffic policies and attach these policies to router interfaces. You configure traffic policies with the **policy-map** command. The policy contains traffic classes that you configure with **class-map** commands, and one or more QoS features. An example QoS feature would be to mark a packet's DSCP value with the **priority** command. You use traffic classes to classify traffic, while the QoS features in the traffic policy determine how to mark the classified traffic.

Example 6-2   *Configuring Layer 3 Packet Marking Using Class-Based Packet Marking*

```
ip cef
access-list 1 permit 10.1.1.0 255.255.255.0
access-list 2 permit 10.1.2.0 255.255.255.0

class-map match-all subnet1
 match access-group 1

class-map match-all subnet2
 match access-group 2

policy-map prioritize_subnets
 class subnet1
  set ip dscp cs5
 class subnet2
  set ip dscp default

interface fastethernet 0/1
 service-policy input prioritize_subnets
```

In Example 6-2, two access lists are created to identify two subnets. You then enter the MQC with the **policy-map** command. The policy named "prioritize_subnets" marks the two subnets with their respective DSCP values, using the **set ip dscp** command. The router classifies the subnets within individual **class-map** modules, assigned the names "subnet1" and "subnet2."

> **NOTE**   Class-based packet marking requires that you first enable CEF on your routers.

IP QoS Group Value

Marking a packet with a QoS group value affects the packet only within the local router that assigns the group value. That is, the router does not modify the packet header ToS field. You can assign up to 100 QoS group values to your applications. You should use the IP QoS group value if changing the IP Precedence or DSCP for the packet is not desirable in your network. You can assign QoS groups based on prefix, BGP autonomous system, or BGP community string. To set the QoS group value in a policy, use the **set qos-group** policy-map class command.

Marking Frames, Cells, and Trunks at Layer 2

For marking at Layer 2, you can use one of the following:

- **Asynchronous Transfer Mode (ATM) Cell Loss Priority (CLP) bit marking**—An ATM cell header contains a 1-bit CLP field indicating that, if you set to the value 1, the cell should be dropped within the ATM cloud during periods of congestion. If your routers interface into ATM networks, you can set the CLP bit for low-priority traffic or applications that can tolerate a minimal amount of lost content in the ATM cloud.

- **Frame Relay Discard Eligible (DE) bit marking**—Similar to ATM CLP marking, the frame relay DE header field indicates that, if you set to the value 1, the frame should be dropped within the frame relay cloud during periods of congestion. If your routers interface into frame relay networks, you can set the DE bit for low-priority application traffic or those that can tolerate lost frames in the frame cloud.

- **Ethernet Class of Service (CoS) bit marking**—The CoS field is a 3-bit value within the 802.1P field used for applying prioritization at Layer 2 to 802.1Q tagged frames. You learned about the 802.1Q frame header in Chapter 3, "Introducing Switching, Routing, and Address Translation." You can set the CoS value on routers or switches and configure your Layer 2 switches to apply QoS policies to the frames. For example, in order to prioritize voice and video traffic over other application traffic, you should separate the voice and video into a different VLAN and configure VLAN tagging throughout your network. Applying VLAN tags is necessary because they carry the priority values used for Layer 2 QoS policy features. Otherwise, you can configure your switch to inspect the IP packet headers for IP Precedence/DSCP values.

> **NOTE** You can perform ATM, frame relay, and CoS marking using class-based marking only.

Network-Based Application Recognition

By statefully inspecting flows as they traverse router interfaces, you can use Network-Based Protocol Recognition (NBAR) to detect applications that are running on your network. Once NBAR detects an application, you can configure class-based packet marking to mark the packet. You can then apply QoS policies to the marked packets throughout the network, including congestion management, congestion avoidance, traffic shaping, and policing.

The major advantage of NBAR over other classification techniques is that it stores transport connection information in RAM, giving it the ability to obtain an accurate picture of the behavior of the application. For example, a peer-to-peer file sharing application may easily use the standard HTTP port (80) but behave completely differently to HTTP. Without stateful inspection, the HTTP port number easily hides the actual behavior of the application. NBAR's stateful inspection engine can easily recognize difficult-to-detect applications that use dynamic TCP/UDP ports, such as peer-to-peer file sharing and instant messaging applications.

To use NBAR, you must enable the NBAR protocol discovery IOS feature to statefully monitor the applications running through router interfaces. To enable protocol discovery on desired interfaces in order to classify packets using class-based packet marking, use the **ip nbar protocol-discovery** interface configuration command.

As discussed previously in Chapter 4, "Exploring Security Technologies and Network Infrastructure Designs," in order to identify most TCP applications, the TCP connection information must be stored in the router's RAM. NBAR provides stateful inspection by storing the connection information as 150-byte entries in RAM. Once the TCP application has completed its three-way handshake, the NBAR engine inspects the payload of the IP packets and classifies the application with high accuracy. The marked values in the packets can then invoke QoS policy at each router within the network.

> **NOTE** Before enabling NBAR, make sure that you know on average how many connections NBAR will be maintaining through your router interface. Multiply the number of connections by 150 bytes to calculate the amount of memory you will need for NBAR connection maintenance. For example, if your router tracks 15,000 concurrent connections on average, then NBAR will use 15,000 * 150 = 2.25 MBs of memory.

Table 6-4 lists applications supported by NBAR that use static ports. The match syntax is the keyword that you use in your class map's **match** clause to match the application.

Table 6-4   *NBAR-Supported Static Port Applications*

Protocol	Match syntax
Border Gateway Protocol	**bgp**
Desktop Video Conferencing	**cuseeme**
Desktop Video Conferencing	**cuseeme**
Dynamic Host Configuration Protocol/ Bootstrap Protocol	**dhcp**
Domain Name System	**dns**
Finger User Information Protocol	**finger**
Internet Gopher Protocol	**gopher**
Hypertext Transfer Protocol	**http**
Secured HTTP	**secure-http**
Internet Message Access Protocol	**imap**
Internet Relay Chat	**irc**
Kerberos Network Authentication Service	**kerberos**
L2F/L2TP Tunnel	**l2tp**
Lightweight Directory Access Protocol	**ldap**
Microsoft Point-to-Point Tunneling Protocol for VPN	**pptp**
Microsoft SQL Server Desktop Video Conferencing	**sqlserver**
NetBIOS over IP (MS Windows)	**netbios**
NetBIOS over IP (MS Windows)	**netbios**
Network File System	**nfs**
Network News Transfer Protocol	**nntp**
Lotus Notes	**notes**
Novadigm Enterprise Desktop Manager (EDM)	**novadigm**
Network Time Protocol	**ntp**
Symantec PCAnywhere	**pcanywhere**
Symantec PCAnywhere	**pcanywhere**
Post Office Protocol	**pop3**
Printer	**printer**
Routing Information Protocol	**rip**
Resource Reservation Protocol	**rsvp**

continues

Table 6-4   *NBAR-Supported Static Port Applications (Continued)*

Protocol	Match syntax
Secure FTP	secure-ftp
Secure HTTP	secure-http
Secure IMAP	secure-imap
Secure IRC	secure-irc
Secure LDAP	secure-ldap
Simple Mail Transfer Protocol	smtp
Simple Network Management Protocol	snmp
Secure NNTP	secure-nntp
Firewall Security Protocol	socks
Secure POP3	secure-pop3
Secured Shell	ssh
Secure Telnet	secure-telnet
System Logging Utility	syslog
Telnet Protocol	telnet
X11, X Windows	xwindows

Table 6-5 lists applications supported by NBAR that use dynamic ports.

Table 6-5   *Dynamic Port Applications That Require Stateful Inspection*

Protocol	Match sytax
Citrix ICA Traffic by Application Name	citrix citrix app
File Transfer Protocol	ftp
MS-RPC for Exchange	exchange
FastTrack	fasttrack
Gnutella	gnutella
HTTP with URL, MIME, or Host Classification	http
Napster traffic	napster
Microsoft Netshow	netshow
rsh, rlogin, rexec	rcmd
Real-Time Streaming Protocol (RTSP)	rtsp
RealAudio Streaming Protocol	realaudio

Table 6-5   *Dynamic Port Applications That Require Stateful Inspection (Continued)*

Protocol	Match sytax
Real-Time Transport Protocol (RTP) Payload Classification	**rtp**
Real-Time Control Protocol (RTCP)	**rtcp**
SQL*NET for Oracle	**sqlnet**
Xing Technology Stream Works Audio and Video	**streamwork**
Sun Remote Procedure Call	**sunrpc**
Trivial File Transfer Protocol	**tftp**
VDOLive Streaming Video	**vdolive**

Table 6-6 lists non-TCP/UDP applications supported by NBAR.

Table 6-6   *Non-TCP/UDP Protocols (Stateful Inspection Not Required)*

Protocol	Match syntax
Exterior Gateway Protocol	**egp**
Enhanced Interior Gateway Routing Protocol	**eigrp**
Generic Routing Encapsulation	**gre**
Internet Control Message Protocol	**icmp**
IP in IP	**ipinip**
IP Encapsulating Security Payload/Authentication Header	**ipsec**

NBAR classifies HTTP packets based on URL, host, or MIME type. For URL classification, NBAR scans the portion of the URL after the hostname. For example, in the URL http://www.cisco.com/support/support-data.pdf, NBAR checks the portion "support/support-data.pdf" for a match during inspection. For host classification, NBAR checks the hostname www.cisco.com. You can also classify packets based on Internet MIME-types.

> **NOTE**   A list of the Internet Assigned Numbers Authority (IANA)-supported MIME types can be found at the IANA website at http://www.iana.org/assignments/media-types/.

When NBAR classifies the first packet of a connection, it assigns all subsequent packets of the connection to the same class. For example, if NBAR detects an HTTP GET request for a file of MIME-type "video/mpeg" from a client, it will also classify the HTTP 200 OK response and data packets from the server containing the MPEG4 file, because they are a part of the same TCP connection.

Example 6-3 uses class-based packet marking and NBAR to give Real-Time Transfer Protocol (RTP) and HTTP streaming video traffic precedence over all other traffic. NBAR marks packets with either types of streaming content with their IP DSCP field as 40 (CS5). Alternatively, all non-streaming traffic is marked with an IP DSCP of 0 (default).

Example 6-3 *Configuring Application Recognition Using NBAR to Prioritize RTP Traffic over Web Traffic*

```
ip cef
interface fastethernet 0/1 ip nbar protocol-discovery
!
class-map match-all streaming
 match protocol http mime video/mpeg
 match protocol rtp
class-map match-all nonstreaming
 match any
!
policy-map video_then_web
 class streaming
  set ip dscp cs5
 class nonstreaming
  set ip dscp default
```

Besides supporting the well-known protocols in Tables 6-4, 6-5, and 6-6, you also can configure NBAR to classify custom applications in your network. For example, if an application in your network is differentiated from others by information in the payload, you can specify what content to match with the **ip nbar custom** command. For example, if your organization's accounting department runs a TCP-based application on port 4777 that contains "PAYABLE=" starting at the 50th byte of the payload, use the following command to enable NBAR to track the application on the router:

```
ip nbar custom acct_app 50 ascii "PAYABLE=" dest tcp 4777
```

To add known protocols supported by NBAR without requiring an upgrade to the IOS on the routers enabled for NBAR, Cisco IOS uses external Packet Description Language Modules (PDLM). Cisco periodically releases PDLMs that you can download from the Cisco.com site. You can install the PDLMs to your router in permanent flash memory and enable them without reloading the router.

NOTE   You must enable Cisco Express Forwarding (CEF) before you configure NBAR.

In this section, you have learned about the ways to inform your routers of traffic that may cause problems if left unchecked. You may find that some of your critical applications are not functioning during times when you would expect them to function properly. Perhaps an application is running during this time that is flooding the network and causing other more critical applications to fail intermittently. If you feel this to be the case, consider classifying and marking the suspect traffic.

When you initially configure congestion marking, you should wait for some time before enabling any of the congestion management techniques that you will learn about next. You should take this time to install traffic sniffers and make sure that the applications you intended to mark are indeed being marked, and that other applications are not unintentionally being marked. You do not want to unwittingly drop packets that belong to a critical application. Once you are sure that traffic is being marked correctly, you should then consider applying the techniques you will learn about next.

Congestion Management

With congestion management, you can control the throughput of packets in your network when it is unable to accommodate the aggregate traffic without dropping packets. You can soften the effects of network congestion by configuring your routers and switches to intelligently queue flows of packets throughout your network. To do so, you can use the following congestion management techniques:

■ Layer 3 Router Packet Queuing

■ Layer 2 Switch Ethernet Frame QoS

Understanding Layer 3 Router Packet Queuing

First-In, First-Out (FIFO) queuing is an unintelligent queuing method that forwards packets in the order in which they arrive at the router. FIFO queuing causes high-bandwidth, delay-insensitive flows, such as file transfers, to take precedence over low-bandwidth, real-time flows, such as voice and video streaming. Packets of a file transfer normally occur in your network in the form of traffic trains—that is, as collective groups of packets flowing through the network at roughly the same time. In contrast, real-time applications generate packets individually and send them as discrete entities through the network. The following congestion management features are available to maintain the quality of real-time flows in your network:

■ Priority Queuing

■ Custom Queuing

■ Weighted Fair Queuing with IP RTP Priority

■ Class-Based WFQ with Low Latency Queuing

Configuring Priority Queuing

Priority queuing (PQ) uses four FIFO queues of different priority to transmit data: high, medium, normal, and low PQ queues. You can configure your router to queue packets into the four queues using criteria, such as incoming router interfaces, source IP addresses, IP protocols, and packet sizes.

A queue at a higher priority receives absolute preferential service over the lower-priority queues. Not until the high queues are empty do low queues receive service from the packet dequeuing (removal) mechanism. As a result, lower-priority queues may starve as the router services high-priority queues. Figure 6-1 shows how a router services the four PQ queues.

Figure 6-1 *The Priority Queuing Mechanism*

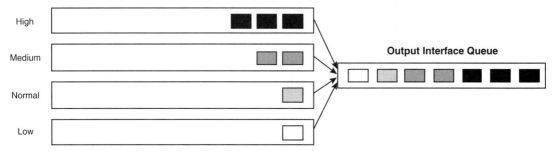

To decrease the probability of queue starvation, you can increase the maximum number of packets allowed in the lower queues, decrease the maximum number of packets allowed in the higher queues, or both. The default values are 20, 40, 60, and 80 packets for the high, medium, normal, and low queues, respectively. To enable priority queuing on an interface, you can use the configuration in Example 6-4.

Example 6-4 *Configuring Priority Queuing*

```
priority-list 1 interface fastethernet 0/0 high
priority-list 1 interface fastethernet 0/1 medium
priority-list 1 interface fastethernet 0/2 normal
priority-list 1 interface fastethernet 0/3 low
priority-list 1 queue-limit 5 30 60 90
interface fastethernet 0/4
  priority-group 1
```

In Example 6-4, the router queues packets from four different Fast Ethernet interfaces into the four PQs. The example decreases the packet count for the high-priority queue, and increases it for the lower-priority queues, so that the queue associated with interface FastEthernet 0/0 does not starve the remaining queues.

> **NOTE**   With any of the congestion management techniques discussed in this section, if the
> queues become full, the router drops packets from the tail of the queue. To avoid tail drop, see
> the section "Configuring Weighted Random Early Detection" in this chapter.

Configuring Custom Queuing

Custom queuing (CQ) provides fair treatment of the queues that PQ lacks. With CQ, you can
configure up to 16 FIFO queues to which you can assign different priorities of traffic. The router
allocates a single queue for system traffic, such as routing updates, and link keep-alives, and
services it until empty. The router services the remaining 16 user queues in a round-robin fashion
by transmitting a configurable number of bytes from each queue every round-robin cycle. Because
a router cannot transmit partial packets, it sends the entire packet, even if the byte count for the
queue is exceeded. To make up for overuse, the router subtracts any excess from the byte count of
that queue for use during the next round-robin cycle. The default byte count for each queue is 1500
bytes. You can change the default byte count by using the following command:

```
queue-list list-num queue queue-num byte-count count
```

Figure 6-2 illustrates how CQ works.

Figure 6-2   *The Custom Queuing Mechanism*

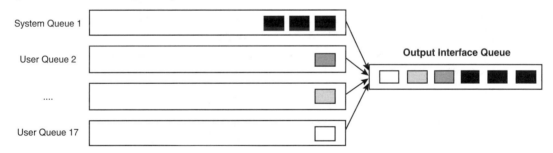

By default, the router classifies a maximum of 20 packets for entry into the queues. You can
classify packets by protocol, access lists, and router interface. You can change the default
maximum number of packets using the command:

```
queue-list list-num queue queue-num limit limit-number
```

Example 6-5 illustrates how to enable CQ with two queues on a Fast Ethernet interface. This
example decreases the byte count for Queue 2 to ensure that packets from Queue 1 receive more
service per round-robin cycle.

Example 6-5 *Configuring Custom Queuing*

```
queue-list 1 protocol ip 1 tcp 6001
queue-list 1 protocol ip 2 udp  5001
queue-list 1 queue 1 byte-count 1400
queue-list 1 queue 2 byte-count 570
interface fastethernet 0/0
  custom-queue-list 1
```

Configuring Weighted Fair Queuing and IP RTP Priority Queuing

WFQ is a flow-based scheduling algorithm that gives low-bandwidth, interactive flows priority over high-demand flows. The fairness of the algorithm comes from the ability to avoid starvation of high-demand flows while fulfilling the network demands of applications with lower bandwidth, smaller packets, and intermittent access requirements.

Fair queuing automatically categorizes traffic into flows with low- and high-demand bandwidth requirements. WFQ assumes that low-demand, interactive flows are those flows with small packet sizes and that high-demand traffic use large packets. WFQ sorts flows in terms of their demand and services them by the packet removal mechanism equally. WFQ gives the low-bandwidth flows priority, while the remaining available bandwidth is shared among the high-demand flows.

WFQ creates a dynamic set of queues for traffic flows, the number of which you can manually set. WFQ assigns each individual flow to a queue and services them with a bit-wise round-robin algorithm, which takes into consideration the size of the packets to decide the order of transmission of the flows. Otherwise, flows with larger packets may starve flows with smaller packets. For example, the packet-based round-robin that PQ uses gives preference over flows with larger packets. WFQ identifies flows by hashing TCP/IP information, such as source/destination IP addresses, TCP/UDP ports, protocol, and IP Precedence. The hashed value provides an index into the individual queue housing the respective flow.

WFQ gives flows with higher precedence a lower weight and therefore a greater allocation of overall bandwidth. The router uses the IP Precedence field to calculate the ratio of the overall link bandwidth with the equation:

$$\text{Link Proportion} = \text{Precedence}_{current} / \text{Precedence}_{sum}$$

For example, three flows that concurrently traverse a 1.544 Mbps T1 serial link have IP Precedences 3, 4, and 5, respectively. The sum of the IP Precedences equals 12. Therefore, the proportions of bandwidth for the three flows are 3/12th (25 percent), 4/12th (33 percent), and 5/12ths (42 percent), respectively. Figure 6-3 illustrates how WFQ treats these three flows within the WFQ queues.

Figure 6-3 *The WFQ Queuing Mechanism*

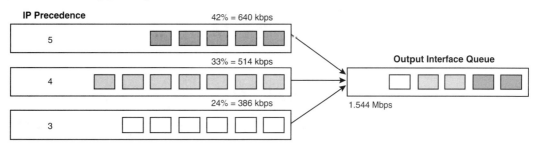

Although WFQ differentiates flows with weights based on IP Precedence, its drawback is that it cannot guarantee bandwidth service to any of the flows. WFQ is fair to all traffic flows, including high-demand applications, which may cause real-time applications to suffer. Furthermore, WFQ is not scalable to higher-speed links. Because the router assigns each flow an individual queue, the number of queues grows substantially for high-bandwidth links. WFQ works well for speeds of 2 Mbps or less, and is therefore enabled by default for links of serial speed or lower. To enable WFQ on a link, use the interface configuration command:

```
fair-queue [congestive-discard-threshold [dynamic-queues [reservable-queues]]]
```

When the proportion of the link bandwidth reaches the congestive discard threshold, the router randomly drops packets (see the section "Congestion Avoidance" for more information on the benefits of randomly dropping packets). The number of dynamic queues is the number of queues for regular flows, and the reservable queues are the number of queues you can configure for Resource Reservation Protocol (RSVP) flows. The default value for the congestive discard threshold is 64 messages. The default number of dynamic queues is dependant on the bandwidth of the interface, and the default for the RSVP queues is 0.

Compared to standard WFQ, PQ provides much better service to higher-priority traffic and is preferable for real-time applications using Real-Time Transport Protocol (RTP), where guaranteed delivery is essential. As a result, you should use IP RTP Priority, also called PQ/WFQ, instead of standard WFQ. With PQ/WFQ, the router assigns a single high-priority strict FIFO queue for RTP traffic, which preempts traffic in other queues. The router services the PQ until it is empty, and services the remaining traffic using a standard WFQ. The drawback of PQ/WFQ is that the PQ can starve the standard WFQ queues. Figure 6-4 illustrates the operation of PQ/WFQ.

Figure 6-4 *Priority Queuing/Weighted Fair Queuing*

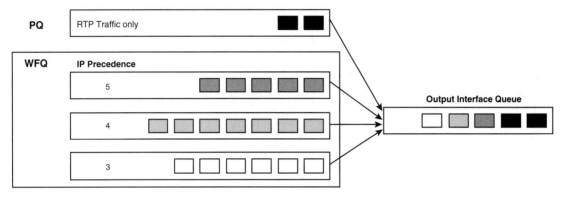

To enable IP RTP priority queuing, use the interface configuration command:

```
ip rtp priority starting-rtp-port-number port-number-range bandwidth
```

Another drawback to PQ/WFQ is that the PQ serves only RTP traffic. Other real-time traffic that requires preferential treatment, including RTCP traffic, is served in the standard WFQ queues, enabling it to be delayed or starved by the PQ. To introduce a strict PQ for real-time traffic of any kind, you should instead use class-based WFQ with Low Latency Queuing (LLQ).

> **NOTE** For more information on RTP and RTCP, see Chapter 9, "Introducing Streaming Media."

Configuring Class-Based WFQ with Low Latency

Class-Based Weighted Fair Queuing (CBWFQ) provides more granularity and scalability than WFQ. With CBWFQ, you can configure different classes and specify the ratio of the available bandwidth for each class. As a result, CBWFQ no longer classifies traffic into flows (see Figure 6-5). CBWFQ is therefore more scalable because each flow does not require an individual queue.

Low Latency Queuing (LLQ) provides a strict PQ to CBWFQ, similar to IP RTP priority. However, the PQ in CBWFQ is monitored to ensure that the fair queues are not forgotten, which differs from the starvation property of the IP RTP Priority mechanism.

Not only can you assign RTP traffic to the PQ using the RTP UDP port range; you can classify any type of traffic as highest priority. For example, you can use access lists to classify traffic based on various IP header fields, such as IP address, TCP/UDP port ranges, IP header DCSP/Precedence fields, IP protocols, and input interfaces. To enable CBWFQ with LLQ, you can use the configuration in Example 6-6.

Figure 6-5   *Class-Based Weighted Fair Queuing with Low Latency Queuing*

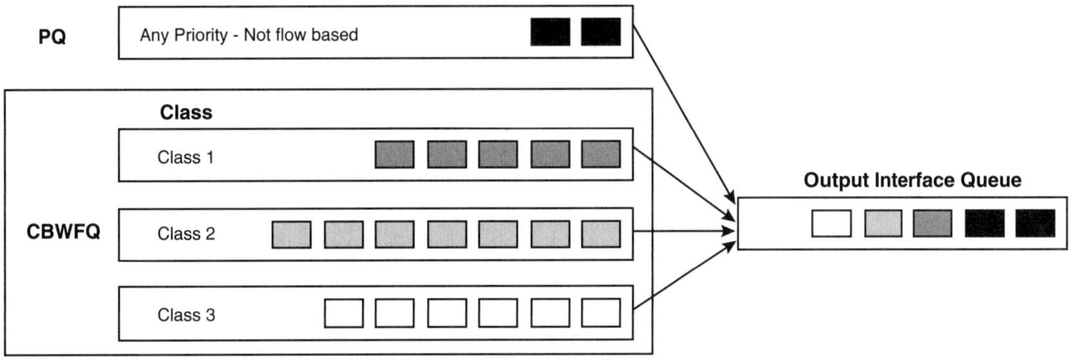

Example 6-6   *Configuring Class-Based WFQ with LLQ*

```
access-list 101 permit udp any any range 16384 65535
access-list 102 permit tcp any any eq telnet

class-map video
    match access-group 101
class-map telnet
    match access-group 102

policy-map diffapps
  class video
     priority percent 60
  class telnet
     bandwidth percent 10
  class class-default
    fair-queue

interface serial 0
  service-policy output diffapps
```

In Example 6-6, the router assigns video traffic matching the class "video" to the PQ. The UDP port range of 16,384–65,535 is used to classify RTP streaming media traffic in this example. CBWFQ does not allocate the video traffic more than 60 percent of the available bandwidth on the Fast Ethernet interface. The router also creates a standard queue for Telnet traffic, within the telnet class. The router allocates 10 percent of the overall bandwidth for Telnet traffic. All other traffic is assigned to WFQ queues.

Understanding Layer 2 Switch Ethernet Frame QoS

You can configure your Layer 2 switches to classify, mark, police, and intelligently queue traffic flowing through switch ports. For traffic that you tag with 802.1P, the switch can trust the existing CoS field in the frame tag in order to classify the frame at incoming (or ingress) switch ports—you learned about the 802.1P field in Chapter 3. For untagged traffic, the switch can inspect the IP header and trust either the IP Precedence or IP DSCP value to classify the frame at ingress ports. Otherwise, if you decide that the switch should not trust the existing values, you can configure default CoS values on the individual ingress switch ports. Based on the priority that you give the frames at the ingress port, the switch queues the frame accordingly at the outgoing (or egress) port.

Table 6-7 gives the default association switches use between CoS and DSCP values. Alternatively, you can re-configure these mappings on your switch.

Table 6-7   *DSCP Values to IP Precedence to CoS Value Mappings*

IP DSCP	IP Precedence	CoS	Purpose
0	0	0	Best effort
8, 10	1	1	Class 1
16, 18	2	2	Class 2
24, 36	3	3	Class 3
32, 34	4	4	Class 4
40, 46	5	5	Express forwarding
48	6	6	Control
56	7	7	Control

The egress ports on Catalyst 29xx/35xx/37xx/4xxx series switches have four queues for the switch to choose from. The switch places traffic in egress queues based on the CoS, IP Precedence, or DSCP value of the frame. Queue 4 is a strict priority queue, and the other three queues are standard queues. The switch services Queue 4 until empty before it services the other queues. The three standard queues are subject to Weighted Round-Robin (WRR) queuing. You can assign the weights to the three standard queues or use the default queuing values, as indicated in Table 6-8.

Table 6-8   *Weights Assigned to 29xx/35xx/37xx/4xxx Transmit Queues*

Queue	CoS value	Queue Weight
4 (priority queue)	5	1
3	3, 6, 7	70
2	2, 4	20
1	1, 2	10

The ingress ports on 29xx/35xx/37xx/4xxx switches have only a single queue. You can configure the switch to classify, mark, and police traffic at the ingress port, but not at the egress switch port.

On the Catalyst 6000, the queuing architecture of a switch port is given using codes. Enter the **show port capabilities** command to see the queue architecture of your switch ports. For example, the code *tx-(1p2q2t)* indicates that the egress port has one strict priority queue (1p), and two standard queues (2q) with two drop thresholds (2t) for each queue. The code *rx-(1q8t)* indicates that the ingress port has one standard queue with eight drop thresholds. You can associate the queues threshold with values, so that low-priority traffic in your network is WRED-dropped before high-priority traffic. Refer to the next section for more information on WRED.

Your switch assigns frames to the queues based on their CoS values. If your switch ports have 1p2q2t/1p1q4t (Tx/Rx) transmit queues, the default CoS assignments and thresholds for your queuing architecture are listed in Tables 6-9 and 6-10.

Table 6-9   *Default Threshold Settings for the 1p2q2t Transmit Queuing Structure*

Transmit 1p2q2t Values	Strict Queue	Queue #1 Threshold #1	Queue #1 Threshold #2	Queue #2 Threshold #1	Queue #2 Threshold #2
CoS Values	5	0, 1	2, 3	4	6, 7
WRED-Drop (Minimum) Threshold	-	40%	70%	40%	70%
Tail-Drop (Maximum) Threshold	-	70%	100%	70%	100%

To change the CoS assignments for the transmit queue structure in Table 6-9, you can use the command:

```
set qos map 1p2q2t tx queue# threshold# cos coslist
```

For example, the command **set qos map 1p2q2t tx 2 2 cos 5 6 7** assigns the CoS values 5, 6, and 7 to Queue #2/Threshold #2.

To change the WRED-drop and tail-drop thresholds, you can use the command:

```
set qos wred 1p2q2t tx queue queue# threshold-list
```

For example, the command **set qos wred 1p2q2t tx queue 1 30:60 60:100** sets the Queue #1/ Threshold #1 values to 30%:60% and Queue #1/Threshold #2 values to 60%:100%.

Table 6-10 gives the default thresholds for the 1p1q4t receive queuing structure.

Table 6-10 *Default Threshold Settings for the 1p1q4t Receive Queuing Structure*

Receive 1p1q4t Values	Strict Queue	Queue #1 Threshold #1	Queue #1 Threshold #2	Queue #1 Threshold #3	Queue #1 Threshold #4
CoS Values	5	0, 1	2, 3	4	6, 7
Tail-Drop (Maximum) Threshold	-	50%	60%	80%	100%

> **NOTE** Notice that the receive queue structure in Table 6-10 does not have WRED-drop thresholds. Therefore, Catalyst 6500 series switches cannot WRED-drop packets at the ingress interface.

To change the tail-drop thresholds for the **1p1q4t** receive structure, you can use the command:

```
set qos drop-threshold 1p1q4t rx queue 1 threshold-list
```

For example, the command **set qos drop-threshold 1p1q4t rx queue 1 30 40 60 100** sets the Threshold #1 value to 20%, the Threshold #2 value to 40, Threshold #3 value to 75%, and Threshold #4 value to 100.

Congestion Avoidance

To configure your network to avoid becoming congested, you have these options at your disposal:

- Weighted Random Early Detection

- Policing and Shaping

- QoS Policy Signaling

Configuring Weighted Random Early Detection

As discussed previously in Chapter 2 TCP senders use TCP slow start or TCP congestion avoidance or both to slow down transmission during periods of congestion. Without WRED enabled, packet dropping occurs from the tail of overloaded router queues, which works well if the congestion affects only a few senders. However, vast numbers of senders may commence TCP slow start at the same time during packet tail-drop. Consequently, traffic temporarily slows down to an extremely low level, and all flows initiate slow-start once again, creating an effect called *global synchronization*.

> **NOTE**   WRED applies only to TCP and does not influence UDP-based traffic. However, real-time UDP applications benefit from WRED by preventing network congestion that is caused by bandwidth-hungry TCP-based applications.

You can configure WRED to randomly dropping packets slightly before congestion occurs. Thus, individual TCP senders initiate TCP slow start or congestion avoidance or both, rather than large groups of senders at once. Routers trigger WRED when its average queue size reaches a minimum threshold, after which it drops certain packets given a drop probability (see Figure 6-6). The drop probability is 10 percent by default, but you can adjust this value depending on your environment. The router randomly drops packets in this way until the average queue size lowers below the minimum threshold or the maximum queue size threshold is reached. Note that traffic in the queues between the minimum and maximum WRED thresholds has an increasing chance of being dropped as the queue fills. When the maximum queue size threshold is reached, the router performs tail-drop.

Figure 6-6   *Weighted Random Early Detection*

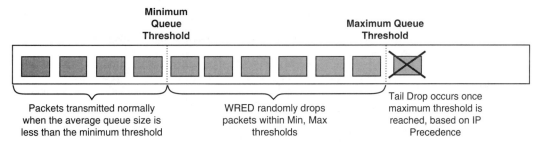

When a packet arrives at an interface, the router calculates the average queue depth. For example, if you configure three CBWFQ, and they currently have queue lengths 50, 75, and 100, then the router calculates the average queue size as 75. If the average depth is less than the minimum threshold, then the router queues the arriving packet. If the average is between the minimum and maximum thresholds, then the router drops the packet based on the probability denominator. If the average queue size is greater than or equal to the maximum threshold, then the packet is dropped.

Enable WRED on an interface with the **random-detect** interface configuration command:

```
random-detect {dscp-based ¦ prec-based}
```

To configure the thresholds and mark probability denominator for WRED, use the command:

```
random-detect precedence precedence min-threshold max-threshold mark-prob-denominator
```

When you enable WRED without parameters in the **random-detect** command, the router uses default values for the drop probability denominator, minimum, and maximum thresholds. The default mark probability denominator is 10 (one out of every 10 packets is dropped). The router calculates the default maximum threshold based on the queue capacity and the transmission speed of the interface. The default minimum threshold depends on the precedence set in the packet. The minimum threshold for IP Precedence 0 is half of the maximum threshold. The values for the IP Precedences one through seven are between half the maximum threshold and the maximum threshold at evenly spaced intervals. That is, higher-priority traffic is less likely to be dropped.

You can manually change the WRED parameters to more accurately reflect the behavior of your queues. For example, if your network contains three classes of traffic with IP Precedence values of three, four, and five, you can enable WRED on your routers with the configuration in Example 6-7.

Example 6-7 *Configuring WRED for Three IP Precedence Values*

```
interface FastEthernet1/0/0
 random-detect prec-based
 random-detect precedence 0 32 128 50
 random-detect precedence 3 64 192 100
 random-detect precedence 4 96 256 150
 random-detect precedence 5 128 320 200
```

Make sure that you monitor average interface queue sizes before you adjust the default values of WRED parameters. Otherwise, the router may drop packets too aggressively, causing global synchronization to occur.

NOTE WRED is RSVP-aware, and it can provide the RSVP controlled-load integrated service, as discussed later in this chapter.

Instead of randomly dropping packets or tail-dropping packets, you can configure your routers to mark packets with the Explicit Congestion Notification (ECN) field. Refer to Chapter 2 for the values of the ECN field. You can configure ECN with WRED using the sample configuration in Example 6-8.

Example 6-8 *Configuring WRED with ECN*

```
policy-map wredecn
 class class-default
 bandwidth percent 100
  random-detect
  random-detect ecn

interface fastethernet0/10
 service-policy input wredecn
```

Because Example 6-8 gives only a single QoS policy, you should configure the default class "class-default" to configure WRED and ECN.

Now, when the average queue length reaches the minimum threshold and the mark probability denominator establishes that the packet should be dropped, the router first checks the ECN value in the packet. If the ECN value is binary 01 (0b01) or 0b10, the router knows that the sending and receiving hosts are capable of understanding ECN. Therefore, instead of dropping the packet, the router sets the ECN value to 0b11, to indicate to the hosts that the network is congested. If the value of the ECN field is already 0b11, the router forwards the packet unchanged. Senders slow down transmission when they receive packets with an ECN value of 0b11.

Understanding Policing and Shaping

You can apply traffic shaping or policing at the edge of your network to control the bandwidth available to your applications within the network. Figure 6-8 illustrates the difference between traffic shaping and policing for the bandwidth graph given in Figure 6-7.

Figure 6-7   *A Typical Bandwidth Graph*

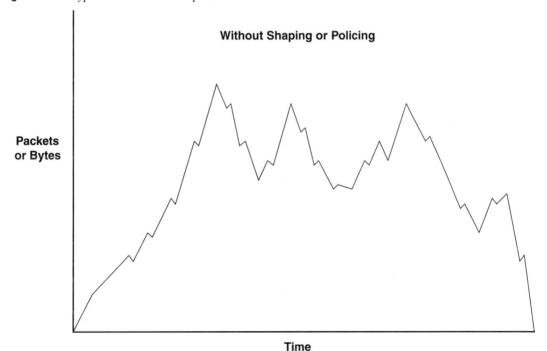

Figure 6-8   *Traffic Shaping Versus Traffic Policing*

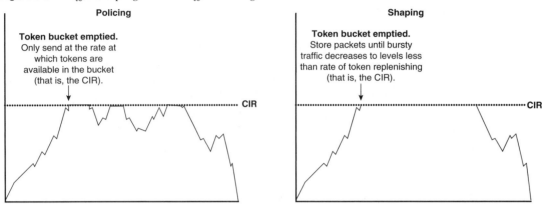

During excessive traffic, routers that you configure with traffic shaping store excessive bursts of packets exceeding committed access rate (CIR) in their queues. When the bandwidth eventually decreases below the CIR, the router can transmit the queued packets. In contrast, traffic policing simply drops traffic exceeding the CIR.

Cisco traffic shaping and policing uses a token bucket metaphor to transmit packets. With traffic shaping, when a router needs to send a packet, it first withdraws a number of tokens from the bucket equal in representation to the size of the packet. The token generator replenishes the tokens at a constant rate that is equal in representation to the configured CIR. However, the bucket will not receive more tokens than its capacity. A full bucket is equal to the amount of the largest available burst in a time interval T, referred to as the committed burst size B_c. For example, if your router sends a burst of packets equal in size to the bucket during one interval T, any more packets are either discarded (when policing is enabled) or held in the queuing system (when traffic shaping is enabled). Shaping holds the packet in the queue until the token generator replenishes the bucket with enough tokens to send the new packet.

As Figure 6-9 illustrates, when the token bucket empties, policing sends only at the CIR, which is the rate at which the token generator replenishes tokens in the bucket. The router drops traffic exceeding the CIR. In contrast, shaping stores bursts in WFQ queues until the level of traffic is less than the token replenish rate, resulting in a smooth traffic curve.

The traffic shaping token generator increments the token bucket periodically with B_c worth of tokens at every constant interval T. You should choose the normal burst (B_c) as half a second's to several seconds' worth of traffic at the configured CIR. Therefore, you may use the following equation to calculate B_c:

$$B_c = (CIR / 8 \text{ bits}) * 0.5 \text{ seconds}$$

> **TIP**   Make sure that you monitor your effective traffic throughput when you enable shaping or policing, to ensure that you have an appropriate value for B_c. A value that is too low may cause your actual throughput to differ from the CIR you configure.

Figure 6-9 *The Token Bucket Mechanism*

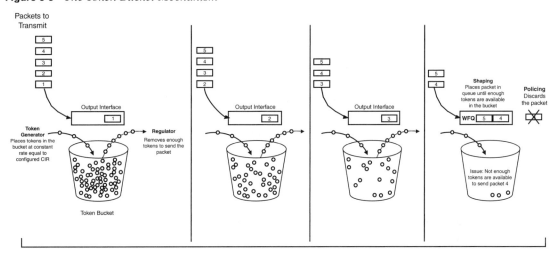

1 Interval

For example, using a CIR value of 100,000 bps would give you B_c = 25,000 bytes. Therefore, every 500 ms, the token generator credits the token bucket with 25,000 bytes worth of tokens. Notice that you can derive the time interval T from the token credits $T = B_c / CIR$.

$$T = B_c / CIR = (25,000 \text{ bytes} * 8 \text{ bits}) * 100,000 \text{ bps} = 200,000 / 100,000 \text{ bps} = 0.5$$
seconds

Therefore, every 500 ms, the token generator credits the token bucket with 25,000 bytes worth of tokens. Notice that you can derive the token credits B_c for the time interval T by using $B_c = CIR / T$. Therefore, with an interval T of 500 ms, you can calculate B_c as follows:

$$B_c = CIR / T = 100,000 \text{ bps} / 0.500 \text{ s} = 200,000 \text{ bits} = 25,000 \text{ bytes}$$

With traffic policing, the token generator does not add tokens to the bucket at every interval T. Instead, policing replenishes the token bucket continuously rather than at constant intervals. That is, the token generator credits the bucket with tokens every time the router sends a packet. The generator uses the inter-packet arrival time (the time between packets) to calculate the amount of new tokens for the bucket. From the example described previously, the CIR is 100,000 bps, and B_c is 25,000 bytes. Assuming that the bucket is idle for some time, it should be full with 25,000 bytes worth of tokens. If a router sends its first packet and has another packet to send 0.05 seconds later, the amount of tokens replenished in the bucket after the second packet is

$$\text{Bucket credit} = \Delta T * CIR = 0.05 * 100,000 = 5000 \text{ bits} = 625 \text{ bytes}$$

Therefore, the token generator credits 625 bytes worth of tokens when the router sends the second packet. For example, with a burst of one 1500-byte packet sent every 0.05 seconds for 0.75

seconds (that is, 15 packets in total), there will still be 9375 bytes (15 intervals * 625 bytes) worth of tokens left in the token bucket, even though the router has sent 22,500 bytes (1500 bytes * 15 packets).

Both traffic shaping and policing have extended capabilities to allow the router to borrow tokens in the event that packets are available to send, but the bucket is empty. B_e is the excess burst associated with the amount of tokens that the router can borrow. As a result, the maximum burst size is now $B_c + B_e$. This borrowing feature is meant to prevent queue tail-drop by applying congestion avoidance using WRED for traffic between the B_c and B_e parameters. If the router sends no packets during an interval, the token bucket may accumulate B_e worth of tokens from the next interval, resulting in maximum of $B_c + B_e$ bytes that are allowed to be transmitted at any given point in time.

To configure traffic shaping, you can use either Generic Traffic Shaping (GTS) or class-based traffic shaping. To configure traffic policing, you can use Committed Access Rate (CAR), class-based policing, or two-rate policing.

Configuring Generic Traffic Shaping

As mentioned previously, the difference between traffic shaping and policing is that, when the token bucket is full, shaping queues packets until congestion decreases.

You can use the following command to enable GTS on a router:

```
traffic-shape rate bit-rate [burst-size [excess-burst-size]]
```

For example, if employees in your organization need to use both real-time and file transfers applications over a T1 link (1.544 Mbps), you should ensure that the file transfers do not flood the T1. To do this, you can constrain file transfers to 70 percent of the T1 on average, but allow 10-second bursts to take up 95 percent of the T1. For your calculations, 70 percent of a T1 is 1,080,800 bps and 95 percent is 1,466,800 bps.

To calculate B_c for traffic shaping, use B_c = CIR * 0.5 seconds = 1,080,800 * 0.5 as with previous examples. Therefore, Bc is 540,400 bits/T. Additionally, bursts at 95 percent of the T1 generates 1,466,800 bits * 0.5 seconds = 733,400 bits of traffic. To calculate B_e, subtract 733,400 from B_c to get 193,000. Use the interface configuration command in Example 6-9 to achieve these requirements.

Example 6-9 *Configuring Generic Traffic Shaping*

```
access-list 101 permit tcp any any ftp
interface serial 1
 traffic-shape group 101 1080800 2161600 14668000
```

Configuring Class-Based Traffic Shaping

Class-based traffic shaping uses the MQC to configure traffic shaping policies. The MQC enables you to shape either incoming or outgoing interface bandwidth. You also can apply shaping to the overall interface traffic, or you can police traffic-based IP address, MAC address, and IP Precedence or DSCP. Use the following command to enable traffic shaping:

```
shape {average ¦ peak} cir [bc] [be]
```

To achieve the results from Example 6-9, use the configuration in Example 6-10.

Example 6-10 *Configuring Class-Based Traffic Shaping*

```
access-list 101 permit tcp any any ftp
class ftp-traffic
 match access-group 101

policy-map shape-ftp
 class ftp-traffic
   shape average 1080800 540400 193000

interface serial 1
 service-policy output shape-ftp
```

Configuring Committed Access Rate (CAR)

CAR is a traffic policer with the ability to police either incoming or outgoing interface bandwidth. Using CAR, you can apply policing to the overall interface traffic, or you can police traffic-based IP address, MAC address, and IP Precedence.

If the traffic rate reaches the CIR (that is, the token bucket is empty), you can configure CAR to drop the packet or borrow more tokens and send the packet. Alternatively, before the router sends packets, you can configure CAR to mark its IP Precedence.

CAR maintains parameters for CIR, B_c, and B_e. Therefore, you can apply actions to traffic conforming to and exceeding these values. Conform actions are applied to bursts less than B_c. Exceed actions are applied to bursts between and B_c and $B_c + B_e$.

To enable CAR on an interface, use the interface configuration command:

```
rate-limit {input ¦ output} [access-group [rate-limit]] [acl-index]
    bps burst-normal burst-max conform-action action exceed-action action
```

In this command, *burst-normal* is B_c and *burst-max* is $B_c + B_e$. For example, if your router has an OC3 interface (155 Mbps), and you want traffic less than 100 Mbps to be marked with IP

Precedence 3, traffic between 100 Mbps and 120 Mbps to be marked as best-effort (IP Precedence 0), and traffic exceeding 120 Mbps to be dropped, use the CAR interface configuration command:

```
rate-limit output 100000000 6250000 7500000 conform-action set-prec-transmit
    3 exceed-action set-prec-transmit 0
```

Using the equation $burst\text{-}normal = B_c = (CIR\ /\ 8\ bits) * 0.5$ seconds discussed previously, burst-normal $= (100{,}000{,}000\ /\ 8) * 2 = 6.25$ MB. Additionally, in this example, burst-max $= B_c * 1.20 = 7.5$ MB, giving $B_e = 1.25$ MB, in order to calculate the maximum burst required to get a peak information rate (PIR) of 120 Mbps.

Configuring Class-Based Policing

Class-based policing supersedes CAR to include support for IP DSCP marking. Additionally, you can specify actions on traffic that exceeds $B_c + B_e$, with the new command parameter **violate-action**. Whereas, with CAR, the router drops traffic exceeding $B_c + B_e$.

To support actions on traffic that exceeds $B_c + B_e$, the router maintains two token buckets: a conform bucket and an exceed bucket. The number of tokens in the conform bucket is equal to B_c, and the number of tokens in the exceed bucket is B_e.

To enable class-based policing, use the following command:

```
police bps burst-normal [burst-max] conform-action action exceed-action
    action [violate-action action]
```

The conform bucket is $burst\text{-}max = B_c + B_e$. The exceed bucket is $B_e = burst\text{-}max - B_c$.

As discussed previously, when a packet arrives at a traffic policer, the generator replenishes the token bucket with tokens representing $\Delta T * CIR$ worth of bytes. Using two buckets, the conform bucket receives the replenish tokens, and the exceed bucket receives the tokens overflowing the conform bucket.

If you are using the bandwidth requirements from the previous example, but instead you want traffic less than 100 Mbps to be marked with IP DSCP 40, traffic between 100 Mbps and 120 Mbps to be marked as IP DSCP 24, and traffic exceeding 120 Mbps as IP DSCP 0, then use the MQC configuration in Example 6-11.

Example 6-11 *Configuring Class-Based Policing for Three Levels of Bandwidth*

```
policy-map police-oc3
 class class-default
  police 100000000 6250000 7500000 conform-action set-dscp-transmit cs5
    exceed-action set-dscp-transmit cs3violate-action set-dscp-transmit
    default


interface pos 0/0
 service-policy output police-oc3
```

When a packet arrives and the conform bucket is not empty, the conform action is applied to the packet. If the conform bucket is empty, the exceed bucket is checked for tokens. If the exceed bucket is not empty, the exceed action is applied to the packet. If the exceed bucket is empty, the violate action is applied to the packet.

Configuring Two-Rate Policing

To improve on class-based policing technologies discussed previously, you can use two-rate policing that also uses two token buckets, but supports frame relay DE and ATM CLP, and MPLS marking. It also uses a much more intuitive command, as follows:

```
Router(config-pmap-c)# police {cir cir} [bc conform-burst] {pir pir}
    [be peak-burst]
```

With this command, you can explicitly configure the CIR, B_c, B_e, and peak information rate (PIR). With early versions, B_e and the PIR are implied within *burst-max*, as discussed previously. To achieve the same results as illustrated in Example 6-11 using two-rate policing, use the configuration in Example 6-12.

Example 6-12 *Configuring Two-Rate Policing*

```
policy-map police-oc3
 class class-default
  police cir 100000000 bc 6250000 pir 120000000 be 1250000 conform-action
    set-dscp-transmit cs5 exceed-action set-dscp-transmit cs3 violate-action
    set-dscp-transmit default


interface pos 0/0
 service-policy output police-oc3
```

QoS Policy Signaling

Besides configuring QoS policies directly on your routers and switches to avoid congestion, you can also configure your routers and hosts to signal QoS policies to one another automatically. You can configure QoS policy signaling using BGP QoS policy propagation or with RSVP.

BGP QoS Policy Propagation

The BGP QoS policy propagation feature enables you to classify packets by IP Precedence based on BGP autonomous system (AS) paths, BGP community lists, and access lists. A BGP router classifies the traffic and associates priority levels using IP Precedence to BGP updates and advertises the updates to remote routers. When remote routers receive the BGP routing updates, they can apply QoS policies, such as traffic policing, shaping, and WRED, to traffic that follows the advertised routes.

Resource Reservation Protocol (RSVP)

RSVP is the only mechanism for hosts to inform the network of end-to-end QoS requirements, such as bandwidth and latency guarantees, before sending the actual data flow. Hosts place reservations using special out-of-band RSVP signaling control packets. Routers perform the QoS features discussed in previous sections with in-band signaling. In-band QoS signaling occurs as traffic flows through the network.

File transfer applications seldom require reservation of bandwidth because their behavior is normally bursty and short-lived. On the other hand, real-time applications generate a constant flow of data and would benefit from a long-lived reservation of network resources. Otherwise, file transfer bursts would cause perceived delay and jitter for your real-time applications.

Using RSVP, you have the ability to provide bandwidth rate guarantees to your applications, such as H.323 video conferencing. H.323 provides constant data encoding and therefore requires a minimum bandwidth. Besides H.323, RSVP also provides delay guarantee to applications, such as streaming media.

RSVP was designed specifically for multicast networks running over simplex UDP flows. The reservation is for one-way resources—in the direction flowing from sender to receiver. However, RSVP can also reserve for any number of senders to any number of receivers.

Clients reserve network resources with either explicit or wildcard *scopes*. With an explicit reservation scope, receivers must specify senders in the reservation request, whereas with a wildcard reservation scope, receivers do not specify the senders. Additionally, RSVP defines the following styles of reservations to differentiate environments containing multiple senders:

■ **Fixed Filter (FF)**—Receivers generate a single reservation per sender. This is useful when individual senders generate distinct flows, such as a video presentation with numerous video sources generating individual streams. The receiver identifies the senders explicitly by IP address within the reservation.

■ **Wildcard Filter (WF)**—Receivers generate a single reservation for a group of senders. You should use WF when individual senders generate a cumulative shared flow, such as in an audio presentation, where only one speaker talks at a time. The receiver does not explicitly identify individual senders; instead, it identifies the group of senders using a wildcard (*) reservation scope.

■ **Shared Explicit (SE)**—SE enables the receiver to identify the senders in a shared flow. With SE, you should first establish a multicast distribution tree within your network using IGMP and PIM. You can then use RSVP for reserving the necessary QoS along the path that the data will flow in the multicast tree, as determined by the underlying unicast or multicast routing protocol.

The IETF Integrated Services suggests two classes of RSVP service: controlled-load and guaranteed QoS. The controlled-load level of service closely approximates best-effort service under unloaded conditions. It does this by specifying traffic shaping (similar to the traffic shaping described previously) and minimal delay-handling capabilities. RSVP achieves minimal delay by borrowing tokens or simply increasing the token bucket size to a value such that it decreases the possibility of queuing. On the other hand, the guaranteed QoS class of service specifies better delay guarantees by setting target values for delay. The routers estimate the queuing delays before the reservation is accepted based on current queue sizes throughout the network. The routers use the estimates as maximum delay guarantees to the application. That is, the delay will never be worse than the computed end-to-end delay.

For example, Figure 6-10 shows how the senders send RSVP PATH messages down the multicast tree. The initial PATH request contains the bandwidth it expects to generate in the "sender TSpec" object. The sender TSpec message contains information about the traffic that the sender will generate, such as the token bucket CIR, B_c, B_e, and minimum and maximum packet sizes. The routers along the path modify these values if they cannot supply the bandwidth that the senders are capable of generating. Additionally, guaranteed QoS accumulates an estimation of the queuing and end-to-end delays at each hop that the PATH message takes toward the receivers, whereas controlled-load does not.

In Figure 6-10, the sender sends its TSpec object down the multicast tree toward the receivers. The intermediary routers make necessary modifications of the sender's requirements, depending on the bandwidth and QoS availability at each hop, while forwarding the PATH message down the tree. The receivers take the accumulated information from the PATH message into consideration while determining what QoS to request from the network. As illustrated in Figure 6-10, modification of the CIR is necessary to accommodate the bandwidth bottlenecks in the network. This is assuming that the flow is able to use the full bandwidth of the link. In Cisco IOS, RSVP enables you to configure the overall bandwidth for RSVP and the rate per application flow, based on the bandwidth of the interface. To enable RSVP on an interface, use the interface configuration command:

```
ip rsvp bandwidth [interface-kbps] [single-flow-kbps]
```

During the PATH message's traversal down the tree, each router stores state information it will use to route the return RESV messages from the receivers on the reverse path the PATH messages take. The senders and receivers send periodic PATH and RECV messages to refresh the soft state tables. This enables routing changes to occur without affecting the reservation.

Figure 6-10 *A Sender PATH Message Flowing Down Toward the Receivers*

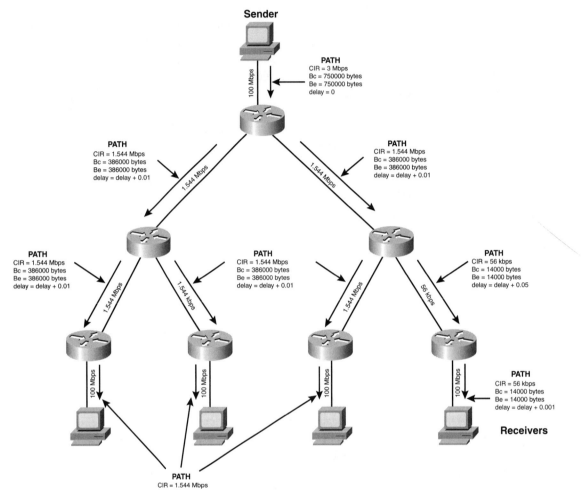

Figure 6-11 shows how, after the receivers process the PATH message, they send a RESV message to request network resources. The routers merge the RESV messages as they progress toward the senders. The RESV message contains a "receiver FlowSpec" object that includes a receiver TSpec and an RSpec. The receiver uses the RSpec to request the guaranteed QoS class of service. The TSpec includes the requested token bucket size, based on information received in the PATH request. The RSpec contains the delay value, obtained from the PATH message that the routers will use to deploy queuing mechanisms along the path. For either controlled-load or guaranteed QoS reservations, you can use PQ/WFQ and WRED. PQ/WFQ is beneficial for guaranteed QoS reservations because strict priority queuing guarantees maximum levels of delay. Recall that you can allocate the number of WFQ queues for RSVP with the **reservable-queues** parameter of the **fair-queue** interface configuration command.

Each router determines whether or not they have the available QoS to allocate for the request. If they have the available resources, the end-to-end reservation is further accumulated by forwarding the request up the tree. Otherwise, the routers send a RESV ERROR message to the receiver(s). The result is essentially a copy of the largest, or most demanding, request made by the downstream receivers arriving at the individual senders. To simplify the illustration, you can consider the merged QoS as the largest of a comparison between absolute numbers. Figure 6-11 illustrates how merging RECV requests results in the senders receiving the QoS pseudo-value of 200.

Figure 6-11 *A Receiver RECV Message Flowing Up Toward the Sender*

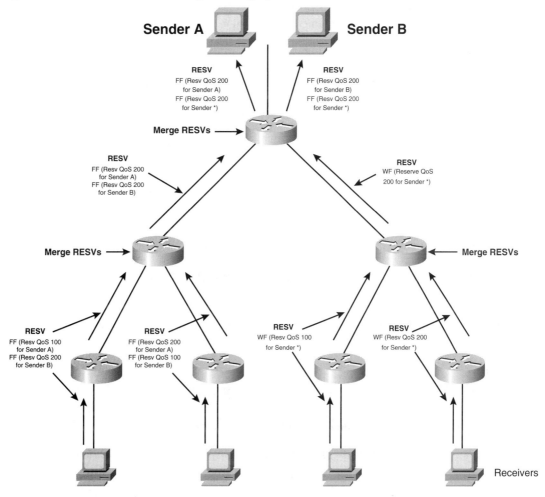

> **NOTE**   RSVP does not permit merging reservations of different styles.

To mark packets that conform to or exceed requested bandwidth resources, you can use the command:

```
ip rsvp precedence {conform precedence-value ¦ exceed precedence-value}
```

Keep in mind the following key items while evaluating RSVP for your network:

■ RSVP works with unicast reservations, but is not as scalable as it is when you use it in multicast reservations.

■ RSVP interoperates with routers that do not support RSVP because most core networks do not run RSVP services. For example, a reservation would terminate at the MPLS edge and take advantage of MPLS engineering in the core. The reservation would then reconvene at the other end of the MPLS tunnel.

■ The drawback to RSVP is the time it takes to set up the end-to-end reservation.

■ RSVP does not work well with LANs. You should use Subnetwork Bandwidth Manager for LANs instead.

Answer these questions before implementing RSVP in your network:

■ How much bandwidth should you allow per end-user application flow?

■ How much overall bandwidth should you allocate for RSVP flows?

■ How many WFQ queues should you allocate to RSVP?

■ How much bandwidth should you exclude from RSVP to allow for low-volume data conversations?

■ Do you have any multiaccess LANs in your network?

Summary

This chapter introduces the reader to Layer 2 and 3 QoS technologies.

■ **Classification and Marking**—Specifies priorities for different groups of applications.

■ **Congestion Management**—Based on priorities, switches packets with various queuing mechanisms and applies shaping or policing.

■ **Congestion Avoidance**—By using congestion avoidance, packets are randomly dropped periodically based on class before congestion occurs. Signaling allocates bandwidth and QoS for traffic flows before sending the application traffic.

Review Questions

1.   What tools can you use to mark IP Precedence? DSCP?

2.   If a router has 100,000 concurrent connections on average, approximately how much memory does NBAR use to store information for those connections?

3.   Why is WFQ not scalable to high-speed links?

4.   What is the difference between standard WFQ and CBWFQ?

5.   How many egress queues do Catalyst 29xx/35xx/4xxx series switches have? What about Catalyst 6500 series switches?

6.   What is the difference between traffic shaping and policing?

7.   How does RSVP differ from other QoS congestion avoidance mechanisms?

Recommended Reading

Richard Froom, Mike Flannagan, Kevin Turek, *Cisco Catalyst QoS: Quality of Service in Campus Networks*. Cisco Press, 2003.

Wendell Odom, Michael Cavanaugh. *Cisco QOS Exam Certification Guide*. Cisco Press, 2004

RFC 791. Internet Protocol. IETF. http://www.ietf.org/rfc/rfc791.txt, 1981.

RFC 2309. Recommendations on Queue Management and Congestion Avoidance in the Internet. IETF. http://www.ietf.org/rfc/rfc2309.txt, April 1998.

RFC 2205. *Resource ReSerVation Protocol (RSVP)   Version 1 Functional Specification. IETF. http://www.ietf.org/rfc/rfc2205.txt,* 1997.

RFC 2814. *SBM (Subnet Bandwidth Manager): A Protocol for RSVP-based Admission Control Over IEEE 802-Style Networks*, IETF. http://www.ietf.org/rfc/rfc2814.txt, 2000.

RFC 3168. *The Addition of Explicit Congestion Notification (ECN) to IP*. IETF. http://www.ietf.org/rfc/rfc3168.txt, 2001.

Part IV: Applications for Serving Content, at the Network Edge

Chapter Goals

In this chapter, you will cover the following topics to learn how to present and transform content:

- **Introducing Markup Languages**— You can use markup languages to format and describe your content.

- **Transforming and Formatting Content**—Powerful tools are available to you for transforming and formatting content.

CHAPTER 7

Presenting and Transforming Content

Introducing Markup Languages

You can use markup languages to manage structured documents in a standard format. To "mark up" a document means to imbed text within the content of the document in order to perform procedures on the data and convey information about it. Today's markup languages form their bases on **procedural markup** languages of the 1960s, when typesetters used proprietary coding for fine control over the font, size, and spacing of printed copy, with the intention of formatting documents destined for paper. For example, some book publishers required authors to submit their manuscript using proprietary procedural markup tags embedded in the text. Procedural coding leaves the task of formatting to the publisher who uses proprietary software to process the tags embedded in the document. This enables the author to concentrate on the content of the document.

Figure 7-1 gives a sample excerpt from the beginning of this book.

Figure 7-1 *A Sample Book Excerpt*

> ### Content Networking Fundamentals, Silvano D. Da Ros
>
> **Chapter 1 – Introducing Content Networks**
>
> **Chapter 1 Goals**
>
> 1.)   To state the purposes of content networking.
> 2.)   To inform the reader of the major protocols of content networking.
> 3.)   To create a framework for configuring content networks.
>
> **The Purposes of Content Networking**
>   The purpose of content networking is to accelerate your applications...
>
> **The Protocols**
>   Each content networking device runs numerous networking protocols...
>
> **Configuring Content Networking**
>   You can configure content networking devices using the command-line interface (CLI) or web interface...

> **NOTE**   Common word processing packages, such as Microsoft Word or Corel WordPerfect, use procedural markup internally to format documents. Each package has its own set of proprietary procedural markup tags for formatting, which is why you normally require a conversion tool to read a document created by one package in the other.

To produce the formatting in Figure 7-1 using procedural markup, you can insert the imaginary procedural marks *!SkipLine=n!*, *!Center!*, *!Bold!*, and *!Indent=n!* in to the text to provide the correct formatting instructions to a word processor, browser, or printer. As you can see from Figure 7-2, the procedural markup tags specify a particular procedure that is to be applied to the text that it references.

Figure 7-2   *A Basic Procedural Markup Example*

```
!Center!!Bold!Content Networking Fundamentals, Silvano D. Da Ros!/Bold!!/Center!
!SkipLine=2!
!Bold!Chapter 1 — Introducing to Content Networks!/Bold!
!SkipLine=1!
!Bold!Chapter 1 Goals!/Bold!
!SkipLine=1!
1.)!Indent=1!To state the purposes of content networking.
2.)!Indent=1!To inform the reader of the major protocols of content networking.
3.)!Indent=1!To create a framework for configuring content networks.
!SkipLine=1!
!Bold!The Purposes of Content Networking!/Bold!
!Indent=1!The purpose of content networking is to accelerate your applications...
!SkipLine=1!
!Bold!The Protocols!/Bold!
!Indent=1!Each content networking device runs numerous networking protocols...
!SkipLine=1!
!Bold!Configuring Content Networking!/Bold!
!Indent=1!You can configure content networking devices using the command-line
interface (CLI) or web interface...
```

Descriptive markup languages, or generic coding, differs from procedural markup languages by describing the structure of the document, leaving the parsers (programs used to display, print, or store the information) to perform the desired procedure. For example, you can use exactly the same text document for printing, monitor display, or even Braille. In contrast, with procedural markup, you would require a separate document for each.

Procedural markup languages have the following disadvantages over descriptive languages for publishing documents on the web:

■   **Inflexible**—The number of commands indicating how the text should be formatted (that is, skip line, indent, and so on) is often cumbersome for effective usage. For example, internally, most word processors contain thousands of tags, which are transparent to you. This number of tags is unmanageable for use in web publishing.

■ **Requires Multiple Document Formats**—Procedural markups are inflexible because, if you require different styles of documents, the text needs to be marked up again for each style. For example, if a document destined for a printer needs to be displayed to a monitor, a new marked-up document is necessary, because even the slightest offset of margins requires reformatting.

Stanley Rice and William Tunnicliffe first conceived of the separation of content from its formatting in 1967. The first formal descriptive markup language was GenCode and was the first general markup specification for the typesetting industry. Gencode recognized the need of different codes for different types of documents. Together, Rice and Tunnicliffe formed the Graphic Communications Association (GCA) Gencode Committee to further develop their ideas into a nonproprietary generic coding markup standard.

IBM then took the ideas behind GenCode to produce Generalized Markup Language (GML—also the initials of its creators, Charles Goldfarb, Edward Mosher, and Raymond Lorie) in 1969, to organize IBM's legal documents into a searchable form. GML automated functions performed specifically on IBM's legal documents. The ANSI Computer Languages group expanded GML in 1980 into the Standard Generalized Markup Language (SGML) for the Processing of Text Committee. In 1984, the International Standards Organization (ISO) joined the ANSI committee to publish the SGML standard based on its sixth working draft in 1986 as an international norm (ISO 8879). The first important users of the standard were the US Internal Revenue Service (IRS) and Department of Defense (DoD).

Figure 7-3 illustrates how to mark up the example described previously using SGML.

Figure 7-3 *A Basic Structural Markup Example Using SGML*

```
<Book title="Content Networking Fundamentals" author="Silvano D. Da Ros">
<Chapter>
<ChapterTitle>Chapter 1 — Introducing Content Networks</ChapterTitle>
<ChapterGoals title="Chapter 1 Goals" >
<Goal>To state the purposes of content networking.</Goal>
<Goal>To inform the reader of the major protocols of content networking.</Goal>
<Goal>To create a framework for configuring content networks.</Goal>
</ChapterGoals>
</Chapter>
<Section title= "The Purposes of Content Networking " >
The purpose of content networking is to accelerate your applications...
</Section>
<Section title= "The Protocols" >
Each content networking device runs numerous networking protocols...
</Section>
<Section title= "Configuring Content Networking" >
You can configure content networking devices using the command-line interface (CLI)
or web interface...
</Section>
</Book>
```

The tags shown in Figure 7-3 group the document into elements. For example, you can use the tags <Book>, <Chapter>, and <Goal> to group the document into elements. Each piece of content has the general form of a start-tag (for example, "<Book>") followed by the content, and ending with the end-tag (for example, </Book>). The title of the <Book> element is an attribute of the element as opposed to being an element itself.

Because the elements, attributes, and overall structure of Figure 7-3 are specific to the application, you should formally define them for the application. This need for formally declaring elements, attributes, and structure gave birth to the Document Type Definition (DTD) file, against which you can validate markup language files. DTD files define the syntax of the markup language. That is, it declares all tags within the markup file and specifies the order with which they should appear, which ones are optional or repeatable, and that they are properly nested. You can use DTD files to establish portability and interoperability and exchange data between organizations with different file formats.

The DTD file for the SGML sample in Figure 7-3 is in Table 7-1. The <!ELEMENT> tag defines each element, preceded by the <ATTLIST> tag, if the element contains any attributes (for example, title and author).

Table 7-1   *A Sample Book.dtd DTD File*

DTD Information	Description
<!ELEMENT book (chapter+)> <!ATTLIST book title CDATA #REQUIRED author CDATA #IMPLIED>	The Book element contains one or more chapter elements. The + indicates that one or more elements may exist. The Book element contains attributes for the required book's title and optional (IMPLIED) author name.
<!ELEMENT chapter (chaptertitle,chaptergoals?,section+)>	Each chapter contains one chapter title, an optional "Chapter Goals" area (as indicated by a question mark), and one or more Sections elements.
<!ELEMENT chaptertitle (#PCDATA)>	The Chapter Title contains parsable character data (meaning it can contain tags within the data), which require special parsing to be rendered properly.
<!ELEMENT chaptergoals (goal+)> <!ATTLIST chaptergoals title CDATA #REQUIRED>	The Chapter Goals area contains one or more Goals Elements.
<!ELEMENT goal (#PCDATA) >	Each goal is parsable data.

Table 7-1   *A Sample Book.dtd DTD File (Continued)*

DTD Information	Description
<!ELEMENT section (subsection*)> <!ATTLIST section title CDATA #REQUIRED>	A section contains a title attribute, optional parsable character data, and zero or more sub-sections.
<!ELEMENT subsection (subsubsection*)> <!ATTLIST subsection title CDATA #REQUIRED>	A subsection contains a title attribute and zero or more subsubsections.
<!ELEMENT subsubsection (#PCDATA)> <!ATTLIST subsubsection title CDATA #REQUIRED>	A subsubsection contains a title attribute and parsable text.

Hypertext Markup Language

HTML was developed as a simple means to publish hyperlinked documents in a standard fashion. HTML enables you to avoid proprietary formats, and thus promote interoperability between the various devices expected to connect to the web. At the time, SGML was considered too bulky and complicated for such a "simple" environment. In general, HTML is an application of SGML, and includes a minor subset of simple tags for organizing content on the web.

> **NOTE**   You can use DTD files to define not only applications of certain markup languages but entire markup languages themselves. For example, just as in the book example above, HTML has its own SGML-compliant structure and subset of tags, which are used to mark up hypertext on the WWW.

In 1990, Tim Berners-Lee, then working at the Organsation Européenne pour la recherche nucléaire (CERN), published the first version of the HTML DTD (that is, HTML 1.0). Tim developed the first prototype browser, supporting HTML transported in HTTP over a TCP/IP network, resulting in the birth of the World Wide Web. The computer community received HTML 1.0 with welcoming arms, and many text-based browsers, such as Viola, Cello, and Lynx, became available shortly after its release.

The IETF published HTML version 2 as RFC 1866 in 1994. Version 2.0 included many new features and fixes to version 1.0, such as support for images and forms. The National Center for Supercomputing Applications (NCSA) developed the first graphical browser for HTML 2.0, then called Mosaic, in late 1993. The developers of Mosaic soon decided that leaving NCSA to form Netscape would be a profitable endeavor.

> **NOTE**   Numerous parties with vested interests in web protocols formed the W3C consortium in 1993 to take web standardization into a nonprofit and unincorporated setting. Soon after work began on HTML version 3.0 at W3C.

In 1993, Netscape developed HTML+ for its Mosaic browser, based on HTML version 2.0, but it included many additional practical features over HTML version 2.0. Numerous competitive companies followed suit with various browsers with support for HTML version 2.0, the largest being Microsoft with Internet Explorer. Although the two largest browser companies developed browsers with close interpretation of the HTML spec, they each developed new and incompatible tags. The browser manufacturers quickly diverged from one another, creating a highly competitive browser market. As a result, the differences between HTTP 2.0 and 3.0 and Netscape's HTML+ were so vast that W3C decided to avoid standardizing 3.0 and instead to include the version 3.0 and HTML+ updates in version HTML 3.2, among various fixes and other new features. Thus, HTTP 3.2 was released in 1997 and included the generally accepted practices at the time, or as general as possible given the major explosion of web applications developed with HTML. HTML 4.0 and 4.0.1 are the most recent versions of documents. The HTML 4.0.1 specification comprises three separate DTDs maintained and published by W3C.

HTML is an excellent markup language for displaying content for humans to read on a screen and for navigation between documents. However, even though the use of HTML is widespread, it soon proved to be insufficient in abstraction and structure for today's increasingly complex content-based applications. Like its procedural markup predecessor, presentation and formatting were given higher priority during the drafting of the HTML DTD than structure and organization, especially since the popularization of style sheets within HTML.

> **NOTE**   You can use style sheets to further separate content from the presentation of content of web documents written in HTML or Extensible HTML (XHTML). You will learn about Cascading Style Sheets (CSS) and XHTML later in this chapter.

Although HTML is a structural markup language based on SGML, the HTML tags do not sufficiently describe the content, and the specification is very loose in terms of syntax and structure as compared to SGML. Due to the explosion of the web, content providers quickly thirsted for control over formatting that was similar to that used with printed copy. Browser developers in conjunction with W3C responded with numerous HTML presentational controls. As HTML matured, its procedural markup features were replaced by mechanisms, such as converting text to images, using proprietary HTML extensions, and style sheets, as simple ways to separate presentation from content without severely changing the markup language specification.

Example 7-1 shows how an HTML file is structured.

Example 7-1 *A Sample HTML Document to Print "Hello World" to a Web Browser*

```
<HTML>
<HEAD>
<TITLE>Hello World Page/TITLE>
</HEAD>
<BODY>
Hello World!
</BODY>
</HTML>
```

To fully overcome the limitations of HTML, people recently favor more robust descriptive markup languages coupled with separate presentational markup languages as successors to HTML. In order to bridge the gap between the structured, self-descriptive nature of SGML and the usability of HTML for visual, interactive web applications, the W3C created the XML family of markup languages to simplify HTML.

Extensible Markup Language

Like HTML, Extensible Markup Language (XML) is an application of the SGML protocol, but includes more of the semantic aspects of SGML. XML is a true structural markup language in that it does not do anything to the data but just describe it. In contrast to HTML, which achieved a certain level of structure with abstractions such as headings, paragraphs, emphasis, and numbered lists, in XML you can create custom XML tags to describe content (for example, Book, Section, and Goals are custom XML tags). HTML has only a specific set of tags available to describe content (e.g., Header, Body, and so on), and vast numbers of tags to perform actions on the data.

> **NOTE**   In contrast to the way you use HTML, you use XML to carry data, not both data and presentation information. In order to present the data, you must use a style sheet or transform the XML document into HTML or XHTML. You will learn how to present XML later in this chapter.

XML was published as a W3C Recommendation in early 1998. Much of the out-of-date features are excluded from XML. For example, SGML typewriter directives are no longer pertinent today. XML also extends SGML with its internationalization features and typing of elements using XML schemas.

With HTML, user agents can accept any syntax and try to make sense out of it, without giving errors. User agents are therefore difficult to write because an enormous number of erroneous pages exist on the web. The validation of XML is much more deliberate, easing the pressure on user agent developers to perform the complex error correction required on poorly written HTML. The downfall is that users must conform to the strict rules imposed by XML to avoid errors in their documents.

> **NOTE**   The term *user agent* refers to any program that fetches, parses, and optionally displays web pages. Search engine robots are user agents, which is why you will not often see the term *web browser* used in most web texts, journals, and standardization documents to refer to all such agents.

Drawing on the ability to create custom elements in XML, numerous associated XML-based languages are available to you for extending the basic functionality of XML. Each requires special applications to recognize and perform actions on their respective custom-defined elements.

- **Extensible StyleSheet Language (XSL) and Extensible Stylesheet Transformation (XSLT)**—You can use the XSL and XSLT languages to display and transform XML documents, for Cisco IP phones, WAP cell phones, and PDAs.

- **Extensible StyleSheet Language-Format Object (XSL-FO)**—You can use XSL-FO to format documents for print, such as Adobe PDF files and barcodes.

- **XPath**—Use XPath to specify locations within XML documents, similar to the way files are organized on a standard computer file system. XPath is not an application of XML, but it is a major component in XSLT. You will see how XPath works with XSLT later in this chapter.

- **XLink**—Use XLink for hyperlinking between XML documents. XLink is similar to HTML links but includes many extensions, such as bidirectional, typed, one-to-many and many-to-many links. You can also use XLink to download links automatically or on user request.

- **XQuery**—You can perform queries on XML files using XQuery, similar to the way in which you use Structure Query Language (SQL) queries in database systems.

- **Synchronized Multimedia Integration Language SMIL**—Use SMIL for the multimedia structured markup. You will learn about SMIL in Chapter 9, "Introducing Streaming Media."

- **Scalable Vector Graphics (SVG)**—Use SVG for structuring graphics.

- **Resource Description Framework (RDF)**—Use RDF for structured metadata markup.

- **MathML**—You can use MathML for mathematical equation structured markup.

Figure 7-4 shows the sample document described previously in Figure 7-1, structured in XML. Notice that the simple SGML example discussed previously in Figure 7-3 is identical when written XML, except for the required "?xml version" header.

Figure 7-4 *Sample XML File*

```
<?xml version="1.0"?>
<!DOCTYPE book SYSTEM "book.dtd">
<Book title="Content Networking Fundamentals" author="Silvano D. Da Ros">
<Chapter>
<ChapterTitle>Chapter 1 — Introducing Content Networks</ChapterTitle>
<ChapterGoals> title="Chapter 1 Goals" >
<Goal>To state the purposes of content networking.</Goal>
<Goal>To inform the reader of the major protocols of content networking.</Goal>
<Goal>To create a framework for configuring content networks.</Goal>
</ChapterGoals>
</Chapter>
<Section title= "The Purposes of Content Networking " >
The purpose of content networking is to accelerate your applications...
</Section>
<Section title= "The Protocols" >
Each content networking device runs numerous networking protocols...
</Section>
<Section title= "Configuring Content Networking" >
You can configure content networking devices using the command-line interface
(CLI) or web interface...
</Section>
</Book>
```

NOTE XML with correct syntax is *well-formed XML*. XML validated against a DTD is *valid XML*. You can optionally specify the DTD to validate an XML file against in the header of the XML document, as show in Figure 7-4. You can also use XML Schemas as an XML-based alternative to the standard DTDs. Relax NG is the schema language by OSI.

Extensible Hypertext Markup Language

Extensible HTML (XHTML) is the next step in the evolution of web documents, and its creation was motivated by the need to deliver content to many different types of devices, such as mobile phones, PDAs, and web kiosks. As the name suggests, it is a combination of XML and HTML. More specifically, the XHTML DTDs are a reformulation of the three HTML 4.0 DTDs, as an application of XML (recall that HTML 4.0 is conversely an application of SGML). In other words, the HTML DTDs where rewritten within the XML DTD, creating the new XHTML DTD. With the new definitions, the old HTML syntax must follow the same strict rules as XML. This leads the way to a more standardized language, as user agents gradually transition to XHTML.

NOTE Because documents in XHTML conform to both XML and HTML 4, you can view them in user agents supporting either type.

Although HTML may never totally retire as a web markup language, it will become much more extensible and standardized under the guise of XML. It will be extensible in that you can create your own tags and standardized in that user agents concern themselves with the standards of the XML specification, not the complex HTML error-correction methods stemming from a lack of standard syntax. Important differences between HTML and XHTML are

- You must nest XHTML elements properly.

- XHTML documents must be well-formed.

- Tag names must be in lowercase.

- You must close all XHTML elements.

Wireless Application Protocol Markup Languages

New business potential in mobile browsing has fostered the development in Wireless Application Protocol (WAP). You can use WAP to supply web content to mobile devices, such as cell phones, pagers, and PDAs. Just as the W3C is responsible for web protocols, the WAP Forum is responsible for its wireless protocol counterparts. The WAP 1.0 protocol is composed of the following specifications:

- **Wireless Markup Language (WML) 1.0 language**—Use WML structural markup language for WAP content rendering. WML is an application of XML and as such strictly adheres to the XML specification.

- **WMLScript language**—A scaled-down scripting language for wireless devices, similar to JavaScript or VBscript for HTML client or server scripting or both.

- **Wireless Telephony Application Interface (WTAI)**—API for making phone calls from data connections.

WAP is an application of XML. Using the analogy of playing cards, WML pages are called decks, and contain one or more cards. WAP devices download all the cards at once but are displayed one at a time to the user. Figure 7-5 illustrates how to publish an online book in WML.

Figure 7-5   *A Sample WML File*

```
<?xml version="1.0" encoding="UTF-8"?>
<!DOCTYPE wml PUBLIC "-//WAPFORUM//DTD WML 1.3//EN" "http://www.wapforum.org/DTD/wml13.dtd">
<wml>
  <card id="ch1" title="Chapter 1 - Introducing Content Networks">
    <p>Chapter 1 Goals<br/>
      1. To state the purposes of content networking.<br/>
      2. To inform the reader of the major concepts of content networking.<br/>
      3. To detail the underlying protocols of content networking.<br/>
    </p>
  </card>

  <card id="ch2" title="Chapter 2 - Exploring the Network Layers">
    <p>Chapter 2 Goals<br/>
      1. To inform the reader of Layers 1 through 4 of the OSI model.<br/>
      2. To give the reader an overview of Ethernet, ARP, and IP routing.<br/>
      3. To illustrate basic TCP operation.<br/>
    </p>
  </card>
</wml>
```

Figure 7-6 shows how you can navigate between individual cards, or chapters, using the WAP device controls.

Figure 7-6   *Navigating a WML Document on a WAP Device*

The W3C specifies a subset of XHTML 1.1 for small devices, called XHTML Basic. However, the WAP Forum created WAP 2.0 to include the XHTML Basic features plus some of the features from the full XHTML 1.1 specification, called the XHTML Mobile Profile (XHTMLMP), or Wireless Markup Language 2.0 (WML 2.0). WAP 2.0 was motivated by advancements in wireless transmission technologies, such as GSM, GPRS, G2.5, and G3.

WAP 2.0 also introduced support for special WAP versions of TCP/IP protocols in order to leverage the same languages and tools for mobile and standard web content (alternatively, WAP 1.0 uses the WAP protocol stack and does not support connectivity to TCP/IP networks). The wTCP/IP protocol supports TCP/IP, HTTP for content transport, and PKI for content security. Additionally, the power of CSS is available to you in WAP 2.0-enabled devices for the possibility to control a document's layout, including the text fonts, text attributes, borders, margins, padding, text alignment, text colors, and background colors to name a few. WAP 2.0 also supports XSLT transformation to transform between WML 1.0 and WML 2.0 documents.

Transforming and Formatting Content

You can use XSL to transform, filter, sort, and format your content. The XSL family consists of XSLT, XPath, and XSL-FO. Use XSLT for transforming XML documents, XPath for defining parts of an XML document, and XSL-FO for formatting XML documents.

You have two options to transform your XML documents for the purpose of publishing them to the web:

- **Transforming XML to XHMTL/HMTL**—You can translate your XML documents into HTML or XHTML and apply CSS's to the documents for display to a web browser.

- **Transforming XML to XSL-FO**—You can translate your XML documents directly into XSL-FO. You can then use a third-party program to convert the standard XSL-FO into HTML/XMTL/CSS (as mentioned previously), Braille, bar-codes, Adobe PDF, PostScript, SVG, Abstract Windowing Toolkit (AWT), or Maker Interchange Format (MIF).

> **NOTE** You can apply XSL stylesheets to your content within your network using the Cisco Application Oriented Network (AON) network modules for the Catalyst 6500 series switches and Cisco 2600/2800/3700/3800 Series routers. For more information on the AON, refer to its product documentation on Cisco.com.

Transforming XML to XHMTL/HMTL

Consider an application where you would like to publish an outline of this book on the web. The outline will contain the book title, author name, and chapter titles followed by the goals within each chapter. The content of each chapter's sections and subsections will not be included in the outline but assume that the entire book is available and marked up with the elements discussed previously in the simple DTD in Table 7-1. Figure 7-7 gives the sample XML file containing the outline of the first two chapters.

Figure 7-7 *A Sample Book Outline XML File*

```
<?xml version="1.0" encoding="UTF-8"?>          The <?xml> element defines the XML version and
                                                character encoding for the XML file.

<!DOCTYPE cnbookoutline SYSTEM "book.dtd">      The DTD file is used to validate the structure of the XML.
<book title="Content Networking Fundamentals" author="Silvano D. Da Ros" >
  <chapter>
    <chaptertitle>Chapter 1 - Introducing Content Networks</chaptertitle>
    <chaptergoals title="Chapter 1 Goals" >
      <goal>To state the purposes of content networking.</goal>
      <goal>To inform the reader of the major concepts of content networking.</goal>    The chapter
      <goal>To detail the underlying protocols of content networking.</goal>            goals element
                                                                                        consists of one
    </chaptergoals>                                                                     or more goals
    <section title="" />
  </chapter>
  <chapter>
    <chaptertitle>Chapter 2 - Exploring the Network Layers</chaptertitle>            The <chapter>
    <chaptergoals title="Chapter 2 Goals" >                                          element contains
      <goal>To inform the reader of Layers 1 through 4 of the OSI model.</goal>       the structure of
                                                                                     each chapter.
      <goal>To give the reader an overview of Ethernet, ARP, and IP routing.</goal>  Note, the chapter
      <goal>To illustrate basic TCP operation.</goal>                                title is includes as
    </chaptergoals>                                                                  an element, as
    <section title="" />                                                             opposed to an
                                                                                     attribute, unlike
  </chapter>                                                                          the<book>
</book>                                 The root element is <book> and                element.
                                        envelopes the source  tree structure.
```

Because you define custom element names in XML, name conflicts may occur when the same name from different DTDs is used to describe two different types of elements. You can use XML namespaces to provide unique element names within an XML document. In Figure 7-8, the namespace is the string "xsl:" that prefixes all of the XSL elements. You are required to use a namespace to differentiate elements among languages. The particular application that parses the document will know what to do with the specific elements based on the prefix. For example, an XSLT parser will look for the xsl: namespace URI and perform the intended actions based on the elements in the document. Alternatively, a XSL-FO parser will see the "fo:" namespace and perform the appropriate actions using the respective elements.

Parsers do not use the URL of the namespace to retrieve a DTD or schema for the namespace—the URL is simply a unique identifier within the document. According to W3C, the definition of a namespace simply defines a two-part naming system and nothing else. However, you must define namespaces of individual markup languages with a specific URL for the parsing application to take action on tags within the context of the language. For example, you must define the XSLT namespace with the URL "http://www.w3.org/1999/XSL/Transform" in your documents. Additionally, you must define the XSL-FO namespace with "http://www.w3.org/1999/XSL/ Format." That said, many simple XML parsing applications do not require namespaces in order to differentiate elements; they simply treat all elements as within the same namespace. However, this chapter uses namespaces strictly for illustration purposes.

In Figure 7-8, the namespace for XSL is defined for the XSLT parser to recognize the XSL specific elements **value-of**, **for-each**, and **number**. An XSLT parser inputs the XSLT file and the XML source file. It processes these two files and outputs an HTML file as a well-formed XML document. There are many other XSLT elements available to you, but you should know at least these three to understand the content transformations in this section.

Figure 7-8 *Sample XSLT File Transforming XML to HTML*

```
<?xml version="1.0" encoding="UTF-8"?>
<xsl:stylesheet version="2.0" xmlns:xsl="http://www.w3.org/1999/XSL/Transform"
xmlns:fo="http://www.w3.org/1999/XSL/Format" >

    <!-- Template to commence processing at the start of the XML document -->
    <xsl:template match="/">

        <!-- Output the HTML headers -->
        <html>

            <head>
                <!-- Output the CSS stylesheet definition to the head
                <LINK REL="stylesheet" TYPE="text/css" HREF="cnbook.css"/>

                <!-- Output the book title and author names -->
                <h1> <xsl:value-of select="book/@title"/> </h1>
                <h1> <xsl:value-of select="book/@author"/> </h1>
            </head>

            <body>
            <!-- eBook Content -->
                <xsl:for-each select="book/chapter">
                    <h2> <xsl:value-of select="chaptertitle"/> </h2>
                    <h3> <xsl:value-of select="chaptergoals/@title"/> </h3>
                    <xsl:for-each select="chaptergoals/goal">
                        <p>
                        <xsl:value-of select="."/>
                        <xsl:number value="position()"/>
                        </p>
                    </xsl:for-each>
                </xsl:for-each>
            </body>
        </html>
    </xsl:template>
</xsl:stylesheet>
```

The HTML head of the result tree document. The CSS style sheet is output to the HTML file here. See the next section for details. The book title and name are output here as well.

The main body of the document contains the control structures for scanning the source tree (XML)

Main for-each loop for iterating through the chapters. This loop displays the chapter title, and goals.

Loops through the individual 'goal' elements and displays the position and goal text.

The HTML document contains a header and a body section.

The XSL stylesheet element requires the template child element with a match clause to indicate where to start scanning the source document. Tell '/' tells the parser to start at the root element of the source tree, in this case, the root is the <book> element.

The XSL stylesheet element defines the namespace URI and XSL version for the xsl element.

The first line in Figure 7-8 defines the XML version and encoding scheme. The second line defines the namespace for the XSL elements within the document. The XSL element "template" imposes a logical template for the whole document. The parser outputs the <head> and <html> tags without modification. The two <h1> tags within the <head> section are output containing the title and author name attributes from the source file.

> **NOTE** The elements <h1>, <h2>, and <h3> have specific implied formats when read by browsers in HTML. However, you can adjust the implied formats of these tags using CSS, as discussed in the next section.

The XSLT language organizes the XML elements into a tree structure, using XPath, similar to the way in which a standard computer file system organizes files. You reference the node elements or attributes by specifying the entire path, starting at the current location in the tree. In this case, the root element contains the desired attribute, so you should use path "book/@title." The "@" character indicates to the parser to select an attribute as opposed to an element.

The parser then reads the content of the book from the XML source file. The **for-each** element iterates through each of the elements given within the **select** attribute. Within the outer **for-each** element, the parser first outputs the chapter goals title and then begins another **for-each** loop to iterate through the list of chapter goals. Figure 7-9 gives the output from the XSLT translation file in Figure 7-8. The text view is the exact text output by the XSLT file, and the browser view is how the HTML looks from an HTML 4.0-based web browser's interpretation of the tags.

Figure 7-9   *Output HTML from XSLT Transformation*

HTML View

A Typical Browser View

Content Networking Fundamentals

```
<html>
  <head>
    <h1>Content Networking Fundamentals</h1><h1>Silvano D. Da Ros</h1>
  </head>
  <body>
    <h2>Chapter 1 - Introducing Content Networks</h2>
      <h3>Chapter 1 Goals</h3>
        <p>1. To state the purposes of content networking.</p>
        <p>2. To inform the reader of the major concepts of content networking.</p>
        <p>3. To detail the underlying protocols of content networking.</p>
    <h2>Chapter 2 - Exploring the Network Layers</h2>
      <h3>Chapter 2 Goals</h3>
        <p>1. To inform the reader of Layers 1 through 4 of the OSI mode.1</p>
        <p>2. To give the reader an overview of Ethernet, ARP, and IP routing.</p>
        <p>3. To illustrate basic TCP operation.</p>
  </body>
</html>
```

Silvano D. Da Ros

Chapter 1 - Introducing Content Networks

Chapter 1 Goals

1. To state the purposes of content networking.
2. To inform the reader of the major concepts of content networking.
3. To detail the underlying protocols of content networking.

Chapter 2 - Exploring the Network Layers

Chapter 2 Goals

1. To inform the reader of Layers 1 through 4 of the OSI mode.1
2. To give the reader an overview of Ethernet, ARP, and IP routing.
3. To illustrate basic TCP operation.

> **NOTE**   To transform the XML source file into a WML file instead, you require a new XSL transformation file. Instead of outputting HTML tags, you output WML tags, leaving the overall flow of the XSLT file the same.

Using Cascading Style Sheets

You can use CSSs to separate the formatting of a web document from the content in the document. Style sheets are useful because you can locate them in files that are separate from the content, allowing for multiple formats for the same content. For example, you can create two versions of your website: a standard style and a style for the visually impaired containing clearer images and larger font. Another example is the format specific to the different series of Cisco IP phones. Each series of IP phone has a different size display and requires special consideration with respect to content placement.

The concept of CSSs gives your authors the ability to blend different style sheets into the same document, as opposed to using completely separate styles for different groups of end users or different displays. For example, the author of a Cisco.com page can apply three different style sheets for a page within the Cisco TAC website. The first style sheet may impose the Cisco corporate look and feel. The second style sheet may apply to the standard TAC presentation, and the third may apply a format for the series of TAC documents that the author is writing for, such as network troubleshooting topics.

You can use the CSS file in Example 7-2 to format the HTML generated in Figure 7-9.

Example 7-2 *Sample CSS File for Formatting a Standard HTML Document*

```
body { background-color: #FFFFFF; }
h1 { font-family: Arial, sans-serif; font-size: 20px; color: #660000; text-align: center}
h2 { font-family: Arial, sans-serif; font-size: 16px; color: #660000 }
h3 { font-family: Arial, sans-serif; font-size: 14px; color: #003333; }
p { font-family: Arial, sans-serif; font-size: 12px; color: #003333;}
```

Alternatively, you can generate HTML using XSLT to include CSS classes. Figure 7-10 illustrates how you can use XSLT to generate HTML with CSS classes, to provide a robust formatting solution to your XML documents.

Figure 7-10 *XSLT for Generating HTML with Embedded CSS Classes*

```
<?xml version="1.0" encoding="UTF-8"?>
<xsl:stylesheet version="1.0" xmlns:xsl="http://www.w3.org/1999/XSL/Transform" >
  <!-- Template to commence processing at the start of the XML document -->
  <xsl:template match="/">
    <!-- Output the HTML headers -->
    <html>
      <head>
      <LINK REL="stylesheet" TYPE="text/css" HREF=" cnbook.css"/>
      </head>
      <body>
      <div class="container">
      <div class="header"><xsl:value-of select="book/@title"/> <br/>
      By: <xsl:value-of select="book/@author"/></div>

      <div class="content">
      <!-- eBook Content -->
      <xsl:for-each select="book/chapter">
        <h2 class="chaptitle"> <xsl:value-of select="chaptertitle"/> </h2>
        <h3 class="goalstitle"> <xsl:value-of select="chaptergoals/@title"/> </h3>
        <p class="goal">
        <xsl:for-each select="chaptergoals/goal">
          <xsl:number value="position()" format="1. "/>
          <xsl:value-of select="."/>
        <br/>
        </xsl:for-each>
        </p>
      </xsl:for-each>
      </div>
      <div class="footer">Copyright &#xA9; 2006 CiscoPress</div>
      </div>
      </body>
    </html>
  </xsl:template>
</xsl:stylesheet>
```

The CSS is linked to the generated HTML document using the LINK directive

CSS classes are used to create numerous areas of the document to define the style of the document.

"container" - encompasses the entire document.

"header" - contains the top area, that will display the title name and author name.

"content" - will contain the outline content. Within the "content" area, **"chaptitle"**, **"goalstitle"**, and **"goal"** classes will further define the style of the book outline.

"footer" - will output copyright information.

The XSLT file in Figure 7-10 will generate the formatted document in Figure 7-11.

Figure 7-11   *Sample HTML Document Formatted with CSS*

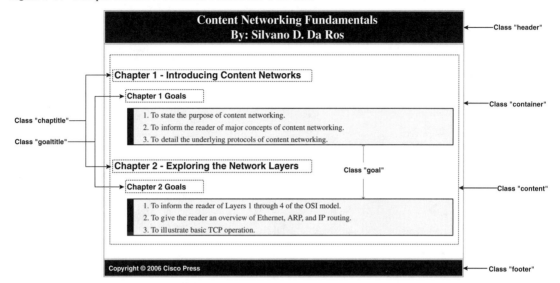

You can use the CSS file in Figure 7-12 to provide the format attributes for the classes described previously.

Style sheets are beneficial when you require rendering a large number of documents into the same style. With a standard XML format, your authors can create content and use a given set of markup tags to describe the content. If the documents require different versions, such as XHTML and HTML for online viewing or Braille and PDF for printing, you will require a separate XSL transformation file for each. At any time, you can create new versions of the content by writing a new transformation file without changing the XML source files. Moreover, you can further separate the style and formatting using CSS. In the future, if a style or layout change to the documents is required, only the style sheets require modification, not the source XML file or XSL transformation file.

Figure 7-12 *Sample CSS File Using Classes*

```
body { background-color: #FFFFFF; }

div.container
{width:100%; margin:0px; border:1px solid gray; line-height:150%;
}

div.header
{
font-family: Times;
font-size: 19px;
text-align: center;
color:white;
background-color:660000;
border:10px solid 0x660000;
line-height: 25px
}

div.footer
{
font-family: Arial;
font-size: 10px;
color:white;
background-color:003333;
border:1px solid white;
margin:0cm 0cm 0cm 0cm
}

div.content
{
border-bottom:1px solid gray;
padding:1em;
}

h1.header
{
font-family: Times, sans-serif;
font-size: 14px;
color: #FFFFFF;
text-align: left;
padding:0; margin:0;
}

h1.title, h1.author
{
font-family: Times, sans-serif;
font-size: 19px;
color: #FFFFFF;
text-align: center;
line-height: 5px}
```

```
p.divhead
{
font-family: Times, sans-serif;
font-size: 20px;
color: #FFFFFF;
text-align: left;
}

h2.chaptitle
{
font-family: Arial, sans-serif;
font-size: 14px;
color: #000000 ;
}

h3.goalstitle
{
font-family: Arial, sans-serif;
font-size: 12px;
color: #000000;
line-height: 1px;
margin-left: 1cm
}

p.goal
{
font-family: Times, sans-serif;
font-size: 11px;
border-color: #003333;
background:EEEFEE;
border-style: solid;
border-left-width: 10px;
border-top-width: 1px;
border-bottom-width: 1px;
border-right-width: 1px;
margin-left: 1cm;
padding-left: 15px;
line-height: 18px
}
```

Transforming XML to XSL-FO

Now that you have a solid understanding of XML, XSL, and CSSs, you can tackle the more complex and highly powerful style sheet formatting language called XSL Format Objects (XSL-FO). Like CSS, you can use XSL-FO to format XML data for output. However, unlike CSS, XSL-FO is XML-based, and you can use it to further mark up XML by including descriptive formatting elements. Once marked up with XSL-FO, the formatted XML files can be output into various formats using third-party XSL-FO processors. The output formats can include any of the online display markup languages discussed in this chapter, such as HTML, XHTML, and WML. However, the most common use of XSL-FO is to produce typeset documents for print in Adobe PDF format.

The XSL-FO in Example 7-3 is the general format for an XSL-FO formatted file. Notice that the "fo:" namespace precedes all the XSL-FO elements in the document.

Example 7-3 *The General Format for an XSL-FO Document.*

```
<?xml version="1.0" encoding="ISO-8857-1"?>
<fo:root xmlns:fo="http://www.w3.org/1999/XSL/Format">

<fo:layout-master-set>
  <fo:simple-page-master master-name="A4">
    <!-- Page template goes here -->
  </fo:simple-page-master>
</fo:layout-master-set>

<fo:page-sequence master-reference="A4">
  <!-- Page content goes here -->
</fo:page-sequence>
</fo:root>
```

The <fo:layout-master-set> element declares the page layout for the document. For your book outline project, you need only a single-page layout. All XSL-FO documents are broken into three areas, **region-before**, **region-body**, and **region-after**, but you can rename them to HEADER, CONTENT, and FOOTER in this example for clarity. Within our page outline, called BOOK-OUTLINE, we define the characteristics of each region. When supplying the content of the page, you reference the outline BOOK-OUTLINE, and the particular regions in which the content will reside.

The last part of the document specifies the actual content for output. The **page-sequence** element specifies the format for each page in your output document and references BOOK-OUTLINE for the placement and structure of content on the page. In the book outline example, the HEADER region contains the book title and author name, the CONTENT region contains the book outline, and the FOOTER region contains the copyright information. The HEADER and FOOTER content do not change. As such, you should define the HEADER and FOOTER content with static-content elements. If the data in this example happened to span multiple printed pages, the header and footer data would not change. Conversely, if content is not destined for print as in previous examples in this chapter, the header and footer remain at the top and bottom of the page. For content that changes from page-to-page, use the <fo:flow> element to output the content. The <block> element specifies each area within a flow. Attributes of the <block> element give the specific formatting for each block. For example, the block containing the content for the chapter goals would contain the formatting attributes in Example 7-4.

Example 7-4 *Sample "Chapter Goal" XSL-FO Block*

```
<fo:block
 background-color="#EEEFEE"
 margin="30px"
 border="1px solid #003333"
 border-left="15px solid #003333"
 text-indent="40px"
 line-height="25px"
 font-family="Times"
 font-size="11pt"
 color="black">
</fo:block>
```

The attributes in Example 7-4 produce the indentation, fonts, and colors that you see in the final output in Figure 7-13. To simplify Figure 7-13, none of the format attributes are included in the XSL-FO output. As an exercise, you can add format attributes based on those provided in Example 7-3 and the CSS example in Figure 7-13 to produce the same results.

Figure 7-13 *Sample XML Document Formatted with XSL-FO and Generated into an Adobe PDF Document Using a XSL-FO Processor*

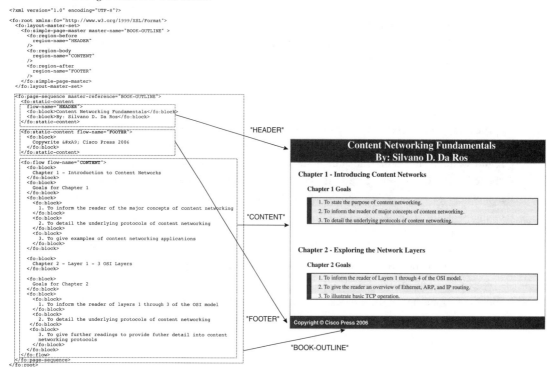

In Figure 7-13, the XSL-FO document includes the content from the source XML file. In order to automatically populate the content from a source XML file, you can use the XSLT document in Example 7-5. The XSLT elements from the previous examples are in bold—the parser generates the non-bolded text as the XSL-FO output in Figure 7-13.

Example 7-5 *XSL File That Generates XSL-FO with Embedded XML Content*

```
<?xml version="1.0" encoding="UTF-8"?>
<xsl:stylesheet version="1.0" xmlns:xsl="http://www.w3.org/1999/XSL/Transform"
    xmlns:fo="http://www.w3.org/1999/XSL/Format" >

  <xsl:template match="/">

    <fo:root xmlns:fo="http://www.w3.org/1999/XSL/Format">
      <fo:layout-master-set>
        <fo:simple-page-master master-name="BOOK-OUTLINE" >
          <fo:region-before
            region-name="HEADER" />
          <fo:region-body margin-top="60px"
            region-name="CONTENT"/>
          <fo:region-after extent="30px"
            region-name="FOOTER"/>
        </fo:simple-page-master>
      </fo:layout-master-set>

      <fo:page-sequence master-reference="BOOK-OUTLINE">
        <fo:static-content
          flow-name="HEADER">
          <fo:block><xsl:value-of select="book/@title"/></fo:block>
          <fo:block>By: <xsl:value-of select="book/@author"/></fo:block>
        </fo:static-content>
        <fo:static-content flow-name="FOOTER">
          <fo:block>
            Copyright &#xA9; Cisco Press 2005
          </fo:block>
        </fo:static-content>
      </fo:page-sequence>
        <fo:flow flow-name="CONTENT">
          <xsl:for-each select="book/chapter">
            <fo:block
              <xsl:value-of select="chaptertitle"/>
            </fo:block>
            <fo:block>
              <xsl:value-of select="chaptergoals/@title"/>
            </fo:block>

            <fo:block>
              <xsl:for-each select="chaptergoals/goal">
```

continues

Example 7-5 *XSL File That Generates XSL-FO with Embedded XML Content (Continued)*

```
            <fo:block>
              <xsl:number value="position()" format="1. "/>
              <xsl:value-of select="."/>
            </fo:block>
          </xsl:for-each>
        </fo:block>
      </xsl:for-each>
    </fo:flow>
  </fo:root>
 </xsl:template>
</xsl:stylesheet>
```

Summary

In this chapter, you learned how to present and transform printed and online content using markup languages. Procedural markup languages are inflexible, information retrieval is difficult, and they require multiple documents for files that require different formats. Descriptive markup languages separate document formatting from document content. This chapter discussed the following descriptive markup languages:

- HTML

- Extensible Markup Language (XML)

- Extensible HTML (XHTML)

- Wireless Application Protocol (WAP) Markup Languages including Wireless Markup Language 1.0 (WML) and XHTML Mobile Profile (XHTMLMP).

- You also learned how to transform XML content into XHTML and HTML using XSLT. Once you transform XML into either of these two markup languages, you can format the content for display using CSSs. As an alternative, you learned how to transform XML into XSL-FO. XSL-FO is a standard formatting output with which you can use XSL-FO processors to parse and output to online or printable form.

Review Questions

1. What are the disadvantages of using procedural markup languages?

2. What is PDATA?

3. What is the purpose of the Document Type Definition (DTD) file and XML schemas?

4. What are the benefits of XHTML over HTML?

5. What are your two options for transforming XML content into a displayable or printable form?

6. What is an XML namespace?

7. What is the benefit of CSS?

8. What is the purpose of the **position**() function in the XSLT examples in this chapter?

Recommended Reading

Erik T. Ray, *Learning XML*, O'Reilly, 2003

Thomas Powell, *HTML & XHTML: The Complete Reference*, McGraw-Hill Osborne Media, 2003

Michael Kay, *XSLT 2.0 Programmer's Reference*, Wrox, 2004

http://www.w3c.org

http://www.w3schools.com

Chapter Goals

You will learn about the following
application layer protocols in this chapter:

- **Hypertext Transfer Protocol
  (HTTP)**—HTTP is the common web-
  based content transfer protocol on the
  Internet.

- **Secure Sockets Layer (SSL)**—You can
  secure your web content using SSL.

- **File Transfer Protocol (FTP)**—FTP is
  used to transfer files over the web.

CHAPTER **8**

Exploring the Application Layer

The application layer is the topmost layer of the OSI model and provides you with high-level application development capabilities. As an application developer, you require little knowledge of how the content of your application traverses the network in terms of characteristics specific to the physical media and what network layer protocols the network uses. However, as a content networking administrator, you require knowledge of how the network functions in addition to how the application layer works.

Some TCP/IP-based application protocols implement the session, presentation, and application OSI reference layers of the OSI reference model. In TCP/IP, the application layer implements the OSI session layer to maintain state across TCP layer connections. For example, HTTP is stateless by design but can use cookies to maintain client state across TCP connections between clients and servers. Secure Sockets Layer (SSL) and Real-Time Streaming Protocol (RTSP), on the other hand, implement the OSI session layer in its specification directly, using a session identifier to associate the TCP connections to an application "session."

Application protocols often refer to well-known applications described in RFCs (for example, FTP, HTTP, SMTP, and Telnet). However, any process, either custom or well-known, that has a structured mechanism for communication between client and server devices is an application protocol. As such, each application layer protocol behaves according to the specifications that you set when developing it. Client-server application protocols are normally text-based, with a specified set of commands and with responses to these commands.

This chapter discusses the following application layer protocols:

- HTTP

- SSL

- FTP

Although Cisco content networking products are aware of many other application layer protocols, these three are primarily used throughout the book in examples and scenarios.

> **NOTE** Because the application layer is Layer 5 of the TCP/IP stack, you may read Cisco.com documents or other books referring to the application layer as "Layer 5" instead of "Layers 5–7."

HTTP

This section provides you with an overview of the HTTP terms, concepts, and features that content networking devices use to enhance content delivery. HTTP is a protocol used to transport web application data across a TCP network. Within the realm of content networking, HTTP clients can be either user agents (web browsers) or content caches. In turn, servers of content can be either origin servers or content caches.

HTTP 1.0 Versus HTTP 1.1

The intent of HTTP 1.1 is to provide a more generic and robust standard than that of HTTP 1.0 to achieve an increase in content optimization, security, and potential for future development. Although HTTP 1.0 reached widespread use through successful implementation into user-agent browsers, such as Microsoft Internet Explorer and Netscape Navigator in the early 1990s, there are many well-known shortcomings of the standard. HTTP 1.1 is backward compatible to HTTP 1.0 and includes the necessary extensibility to avoid the creation of a new version for every extension, or new header, to the protocol. As long as the general message parsing algorithm remains the same, the HTTP version number does not change.

> **NOTE** You should prepend your custom HTTP headers with "X-." For example, proxy caches often use the "X-Forwarded-For:" header to indicate the IP address of clients it proxies.

To allow for future headers, HTTP 1.1 requires transparent proxies, such as caches and security proxies, to ignore unrecognized HTTP headers and forward the packets directly to the origin server. This enables easy deployment of new headers into production without first changing every device in the content network—only the participating devices require the intelligence to process the new headers. As such, the HTTP 1.1 standard allows for significant enhancements to HTTP 1.0, including new caching, security, connection management, and client state recognition functionality.

> **NOTE** HTTP 1.0 does not include the server domain name within GET requests. The assumption by its developers was that the IP address would suffice to uniquely identify the site. HTTP 1.1 included a "Host:" header to denote the domain name for use in hosting environments where multiple sites reside on a single physical server.

HTTP Transactions

HTTP is a text-based protocol, with each line terminated with a CRLF (Carriage Return/Line Feed) pair. Text-based protocols make it simple to add headers, thus making the protocol more expandable. In other words, the HTTP RFC 2616 does not contain packet formats as the TCP and IP RFCs do.

HTTP clients and servers communicate with methods for either requesting or supplying content. A client request normally contains a method, URL, the HTTP version number, and headers that pertain to the request, such as the type of client web browser or client security credentials. The response from the server contains a result code and may or may not contain the requested data, depending on factors such as the object's freshness, HTTP version support, or the client's privileges. Table 8-1 gives some common HTTP 1.1 methods.

Table 8-1 *Common HTTP 1.1 Methods*

Method	Description
OPTIONS	Used by the client to request available options of the URI. For example, the server can respond to an OPTIONS request with the Allow: header in its 200 OK response. The "Allow:" header lists the available methods that the client can send to the server for that URI.
GET	Retrieves the requested URI, including the headers and body (that is, the content).
HEAD	Retrieves only the headers for the requested URI and not the body.
POST	Sends information to the server from HTML forms.
PUT	Uploads the file indicated in the URI to a server.
DELETE	Deletes the URI from a server.
TRACE	Used to troubleshoot communications to web servers.
CONNECT	Used for proxy server content tunneling.

Table 8-2 gives the available HTTP 1.1 return codes.

Table 8-2 *Available HTTP 1.1 Return Codes*

Return Code	Description
Informational 1xx	
100	Continue
101	Switching Protocols
Successful 2xx	
200	OK
201	Created

continues

Table 8-2 *Available HTTP 1.1 Return Codes (Continued)*

Return Code	Description
202	Accepted
203	Non-Authoritative Information
204	No Content
205	Reset Content
206	Partial Content
Redirection 3xx	
300	Multiple Choices
301	Moved Permanently
302	Found
303	See Other
304	Not Modified
305	Use Proxy
306	(Unused)
Client Error 4xx	
400	Bad Request
401	Unauthorized
402	Payment Required
403	Forbidden
404	Not Found
405	Method Not Allowed
406	Not Acceptable
407	Proxy Authentication Required
408	Request Timeout
409	Conflict
410	Gone
411	Length Required
412	Precondition Failed

Table 8-2   *Available HTTP 1.1 Return Codes (Continued)*

Return Code	Description
413	Request Entity Too Large
414	Request-URI Too Long
415	Unsupported Media Type
416	Requested Range Not Satisfiable
417	Expectation Failed
Server Error 5xx	
500	Internal Server Error
501	Not Implemented
502	Bad Gateway
503	Service Unavailable
504	Gateway Timeout
505	HTTP Version Not Supported

HTTP Connection Persistence and Pipelining

When a client requires content from a web server, it first establishes a TCP connection to the server to send a content request over. The server then sends its response over the same TCP session. However, websites often provide multiple URLs in their HTML files that contain ads, images, or other embedded content. If the client creates a new TCP connection for each URL of these embedded objects, the number of TCP connections grows quickly in a short time. HTTP 1.0 introduced the concept of persistent connections where a single TCP connection is used to transport numerous transactions between the client and server. Persistent connections decrease the additional bandwidth created by the overhead from creating multiple TCP connections. Additionally, connection persistence does not incur the round-trip time delays caused from opening new TCP connections. The result is that you perceive faster download times.

Figure 8-1 illustrates how a client establishes two TCP connections to request two objects from an HTML page. The first request is for the index.html main page of Cisco.com, and the second is for an image within the page. The client's browser obtains the image URL from within the index.html page.

Figure 8-1 *HTTP Requests Using Individual TCP Connections*

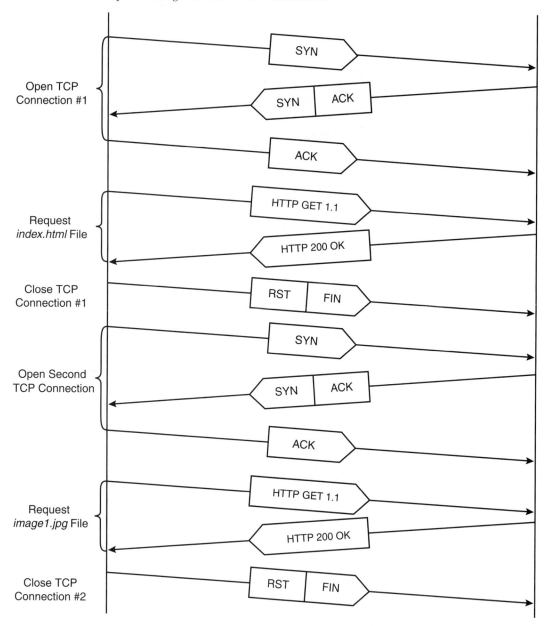

HTTP 1.0 introduced the "Connection:" header for client requests. Using this header in the HTTP GET request with a value of "Keep-alive," clients can request HTTP persistence from the server. If the server supports HTTP connection persistence, it will include the "Connection:" header with

the value "Keep-alive" in its HTTP 200 OK response. Persistence was a negotiated feature between the client and server in HTTP 1.0 but is enabled by default in HTTP 1.1.

Figure 8-2 illustrates HTTP persistence where the client requests the image within the same TCP connection.

Figure 8-2 *HTTP 1.0 Persistence*

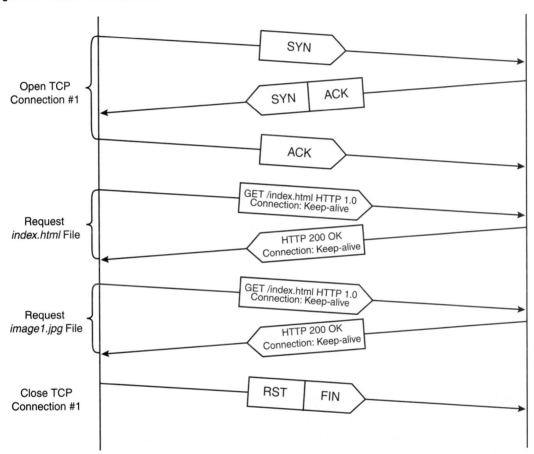

Even with persistent connections, the roundtrip wait for each response to URL requests created additional noticeable delay. Therefore, HTTP 1.1 introduced pipelined requests, where the client does not require waiting for the response to a request before sending another request. Figure 8-3 illustrates HTTP persistent and pipelined requests.

> **NOTE**   Although HTTP 1.1 supports pipelined requests, many clients are not yet implementing this behavior.

Figure 8-3   *HTTP 1.1 Persistence and Pipelining*

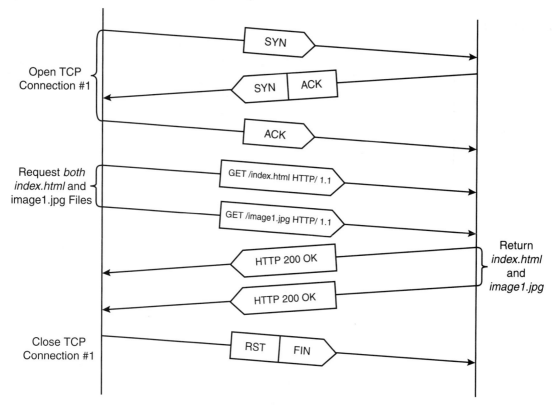

Maintaining Client-Side State with HTTP Cookies

The HTTP 1.1 standard is a generic stateless protocol. Therefore, to extend the HTTP 1.1 protocol to enable participants to maintain the state of the HTTP session, cookies were added. Cookies come in two flavors, both created by the server using the same "Set-Cookie:" header. The two types of cookies are session cookies and persistent cookies. Your web browser stores session cookies in RAM only for the life of your HTTP session and removes them when your session ends. That is, when you close your browser window, the client deletes the cookie from memory. In contrast, your web browser stores persistent cookies to disk for future visits to the site, for a period specified by the server in the "Set-Cookie:" header. The server sets session cookies by not including an expiration time in the header, which indicates to the client to remove the cookie after the session ends. Servers set cookies using the HTTP header:

```
Set-Cookie: name=value; expires=DATE;
```

When a client sends a request for a URI to a server, the server responds with the "Set-Cookie:" header, set to a unique value to identify the session on the server. In all subsequent requests, the client includes the "Cookie:" header with the value set by the server. This way, the server is able to maintain the state of the session. For example, the server may set a session cookie using the header:

```
Set-Cookie: Session-ID=071344326745213
```

As a result, the client will include the following header in all subsequent HTTP transactions with the server.

```
Cookie: Session-ID=071344326745213
```

> **NOTE** Sessions cookies are useful to keep track of user information as they browse from page to page on a website. Session cookies are also an important aspect for SLB Stickiness, which you will learn about in Chapter 10, "Exploring Server Load Balancing."

HTTP Authentication

HTTP 1.0 enables you to provide basic authentication to clients using clear text passwords. For HTTP message digest authentication, you need to use the extension to HTTP 1.1 that is defined in RFC 2617.

With basic authentication, your browser sends your credentials over the network unencrypted using Base64 encoding. For example, the username and password string "sdaros:cisco" (without the quotes) is "c2Rhcm9zOmNpc2Nv" in Base64. Base64 encoding may appear encrypted but it is easily reversible. For example, try cutting and pasting the Base64 encoded string "c2Rhcm9zOmNpc2Nv" into any publicly available Base64 tool on the Internet, and you will see how quickly it can be reversed into the original source string "sdaros:cisco."

With message digest authentication, your browser encrypts your credentials by computing a message digest before sending them over the network. First, to authenticate you, the server challenges your browser with a nonce value. Your browser uses this nonce, along with the username and password that you supply, as input to a hash algorithm. A nonce is a one-time random number that HTTP 1.1 uses to prevent replay attacks.

> **NOTE**   A hash function is a function that takes input values and performs a mathematical computation, resulting in a single (smaller) value that is impossible to determine the original values from. These functions are also called one-way hash functions because they are considered impossible to reverse. You can use Message Digest 5 (MD5) and Secure Hash Algorithm 1 (SHA-1) hash algorithms for your web applications to compute public keys from private keys. MD5 provides hashes 128 bits in length, and SHA-1 provides 168-bit hashes. Hash functions are also used in many other areas in content networking, ranging from public-key cryptography, X.509 certificate authentication, and message integrity, to server/cache selection in server load balancing (SLB) environments.

A replay attack occurs when a malicious third party somehow intercepts the checksum containing your credentials and attempts to use them to connect to the same server. Because the credentials that the third-party intercepts contain a nonce value that you have previously used to authenticate with that server, the server refuses the malicious authentication attempt. The nonce value forces your credentials to change on the network for every login attempt, even though your username and password stay the same.

A message digest is a one-way hash algorithm, in which the algorithm uses the inputs to compute a single 128 bit (that is, 16 bytes and is visually represented as 32 hexadecimal digits). HTTP message digest authentication uses the MD5 message digest algorithm. For example, the MD5 message digest value for the username and password string "sdaros:cisco" is

```
"5c2667a142f833bdb8ad06894786552d"
```

Consider the following string containing a username, password, and nonce value of "64b0a095cfd25133b2e4014ea87a0680":

```
"sdaros:cisco:64b0a095cfd25133b2e4014ea87a0680"
```

The MD5 digest value for this string is

```
"cacdf924bcbb809b49c75cf967098fc1"
```

To generate nonce values, servers normally use the current timestamp in conjunction with its private key (if it has a private key) and the "ETag:" HTTP headers in the client's requests. You will learn about the "ETag:" header and private keys later in this chapter.

When you attempt to access an object on a server that requires authentication, the server sends the "HTTP 401 Unauthorized" response to challenge your browser for your credentials. This challenge from the server includes the "WWW-Authenticate:" header, which specifies the type of authentication that your browser should use and the realm that the server is authenticating you within. Some common values for this header are "Basic," "Digest," "Kerberos," and "NTLM." The server maintains a list of objects that you can access associated to the particular realm.

Your browser then prompts you for your username and password with a popup window and sends your credentials to the server, with the HTTP "Authenticate:" header. You do not need to enter your password for every object within the realm you request during the HTTP session because your browser automatically sends your credentials during your session. For example, your server challenges your browser to authenticate you with the header:

```
WWW-Authenticate: Digest realm="CUST_RELATIONS"
nonce="64b0a095cfd25133b2e4014ea87a0680"
```

Then your browser includes the following header to the server:

```
Authorization: Digest "cacdf924bcbb809b49c75cf967098fc1" realm="CUST_RELATIONS"
```

NTLM and Kerberos authentication are available for intranet or extranet HTTP access. NTLM servers issue the "WWW-Authenticate: NTLM" header and Kerberos issue "WWW-Authenticate: Negotiate" to clients. These two protocols are similar to Digest authentication in that they both use a one-time nonce value to authenticate clients. However, they are different in that they both automatically supply your Windows user credentials automatically through HTTP to the site to which you require access. If you attempt to log in to the site from a workstation that is not part of a Windows domain, you will have to enter your Windows credentials in a popup window provided by the browser. You will see in Chapter 13, "Delivering Cached and Streaming Media," how NTLM and Kerberos are also useful with the Cisco Content Engine request authentication and authorization feature.

HTTP Caching Controls

As you will learn in Chapter 13 you can use caches in your network when you require reductions in bandwidth and response times. You can place caches between clients and servers to inspect requests and responses to intelligently cache and respond to client requests on the server's behalf. HTTP provides implicit and explicit cache controls.

Implicit Cache Controls

HTTP provides clients and servers with the ability to supply information to caches to ensure that cached information is as fresh as the content residing on the origin server. When a cache requires the validation of a piece of cached content, it sends a GET method to the origin server, with conditional directives. The cache converts the client GET request to a conditional GET request by adding the headers "IF-Modified-Since:" or "IF-Match:" to the request. The response by the server contains only the requested object, depending on the results of a comparison between the freshness of cached content and the original content. If the comparison fails, the server sends the object to the cache; otherwise, the server considers the cached content fresh, and the cache avoids having to download the object from the origin server.

> **NOTE** Some browsers send a conditional GET request to the server when you click the Reload button on your web browser. If the content has not changed on the origin server, then your browser uses files and images obtained from its local cache located on your hard disk. Try using a network packet sniffer the next time you click **Reload** on your browser.

In HTTP 1.0, when a cache originally receives a copy of an object, it stamps the object with an absolute expiration time specified in the "Expires:" header that it receives in server responses. If the origin server wants the cache to validate the object immediately upon receiving the object, the "Expires:" header contains the current time. Otherwise, the cache does not validate the object until the time in the "Expires:" header is reached. To compare the freshness of two pieces of content, the "If-Modified-Since:" header provides a way for the server to determine if the requested content has been modified since the expiration time. The cache issues a conditional GET request to the server with the original expiration time in the "If-Modified-Since:" header. The server then compares the time value in the header from the cache with the modified date on the object in the file system. If the object has not changed, the server returns the "HTTP/1.0 304 Not Modified" response. Otherwise, the server sends a fresh copy of the updated object to the cache. For example, a cache may send the following conditional request to an origin server to validate a piece of requested content:

```
GET /index.html HTTP/1.0
If-Modified-Since: "Sat, 23 Mar 2006 19:43:31 GMT"
```

If the server determines that the content has not changed (a cache hit has occurred), it sends the following response to the cache:

```
HTTP/1.0 304 Not Modified
```

If the server determines that the content has changed (a cache miss has occurred), it sends the following response to the cache:

```
HTTP/1.0 200 OK
*Data*
```

This time-based validation mechanism provided by HTTP 1.0 proves to be problematic. That is, if the clocks between the cache and server are not synchronized, this method does not provide the correct response. Therefore, HTTP 1.1 enhanced this method by using the "E-Tag:" header. This header avoids using dates by instead maintaining version numbers for objects. When a cache originally stores an object, it also stores the E-Tag value supplied by the server. When the cache validates the content, the GET request contains a conditional "IF-Match:" header containing the original version code. If the origin server's version code for the object is different from the version supplied by the cache, then the server returns the object to the cache. Otherwise, the server sends the "HTTP/1.1 412 Precondition Failed" response, indicating that the content is fresh. For example, a cache may send a conditional GET request as follows:

```
GET /index.html HTTP/1.1
If-Match: "4cf0a-8f3-345e03ab"
```

For a cache hit, the server will respond with:

```
HTTP/1.1 412 Precondition Failed
```

For a cache miss, the server will respond with:

```
HTTP/1.1 200 OK
*Data*
```

Table 8-3 lists the HTTP implicit cache control headers.

Table 8-3   *Implicit Cache Control Headers*

Value	Description
Expires	Set by the server, this value specifies the absolute time until which the server considers a piece of content to be fresh. The cache uses this value to stamp incoming cacheable content.
IF-Modified-Since	Set by the cache and sent to the server to determine if a piece of content has been modified.
IF-Not-Modified-Since	Set by the cache, using the Expires timestamp listed previously, and sent to the server to determine if a piece of content has not been modified.
E-Tag	Set by the server to indicate to caches the version number of the document.
IF-Match	Set by the cache with the value given by the E-Tag version number, in validation requests.
If-None-Match	Same as If-Match, but for more than one object.

Explicit Controls

You learned that servers can provide implicit controls in response to directives sent by caches through conditional validation requests. In contrast, HTTP 1.1 provides a mechanism for clients and servers to send *explicit* directives to caches, using the "Cache-Control:" header, regardless of the possible directives in the request that a cache may insert. The "Cache-Control:" header provides the values listed in Table 8-4 that pertain to caching mechanisms in Cisco content networking products.

Table 8-4   *Explicit Cache-Control Header Values*

Value	Description
public	Indicates that an authenticated response is cacheable.
expires	Indicates to the cache when the content should be considered stale.
max-age	Specifies the maximum time that an object is considered fresh. This time is relative to the request time, not the absolute expiry time that the expires header uses.

continues

Table 8-4 *Explicit Cache-Control Header Values (Continued)*

Value	Description
no-cache	Forces the cache to validate the object, using E-Tags or dates, for every request. However, if an HTTP header is included after the no-cache directive, only that header needs to be revalidated, not the entire object. For example, **Cache-Control: no-cache="Set-Cookie"** indicates that the cache must retrieve a new cookie from the origin server before sending the requested object to the client.
no-store	Prevents the cache from storing the object.
must-revalidate	Some caches may be configured to return stale objects, unless the object has the "must-revalidate" explicit cache directive set. This directive forces the cache to revalidate the object, even if it is configured to return a stale object.

For example, in response to a client's request, an origin server may indicate that intermediary caches should re-validate the "Set-Cookie" header before returning the header in the object to requesting clients.

```
HTTP/1.1 200 OK. Cache-Control: no-cache
```

This completes the overview of the HTTP protocol. So far you have learned the basic features of the HTTP web protocol, including how transactions are executed using persistence and pipelining, how HTTP authentication takes place, and how HTTP uses caching controls for efficient content caching. These features are important to grasp for further study of content networking. However, by themselves most of these provide functionality that, if left as cleartext on your network, could lead to a compromise of your organization's private information.

Because of the growing importance of information security on the Internet, the rest of the chapter will cover how to secure HTTP using the Public Key Infrastructure (PKI).

Public Key Infrastructure

Growing concerns by organizations with e-commerce presence for data security has fostered the adoption of a standard Internet security framework. PKI addresses issues such as data confidentiality, integrity, and authentication.

Secret Key Cryptography

Cryptography deals with keeping data confidential between clients and servers in a public insecure network. With secret key cryptography, both the client and server must each have a secret key in their possession that they both agree upon before any encryption can take place. They use their secret (or private) keys for both encrypting and decrypting information exchanged between them. The process is also called symmetric key cryptography because you can easily derive the two keys from one another mathematically. The keys are either the same or one is a transformation of the other using a mathematical function. Common symmetric key protocols are Data Encryption Standard (DES), Triple DES (3DES), Rivest Cipher 2 (RC2), and Rivest Cipher 4 (RC4). Figure 8-4 illustrates secret key cryptography.

Figure 8-4 *Secret Key Cryptography*

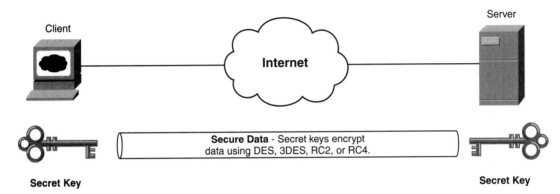

You can use two forms of ciphers to encrypt your data:

■ **Stream Ciphers**—Stream ciphers enable network devices to encrypt the individual bytes of the data stream. RC2 and RC4 are examples of symmetric key stream ciphers.

■ **Block Ciphers**—Block ciphers enable network devices to encrypt blocks of data containing many bytes each. DES and 3DES are examples of symmetric key block ciphers.

With the symmetric/secret key method of encryption, the question arises of how to exchange private keys without an existing private exchange mechanism available beforehand—especially between a server and a large number of clients on the Internet. Public-key cryptography helps resolve this issue.

Public-Key Cryptography

Public-key cryptography circumvents the need to exchange a single private encryption/decryption key for secure communication to take place. Instead, the server generates two keys: a private and a public key. The server keeps the private key secret and makes the public key available for anyone to see. These two keys make it possible for the public key to decrypt information encrypted by the private key and for the private key to decrypt information encrypted by the public key. The keys also have the asymmetric property that enables you to easily derive the public key from the private key using a hash function, but you cannot derive the private key from the public key. This scheme is called asymmetric key cryptography. Digital Signature Algorithm (DSA) and Rivest Shamir Adleman (RSA) are common encryption algorithms that you can use in public key cryptography.

Consider an example in which a client, C, needs to send a message to a server, R. The following then occurs, based on the diagram in Figure 8-5:

1. R generates a private/public key pair.

2. R sends the public key to C, and keeps the private key to itself.

3. C can now encrypt a message using R's public key and send it over the insecure network. R is the only one who can decrypt the message from C because nobody else has access R's private key but R.

Figure 8-5 illustrates public key cryptography.

Figure 8-5 *Basic Public Key Cryptography*

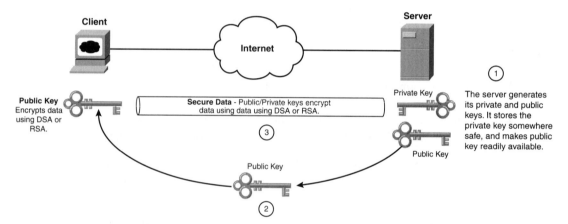

Because public keys are available to anyone, they need to be very large (for example, 1024-bit RSA public keys are common) in order to ensure the security of the messages that you transmit. In practice, computational load drastically increases on both C and R for keys large enough to avoid any possibility of brute force on the encryption algorithm compromising the keys. Symmetric keys prove much more practical for encrypting large amounts of traffic because they are private and can be shorter than asymmetric keys. For example, 128-bit RC4 and 56-bit DES keys are common. As such, most public key environments use a hybrid approach, combining the key exchange capabilities of public key schemes and processing efficiency of private key schemes.

In the example discussed previously, the following takes place using public-key cryptography, as illustrated in Figure 8-6.

1. The server R generates its private and public keys.

2. R sends its public key to client C.

3. Once C receives R's public key, it generates a random number.

4. C encrypts the random number using the server's public key and sends it to R.

5. R then decrypts the random number using its private key and uses the random number to create a symmetric key for further data encryption and decryption.

6. Further two-way secure communication between C and R occurs using a secret symmetric key based on the shared random number generated by C, as Figure 8-6 illustrates.

Figure 8-6 *Hybrid Public-Key Cryptography*

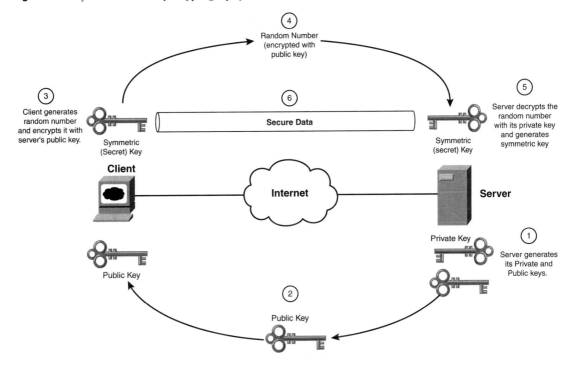

Using public-key cryptography, the server R maintains a single private/public key pair. The server's public key is available to any client that requires secure communication between itself and the server. The client and server generate a unique symmetric key for use during each session, which they discard at the end of the session. Combining asymmetric and symmetric keys provides a more practical hybrid encryption mechanism for encrypting bulk data. PKI uses public-key cryptography.

NOTE   Internet Key Exchange (IKE) also uses public-key cryptography to exchange secret keys for the symmetric encryption performed by IPSec, the popular site-to-site and remote access Virtual Private Network (VPN) protocol.

> **NOTE** Instead of using RSA or DSA to exchange a master secret key, you can use Diffie-Hellman key agreement. Diffie-Hellman is the protocol commonly used in IKE, but it can also be used in PKI.

Identity Theft Prevention Using Certificates

The nature of public-key cryptography allows for a malicious third party to create a separate private/public key pair and pose as a valid server. The client unknowingly uses the malicious server's public key to encrypt the random number. Once that happens, only the malicious server can decrypt with its private key. The client is unaware of the exchange because it did not verify that the public key actually belongs to the server in question. As a result, public key certificates are available for you to verify the authenticity of public key owners. Figure 8-7 illustrates how a malicious third party can pose as a valid server.

Figure 8-7 *A Malicious Third Party Posing as a Valid Server*

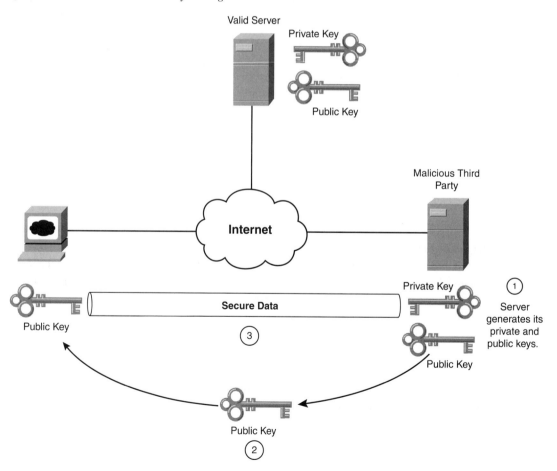

In Figure 8-7, the following sequence takes place:

1. The malicious server generates its private and public keys.

2. The client downloads the malicious server's public key, thinking that it is the valid server's public key.

3. The client and malicious server establish a secure connection to one another. The valid server remains unaware of the transaction.

Figure 8-8 shows how a CA creates a certificate to enable you to avoid the possibility of a malicious third-party server posing as your server. Based on the flow in Figure 8-8, the following sequence occurs:

1. When your server generates a private/public key pair, it also generates a Certificate Signing Request (CSR), containing the public key and other information to prove your identity (for example, your company name, address, and phone number).

2. You manually send the CSR that was generated by the server to a CA, normally via cut/paste onto the website of the CA.

3. The CA verifies the CSR with the Registration Authority (RA), thus making sure your organization is who they claim to be. The RA is a part of the PKI and is responsible for verifying requestors by looking them up in official business directories, calling them on the phone, or other such methods. If the RA verifies your organization, the CA will sign the CSR to vouch for your server.

4. The CA issues you a certificate for public use, including the expiration time of the certificate.

5. You can then install the certificate on your server. When a client accesses your server over the Internet, your server sends the certificate to the client so that it can verify that the public key belongs to you.

Figure 8-8 *A Certificate Authority Signing a Certificate for a Server*

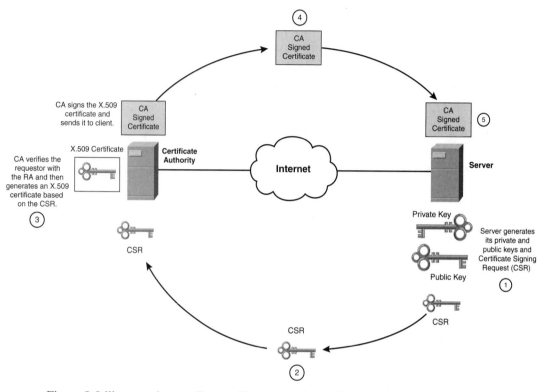

Figure 8-9 illustrates how a client verifies a server's certificate and generates the symmetric session key. Before the CA issues you a certificate, it signs the certificate with its digital signature. The CA creates a digital signature by first computing a hash on the contents of the certificate. The CA then encrypts the hashed value using its private key to produce its digital signature.

The following sequence takes place in Figure 8-9:

1. To verify the authenticity of origin server R's public key, the client browser, C, first downloads the CA-signed certificate from R.

2. C runs the same hash function that the CA ran on the certificate contents during the signing process.

3. C decrypts the CA's signature using the CA's public key and compares its hash to that of the CA. If the two hash values are the same, C can rest assured that the public key belongs to R, and no one else.

4. C extracts the server's public key from the certificate.

5. C generates a random number, encrypts it with R's public key, and generates the symmetric key.

6. C sends the encrypted random number to R.

7. R decrypts the random number with its private key and generates the symmetric key.

8. C and R exchange private information over the Internet using the symmetric secret key.

Figure 8-9 *Client Verifying a Server's Certificate*

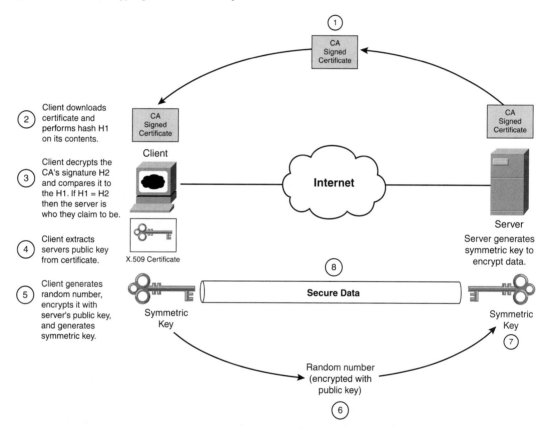

NOTE   Cisco content networking SSL-offloading devices use X.509 version 3 format certificates.

CAs also require certificates to verify their own authenticity in the PKI system. CA certificates are in the same form as regularly issued certificates. Root CAs, which are the largest CA providers, provide self-signed certificates. Verisign is an example of a root CA. Smaller intermediary CAs that want to provide CA services require root CAs to sign their certificates. When a server sends the client its certificate, it must also send the hierarchy of CA certificates involved in the certification chain. Certificate chains offer a means for a server to represent to the client the structured hierarchy of the CAs that are involved in the certificate authorization process. This ensures that a few well-known CAs are at the top of the hierarchy. When a client verifies the server certificate, it traverses the certificate chain until it detects a known certificate. The client then compares the CA's public key supplied by the server to the public key stored locally for the CA.

> **NOTE** All well-known certificates are stored directly on the client in a certificate store for comparison during the certificate verification process. In the case of SSL for use in HTTP web browsing, client browsers require obtaining the root CA certificates through a direct exchange. Most browser vendors include the common root CAs in the default browser download/ installation.

Some common certificate formats are:

- **X.509 Privacy Enhanced Mail (PEM)**—RFCs 1421–1424 specify the X.509 PEM format. You must encode your PEM certificates in Base64, enclosed between "-----BEGIN CERTIFICATE-----" and "-----END CERTIFICATE-----." Base64 is similar to ASCII, so you can cut/paste your certificates into your application's certificate import window. Your PEM-file may contain certificates, private keys, and CSRs (see Figure 8-8) also enclosed between the appropriate BEGIN/END-lines. X.509 PEM files may have ".crt," ".pem," or ".csr" file extensions.

- **Public-Key Cryptography Standard (PKCS)**—PKCS is an RSA Data Security, Inc., standard that provides an industry standard interface for public-key cryptography. It provides a format for transferring data based on a public-key cryptography and an infrastructure to support that transfer.

  — PKCS #7 is a standard for signing or encrypting data but cannot contain your private keys. PKCS #7 may contain your certificate chain. PKCS #7 files have a ".p7c" file extension.

  — Personal Information Exchange (PFX)/PKCS#12 formatted certificates contain a certificate chain and a private key. These files have either a ".pfx" or a ".p12" file extension.

- **Distinguished Encoding Rules (DER) and Canonical Encoding Rules (CER) certificates**—DER encodes files in binary X.509 format with the extension ".der" and CER as Base64 X.509 format with the extension ".cer."

> **NOTE** You can use Openssl freeware utility to convert between these certificate formats.

PKI typically uses X.509 certificates for server authentication. They contain the following information:

- **Version**—The version of the X.509 standard that applies to your certificate. There are three versions currently defined: versions 1, 2, and 3.

- **Issuer Name**—The issuer is the name of the entity that signed the certificate. The issuer is most often a CA. However, you can also issue yourself certificates using third-party certificate-signing utilities.

> **NOTE** You can create and self-sign X.509 certificates if you require them for your internal applications only. However, if you will give public access to your certificates, then you should acquire them from a public CA.

- **Serial Number**—The CA or certificate utility generates a serial number distinguishing it from other certificates that it issues.

- **Signature Algorithm Identifier**—The CA or certificate utility must identify the algorithm that it uses to sign the certificate.

- **Validity Period**—Your CA or certificate utility specifies the period for which the certificate is valid.

- **Subject Name**—This is the Distinguished Name (DN) of your organization or entity. For example, the values "CN=www.contentnetworking.com," "OU=Network Engineering," "O=Cisco Systems Inc.," and "C=US" identify a sample subject. These refer to your common name, organizational unit, organization, and country.

- **Public Key Information**—Your public key that clients use to encrypt a master secret.

Some common private key formats are:

- **PKCS#8 format**—An encrypted private key format with the extension ".p8c."

- **NET**—The NET format is a format that is compatible with older Netscape servers and Microsoft IIS .key files. NET is not very secure, so you should use this format only when necessary.

- **PEM and DER**—You encrypt your private keys alone within PEM and DER formatted files.

Secure Sockets Layer

SSL provides a secure infrastructure for the exchange of information over public networks, between public web servers and anonymous clients on the Internet. SSL is a protocol of the PKI that applications, such as HTTP, FTP and SMTP, use to provide content confidentiality and integrity. Netscape originally developed SSL in 1994, but the IETF formally drafted RFC 2246, "The TLS Protocol Version 1.0" version 1 protocol based on SSL version 3.

SSL achieves confidentiality by using symmetric key encryption, with RC4 or DES protocols, to encrypt packets. SSL ensures integrity by appending a Message Authentication Code (MAC) to the SSL packet header. The major difference between TLS and SSL is that TLS 1.0 uses Keyed-Hashing for the Message Authentication Code (HMAC) algorithm for message integrity, as specified in RFC 2104. The difference between MAC and HMAC is that HMAC uses the shared symmetric key along with the underlying hash function (MD5 or SHA-1) to create message digests, whereas MAC uses only the underlying hash function. As a result, TLSv1 and SSLv3 do not interoperate.

You can think of SSL as residing in the session layer of the OSI reference model, as Figure 8-10 illustrates.

Figure 8-10   *SSL Layers*

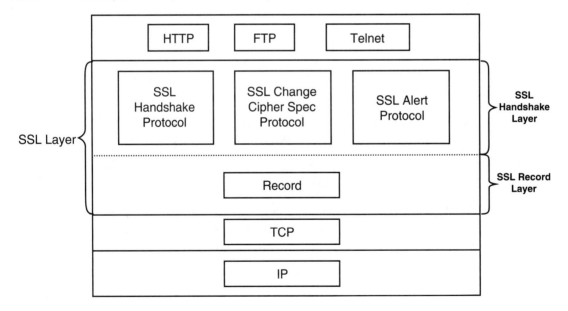

SSL uses the following protocols:

- **SSL Handshake Layer**—The SSL Handshake Layer includes three subprotocols and negotiates session information between the client and server. The session information includes:

  — **Shared secret**—The shared secret is the random number that is used to create the symmetric key for encrypting bulk data.

  — **Session identifier**—Participants use the session identifier to identify the SSL session. Content switches use this session identifier for SSL session stickiness, discussed in Chapter 10.

  — **Server and client certificates**—Client certificates are optional, and not typical for most public Internet sites.

  — **Cipher suite**—The cipher suite includes the protocol (TLS or SSL), asymmetric algorithm used for key exchange (RSA or DSA), the symmetric algorithm used for bulk encryption (DES or 3DES), and the hash algorithm for message integrity (MD5 or SHA-1). An example cipher suite string is "TLS_RSA_WITH_RC4_128_MD5."

- **SSL Change Cipher Spec Protocol**—Clients or servers use the SSL Change Cipher Spec Protocol during a full handshake to indicate to the other to use the negotiated keys for the current session. It is also used to resume an idle session, thus avoiding having to perform another full handshake.

- **Record Protocol**—The Record Protocol performs the bulk SSL encryption, using the shared secret key established in the handshake.

- **SSL Alert Protocol**—The SSL Alert Protocol signals problems with the SSL session ranging from unknown, revoked, or expired certificates to fatal error messages that will terminate the SSL connection.

SSL uses the four-phased handshake shown in Figure 8-11 to establish an SSL connection between a client and server.

Figure 8-11 *The Four-Phased SSL Handshake*

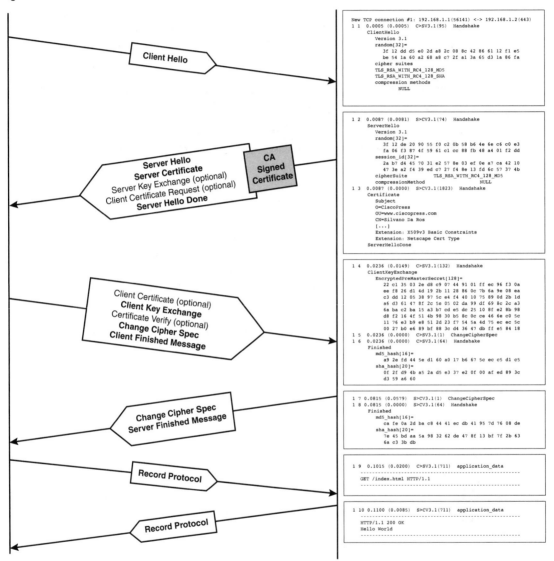

> **NOTE** Due to its increased popularity resulting from its strong security mechanisms, SSL is also used in VPN for remote access to corporate resources (SSL-VPN). SSL-VPN uses SSL client certificates for client authentication.

Typically, the client initiates a session to the server by sending a Client Hello message to the server. The server responds with a Server Hello message and its server certificate. The server can optionally request a certificate from the client, but this is not normal practice for most Internet applications. If the server certificate does not contain a public key, which again is not normal practice, the Server Key Exchange message can optionally contain a temporary key for the client to encrypt the master secret.

The Client Hello packet contains the SSL version number, random number, and supported cipher suites. The Server Hello packet contains the SSL version number, random number, session ID, and supported cipher suites. The version number is the highest version that the client supports. SSL uses "Version 2" for SSLv2, "Version 3" for SSLv3, and "Version 3.1" for TLS 1.0.

The client then computes a master secret key using its random number and the random number received from the Server Hello message. The client then encrypts the master secret with the public key located in the server's certificate (or with the temporary key from the Server Key Exchange message if no public is available in the certificate) and sends the result back to the server within the Client Key Exchange message. Both parties now have a master secret key with which they can derive a master symmetric encryption key for use by the Record Protocol to encrypt data between the client and server.

The handshake protocol then completes, as shown in Figure 8-11, by each party sending a Change Cipher Spec message and a Finish message. The Record Protocol then performs the RC4 encryption and HMAC message integrity checks on the application data. The participants fragment and optionally compress each application payload into sizes appropriate for the encryption mechanism. The participants also compute the MAC or HMAC and append it to the application payload. They then can encrypt the fragmented and compressed payload containing the hash using the shared secret key and send it to their SSL peer.

If you leave an SSL session idle for an extended time, SSL may resume the session without requiring a full handshake. Avoiding the full handshake is beneficial because, as you learned previously, asymmetric key cryptography, which is used during the SSL full handshake to exchange the session keys, is much more computationally intensive than symmetric (session) key cryptography. Figure 8-12 shows sample TLS 1.0 dump output for resuming an SSL session between a client and a web server. Because the client already possesses the server's certificate, the server does not resend its certificate to the client, resulting in only a three-way handshake to reestablish the SSL session.

Figure 8-12 *Three-Way Handshake to Resume an SSL Session*

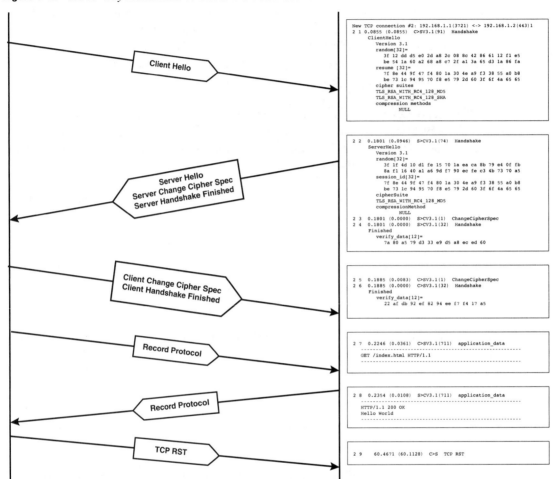

File Transfer Protocol

FTP is commonly used to transfer files between computers on the Internet. There are two types of FTP: active- and passive-FTP. Both use two TCP connections for the FTP transaction:

■ A *control* connection for authentication.

■ Negotiation of options for use during the *data* connection, over which the data transfer takes place.

With both active- and passive-FTP, the client initiates a control connection to the server, but with active-FTP the server in turn initiates the data connection to the client. In contrast, with passive-FTP, the client also initiates the data connection after the control connection.

Figure 8-13 illustrates active-FTP.

Figure 8-13 *Active-FTP*

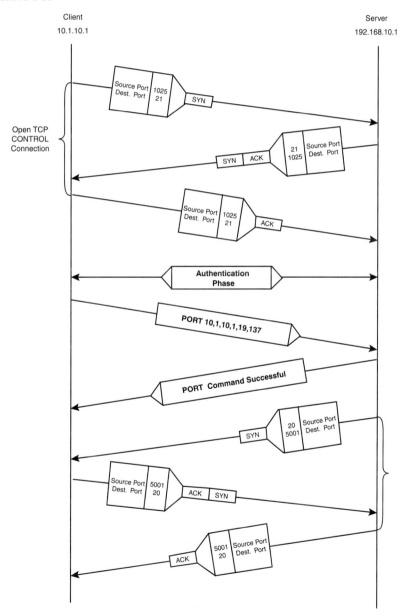

As you can see from Figure 8-13, the client initiates the control connection, performs the authentication, and sends the command **PORT 10,1,10,1,19,137** to the server. The first four octets given in the **PORT** command supply the IP address the server should connect to (that is, 10.1.10.1). To find the actual port the server should connect to, the server multiplies the fifth octet by 256 and then adds the sixth octet to the total (that is, 19 * 256 + 137 = 5001). The server then initiates the DATA connection to TCP port 5001, using the reserved active-FTP data source port 20.

With passive-FTP, the client initiates the control connection and issues the **PASV** command to the server. The server responds with "Enter Passive mode (192,168,10,1,98,16)." The client deciphers the fifth and sixth octet in the same manner as mentioned previously to determine the TCP port it should use for the data connection (that is, 98 * 256 + 16 = 25,104). The client then opens the FTP data connection to the server. Notice that in passive-FTP, the client does not use reserved TCP port 20 for the source port of the data connection. Figure 8-14 illustrates passive-FTP.

NOTE   For information on how to deal with active- and passive-FTP in a Firewall Load Balancing (FWLB) environment, refer to Chapter 11, "Switching Secured Content."

Figure 8-14   *Passive-FTP*

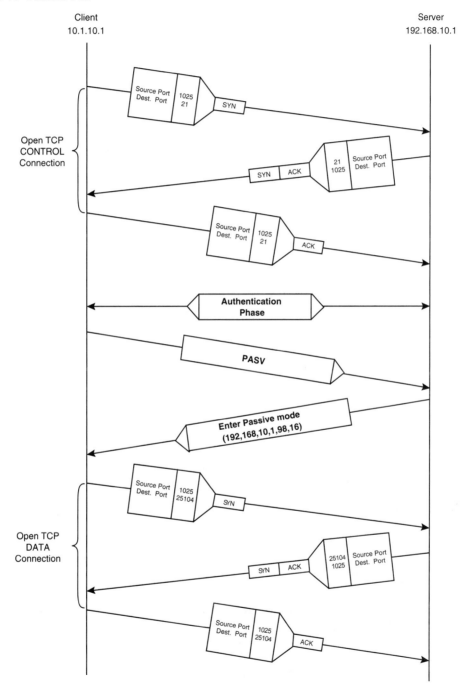

Summary

In this chapter, you learned about the following application layer protocols:

- **HTTP**—You learned how HTTP optimizes web content delivery between origin servers and user agents, using HTTP persistence, pipelining, and cache controls. You also learned the differences between HTTP 1.0 and HTTP 1.1, the major being the ability to extend the functionality of HTTP 1.1 by adding HTTP headers without changing the protocol itself.

- **SSL**—You learned how to secure your web content using the PKI encryption and certificates specific to the SSL protocol.

- **FTP**—You learned how FTP works, and in particular the differences between active- and passive-FTP.

Review Questions

1. What is an application layer protocol?

2. What is the difference between HTTP persistence and pipelining?

3. What is the HTTP header and value that servers use to issue session cookies to clients?

4. What is the difference between basic and message digest authentication?

5. What is the difference between explicit and implicit cache controls?

6. List the three types of security schemes and the available algorithms that PKI systems commonly use.

7. How do CAs generate digital signatures for signing a server's certificate?

Recommended Reading

RFC 2616. *Hypertext Transfer Protocol   HTTP/1.1*. IETF. http://www.ietf.org/rfc/rfc2616.txt, 1999

RFC 2617. *HTTP Authentication: Basic and Digest Access Authentication*. IETF. http://www.ietf.org/rfc/rfc2617.txt, 1999

RFC 2104. HMAC: *Keyed-Hashing for Message Authentication*. IETF. http://www.ietf.org/rfc/rfc2104.txt, 1997

RFC 2246. HMAC: *The TLS Protocol Version 1.0*. IETF. http://www.ietf.org/rfc/rfc2246.txt, 1999

Chapter Goals

In this chapter, you will learn the basic concepts required to stream content on your network, which include the following topics:

- **Streaming Media Files and Content Playback**—You can encapsulate streaming media in container files. Users who request these container files can play back the content in their media players.

- **Delivering Streaming Media**—To transport streaming media on your network, your streaming media application requires a real-time transport protocol, such as RTP. To enable further control and scalability of your network resources, you can configure quality of service (QoS) and IP Multicast.

CHAPTER 9

Introducing Streaming Media

Streaming media enables you to distribute digital voice, video, and data over an IP network and is analogous to conventional analog television broadcasting. With conventional TV, you see frames on the TV screen as they arrive from a cable or antenna feed. In the past, digital media files required you to download the entire audio, video, or data file before viewing the content. You can now format streaming media files such that your media player can display the content to you in smaller chunks, as you download them individually.

In the context of content networking, there are two components to streaming media.

- **Streaming Files and Playback**—The first component includes the media file storage formats and client playback mechanisms.

- **Delivering Streaming Media in Real-Time**—The second component contains the set of network protocols for delivering streaming content.

This chapter covers both of these components. However, you can further optimize networks for streaming by using technologies discussed in Chapter 13, "Delivering Cached and Streaming Media."

Streaming Files and Content Playback

You can stream media files live, as a scheduled rebroadcast of a live event or on-demand. Live streaming involves capturing the event with a video camera, an audio recording system, or both. You can then encode the live event into a digital network-ready format as it occurs and send it over the network to active receivers. Schedule rebroadcast and on-demand streaming involves encoding the media for storage and later viewing.

Streaming introduces the concept of progressive downloading, in which you view the multimedia session after a momentary delay to allow data buffering to take place in order to reduce packet jitter. The result is an almost immediate playback of the streaming content.

Figure 9-1 illustrates a basic streaming media solution. The audio–video recorder transmits raw media to the conversion device. You can use either analog or digital video transmission standards to transmit the raw content to the streaming data converter. Common analog standards include composite video (such as Phase Alternation Line [PAL] National Television Standards Committee [NTSC]), and S-Video, and Component Video. Digital audio–video recording devices commonly use Firewire or USB interfaces into conversion devices. The conversion device then encodes the data for storage either to a video-on-demand/live origin server or transmission to a network for live viewing. The origin server can receive the live stream from the data converter and deliver it directly to clients live or store it for later viewing. You also can configure some streaming data converters to deliver the live stream to clients directly.

Figure 9-1 *A Sample Streaming Media Network Environment*

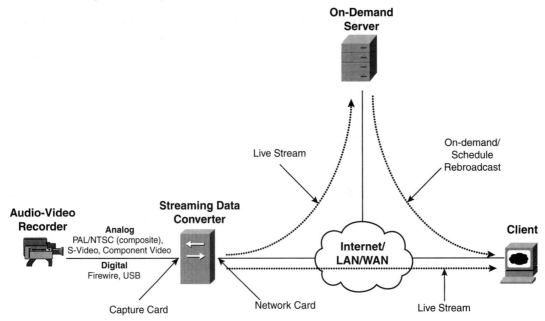

PAL and NTSC are the most widely used analog television and motion picture standards, and are commonly known as composite video. NTSC is used in North America and PAL in Europe. Systeme Electronique Couleur Avec Memoire (SECAM) is another analog protocol that is used in France. You choose the format depending on where you will be viewing the content.

Raw audio-video from analog recording devices normally originates from one of these three formats. You can convert these formats digitally for delivery over a network using codecs. You also can stream from digital audio–video recorders directly, if you have the appropriate hardware to convert the digital formats into streaming formats.

The encoding format you select, whether analog or digital, will dictate playback quality. Make sure that you understand each format in terms of its playback quality before selecting a format. Additionally, when encoding your presentation from the recording device, using too few scanlines will ultimately affect the viewer's experience.

> **NOTE** The word *codec* is short for compress-decompress and sometimes code-decode. You can use codecs to translate raw media into compressed streaming media, for viewing or listening over a network. Your media player uses the same codec to piece the data back together for viewing that you used to compress the data. Some codecs are lossy, whereas others are lossless, implying a difference in the bandwidth required to transport the resulting information.

You can encode, deliver, and play back streaming content using a streaming media solution that you choose. Streaming media vendors offer you the ability to stream live, scheduled rebroadcast, or on-demand video, audio, and data. Media servers provide encoding of the inputs using audio–video hardware interface capture cards. You can install the capture cards on the streaming data converter server that was shown in Figure 9-1 to provide the interface between the audio–video recording hardware and the network.

Table 9-1 lists the popular streaming media products and standards.

Table 9-1 *Streaming Media Products and Standards*

Streaming Vendor/Software	Player	Container file extension	Transport Protocols	DRM	Meta-File
Windows Media Technology (WMT)/ Windows Media Services (WMS)	Windows Media Player	ASF	MMS WMT RTSP RTP (UDP) HTTP	Yes	ASX
RealNetworks/Helix Univeral Server	RealPlayer	RM	Real RTSP G2 and Real PNA RTSP MMS RTP (UDP) RealNetworks' Real Data Transport (RDT) HTTP	Yes	SMIL

continues

Table 9-1 *Streaming Media Products and Standards (Continued)*

Streaming Vendor/Software	Player	Container file extension	Transport Protocols	DRM	Meta-File
Apple QuickTime Streaming	Apple Quicktime	QT	RTSP RTP (UDP) HTTP	Yes	SMIL
MPEG4	RealPlayer and Apple Quicktime	MPEG4 (based on QT)	Not specified	No, but includes proprietary interfaces	SMIL

NOTE WMT uses its own version of RTSP and a proprietary streaming control protocol called Microsoft Media Services (MMS) to control streaming flows. MMS provides similar functionality to RTSP but uses TCP/UDP port 1755 for control and UDP ports 1024–5000 for data transmission.

Raw video content contains rich color, movement detail, and sound quality. As a result, raw uncompressed video can consume a great deal of your server and network resources. Consider a typical television show that produces millions of colors on the screen that change every fraction of a second. A computer that could capture and process these pixels and their changes in real-time would require vast amounts of CPU power, disk storage space, and bandwidth. Therefore, you should use codecs to compress media before network transmission.

Stills-based codecs, such as JPEG and GIF, are good at removing any unnecessary information within an individual image. Similar to stills, motion-based codecs perform encoding of individual frames, but also remove unnecessary information between frames. For example, MPEG records only changes to images across frames—information that has not changed in the current frame remains the same as the previous frame. For uncompressed voice, 64 kbps per stream is typical; however, voice codecs such as G.711 can deliver business-class voice at less than 10 kbps per voice stream.

Table 9-2 lists the codecs available for streaming audio–video media. Digital Rights Management (DRM) embeds pay-per-view, pay-per-subscription, and user authentication into the streaming media solution. DRM protection provides a way for organizations to generate revenue and prevent piracy.

Table 9-2   *Common Audio–Video Codec Algorithms Available for Streaming Media*

Codec Name (ITU-T/ISO-IEC)	Type of Codec	Typical Use	Required Bandwidth
MPEG1	High-quality video codec	CD encoding	500 kbps–10+ Mbps
MPEG2	High-quality video codec	DVD/HDTV enconding	500 kbps–10+ Mbps
MPEG4	Medium-quality video	Live, on-demand Internet streaming and HDTV	100 kbps–1 Mbps
H.263	Low-quality codec	Originally for ISDN video conferencing	128 bps
Motion-JPEG	Video Codec (Frame-by-frame)	Internet Streaming	-
JPEG	Image encoder	Still images	-
G.711	Audio codec	Raw voice transmission	64 kbps
G.729	Audio codec	Voice over IP (VoIP)	8 kbps
MP3	MPEG1 Layer III Audio Codec	Music download-and-play or streaming	-

Streaming vendors normally use codecs containing licensed or open-source software from the standards in Table 9-2 or proprietary codec algorithms. Due to the popularization of the codec algorithms given in Table 9-2, the number of manufacturers that provide commercially available codecs based on these algorithms has dramatically increased. To differentiate among codecs, you should refer to their Four Character Code (FourCC). For example, DivX, the popular audio–video codec manufacturer, has numerous codecs each given unique FourCC identifiers (for example, DX50 and DivX).

> **NOTE**   Visit fourcc.org for a list of common codec algorithms and their respective FourCC identifiers.

Creating Streaming On-Demand Container Files

Streaming server vendors provide the ability to store multiple streams of data that form a multimedia session into a single file called a streaming container. These container files are suitable for playback that is live in nature or on-demand, whether you stream over a network or play the file locally. The underlying transport protocols (for example, RTP, UDP, and RTSP) of Windows Media and RealNetworks are independent of the container file and do not represent specifications of the container file for transmitting streams over a network. With Apple QT and MPEG4, the underlying protocols are part of the container file specification. Each vendor has its own proprietary container format, with the exception of MPEG4. MPEG4 is a standard streaming format to organize multiple audio, video streams, and multimedia streams, but is based closely on the Apple QT format.

To stream audio–video media, your solution first compresses and encapsulates the audio–video data. Codecs are available for media compression and decompression. The encapsulation includes application-layer headers containing information on how your client media player should play back the file to you. The headers include index information, bandwidth rate limits, and types of media contained in the file. The media may contain audio, video, or slideshow presentation media. When a player receives the streamable file over a network, it first reads the headers instructing the player on how to play the chunks of media in the file. Figure 9-2 diagrams a typical container file format.

Figure 9-2   *A Typical Streaming Container File*

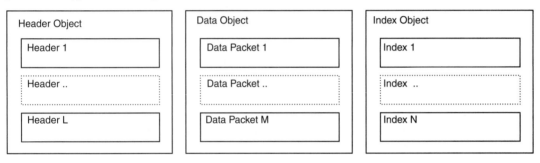

The container file in Figure 9-2 includes the following information.

- **Headers**—The container headers include information about the streams, such as the stream size and codecs. Other information, such as the bit rates of the streams and offset between the individual packets within the streams, is included in the headers as well.

- **Data Packets**—The list of data packets, in order of delivery. Because container files normally deliver multiple streams, the data packets from each stream are interleaved. This enables your media player to render and synchronize the different streams together as they arrive from the network.

> **NOTE**   The intention of the container file is to organize the streams for transmission. Your streaming solution can deliver the data packets using any of the mechanisms described later in this chapter, such as RTP, RTCP, and RTSP.

- **Index**—Because the container file interleaves the data packets, it uses an index for each stream to enable your media player to efficiently seek through the media once the entire file is downloaded.

> **NOTE**   Solutions using the container format in Figure 9-2 send the application headers using the same underlying transport (for example, RTP) as they use to transport the data packets and index information.

A container can encapsulate audio and data streams for different bit rates and languages. For example, you can encapsulate a presentation containing both French and English 10 kbps audio streams and a video stream for bandwidths 56 kbps, 100 kbps, 500 kbps, and 1 Mbps. You can publish this presentation to a website and allow your users to select their preferred bandwidth and language from the site. The server then sends the headers and the appropriate bandwidth and language from the file. When the header arrives, the player can determine the appropriate codecs for rendering the presentation and display the data packets as they arrive from their respective streams. A player can start rendering the audio and video content as soon as it reads the header and at least a single data packet from the network. By design, containers are media-independent. For example, you also can encapsulate audio, video, 3D objects, Macromedia Flash objects, sprites, and text into a container file. SDP session information about the session for use during session transmission also can be stored in the container.

You can convert your streaming content into a container format, for delivery into the respective vendor's streaming player. Alternatively, you can imbed a player into a web browser using the vendor's Software Development Kit (SDK). The SDKs include programming interfaces to languages such as C++ and Java.

To provide streaming media to your users, you can insert URLs in your HTML pointing to the streaming container files. Your client's web browsers will launch the respective media player based on the MIME-type of the container file. For example, with WMT, the browser recognizes the ".asf" extension and launches Windows Media Player. Example 9-1 shows how you can insert a WMT file into your HTML.

Example 9-1   *A Sample HTML Document Linking Users to a Windows Streaming Media Clip/Container*

```
<HTML>
<HEAD>
<TITLE>A Sample Video Stream/TITLE>
</HEAD>
<BODY>
<A HREF="mms://cisco.com/wmt/helloworld.asf">Hello World!</A>
</BODY>
</HTML>
```

As mentioned previously, containers (or clips) may hold multiple inputs, such as audio, video, and whiteboards. For example, the streaming file helloworld.asf in Example 9-1 is an audio–video clip. To provide enhanced synchronization of individual streaming clips, you should use meta-files.

Describing Streaming On-Demand Content with Meta-Files

You can use meta-files to describe how to display streaming content to a web browser. Meta-files provide the interface between web browsers and proprietary container files. Instead of embedding the URLs of the media files directly into your HTML, you can point your users to the URL that houses the meta-file. Your user's web browser launches the media player and passes the meta-file to the player. The player reads the contents of the meta-file and performs the appropriate actions on the streaming media clips in the meta-file. You can write your meta-files using the Synchronized Multimedia Integration Language (SMIL) or with Windows Advanced Stream Redirector (ASX) files. SMIL is an XML-based standard meta-file language. Windows streaming uses ASX files, and both RealNetworks and Apple QuickTime uses SMIL. Example 9-2 shows how a browser can open two different WMT clips in sequence using ASX.

Example 9-2 *A Sample ASX File for Streaming Two WMT ASF Clips in Sequence*

```
! HTML referencing an ASX File:
<HTML>
<HEAD>
<TITLE>A Sample Video Stream/TITLE>
</HEAD>
<BODY>
<A HREF="http://cisco.com/wmt/helloworld.asx">Hello World!</A>
</BODY>
</HTML>
```

```
! helloworld.asx ASX File:
<ASX version="3.0">
<Entry>
<ref HREF="mms://cisco.com/wmt/helloworld.asf"/>
</Entry>
<Entry>
<ref HREF="mms://cisco.com/wmt/goodbyeworld.asf"/>
</Entry>
</ASX>
```

Example 9-3 shows how you can write a SMIL file to deliver two RealNetworks clips in sequence. You also can use SMIL to include images, text, and graphics in your presentation, not just video clips.

Example 9-3 *A Sample SMIL File for Streaming Two RealNetworks RM Clips in Sequence*

```
<smil xmlns="http://www.w3.org/2001/SMIL20/Language"
xmlns:rn="http://features.real.com/2001/SMIL20/Extensions">
 <body>
   <video src="rtsp://cisco.com/real/helloworld.rm "
   <video src="rtsp://cisco.com/real/goodbyeworld.rm "/>
 </body>
</smil>
```

RealNetworks supplies extensions to the standard set of XML tags defined in SMIL 2.0. Some extended features include changing the opacity and color of static images such as JPEG, GIF, and PNG files. To access RealNetworks' customize XML tags, you need to declare the RealNetworks namespace **xmlns:rn=http://features.real.com/2001/SMIL20/Extensions.**

You must prefix all RealNetworks custom XML tags with this namespace. Refer to Chapter 7, "Presenting and Transforming Content," to understand custom namespaces. The namespace defined with **http://www.w3.org/2001/SMIL20/Language** is the standard SMIL 2.0 namespace. All elements not defined with the "rn:" prefix will assume this namespace. In your HTML, you would link users to the SMIL file with **<A HREF="http://cisco.com/wmt/helloworld.smil">Hello World!</A>**.

With SMIL and ASX meta-files you can:

■   Time and control your streaming media presentation.

■   Apply advanced layouts to your presentation.

■   Stream clips from different servers.

■   Include ads in your streaming media presentation.

Streaming with Microsoft WMT, Real Networks, and Apple QuickTime

The proprietary RealNetworks and Windows file formats are very similar to the generic container shown previously in Figure 9-2. However, the Apple and MPEG4 file formats use a much different format. The QuickTime format does not inherently organize the different media streams of a multimedia session into interleaved data packets for streaming media transmission, as the Real and WMT formats do.

> **NOTE**   The MPEG4 container format is based on QuickTime's container file format.

Apple QT and MPEG4 organize the media streams into virtual packets with the use of hint tracks, thus preserving the continuous nature of the media. During transmission, QT and MPEG4 uses the hint tracks to divide the data into packet-sized chunks for transport over RTP/UDP. The hint tracks contain pointers to locations within the media streams. The hint tracks also contain necessary transmission timing information to rebuild individual streams and for synchronizing multiple streams together. Unlike RealNetworks and WMT, when an Apple QT or MPEG4 streaming server sends packets over the network, there is no QuickTime- or MPEG4-related header information embedded in the packets, just the standard application transport header and payload format information.

> **NOTE** The container defined in Figure 9-2 (for Real and WMT) does not specify anything related to lower-level transport. Because Apple and MPEG4 packetize the media on-the-fly, they must store lower-layer transport information in the container.

Vendors develop proprietary versions of streaming protocols, such as Windows MMS, Real RTSP G2, and Real PNA. The vendors develop these to provide additional features, such as stream thinning and failover to HTTP streaming. Stream thinning involves signaling between the client and server to automatically detect decreases in network bandwidth. If the bandwidth decreases, WMT and RealNetworks servers can automatically decrease the transmission rate to the clients. Additionally, the MMS and RTSP protocols generate random transport (TCP or UDP) port numbers for the RTP stream. Because some firewalls may not have the RTP, or RTSP/MMS UDP ports opened, MMS and Real RTSP streaming protocols offer proprietary HTTP streaming failover mechanisms, because HTTP is readily available through firewall devices.

Each vendor strives toward adoption of the MPEG family of transport and signaling protocols. Phasing out proprietary protocols remains in discussion by Windows and RealNetworks. However, the MPEG standards will require extensions such as stream thinning and HTTP failover to be part of the standards before the vendors consider a complete phase-out of their proprietary solutions.

Streaming Motion Picture Experts Group

The Motion Picture Experts Group (MPEG) working group initiated development of the video standards in the late 1980s to address digitization and storage of video and audio media. The International Telecommunications Union (ITU) currently maintains the MPEG standard documents.

> **NOTE** You can consider the MPEG family as residing in the MPEG standards Presentation and Session layers of the OSI reference model.

The following MPEG standards are currently available to you for compressing and decompressing video data.

- **MPEG1**—Developed in the late 1980s–early 1990s for the storage and retrieval of video and audio on storage media, such as high-capacity tapes and CD-ROMs.

- **MPEG2**—Developed in the mid-1990s for the TV broadcasting industry's transition from analog to digital television (DTV). Most DVDs today store content in MPEG2 format. MPEG3 was merged into MPEG2. The playback of MPEG2 at the desktop is a licensed function. Typically, the license agreement and fees are accounted for when you purchase the MPEG2 player.

- **MPEG4**—Developed in the late 1990s and introduced the concept of storing content as objects capable of being individually or collectively manipulated. Although MPEG4 is a standard, the software requires special royalty-based software licensing. MPEG4 has no built-in DRM; however, it can hook in to proprietary DRM solutions. The MPEG4 file format is based on the Apple QuickTime file format.

> **NOTE**   MPEG4 is the only MPEG4 standard with inherent streaming capabilities.

- **MPEG7**—Currently a draft under development to provide a multimedia description interface.

- **MPEG21**—Also currently a draft under development. MPEG21 is a multimedia framework that covers the entire multimedia content delivery chain, including content creation, production, delivery, trade, and consumption.

Delivering Streaming Media

To accommodate multimedia applications requiring delay-sensitive delivery, use real-time media transfer protocols such as Real-Time Transport Protocol (RTP), and its partner control protocol Real-Time Control Protocol (RTCP). To provide additional control to the media transfer, use signaling protocols such as Real-Time Streaming Protocol (RTSP), SIP, and H.323. You also can specify these signaling protocols to use Session Description Protocol (SDP), XML, or SMIL to supply the information related to the session to the participants.

Table 9-3 outlines the real-time protocols discussed in this chapter.

Table 9-3   *Streaming Media Protocols*

Protocol	Usage	Related Standards, RFC(s),W3C documents	Protocol Versions Available
Real-Time Transport Protocol (RTP)	Media Transport protocol	RTP Standard RFC 3550 (obsoletes RFC 1889) RFC 3551 RTP Audio/Video Profile (extends RFC 3550)	No version numbering
Real-Time Control Protocol (RTCP)	RTP control for reporting, timing and statistics calculation.	Defined within RFC 3550	No version numbering
Real-Time Streaming Protocol (RTSP)	Signaling protocol for controlling RTP sessions. Provides VCR-like controls. Uses TCP port 554.	RFC 2326 (April 1998)	Version 2
Session Initiation Protocol (SIP)	Signaling protocol for inviting participants to a session.	RFC 3261 (obsoletes RFC 2543)	No version numbering

continues

Table 9-3 *Streaming Media Protocols (Continued)*

Protocol	Usage	Related Standards, RFC(s),W3C documents	Protocol Versions Available
H.323	Signaling protocol for inviting participants to a session. Originally meant for fixed bandwidth (e.g., ISDN) conferencing, but now used for scalable real-time video conferencing, such as Microsoft NetMeeting.	Not an Internet Draft RFC. Managed by ITU-T	Version 5 (2003)
Session Description protocol (SDP)	Used by RTSP and SIP to describe the session to participants.	RFC 2327	No version numbering
SMIL	Used for rich multimedia presentations which integrate streaming audio and video with images, text, or any other media type.	http://www.w3.org/ AudioVideo/ http://www.w3.org/TR/ SMIL2/	Version 2

Transferring Streaming Media with the Real-Time Transport Protocol

RTP provides the transport for audio and visual media transmission over an IP network. The Layer 4 transport can be over UDP or TCP, but more often UDP is used as the transport protocol. For real-time applications, UDP provides less packet delay than TCP. Recall from Chapter 2, "Exploring the Network Layers," that delays occur using TCP and are associated with retransmissions from packet loss and the TCP slow start congestion control algorithm. Furthermore, most real-time applications prefer to conceal packet loss rather than retransmit lost packets. As such, RTP provides mechanisms to handle network issues, such as jitter and packet loss, on its own at the application layer of the OSI model.

> **NOTE** You can scale RTP by using IP Multicast Layer 3 forwarding, provided that you enable IP Multicast features in your network infrastructure, such as PIM-SM and Bidir-PIM. You also can use unicast-UDP to transport RTP sessions.

RTP is flexible as it specifies the transport mechanism, not the payload formats and algorithms for the underlying real-time media. RTP can transport a number of video formats, such as MPEG-4, H.261, JPEG compressed video, and many more. However, each payload format is normally specified separately in its respective RFCs or ITU document, in order to provide format-specific header values and controls. For example, in the case of H.261, RFC 2032 specifies Negative Acknowledgements to control video flow and handle retransmission of lost packets.

Because RTP uses UDP as its transport protocol to deal with delays associated with network errors resulting in lost or out-of-sequence packets, RTP packets include timestamps and sequence information in their application headers. RTP uses the timing information to synchronize different sources involved in a multimedia presentation, such as audio and video. For example, lip movements require synchronization with the voice of someone presenting over a video conference or corporate communication. RTP also includes sequence numbers to determine lost or out-of-sequence packets. In contrast to the mechanism TCP uses to retransmit and reorder in the event of errors, RTP uses sequence numbers to detect packet loss in order to conceal rather than correct errors. The assumption is that a video frame received out-of-sequence is better discarded than displayed to the viewer out-of-sequence.

> **NOTE**   Although RTP uses a short playout buffer, it is meant to alleviate packet jitter and is not suitable for buffering, retransmitting, and reordering packets.

RTCP is the protocol within RTP for session monitoring and control but does not provide any delivery guarantee. RTCP maintains the state of RTP sessions using a unique identifier, called CNAME, for each group of RTP-UDP connections. RTCP uses this state to group the different feeds into a single multimedia session. Based on the session that the RTP-UDP connections belong to, synchronization can take place using the timing information that is included in the session information embedded within each RTP and RTCP UDP connection. However, the timestamps in the RTP packets originating from different servers may skew from one another, making synchronization difficult. As a result, RTCP provides a reference clock (or wallclock) to reconcile timestamps from different RTP streams for synchronization purposes. You can derive the RTCP wallclock from an external Network Time Protocol (NTP) source. NTP is accurate enough to provide time resolution appropriate for any of today's streaming media applications. The streaming media application can use the RTCP time reference to calculate jitter, data packet rates, and clock skew in the individual RTP connections.

RTCP also provides congestion control through client-side reporting on the quality of the streaming data reception. RTCP sender reports (SR) are sent periodically (for example, every 5 seconds) to receivers indicating the quality of the stream. Based on these reports, participants can calculate statistics, such as number of lost packets, round trip times, and inter-arrival jitter. Optionally, RTCP also can send participant information such as participant name, e-mail address, phone number, and location in the SRs.

RTCP sends packets periodically to all participants in the session, using a different port number than the RTP streams. This way, all participants can evaluate the total number of participants. Packets are sent using the same distribution as the RTP streams, either UDP unicast or multicast. RTCP traffic normally does not exceed 5 percent of the total session bandwidth, with at least 25 percent of that being for source reports.

Table 9-4 lists the available RTCP commands.

Table 9-4   *Available RTCP Commands*

Packet Code	Description
SR	Sender Report—transmit and receive reports for active senders to all participants
RR	Receiver Report—transmit and receive reports for receivers to all participants
SDES	Source description—describe the source of session, including the CNAME
BYE	Explicit leave
APP	Application specific extensions

RTP organizes data into payloads such that each packet contains an independently decodable unit. If possible, each frame of a video feed is compressed and sent in a single packet, so that the user can decode the packet as it arrives on the network. If a source sends a single frame across multiple packets, the RTP timestamp is the same for each packet.

> **NOTE**   RTP uses the RTP UDP port range 16384–32767. RTP uses the even numbers in this range; RTCP uses odd numbers within the range.

Real-time Data Control with Real Time Streaming Protocol

RTSP acts as a TV remote control, enabling the recipient to use functions, such as play, pause, record, fast-forward, and rewind, to control the delivery of media from the origin server to clients.

RTSP is similar to HTTP with the following major exceptions:

- RTSP maintains session state by default. RTSP requires session state for normal operations, whereas HTTP requires state only for session-stickiness.
- Servers can contact clients using an existing persistent connection.
- RTSP does not transport the stream. The data RTSP transports is the meta-information for the stream.
- RTSP clients must specify the host portion of the URL within the RTSP commands, whereas, HTTP allows clients to specify the relative path of the URL within the requests and use a **Host:** header to specify the host portion of the URL.

Table 9-5 lists the common RTSP messages that clients and servers use.

Table 9-5   *Available RTSP Control Messages*

Method	Method Direction (i.e., Client *Direction* Server)	Description
DESCRIBE	->	Requests the description file of a session.
ANNOUNCE	<->	The client publishes a new description file to a server using the ANNOUNCE method. If sent to the client by the server during a real-time session, an update to a description file is sent.
SETUP	->	Sent by the client to a server to specify the transport protocol to be used in the session, for example, Real-Time Transport Protocol/Audio Video Profile (RTP/AVP).
PAUSE	->	Causes the server to temporarily suspend the media. Not yet used for live feeds.
TEARDOWN	->	Requests the server to stop the session.
PLAY	->	Tells the server to start sending the streaming data over the transport indicated in the SETUP method.
RECORD	->	Indicates to the server to store the streaming media content, useful in live streaming.
REDIRECT	<-	Informs the client that it must connect to another location.
SET_PARAMETER	<->	Assigns a value of a session-specific parameter. These parameters are dependant on the implementation.
GET_PARAMETER	<->	Requests a value from the server of a session-specific parameter.
OPTIONS	<->	Identical to the HTTP 1.1 Options header. The server must return the available methods for the URI specified.

A client must have information about the following components to request and receive a stream.

- **Media types**—The media types in use, such as audio, video, and whiteboards

- **Network protocols used**—The network protocols in use, such as RTP, UDP, and IP

- **Codecs**—Information to determine the codec algorithms in use, such as H.261 and MPEG4

- **IP addresses and ports**—The multicast or unicast IP addresses that are in use, whether TCP or UDP is used as the transport protocol, and the TCP or UDP port numbers that are in use

RTSP can use Session Description Protocol (SDP), SMTP, XML, or SMIL or inform clients of this information. In Figure 9-3, a client uses HTTP to request a description of the streaming content from the server. You identify the streaming content by URL in the same way that HTTP identifies web content. The server responds with a detailed SDP description of the streaming media, including the media types, transport protocols, the multicast or unicast IP addresses of the sources, and codecs. Figure 9-3 shows a typical RTSP flow in which the client retrieves the SDP file using HTTP.

Figure 9-3 *Sample RTSP Flow for Controlling a Multimedia Session*

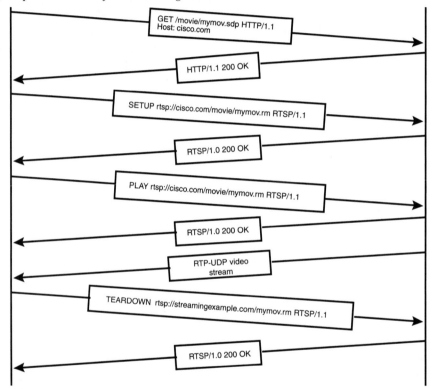

You also can send SDP description files to clients using RTSP in response to the DESCRIBE method. Example 9-4 is a description file in SDP format for an on-demand Windows streaming media session within an .asf file containing three streams: an audio, video, and whiteboard stream.

> **NOTE**   The W3C defines custom XML tags that enable you to implement the SDP fields given in Example 9-4 using SMIL. To use the custom tags, you need to define the SDP namespace **<smil xmlns:sdp="http://www.w3.org/AudioVideo/1998/08/draft-hoschka-smilsdp-00">** in your SMIL file.

Example 9-4   *Sample Session Description File to Describe a WMT Stream*

```
v=0                                              - protocol version
o=sdaros 2890844526 2890842807 IN IP4 10.1.2.11  - owner information
s=Content Networking Fundamentals                - session name
i=A Seminar on Content Networking Concepts        - session description
u=http://www.cisco.com/cn.pdf                    - URL of user-friendly description
e=sdaros@ssdl.com (Silvano Da Ros)               - owner e-mail
c=IN IP4 10.1.3.11/127                           - IP address of
t=2873397496 2873404696                          - time range of session
a=recvonly                                       - direction of the session
m=audio 3456 RTP/AVP 0                           - media types and port numbers
m=video 2232 RTP/AVP 31
m=whiteboard 32416 UDP WB
a=orient:portrait                                - Orientation = landscape or portrait.
```

> **NOTE**   If you are using RealNetworks or WMT, you can package the SDP file directly into the proprietary container file headers.

When the client receives the SDP file, it sends a SETUP method to the server to initialize the requested session. The SETUP includes the transport and the port numbers that the client requires.

```
SETUP rtsp://ssdl.com/test.asf RTSP/1.0
       CSeq: 101
       Transport: RTP/AVP;unicast;client_port=2301-3202
```

The server responds with a RTSP 200 OK that includes a sequence number for the current method, and an identifier for the client to use in subsequent RTSP methods as a reference to the session. The server confirms the transport (RTP/AVP;unicast) and client ports (client_port), and informs the client as to the server ports (server_port) to use for the RTP connection, within the **Transport:** RTSP header.

```
RTSP/1.0 200 OK
       CSeq: 101
       Date: 23 Aug 2005 15:35:06 GMT
       Session: 47112344
       Transport: RTP/AVP;unicast;
          client_port=4589-4589;server_port=6256-6257
```

By keeping track of session state, a participant may send many RTSP messages over short-lived TCP connections, throughout the timeline of the presentation. By providing the session identifier in every RTSP request or response, an RTSP session can span multiple TCP connections. RTSP supports pipelining as well and works with either unicast or multicast.

The server then sends a PLAY method notifying the server that it should start the RTP session. In this example, the server sends the three streams that are indicated in the SDP file over three independent UDP streams. The client and server use a fourth RTCP TCP stream to synchronize the three streams. The client and server establish these four streams transparently to RTSP. The client includes the time range of the session that it wishes to view in the PLAY method.

```
PLAY rtsp://ssdl.com/test.asf RTSP/1.0
          CSeq: 102
          Session: 47112344
          Range: npt=1-40
```

NOTE RTSP reuses HTTP Basic and Message digest authentication to authenticate users.

The server responds with a 200 OK indicating to the client that it should initiate the three RTP UDP streams and the single RTCP TCP connection to the server.

```
RTSP/1.0 200 OK
          CSeq: 102
```

When the client wants to stop or pause the session, it sends a TEARDOWN or PAUSE method to the server. Figure 9-4 illustrates the finite state machine (FSM) that RTSP uses to transition between *idle*, *ready*, and *playing/recording*.

Figure 9-4 *RTSP State Diagram*

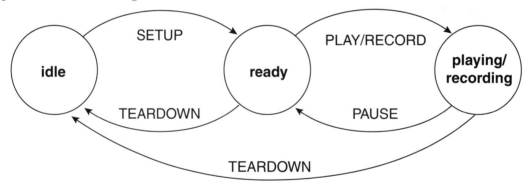

NOTE RTSP supports cache control mechanisms in a similar manner to HTTP.

If your clients are behind a Cisco PIX firewall performing NAT, you can use the PIX application recognition (fixup) feature to rewrite private NAT addresses in the payload with registered public IP addresses. To enable RTSP fixup, use the command **fixup protocol rtsp**. If instead your Cisco IOS router is performing NAT, you can use NBAR to recognize/rewrite RTSP. To enable NAT RTSP support on your router, use the **ip nat service rtsp port** global configuration command.

Fast-Forwarding and Rewinding a Stream with RTSP

RTSP clients can use the **Scale:** header in conjunction with the PLAY method to indicate the speed and direction that the server should stream the media to the client. As an example, if the client sets the header as **Scale: 2**, it will receive the stream at twice the normal rate. Also, if **Scale: 0.5**, the server sends the stream at half the rate. Negative **Scale:** values instruct the server to deliver the stream in reverse direction. That is, the client requests to rewind the stream.

The client also uses the **Range:** header in the PLAY method to seek through various parts of the stream. The **Range:** header takes three different timestamp types as parameters.

- **Normal Play Time (NPT)**—NPT starts at time zero and increases time as the session proceeds. NPT is the equivalent to the time you see on our VCR or DVD display while watching a movie. For example, 00:19:03.3 indicates the session has progressed for just over 19 minutes (19 minutes and 3.3 seconds).

- **Society of Motion Picture and Television Engineers (SMTE) relative time codes**— SMPTE relative time codes enable direct labeling of the 30 individual frames sampled every second during a video stream. For example, 00:19:02:20 indicates the 20th frame of second 2 in minute 19.

- **Absolute time**—Absolute time expresses the range values in Greenwich Mean Time (GMT), or Coordinated Universal Time (UTC) as specified by ISO 8601 timestamps. For example, 20061016T144523.45Z expresses the timestamp from October 16, 2006, at 14:45:23.45 GMT.

Table 9-6 gives samples of each timestamp type.

Table 9-6   *Samples of NPT, SMTE, and UTC Timecodes*

Timestamp Type	Sample Ranges	Description of Seek
NPT	Range: npt=00:07:33-	Start at 00:07:33; with no end-time specified.
	Range: npt=00:07:33-00:18:23	Start at 00:07:33; end at 00:18:23
SMPTE	Range: smpte=00:07:33:15-	Start at 00:07:33; with no end-time specified.
UTC	Range: 20061016T144523.45Z-20061016T145013.15Z	Start October 16, 2006, at 14:45:23.45 GMT; End October 16, 2006, at 14:50:13.15 GMT

Using Quality of Service and IP Multicast with Streaming Media

Streaming video normally produces constant data rates with frames arriving at constant intervals. However, as you learned in Chapter 6, "Ensuring Content Delivery with Quality of Service," networks can introduce packet loss, packet delay, and jitter between frame inter-arrival times. To reduce the effect of these network-related issues on your applications, you should use the following QoS features that you learned in Chapter 6, to prioritize your streaming media applications over less-critical applications.

- **Classifying and Marking Streaming Applications**—You can classify and mark your streaming content using the schemes you learned in Chapter 6. For example, you can use the RTP, RTCP, and RTSP protocol classification mechanism in NBAR to classify and mark streaming media packets. You can then apply CBWFQ to the marked packets to give priority to the streaming applications in your network.

- **Class-Based Weighted Fair Queuing (CBWFQ) with Low Latency Queuing (LLQ)**— You can configure a number of queues for your marked streaming protocols, such as RTSP and RTCP, and specify the overall bandwidth of each application. You also can allocate a priority queue (PQ) to your transport protocols, such as RTP and RTCP, to ensure that streaming content has priority over less-critical traffic.

- **Resource Reservation Protocol (RSVP) and Traffic Policing**—Your eyes are not able to notice frame discontinuity, or flicker, at rates greater than 30 frames/sec (fps). Indeed, movies that you watch in theaters display at 24 fps. Encoding video frames at rates between 10 and 30 fps can deliver data rates ranging from 40 kbps to over 1 Mbps per stream. If your streaming applications support RSVP, you can enable RSVP in your network to allow receivers to signal their desired resource requirements per streaming flow. Alternatively, you can enable traffic policing to give flows appropriate levels of bandwidth to avoid having other less critical applications flood your WAN links.

> **NOTE** To reduce the amount of bandwidth required by RTP on serial links of 2 Mbps or less, you can compress RTP headers using the **ip rtp header-compression** configuration command.

- **Layer 2 QoS**—To ensure that your Layer 2 network does not drop audio–video traffic, you can enable the Layer 2 QoS features you learned in Chapter 6.

Most streaming applications are uni-directional, so you can enable PIM-SM to scale the application on your network. However, if your application requires bidirectional communication, you can enable Bidir-PIM, as you learned in Chapter 5, "IP Multicast Content Delivery."

Summary

In this chapter, you learned how to package and deliver streaming media on your network. Packaging streaming media involves using third-party software, such as Windows Media Technologies, Apple, or RealNetworks, to insert your streaming flows into container files.

Users can request streaming content either live or on-demand. You can deliver the streaming content using RTP-UDP streams. To provide granular control over the streams, your users can use RTSP controls to initiate, pause, fast-forward, and rewind the streams.

The streams can be multicast to a large audience to scale the application in your network. You also can apply QoS in your network to ensure high quality picture and audio of the streaming content.

Review Questions

1.   What is progressive download?

2.   What are the three major streaming media vendors?

3.   What is the purpose of a streaming meta-file?

4.   What is the relationship between "streaming containers," "codecs," "FourCCs," and "RTP-UDP"?

5.   What is the difference between the way Apple/MPEG and Windows/Real structure their container files?

6.   Does RTP provide sequence numbers to reorder out-of-sequence packets?

7.   What is the difference between RTCP and RTSP?

8.   What port numbers does RTP use? What about RTSP, WMT, and Real?

9.   What is the purpose of streaming media session description files? How do they differ from meta-files?

Recommended Reading

Steve Mack, *Streaming Media Bible*, Wiley, 2002

RFC 2326, *Real Time Streaming Protocol (RTSP)*, IETF, http://www.ietf.org/rfc/rfc2326.txt, 1998

RFC 3550, *RTP: A Transport Protocol for Real-Time Applications*, IETF, http://www.ietf.org/rfc/rfc2326.txt, 2003

http://www.fourcc.org

Part V: Application Layer Services for Content, within the Network

Chapter Goals

You will learn about the following core content switching concepts in this chapter:

- **Content Switch Operational Modes**— You can configure your content switch in router or bridge mode.

- **Load Distribution Algorithms**— Round robin, least connections, source IP address hashing, and server load are available for distributing content requests across your servers.

- **Layer 5–7 Load Balancing**—Content switches can inspect requests at Layers 5–7, in order to intelligently select server farms to service client requests.

- **Health Checking**—To determine the availability of servers, content switches use in-band or out-of-band health checks.

- **Session Persistence**—To forward client requests to the same server for the duration of a session, content switches can use session persistence technologies.

- **Content Switch High Availability**—To forward client requests to the same server for the duration of a session, content switches can use session persistence technologies.

CHAPTER 10

Exploring Server Load Balancing

Server Load Balancing (SLB) involves three elements: real servers, server farms, and virtual servers. The primary element is the real server that contains the origin server content. Real servers are logical units and may not be associated with a physical server. For example, you may have multiple logical real servers on a single physical server. A server farm is a group or pool of real servers. You can create server farms by replicating a single real server to scale the performance and provide redundancy to your application. Each real server in a server farm responds to requests for the same content. Lastly, virtual servers are the client-facing element of an SLB environment. You can configure your virtual servers by specifying Layer 3 and 4 policies for your content, such as IP address or range of addresses, IP protocol, and TCP/User Datagram Protocol (UDP) ports. You can also configure Layer 5–7 policies to further narrow your virtual servers down to specific functionality, based on such criterion as HTTP headers and URLs.

The virtual server provides your clients with access to the server farm, as Figure 10-1 illustrates.

Figure 10-1 *A Typical Server Farm*

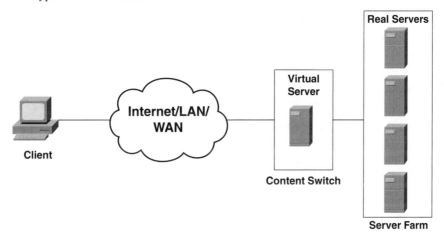

> **NOTE** Although Figure 10-1 shows a single server farm environment with standard client-to-server load balancing, Cisco supports hundreds of server farms with server-to-server load balancing.

Virtual servers contain the policies that content switches use to match content requests to make load balancing decisions. The content switch performs a virtual server lookup by matching the client's requests to the virtual server that contains the largest number of identical policies. For example, you may have Secure Socket Layer (SSL) available on your website. You would then have two virtual servers differentiated by TCP port, but otherwise the configuration would be the same. You would normally configure port 80 for your HTTP virtual server and port 443 for your SSL virtual server. Even your configured real servers would be the same, unless you are offloading your server's SSL processing to a dedicated device, which you will learn about in Chapter 11, "Switching Secured Content." Example 10-1 shows how you can configure a single server farm and two virtual servers on the Cisco Content Services Switch (CSS).

> **NOTE** The terms "real server," "server farm," and "virtual servers" are Content Switching Module (CSM)-specific terms. In contrast, "services" and "content rules" are used for CSS-specific explanations—there is no CSS-equivalent terminology for server farms. Because the CSS and CSM share the majority of the same *concepts*, this chapter will use the CSM-specific terms when referring to concepts from either product, primarily because of the additional term for server farms. When referring to the *configuration*, this chapter will refer to the product-specific terminology (that is, services and content rules for CSS configuration and real servers, virtual servers, and server farms for CSM configuration).

Example 10-1 *Configuring Two Virtual Servers Using a Single Server Farm on a CSS*

```
service web01
 ip address 209.165.200.225
service web02
 ip address 209.165.200.226

content http-vip
 vip address 209.165.201.1
 protocol tcp
 port 80
 add service web01
 add service web02

content ssl-vip
 vip address 209.165.201.1
 protocol tcp
 port 443
 add service web01
 add service web02
```

Clients send requests to the virtual IP address (VIP) of the virtual server, which is the client-facing IP address for the server farm, resident on the content switch. For most organizations, the VIP of a site is normally a registered IP address available in the public Domain Name System (DNS) for client use. However, you can also use a private IP address for internal or public applications. If you use a private IP address for public applications, you will require a firewall to source-Network Address Translation (NAT) to a publicly routable IP address. When the content switch receives the client request, it performs a virtual server lookup. The content switch load balances the request to a real server within the server farm associated with the resultant virtual server. The content switch forwards the request to the real server in one of two modes:

- **Destination-NAT or directed mode forwarding**—With destination-NAT mode forwarding, the content switch modifies the packet's destination MAC address and IP address before forwarding the packet to the real server. The content switch rewrites the request's destination IP address (that is, the VIP) and the MAC to the selected real server's IP address and MAC address, respectively. The content switch rewrites the real server's response back to the VIP before sending it to the requesting client.

  > **NOTE**   You can perform source-NAT on the client IP address when your real servers require originating connections to virtual servers, as you will learn in the section "Content Switch Operational Modes."

- **Dispatch-mode forwarding**—In dispatch-mode, the content switch only rewrites the destination MAC address before forwarding the request to the real server—the content switch preserves the original destination IP address. Dispatch-mode is useful in server acceleration environments, such as SSL offloading and firewall load balancing, in which you require the original destination IP address to apply security policies against and for accounting purposes. You will learn about server acceleration in Chapter 11 and Chapter 13, "Delivering Cached and Streaming Media."

To send an application request to the content switch, the client sends a TCP SYN segment to the content switch. When the content switch receives the TCP SYN segment, it performs a virtual server lookup, by matching the Layer 3 and 4 fields in the segment to policies that you configure for your virtual servers. If you configure your virtual server with additional Layer 5–7 policies, such as URL file extensions, cookies, and HTTP headers, the content switch proxies the TCP connection to the client in order to inspect the client's application request. Otherwise, the content switch simply selects a real server, translates the destination address to that of the real server, and forwards the TCP SYN request to the real server. When the real server receives the request, it sends a TCP SYN-ACK response back through the content switch. The content switch translates the source address back to the virtual server address, and forwards the TCP SYN-ACK to the client directly. The client's TCP ACK completes the TCP three-way handshake with the real server.

> **NOTE** Because the content switch rewrites the destination IP address in the IP packet, it must recalculate the IP checksum, encompassing the header of the IP packet.

For Layer 5–7 policies, the content switch must complete the TCP connection with the client on behalf of the real server—the content switch performs delayed binding to inspect the application request. The content switch can then match content in the application request to the Layer 5–7 policies of your virtual servers. For example, you can configure a virtual server policy to match all HTTP GET requests containing the string "*.jpg" and another virtual server policy to match requests containing the string "*.html." Based on the matched policies, the content switch selects a real server from the configured server farm to forward the request to. Figure 10-2 illustrates how delayed binding works.

Figure 10-2 *Content Switch Delayed Binding*

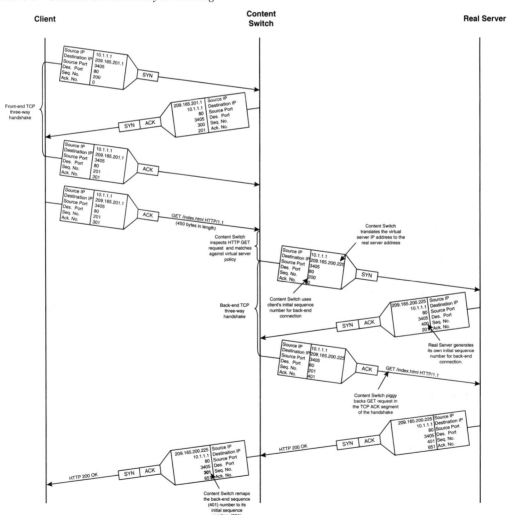

The content switch generates an initial sequence number for the front-end TCP connection. As a result, the content switch is responsible for sequence number remapping. Remapping involves the content switch rewriting the sequence number generated by the real server throughout the TCP flow, as Figure 10-2 illustrates. Because the content switch rewrites the sequence numbers in the TCP segment, it must also recalculate the TCP checksum, to encompass the entire TCP segment.

The benefits of delayed binding are twofold. The first benefit is ensuring that clients open valid TCP connections before the content switch establishes connections to back-end real servers. This is beneficial because the CSS can detect and drop denial-of-service (DoS) attack TCP SYN segments before forwarding them to real servers. The second benefit is that the content switches can inspect the payload of the client's request in order to make intelligent Layer 5–7 decisions. For example, you can configure your content switch to inspect HTTP headers or URLs and forward requests to real servers based on that information.

Content switches can also process pipelined HTTP requests. Recall from Chapter 8, "Exploring the Application Layer," that, with persistent HTTP connections, clients send multiple requests over the same TCP connection. With HTTP pipelining, the client does not wait for the HTTP responses from the server before sending additional requests. Persistence and pipelining avoid overhead that is associated with establishing multiple TCP connections, and the delay associated with waiting for server responses for each HTTP request. Figure 10-3 shows how a content switch forwards two requests to the same real server, using delayed binding.

> **NOTE**   Delayed binding is not required for forwarding pipelined persistent requests, unless you configure Layer 5–7 policies for the virtual server.

Alternatively, content switches can distribute non-pipelined persistent requests across real servers by extracting each HTTP request from within the persistent HTTP session. The server can then send the requests to individual back-end real servers. Figure 10-4 illustrates HTTP rebalancing multiple persistent requests with HTTP 1.1.

> **NOTE**   If a request spans multiple packets, the CSS buffers a configurable number of packets, with the **spanning-packets** command on the CSS, before making a load-balancing decision.

Figure 10-3 *Forwarding Pipelined Persistent Requests to a Single Real Server*

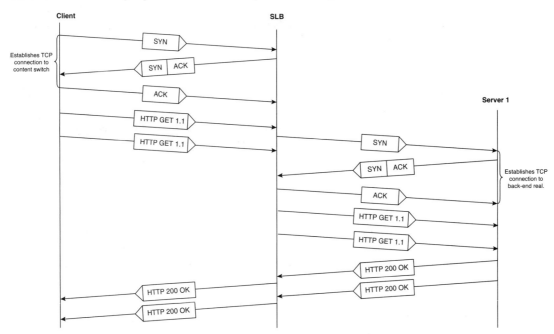

> **NOTE** Rebalancing HTTP requests to different servers is of particular interest in caching
> environments where even distribution of files across a pool of caches is desirable. You will learn
> about cache load-balancing in Chapter 13.

By default, the CSS distributes all subsequent GET requests within an HTTP persistent TCP
connection to the originally selected real server (unless the CSS matches a subsequent request
with a different virtual server that does not contain the originally selected real server). However,
you can configure your CSS to rebalance back-end real server connections, using the content rule
configuration command

    no persistence

By issuing this command, when the CSS receives a new GET request for the current real server,
the CSS sends a TCP RST to the current real server and an HTTP 302 Object Moved to the client
to remap the connection to another real server. The client generates the GET request again, which
the CSS uses to select another back-end real server for the request. As Figure 10-4 illustrates, to
enable the CSS to instead remap the back-end connection to a new real server automatically, you
can use the content rule configuration command

    persistence reset remap

With this command, the CSS sends a TCP RST to the current real server, establishes a TCP
connection to the new real server, and sends the GET request to the new real server.

Figure 10-4 *Rebalancing Multiple Persistent Requests to Different Servers*

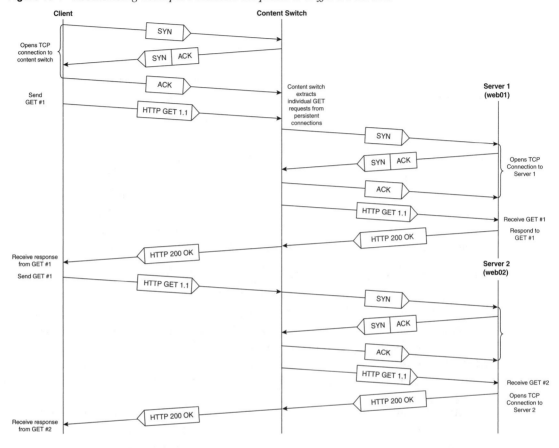

To revert back to HTTP 302 redirection, you can manually use the command

```
persistence reset redirect
```

The CSM does not support HTTP 302 redirection. However, you can enable your CSM to rebalance back-end real server connections automatically using the virtual server configuration command:

```
persistent rebalance
```

Exploring Your Server Load-Balancing Devices

Cisco developed the Local Director, its first standalone load-balancing appliance, in the mid-1990s. Toward the late1990s, Cisco embedded the IOS SLB feature within the Cisco IOS for basic SLB functionality. Cisco retired the Local Director in 2001 and concerted content switching development efforts on the more powerful CSS and CSM products. Although SLB has been available in Cisco IOS since the late 1990s, and you can still use it for very small data center environments, the CSS and CSM provide you with a superior hardware platform and robust SLB feature support.

Unique to the CSS and CSM is their customized hardware for connection processing, packet forwarding, and control processing.

- **Connection processing hardware**—Content switches use specific connection processing hardware for TCP/UDP connection maintenance, virtual server lookups, delayed binding, Layer 5–7 load-balancing decision making, in-band health checking, and the required packet transforms (that is, sequence number remapping or NAT translations or both). The connection processor processes persistent HTTP 1.1 requests, in order to perform HTTP request rebalancing.

- **Packet forwarding hardware**—The packet forwarding hardware is responsible for forwarding packets that are part of existing TCP/UDP connections, enabling packets to bypass the connection processor, thus effectively streamlining packet flow. The forwarding hardware can also perform packet transforms on packets of existing connections, if the connection processor instructs it to do so. The packet forwarding hardware is highly optimized, because it processes many more packets than the connection processing hardware.

> **NOTE**   The connection processing and packet forwarding hardware are not necessarily separate hardware but are together logically called the *datapath* because they carry out operations on live data traffic. The connection processing hardware is sometimes called the *session processing path*, and the packet forwarding path is also called the *fastpath*. For complex operations, such as HTTP 1.1 persistent connections and Layer 5–7 load balancing, these two paths may work together.

- **Control processing hardware**—In addition to the connection and forwarding hardware, the CSS and CSM have special control processing hardware. The control processor handles all control traffic, such as ARP, HSRP, and ICMP, to the VIPs and operational management functions, such as the command line, web, XML, Dynamic Feedback Protocol (DFP), and SNMP interfaces. The control processor is also responsible for the systems management functions, including management of configuration files, system images, booting, and diagnostics. The control processor manages the status of real and virtual servers and actively takes servers on- and offline, when necessary. To do so, the control processor issues out-of-band health checks and inspects the responses from the real servers, resulting in a high level of administrative overhead. The control processor is a shared component of the CSM architecture—the other two hardware components access the control processor through a shared hardware bus, as you will learn later in this chapter.

> **NOTE**   The control processing hardware is also called the *slowpath*.

Content Services Switch

The CSS 11500 series is a standalone modular appliance, designed for any size of data center environment. The following module types make up the architecture of the CSS:

- **Switch Control Modules (SCM)**—The SCM is the central management module containing the control processor. The SCM comes with 2-Gigabit Ethernet ports supporting small-form factor pluggable gigabit interface converters (SFP GBICs), a console port, and Ethernet port for management. The SCM also has two PCMCIA slots that each support 256-MB flash memory disks or 512-MB hard disks.

- **Input/Output (I/O) modules**—I/O modules are available in the following port densities:

  — Two-port Gigabit Ethernet

  — Sixteen-port Fast Ethernet

  — Eight-port Fast Ethernet

- **Session Acceleration Modules (SAM)**—The SAM offers an increase in performance, without the cost of additional ports. The SAM provides the same flow setup mechanism as the other modules.

- **SSL processing modules**—The SSL module adds hardware-based encryption capabilities for e-commerce applications. The SSL module delivers 1000 SSL transactions per second and 250 Mbps of RC4 symmetric key bulk data encryption. The SSL module also offers accelerated Rivest, Shamir, and Adelman (RSA) public key encryption for establishing SSL sessions.

Each of the modules in the preceding list includes a network processor (NP), which is responsible for the forwarding processing. Additionally, the NP interfaces the module into the switch fabric. Each module also contains a classification engine (CE) for accelerating access control list (ACL) processing and address resolution protocol (ARP) table lookups.

The NP contains four 200-MHz CPUs, each with its own direct access to the CE, thereby substantially decreasing the load on NP resources so that it can concentrate more on packet forwarding. The forwarding processors within the NP use the DRAM memory for packet buffering. The session processor (SP) is responsible for the connection processing of the switch and control processing on the SCM.

The beauty of this architecture is that it is scalable, enabling an increase in overall performance with the addition of any type of module to the chassis. In other words, the NP, SP, and CE within any module can process their own packets, or the packets of any other module. The SAM module always processes packets of other modules, because it does not have any I/O interfaces of its own. Figure 10-5 illustrates the CSS switching architecture.

The CSS I/O modules distribute incoming flows evenly across the available modules. For example, if three clients initiate flows from the I/O module in Figure 10-5, the I/O module switches one request to the SCM and another to the SAM, and processes one itself.

CSS Packet Flow

Consider an example in which a client, located upstream via the Fast Ethernet I/O module B in Figure 10-6, issues a single HTTP request for the virtual server configured previously in Example 10-1. The real servers for this virtual server are reachable via Fast Ethernet ports on a different module within the CSS chassis (I/O module A). Figure 10-6 illustrates the flow of this packet through the CSS.

Figure 10-5 *The CSS Switching Architecture*

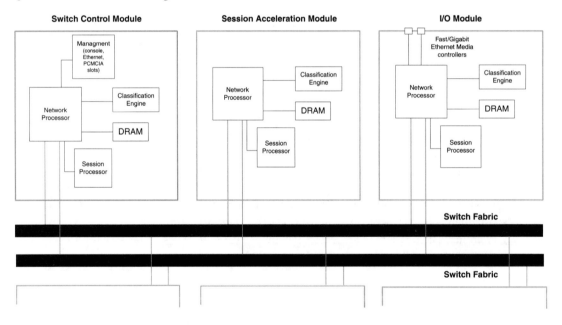

Figure 10-6   *CSS Packet Flow*

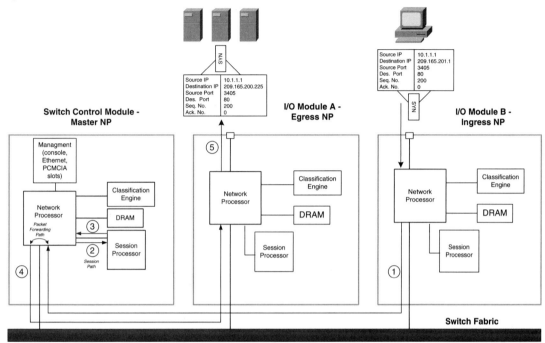

The packet takes the following steps through the CSS:

Step 1   The NP in I/O module B receives the TCP SYN segment from the upstream client and arbitrarily selects the SCM as the master NP to switch the request to.

Step 2   The master NP determines that the packet is for a new connection and performs an ARP and ACL lookup in the CE. The NP forwards the packet and the results of the ARP and ACL lookups to the master SP. The master SP then performs a virtual server lookup. The SP finds a matching virtual server, based on Layer 3–4 rules. The master SP then selects the real server to forward the request to, NATs the packet to the real server IP address, and recalculates the packet checksum.

> **NOTE**   If the CSS in this example were to use a virtual server configured with Layer 5–7 policies, the master SP would perform delayed binding with the client before continuing to step 3.

Step 3   The master SP informs the master NP of the NAT requirements for subsequent packets of the flow, thereby enabling the rest of the flow to bypass the connection processing function of the SP. The NP also stores the return path at this step, enabling return packets to be NATed in the reverse direction.

> **NOTE**   Steps 2 and 3 make up the session path that packets take for new connections. Packets of existing connections skip steps 2 and 3. Instead, they follow the packet forwarding path, as shown in Figure 10-6.

Step 4   The master SP then selects which egress NP it will forward the packet to, based on MAC and ARP address tables maintained within the CE.

Step 5   The Egress NP then forwards the packet to the downstream server and stores connection information for the packet, such that it selects the same master NP for the return packets.

In the example in Figure 10-6, the single I/O distributes the total load between three modules. If you add another SAM to this CSS, the I/O module would further distribute the load across four modules.

CSS Models

The CSS chassis is available in three different form factors, each with the NP/SP/CE architecture described previously:

■   **CSS 11501** — As a fixed-configuration 1 rack-unit (RU) stackable switch, this switch includes an embedded SCM module and does not support the addition of other modules. It has a console port, an Ethernet management port, two PCMCIA slots for a combination of 256-MB flash or 512-MB hard disks, eight 10/100 ports, and one Small Form Factor Pluggable (SFP) GBIC Gigabit Ethernet port. The CSS 11501 does not support the modules, memory, and SFP GBICs as do the other modules. The CSS 11501 supports 6-Gbps aggregate throughput. Figure 10-7 shows the front of a CSS 11501 chassis.

Figure 10-7   *The CSS 11501 Content Switch*

- **CSS 11501 with SSL termination**—The same specifications as the CSS 11501 but includes embedded SSL termination. The CSS 11501 with SSL supports 1000 SSL transactions per second and 250 Mbps of RC4 symmetric key bulk data encryption. The SSL module also supports data GZIP/deflate compression.

- **CSS 11503**—Supports one SCM, and any two of the I/O, SAM or SSL modules. Only a single switch fabric and power supply is available in the CSS 11503. Each module has 1.6 Gbps connectivity to the switch fabric, resulting in 10 Gbps aggregate throughput. Figure 10-8 shows the front of a CSS 11503 chassis.

Figure 10-8 *The CSS 11503 Content Switch*

- **CSS 11506**—Supports two SCMs (with one in standby mode) and any five (four, if you are using a standby SCM) of the I/O, SAM, or SSL modules. Like the CSS 11503, each module has 1.6 Gbps connectivity but includes dual switch fabrics, resulting in 20 Gbps aggregate throughput. The CSS 11506 (see Figure 10-9) supports an additional power supply.

Figure 10-9 *The CSS 11506 Content Switch*

Table 10-1 gives the specifications for these content switches.

Table 10-1   *Cisco CSS Series Content Switch Specifications*

	Cisco CSS 11501	Cisco CSS 11503	Cisco CSS 11506
# of Available Modules	0 (Fixed Configuration)	3	6
Default Hardware	Switch Control with 8 10/100 Ethernet and 1 Gigabit Ethernet (GBIC) Port	Switch Control Module with 2 Gigabit Ethernet (GBIC) Ports	Switch Control Module with 2 Gigabit Ethernet (GBIC) Ports
Maximum 2-port Gigabit Ethernet I/O Module	-	2	5
16-port 10/100 Ethernet I/O	-	2	5
8-port 10/100 Ethernet I/O	-	2	5
SSL Modules	-	2	4
Session Accelerator Modules	-	2	5
Maximum Gigabit Ethernet Ports	1	6 (includes 2 on the SCM)	12 (includes 2 on the SCM)
Maximum 10/100 Ethernet Ports	8	32	80
SSL Termination Available?	Yes, as a separate appliance	Yes	Yes
Redundancy Features	· Active-active Layer 5 Adaptive Session Redundancy (ASR) · VIP redundancy	· Active-active Layer 5 Adaptive Session Redundancy · VIP redundancy	· Active-active Layer 5 Adaptive Session Redundancy · VIP redundancy · Active-standby SCM · Redundant switch fabric module · Redundant power supplies
Height	1.75 in. (1 rack unit)	3.5 in. (2 rack units)	8.75 in. (5 rack units)
Bandwidth Aggregate	6 Gbps	20 Gbps	40 Gbps
Storage Options	512-MB hard disk or 256-MB flash memory disk	512-MB hard disk or 256-MB flash memory disk	512-MB hard disk or 256-MB flash memory disk
Power	Integrated AC	Integrated AC or DC	Up to 3 AC or 3 DC

Content Switching Module

The Content Switching Module (CSM) is an integrated services module that you can install in your Catalyst 6500 series switch or Cisco 7600 Series Internet routers. Figure 10-10 shows the CSM.

Figure 10-10 *The Content Switching Module*

The CSM supports four 1-Gigabit connections into the switching fabric, which the CSM multiplexes into the processing fabric. The CSM has a pipeline NP architecture in which packets traverse a series of stages that apply logic or modifications to the packet. Figure 10-11 illustrates the CSM pipelined architecture.

Figure 10-11 *CSM Pipelined Architecture*

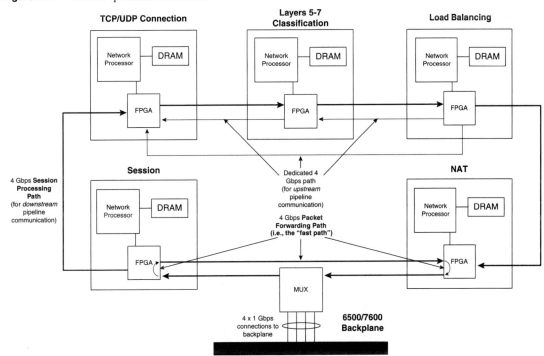

> **NOTE** Do not confuse HTTP "pipelining," which you learned about previously, with the
> CSM "pipeplined" architecture—they refer to different concepts.

Each stage contains a Field Programmable Gate Array (FPGA), 128 MB of DRAM memory, and
an NP. Each NP has an Intel IXP 1200 processor containing six RISC microengines (uE) and a
RISC core, as Figure 10-12 illustrates. The seven IXP subprocessors can operate in parallel on
packets from different flows. A particular IXP provides 1 billion operations per second, giving the
CSM an aggregate 5 billion operations per second across the five stages of the pipeline. The
FPGAs are the physical connection points between each stage of the architecture, providing an
addressable communications mechanism between the NPs. For example, if one stage needs to
communicate with another in the pipeline, the intermediary FPGAs simply forward the packet to
the next FPGA until the packet reaches the requested stage.

Figure 10-12 *Network Processor Architecture*

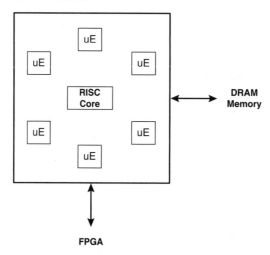

> **NOTE** You can view the use of the CSM IXPs using CiscoView Device Manager for the
> CSM. You can also see the statistics for individual IXPs using the command **show module csm**
> *mod-num* **tech-support processor** *IXP-num* command. You can also use the **show module csm**
> *mod-num* **tech-support fpga** command to display the FPGA statistics.

The NPs within each stage also maintain a connection to a shared PCI bus. The control processor provides a dedicated general-purpose PowerPC CPU for performing out-of-band health checking and configuration management to avoid increases in administrative processing from affecting the session or forwarding paths. Additionally, because the control processor is a general-purpose CPU, its functions are performed in software, as opposed to in hardware that uses IXPs, and the functions are therefore much more flexible (albeit slower) when performing the control functions. Figure 10-13 illustrates the control processor's placement in the CSM.

Figure 10-13 *The Shared PCI Bus for Control Processing*

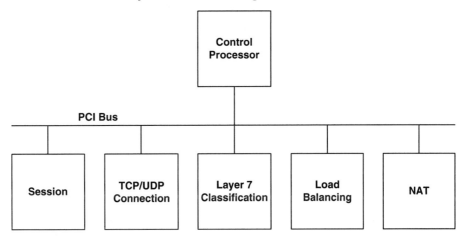

The CSM pipeline operates in a manner that is similar to an automobile assembly-line system. While some algorithms are being computed at one stage of a data pipeline, others are computed at a later stage of the same pipeline.

When a packet arrives at the CSM, the session stage is the first to process the packet, as you saw previously in Figure 10-11. The session stage determines whether the packet is part of an existing connection or a modification of an existing connection, such as an HTTP pipelined GET request. If it is part of an existing connection, the session stage sends the packet directly to the NAT stage through the packet forwarding path, completely bypassing the session forwarding path. Otherwise, the session stage forwards the packet through the session forwarding path to the TCP/UDP connection stage.

The TCP/UDP connection stage maintains the connection information for the flow, ranging from creating and removing entries from its connection state table, and performing delayed binding on flows matching Layer 5–7 policies, to performing virtual server lookups. For flows matching Layer 5–7 policies, the TCP stage passes the packet and its virtual server lookup results to the Layer 5–7 classification stage. The Layer 5–7 stage parses the content of the packet for cookies or URLs, using regular expressions that you configure on the CSM, and passes the packet and its results to the load-balancing stage.

For Layer 3 and 4 policies, the TCP/UDP stage bypasses the Layer 5–7 stage by addressing the FPGA of the load-balancing stage instead. That is, the load-balancing stage can receive packets from either the TCP connection or Layer 5–7 stages. The load-balancing stage applies the load-balancing algorithm, persistence policy, and fail-over mechanism associated with the virtual server you configured for the flow. For flows that require modification to the TCP connection entry during the load balancing or Layer 5–7 inspection process, both the load balancing or Layer 5–7 stages may communicate directly with the TCP stage over a secondary 4 Gbps communication path, as Figure 10-11 illustrates. The load-balancing stage then passes the packet and results to the NAT stage. The NAT stage is the final stage in the pipeline and is responsible for performing the packet transforms, such as NAT and sequence number remapping, and forwarding the packets to the MUX for transmission to the real servers or clients.

Content Switch Operational Modes

This section provides a conceptualization of the different content switching modes to enable you to understand the underlying configuration that is explained later in this chapter. You can either configure your content switch as one-armed or inline.

In one-armed mode, the content switch receives requests from clients, and forwards these requests to real servers on a single VLAN. In turn, the content switch receives the responses from real servers, and forwards these responses to the clients on the same VLAN. You require configuring Policy-Based routing (PBR) on an IOS router or NAT on a firewall to direct client requests to the VIPs configured on the content switch in one-armed mode. Figure 10-14 illustrates a content switch in one-armed mode.

Figure 10-14 *One-Armed Content Switching*

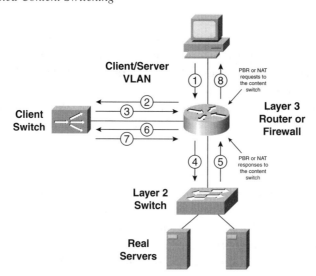

To get started with your inline mode configuration, there are two VLANs that you must include when designing your server farms:

- **Client VLAN**—Client VLANs contain the client-facing virtual servers.

- **Server VLAN**—Server VLANs contain the server farms that you want to load balance.

> **NOTE**   You can also put clients and servers that you do not intend to load balance in your client VLAN. There they can access the virtual servers themselves, if necessary.

As an example, a client directly behind the Layer 3 router in Figure 10-15 sends a TCP SYN request to the virtual server. When the router receives an Ethernet frame for the virtual server, it performs a routing table lookup and determines that the destination address of the packet is reachable via its directly connected interface. Next, the router determines the MAC address of the virtual IP address (VIP) by sending an ARP request on the client VLAN. The content switch responds with its Ethernet interface MAC address. In fact, all virtual servers that you configure on the content switch in the client VLAN 10 resolve to the MAC address of the content switch's client VLAN Ethernet interface. The Layer 3 router then forwards the packet to the content switch's MAC address at Layer 2. The content switch receives the TCP SYN and, in this example, performs delayed binding by responding to the client with a TCP SYN/ACK response. When the handshake completes, the content switch chooses the real server with IP address 10.1.10.100 for the request. The content switch performs the TCP three-way handshake and bridges the HTTP GET request to the real server. Figure 10-15 illustrates this flow.

Figure 10-15   *Tracing a Flow in Content Switching*

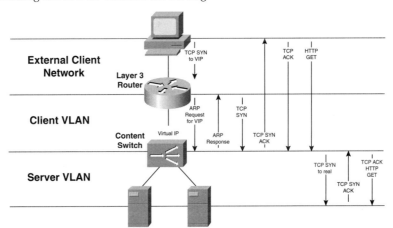

You can configure your content switches to behave as either routers or bridges.

Bridge-Mode Content Switching

To configure your CSS in bridge mode, you simply configure your client and server VLANs with the same VLAN number. You must also configure the client and server subnets as the same. Figure 10-16 illustrates a CSS in bridge mode.

Figure 10-16 *A CSS in Bridge Mode*

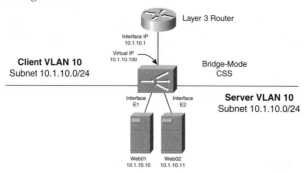

NOTE Because the CSS handles bridged packets in software, unless absolutely necessary, you should avoid configuring your CSS in bridge mode. Instead, you should configure your CSS in router mode, where packets are processed in hardware. Alternatively, the CSM handles both bridge- and router-mode traffic in hardware.

To configure your CSS for bridge mode, you can use the configuration in Example 10-2. You must configure the default gateway of your servers as the IP address of the Layer 3 router (10.1.10.1).

Example 10-2 *Bridge-Mode CSS Configuration*

```
!************************** INTERFACE ************************
interface e1
  bridge vlan 10

interface e2
  bridge vlan 10

interface e3
  bridge vlan 10

!************************** SERVICE ************************
circuit VLAN 10
ip address 10.1.10.1 255.255.255.0
service web01
 ip address 10.1.10.10
 active

service web02
 ip address 10.1.10.11
 active
```

Example 10-2 *Bridge-Mode CSS Configuration (Continued)*

```
!*************************** OWNER ***************************
owner cisco
 content http-vip
  vip address 10.1.10.100
  protocol tcp
  port 80
  add service web01
  add service web02
  active
```

> **NOTE**   In Example 10-2, the owner section specifies your virtual servers (with the **content** command). The owner concept comes from the managed hosting industry where an ASP manages the content switch on behalf of multiple clients.

You can also configure the CSS using the XML interface, as Example 10-3 illustrates. You must use HTTP to publish the XML configuration to the CSM. Some network management stations offer you the ability to post XML to network devices—refer to your specific network management station documentation for more details.

Example 10-3 *Bridge-Mode CSS XML Configuration*

```
<?xml version="1.0"?>
<config>

  <action>interface e1 </action>
  <action>bridge vlan 10 </action>

  <action>interface e2 </action>
  <action>bridge vlan 20 </action>

  <action>interface e3 </action>
  <action>bridge vlan 20 </action>

  <action>circuit VLAN0 </action>
  <action>ip address 10.1.10.1/24 </action>

  <service name="web01">
    <ipaddress>10.1.10.10</ipaddress>
    <action>active</action>
  </service>

  <service name="web02">
    <ipaddress>10.1.10.11</ipaddress>
```

continues

Example 10-3 *Bridge-Mode CSS XML Configuration (Continued)*

```
      <action>active</action>
   </service>

   <owner name="cisco">
     <content name="http-vip">
        <vip_address>10.1.10.100</vip_address>
        <protocol>tcp</protocol>
        <port>80</port>
        <add_service>web01</add_service>
        <add_service>web02</add_service>
        <action>active</action>
     </content>
   </owner>
</config>
```

To configure your CSM in bridge mode, you configure the server VLAN in the same IP subnet as the client VLAN, but you configure them with different VLANs. That is, you separate them at Layer 2 with VLANs, but not at Layer 3 with IP subnets. The CSM bridges IP traffic between the two VLANs, creating a single Layer 3 subnet. Figure 10-17 illustrates a CSM in bridge mode. Notice that the highlighted IP addresses in the configuration are the same—identical IP addresses on the server and client VLANS make the CSM work in bridge mode.

Figure 10-17 *CSM Bridge-Mode Configuration*

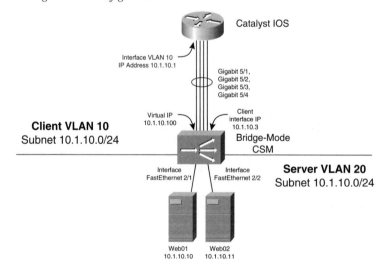

To configure your CSM for bridge mode, you can use the configuration in Example 10-4.

Example 10-4 *Bridge-Mode CSM Configuration*

```
interface vlan 10
 ip address 10.1.10.1

interface fastethernet 2/1
 switchport vlan 20

interface fastethernet 2/2
 switchport vlan 20

module ContentSwitchingModule 5

vlan 10 client
  ip address 10.1.10.2 255.255.255.0
  gateway 10.1.10.1

vlan 20 server
  ip address 10.1.10.2 255.255.255.0

serverfarm webfarm
 nat server
 no nat client
 real 10.1.10.10
  inservice
 real 10.1.10.11
  inservice

vserver webvip
 virtual 10.1.10.100 tcp www
 serverfarm webfarm
 persistent rebalance
 inservice
```

To configure your CSM for bridge mode using the CSM XML interface, you can use the configuration in Example 10-5. Refer to your CSM product documentation for the full CSM DTD that contains all the available XML tags for our CSM configuration. Notice that, unlike with the CSS, you cannot configure the MSFC interfaces and VLANs using XML.

Example 10-5 *Bridge-Mode CSM XML Configuration*

```
<?xml version="1.0"?>
<csm_module slot="5">
  <vlan id="10" type="client">
    <vlan_address ipaddress="10.1.10.2" ipmask="255.255.255.0"/>
    <gateway ipaddress="10.1.10.1"/>
```

continues

Example 10-5 *Bridge-Mode CSM XML Configuration (Continued)*

```
    </vlan>
    <vlan id="20" type="server">
      <vlan_address ipaddress="10.1.20.2" ipmask="255.255.255.0"/>
    </vlan>

    <serverfarm name="webfarm">
      <server_nat id="server"/>
      <server_nat id="client" sense="no"/>
      <predictor value="leastconns"/>
      <real_server ipaddress="10.1.10.10">
        <inservice sense="yes"/>
      </real_server>
      <real_server ipaddress="10.1.10.11">
        <inservice sense="yes"/>
      </real_server>
    </serverfarm>

    <vserver name="webvip">
      <virtual ipaddress="10.1.10.100" protocol="tcp" port="80"/>
      <serverfarm_ref name="webfarm"/>
      <inservice sense="yes"/>
    </vserver>
</csm_module>
```

Although you configure the CSM using the Catalyst 6500 or Cisco 7600 series command line and XML, Figure 10-17 illustrates that you should consider the CSM as a logically separate device that is one "router-hop" away from the Catalyst 6500 Layer 3 switch or Cisco 7600 series router. If you do not use your Layer 3 Multilayer Switch Feature Card (MSFC) in your switch to route packets to/from the CSM, then it's much easier to see that the CSM is one router hop away from your next-hop external router.

> **NOTE** The CSM is not supported in the Catalyst 6500/7600 without an MSFC present.

You learned previously from Figure 10-11 that the CSM has four Gigabit Ethernet connections switch fabric. Because the CSM in Example 10-4 is installed in module 5, the interface between the CSM and the Catalyst switch is four Gigabit Ethernet interfaces with the names Gigabit 5/1–4. You can verify these interfaces using the **show interfaces** exec command.

In Example 10-4, the **interface vlan** command configures the logical interface of the Catalyst 6500 MSFC facing the CSM. You assign an IP address to the interface of the CSM that is facing the Catalyst switch using the **ip address** command in VLAN client/server configuration mode on the CSM. The VIPs that you configure on the CSM with the **virtual** command will appear in the

ARP tables of the MSFC that is connected to the CSM client VLAN interface. As such, the CSM responds to ARP requests from the MSFC for its VIPs, as you learned previously in Figure 10-15. The **switchport access** command assigns the server VLAN to the ports to which the real servers connect.

To configure the CSM, you must enter the **module ContentSwitchingModule** command, or **module csm** for short, specifying the module number into which you installed the CSM. The configuration that tells the CSM to enter bridge mode is identical IP addresses assigned to both CSM client and server VLANS, as highlighted in Example 10-4. You should use the **gateway** command in client VLAN configuration mode to configure the CSM to route its traffic to the client VLAN interface you configure in the Catalyst MSFC. If you want to bypass your MSFC, configure the gateway to point to the next-hop router or firewall toward your clients. As you learned previously, to enable the CSM to inspect HTTP 1.1 requests for persistent GET requests, use the **persistent rebalance** command.

CSM bridge-mode is useful when your non-load balanced servers are in the same subnet as your server farms. For example, in case you want to introduce the content switching to a subnet of servers without changing the IP address configuration on the servers, you can use bridge mode content switching. You simply need to add a new server VLAN, and allocate the existing VLAN as the client VLAN. This way, all devices in the client VLAN can directly access the virtual servers you configure in the client VLAN. Notice that Example 10-4 does not configure the client VLAN on any Catalyst ports, but in this case, you would leave your existing ports assigned with the client VLAN.

If real servers within your server farms require originating connections to other virtual servers whose real servers are in the same VLAN/Layer 2 broadcast domain, you must make concessions to avoid the origin server using an optimal route to the requesting server. This concept is also known as *triangulation*, because the traffic flows in a triangular shape, with the requesting server, content switch, and origin server as the corners of the triangle. For example, in Figure 10-18, the real server Web02 from within the server farm WebFarm requires sending mail to the virtual server MailVIP. The content switch receives the TCP SYN request for its VIP, and selects real server Mail01 to send the TCP SYN request to. The content switch then performs destination NAT on the TCP SYN packet to the real IP address of Mail01. However, Mail01 will recognize that the Web02 is on the same subnet as itself, based on its routing table entry for 10.1.10.0/24, and will therefore send an ARP request directly for the MAC address of Web02. When the SYN/ACK packet from Mail01 reaches the Layer 2 switch, the Layer 2 switch forwards the SYN/ACK packet directly to Mail01. Because the Layer 2 switch has the switch port-to-MAC address mapping in its forwarding tables, the SYN/ACK never reaches the content switch. The content switch must receive the return SYN/ACK in order to perform DNAT, because Web01 is expecting the SYN/ACK response from the content switches' VIP, not Mail02's real server IP address. When Web01 receives the SYN/ACK, it terminates its connection by not sending its TCP ACK to complete the connection.

Figure 10-18 *Server Farms Accessing Each Other in Bridge Mode*

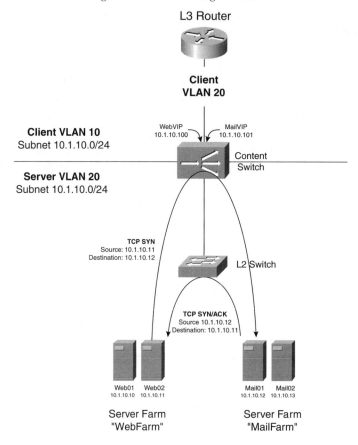

You can avoid bypassing your content switch at Layer 2 in four ways, and thus force return packets back through the content switch.

- **CSS Direct Cabling**—If you directly cable your real servers to your CSS, then the CSS DNATs the return TCP SYN-ACK segment with the VIP address before switching the return TCP SYN-ACK segment to the requesting client.

- **Enable router-mode**—By creating separate subnets in addition to VLANs, the default gateway of the real servers of MailFarm in Figure 10-18 routes all return traffic back through the content switch.

- **Use source-NAT (SNAT)**—If you SNAT the IP address of Web01 in Figure 10-18 on the content switch, then the content switch also changes the MAC address of the frame to its own MAC address. Therefore, Mail01's ARP entry for Web01 now points to the content switch. To enable source NAT on the CSM, first create a NAT pool using the command:

```
natpool pool-name beginning-address ending-address netmask mask
```

You then assign this pool to the server farm with the **nat client** *pool-name* virtual server command. For example, the following command creates a pool to SNAT server-originated connections:

```
natpool src-nat-pool 10.1.10.100 10.1.10.100 netmask 255.255.255.255
```

To configure your CSS to NAT real servers that originate connections, you can use a source group as follows:

```
group web_group
  vip address 10.1.10.100
  add service web01
  add service web02
```

Source groups NAT the source IP address of the real server's outgoing packets to the VIP you configure for the group. If you want to instead NAT incoming requests to the mail farm, you can create a source group to NAT all incoming requests to the VIP of the source group. The following configuration triggers when clients (that is, one of the web servers) access the virtual server of the farm MailFarm. This also ensures that your mail servers respond through the CSS:

```
group mail_group
  vip address 10.1.10.101
  add destination service mail01
  add destination service mail02
```

Be aware that all requests to the server farm will be source NATed with this configuration, precluding the use of source IP address auditing on your real servers.

■ **Use manual host routes**—You can manually specify host routes on the real servers in MailFarm to the real servers of WebFarm, pointing to the content switch. By creating individual host routes (for example, "static 10.1.10.100/32 gw 10.1.10.11") for all your real servers in WebFarm on all your real servers in MailFarm, you force return traffic through the CSS. However, this solution is difficult to manage because every time you add a new server to WebFarm, you need to add a new host route entry to each of the real servers in WebFarm.

Router Mode Content Switching

In secure router mode, you separate the client and server VLANs at both Layer 2 and Layer 3, and the content switch can then route between the two VLANs. Figure 10-19 illustrates a CSS in router mode. You should configure the default gateway of the servers as the content switch in router mode.

Figure 10-19 *A CSS in Router Mode*

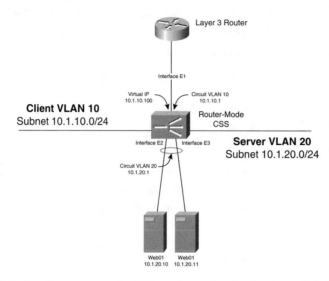

Example 10-6 gives the router-mode CSS configuration for the network in Figure 10-19. The circuit VLAN 20 interface is the default gateway of your real servers. The CSS routes between circuit VLAN 10 and VLAN 20.

Example 10-6 *Configuring Your CSS in Router Mode*

```
!*********************** INTERFACE ***********************
interface e1
  bridge vlan 10

interface e2
  bridge vlan 20

interface e3
  bridge vlan 20

!*********************** CIRCUIT ***********************
circuit VLAN10
  ip address 10.1.10.1 255.255.255.0

circuit VLAN20
  ip address 10.1.20.1 255.255.255.0

!*********************** SERVICE ***********************
service web01
 ip address 10.1.20.10
 active
service web02
```

Example 10-6 *Configuring Your CSS in Router Mode (Continued)*

```
ip address 10.1.20.11
active
!************************* OWNER *************************
owner cisco
 content http-vip
  vip address 10.1.10.100
  protocol tcp
  port 80
  add service web01
  add service web02
  active
```

To configure a CSM in router mode, you can use the configuration in Example 10-7, based on the design in Figure 10-20. The configuration that enables the CSM in router mode is the different IP address highlighted in Example 10-7. The server VLAN interface is the default gateway of your real servers. The CSM routes between server VLAN 10 and VLAN 20.

Figure 10-20 *A CSM in Router Mode*

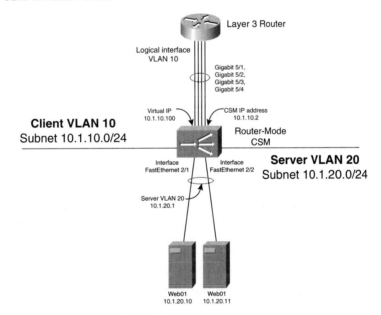

Example 10-7 *Configuring Your CSM in Router Mode*

```
interface vlan 10
 ip address 10.1.10.1

interface fastethernet 2/1
 switchport vlan 20

interface fastethernet 2/2
 switchport vlan 20

module csm 5

vlan 10 client
  ip address 10.1.10.2 255.255.255.0
  gateway 10.1.10.1

vlan 20 server
  ip address 10.1.20.2 255.255.255.0

serverfarm webfarm
 nat server
 no nat client
 real 10.1.20.10
  inservice
 real 10.1.20.11
  inservice

vserver webvip
 virtual 10.1.10.100 tcp www
 serverfarm webfarm
 persistent rebalance
 inservice
```

By default, the CSM denies access to your real servers, which is why the common term for CSM router mode is "secure" router mode. To enable direct access to your real servers, you can add the configuration in Example 10-8 to your MSFC (or next-hop router) and CSM. The static route informs the MSFC router to route all packets destined to the subnet of the real servers (10.1.20.0/ 24) to the CSM IP address (10.1.10.2). You need to create a new server farm and specify the load-balancing algorithm with the command **predictor forward**. This tells the CSM to route packets according to the CSM routing table. In this case, the real subnet is directly connected to the CSM, so the CSM forwards packets directly to the real servers. Your new virtual server matches the subnet of the real servers for packets of any protocol, as specified with the **any** keyword.

Example 10-8 *Configuring Direct Access to Real Servers*

```
ip route 10.1.20.0 255.255.255.0 10.1.10.2

module csm 5

serverfarm forward-route
  no nat server
  no nat client
  predictor forward

vserver direct-access
  virtual 10.1.20.0 255.255.255.0 any
  serverfarm forward-route
  inservice
```

Load-Distribution Algorithms

In order to distribute requests among real servers, you can use any of the following load-balancing algorithms:

- Round Robin

- Least Connections

- Server Load

- Hash Distribution

- Layer 5–7 Load Balancing

- Equal-Cost Multi-Path (ECMP) Router Load Balancing

Round Robin

Round robin is the most basic prediction algorithm. As requests arrive, the content switch forwards them blindly to its list of real servers starting with the real (short for real server) that you configured first, and ending with the last real you configured. With round robin, during one cycle, the content switch sends only one connection to each real server. If a server farm has N servers, a single cycle represents N connections. Alternately, with weighted round robin (WRR), each cycle provides multiple connections to each real. You can assign to each real a weight—those reals with a higher weight receive a larger number of the available connections. Now the sum of all the weights of the real servers represents the number of connections issued by the content switch during one round-robin cycle. With WRR, you can assign different weights to subgroups of real servers within a server farm. For example, the assigning of weights is beneficial if your server farm has numerous real servers running on a few different hardware platforms, with various memory capacities and CPU speeds. Table 10-2 illustrates a server farm consisting of four groups of six real servers in total that are assigned various weights. The total number of connections per cycle in this example is 27.

Table 10-2   *Sample WRR Weights*

Sub-Group	Server	Weight / Connections per Cycle
1	S1	8
1	S2	8
2	S3	2
2	S4	2
3	S5	4
4	S6	3
	Total	**27**

To configure WRR on your CSS, use the **balance weightedrr** command in your content rule. To specify the weights for the real, use the **weight** command in service configuration mode on the CSS. To configure least connections on your CSM, use the **predictor leastconns** command in your server farm configuration. You can configure the weights using the **weight** command in real configuration mode on the CSM.

You can manually weight your reals, as Table 10-2 illustrates, or you can automatically weight them using DFP. DFP requires that you install a software agent on your real servers. DFP agents are commercially available from third-party software vendors. If the installed agent recognizes that resources are low on its real server, it can send a DPF message to the content switch to modify its weight within the server farm. Your content switches act as DFP managers. The DFP manager actively probes the agents for status information, such as whether the real server is over- or underused. To configure your CSS as a DFP manager, use the following command in global configuration mode:

```
dfp ip_address {port} {key "secret" ¦ [des-encrypted encrypted_key ¦
   "encrypt_key"]} {timeout seconds} {retry count} {delay time} {max-agent-wt weight}
```

The *ip_address* value indicates the IP address of the DFP agent. To encrypt the information exchanged between the DFP agent and manager, you can enter an MD5 key as a quoted string, using the **key** parameter. Alternatively, you can perform DES encryption by providing an encrypted unquoted key (that has already been encrypted by the CSS) or quoted unencrypted key (that the CSS encrypts for you), using the **des-encrypted** parameter. The CSS encrypts your key, if necessary, before saving it to the running configuration. The **timeout** value indicates the inactivity period before the manager closes the connection to the agent. The **retries** value specifies the number of times the manager attempts to connect to the agent. The **delay** value indicates the length of time that the DFP manager waits between each retry. All time units are in seconds. The default TCP port for DFP is 14001. For example, you can use the following command to configure your CSS to connect to the real 10.1.10.11:

```
dfp 10.1.10.11 14001 key "cisco" timeout 300 retry 3 delay 15
```

To configure your CSM as a DFP manager, use the following commands in CSM configuration mode:

```
dfp [password password]
agent ip-address port [activity-timeout [retry-count [retry-interval]]]
```

For example, you can use the following commands to configure your CSM to connect to the real 10.1.10.11:

```
dfp password cisco
agent 10.1.10.11 14001 300 3 15
```

A drawback to round robin is that it can cause an uneven distribution of concurrent connections in volatile environments where real servers fail frequently. In the event of a real failure for a period of time, the remaining servers absorb the load. Even when the failed real comes back online, its concurrent connections may not catch up to the others, unless they also fail for the same duration and frequency. To provide an even distribution of connections to your reals in volatile environments, use the least-connections distribution algorithm.

Least Connections

With the least-connections algorithm, as the name suggests, the content switch forwards new requests to real servers with the fewest connections. The content switch maintains the concurrent number of existing connections to each real. When a real receives a new connection, the content switch increments the count. When clients or servers tear down connections, the content switch decrements the amount. The benefit of the least-connections load distribution mechanism is that it creates an even distribution of connections across your reals.

Real server weighting is also available for the least-connections predictor algorithm—those reals with higher relative weights receive a larger proportion of the available connections. The difference with least-connection weighting and the weighting mechanism in WRR is the way in which the content switch uses the weight to determine the distribution of connections. For example, say that you give the same weights to subgroups of reals within your server farm as given previously in Table 10-2. Consider a server farm consisting of N subgroups of reals, with N different weights 1, 2, ... N. During one cycle, the real subgroup with weight 1 would receive $1 / (1 + 2 + ... + N)$ connections, the real with weight 2 would receive $2 / (1 + 2 + ... + N)$ connections, and so forth. Table 10-3 illustrates how the least-connections algorithm distributes the load with the same weights as given previously with WRR in Table 10-2.

Table 10-3 *Sample Weighted Least-Connections Proportion Calculations*

Server	Weight	Percentage of Connections
S1	8	8/27 = 29%
S2	8	8/27 = 29%
S3	2	2/27 = 7%
S4	2	2/27 = 7%
S5	4	4/27 = 14%
S6	3	3/27 = 11%
Total	27	27/27 = 100%

To configure least connections on your CSS, use the **balance leastconn** command in your content rule. The CSS does not use the service weight with least connections—it assumes that every service has the same weight.

To configure least connections on your CSM, use the **predictor leastconns** command in your server farm configuration. You configure the weight in real configuration mode on the CSM, using the **weight** command. You can also use DFP as discussed previously to automatically adjust the weights of your real servers.

A drawback to least connections is that, when real servers fail or when you add a new real server to the farm, the CSS sets the real's connection count to zero. When they come online again, the content switch may overload them with connections to bring them up to the level of connections that are on the rest of the available reals in the server farm. To overcome the possibility of overloading a real when it comes back online, the CSM least-connections algorithm provides an inherent slow-start mechanism to avoid overloading real servers when they come online.

If you find that your servers tend to fail repeatedly when they come online on your CSS, you should consider using weight round robin—the CSS least connection algorithm does not provide connection slow start. When you add the real server to the farm, make sure that its weight is very low, and then gradually increase its weight manually to provide a similar function to slow start.

Both round robin and least connection load-balancing methods enable you to configure connection thresholds. Once you configure the connection thresholds, the content switch will take a real server out of the rotation, leaving existing connections intact. To define the maximum number of connections of a real server on the CSS, use the following command in service configuration mode:

```
max connections max-conns
```

Once the CSS reaches the maximum connections for the real, it will not issue connections until the connections drop below the maximum threshold.

To define the maximum number of connections of a real server on the CSM, use the following commands in real server configuration mode:

```
maxconns max-conns
minconns min-conns
```

Once the CSM reaches the maximum connections for the real, it will not issue connections until the connections drop below the minimum threshold.

Configuring Server Load

Your CSS can estimate the average load of a real server by calculating its average response times that are obtained from live traffic over a period of time. The content switch uses response times from both TCP connection setup and application layer requests/responses for live flows in its calculations. The content switch forwards requests to the real servers based on their load—the reals with a higher load receive fewer requests than those with a lower load.

The CSS implements a proprietary algorithm called Arrowpoint Content Awareness (ACA) to calculate the real-time server load based on the average response time over a period of time. ACA is not useful in small server farms (for example, server farms with only two or three reals). To enable ACA, use the **balance aca** content rule command. You can then configure either relative or absolute server load calculations.

> **NOTE**   As an alternative to ACA, you can also use the **load** *value* service configuration command to manually specify the load of a server. The CSS considers a real with a value of 254 configured with this command as out of service. This command bypasses the ACA load calculation and can be set using XML, SNMP, or the command line. To use the **load** command, you must first disable load reporting by using the **no load reporting** global configuration command.

Calculating Relative Load

With relative load calculations, the CSS computes the load for each real to a value between 2 and 254, where 255 is fully loaded and therefore ineligible for content requests. The CSS computes two different load numbers for each server—one for large files (greater than 15 KB) and one for small files (less than 15 KB)—and then averages the two.

The load step is a value that the content switch uses to determine whether a significant difference exists between the average response times of different servers. The greater the step, the less likely it is that the average response times of the reals servers will be different. You can manually set the load step yourself, using the command

    `load step` *step* `static`

Alternately, you can configure the CSS to automatically calculate the load step for you by using the command

    `load step` *step* `dynamic`

With the **load step dynamic** command, you must configure an initial load step, but the CSS modifies it after the CSS collects sufficient response times.

The CSS takes a real server out-of-service when its load surpasses a load threshold that you configure with the command

    `load threshold` *load*

To calculate the load of the real $Real_i$, where i is the index of real within the server farm, the CSS uses the following function to normalize the load against the fastest responding real MinimumRespTime:

$$Load(Real_i) = [(RespTime(Real_i) - MinimumRespTime)/LoadStep] + 2$$

The content switch assigns the real server with the lowest response time (MinimumRespTime) with a load of 2. All other real servers' loads are based on the response time of that real. For example, Table 10-4 shows four servers with response times of 100 ms, 200 ms, 600 ms, and 700 ms. The lowest response time is that of server S1 at 100 ms. The load is calculated for the remaining services in Table 10-4 using a MinimumRespTime of 100 ms and a load step of 10 ms.

Table 10-4   *Sample Load Calculations with Load Step of 10 ms*

$Real_i$	RTT	$Load(Real_i)$
S1	100	Lowest Load = 2
S2	200	2 + (200 − 100)/10 = 12
S3	600	2 + (600 − 100)/10 = 52
S4	700	2 + (700 − 100)/10 = 62

If you use a load step of 100 ms instead, you will get the loads calculated in Table 10-5. Because the difference in response times between S1 and S2 is equal to 100, their load numbers are the same, and therefore they will receive the same amount of connections from the CSS. Also, notice that, the higher you choose the load step, the closer the load numbers are for the reals.

Table 10-5   *Sample Load Calculations with Load Step of 100 ms*

Real$_i$	RTT	Load(Real$_i$)
S1	100	Lowest Load = 2
S2	200	2 + (100 − 100)/100 = 2
S3	600	2 + (600 − 100)/100 = 7
S4	700	2 + (700 − 100)/100 = 8

The CSS recalculates the load numbers for each real server when the load-teardown timer expires. To configure the load-teardown timer, use the following command:

```
load teardown-timer interval
```

The CSS uses an age-out mechanism to test real servers whose performance has dropped substantially for an extended time, but that may be back to normal by the end of the age-out timer. When the age-out timer expires, the content switch resets the load to a value of two of all reals whose load has not changed since the beginning of the age-out timer. This way, the content switch can issue more connections to the reals in order for the tear-down reports to accumulate more flow information and more accurately calculate the load for the server. To change the age-out timer, use the following command:

```
load ageout-timer seconds
```

The default setting for the tear-down and age-out timers are 20 and 60 seconds, respectively.

Calculating Absolute Load

As you learned with relative load calculations, the content switch normalizes the response time values with the fastest responding real while calculating the load of the remaining real servers. However, if you use your CSS to switch content for multiple applications, relative load normalizes the load values of services of a slower application with the response time of the fastest service of the faster responding application. For example, the average response times of application A is 50 ms and application B is 700 ms. Furthermore, the response time of the fastest responding service is 20 ms for a service within application A. In this example, the CSS normalizes all services within applications A and B using the response time of 20 ms. If you want to use ACA for multiple applications on a single CSS, you should use absolute load calculations instead of relative load.

Absolute load calculations take into account only the actual perceived load of the server. With absolute load calculations, the CSS divides the load number scale into 16 ranges of load numbers. The CSS assigns individual load steps to the ranges, depending on the granularity of the response times of your applications. Ranges are groups of consecutive load numbers that share a common load step between numbers. You can adjust the load step and maximum response times for the ranges by using the command

```
load absolute-sensitivity number
```

The CSS uses a sensitivity of 21 by default. Table 10-6 gives the load step and maximum response time values for the 16 ranges, based on a sensitivity of 21. With this sensitivity, the upper boundaries for the load step and maximum response time are 65,536 ms and 33 minutes, 51 seconds, respectively.

Table 10-6   *Absolute Load Values for Sensitivity of 21*

Range Number	Load Numbers	Step Size (ms)	Maximum Response Time (ms)	Maximum Response Time (h:m:s)
1	2-15	2	32	0: 0: 0
2	16-31	4	96	0: 0: 0
3	32-47	8	224	0: 0: 0
4	48-63	16	480	0: 0: 0
5	64-79	32	992	0: 0: 0
6	80-95	64	2016	0: 0: 2
7	96-111	128	4064	0: 0: 4
8	112-127	256	8160	0: 0: 8
9	128-143	512	16,352	0: 0:16
10	144-159	1024	32,736	0: 0:32
11	160-175	2048	65,504	0: 1: 5
12	176-191	4096	131,040	0: 2:11
13	192-207	8192	262,112	0: 4:22
14	208-223	16,384	524,256	0: 8:44
15	224-239	32,768	1,048,544	0:17:28
16	240-254	65,536	2,031,584	0:33:51

With absolute load calculations, the CSS groups services from your faster applications into the lower ranges. The maximum response time value in Table 10-6 separates your slower applications from faster applications. Additionally, real servers of slower-responding applications tend to have larger differences in response times. Therefore, the CSS increases the load step as the maximum response time increases, as Table 10-6 illustrates.

As an example, Table 10-7 gives sample absolute load calculations for two applications with three reals each. Based on the perceived response times, the CSS assigns application A to range 1 and application B to range 5.

Table 10-7 *Sample Absolute Load Calculations for Two Applications with Three Servers Each*

Application	Real$_i$	RTT	Load(Real$_i$)	Range
A	S1	45	19	1
A	S2	50	20	1
A	S3	55	21	1
B	S1	670	70	5
B	S2	700	71	5
B	S3	730	72	5

Increasing the sensitivity increases the upper load step size and maximum response time boundaries, and thus decreases the load numbers that the CSS assigns to your reals. For example, if you change the sensitivity to 22 using the command **load absolute-sensitivity 22**, the CSS would assign lower load numbers to the reals of application B in Table 10-7.

Hash Distribution

In previous chapters, you learned that hashing can be used to check the integrity of SSL segments, authenticate HTTP requests, and compute hash values from keys used in hash table lookups during CEF adjacency determination. You can also use hashing for distributing load across real servers.

With simple hash distribution, the content switch extracts the input to its hash function from fields within the incoming IP packet and TCP/UDP segment headers, including source/destination IP addresses and TCP/UDP ports. The content switch computes the hash as a value between 0 and a number that is usually quite a bit larger than the number of reals. The content switch then divides the hash value by the number of reals N, with the remainder being in between 0 and N − 1. The remainder of the division provides the real server to forward the request to.

NOTE To determine the remainder of a division between two numbers, the content switch uses the modulus or "mod" operator.

A benefit of hashing in general is that, because the content switch hashes every packet of a flow, it does not need to store the associations of the client's connection to the selected real server in RAM. As a result, hashing is a stateless distribution method, whereas the methods described previously are all stateful because the content switch must store the mappings in RAM in order to know where to forward subsequent packets of the client's flow.

Hashing the packet's source IP address is useful only in environments where there are vast numbers of clients, because the same keys provide the same hash value. A small number of clients may cause an over-selection of particular real servers. Additionally, some ISPs use mega-proxy servers to NAT hundreds or even thousands of clients to a single IP address. As a result, your content switch will forward all requests from clients behind the proxy to the same real server, potentially causing that real server to overload.

You can configure your content switch to hash the following information for selecting real servers:

- **Source IP address hashing**—A benefit of source address hashing in some environments is that the client connects to the same server for every request, causing the client to stick to the same real server for all requests to the virtual server. This benefit proves useful for e-commerce applications that store client-specific information across content requests. You will learn more about session stickiness later in this chapter.

- **URL, domain name, and destination IP address hashing**—URL hashing is useful in caching environments in which the content is not duplicated across the real servers. Cache load balancing requires the content switch to distribute files evenly across available CEs. Delayed binding enables the content switch to extract the URL in the request before choosing a real server. You will learn more about cache load balancing in Chapter 13.

Layer 5–7 Load Balancing

In order to match a client request to a virtual server, you can configure your CSS to inspect application layer headers as matching criteria. By enabling application-layer load balancing, you can assign client requests to virtual servers given the following criteria:

- **URLs and file types**—URLs contain information that you can use to divide your content into various groups. For example, you can distinguish between static and dynamic content using file extensions.

- **Languages**—Content for various demographics can reside on dedicated servers or server farms.

- **Browser types**—Palm, PDA, or cell phones may have different screen resolutions than regular PCs or interpret markup languages other than HTML, such as Wireless Markup Language (WML) or extensible HTML (XHTML). You can house a transformed version of content for these clients on a dedicated server. See Chapter 7, "Presenting and Transforming Content," for more information on content transformation.

- **Search engine services**—Search engine services and wireless application protocol (WAP) gateways sometimes send requests that contain distinguishable characteristics from regular client requests. For example, a request for uniform resource identifier (URI) /robots.txt is probably from a search engine, in which case you can handle the requests differently than regular content requests. Search engines may also use specific user-agent header values to distinguish themselves, such as "Googlebot" and "YahooSeeker."

- **Cookies**—Cookies can be used as criteria for inspecting customized content for clients. You will learn about connection stickiness later in this chapter.

- **Bypass noncacheable traffic**—When selecting whether a request should be forwarded to a cache engine, the HTTP "Cache-Control:" header can be inspected by the content switch for a value of "no-cache" or "no-store." Recall from Chapter 8 that these values indicate that content must be validated for every request. Therefore, there is no reason to send the request to a cache engine; rather, simply send the request to the virtual server of the origin server where the content resides.

Figure 10-21 illustrates how you can configure a CSS with two virtual servers for the same content. The content switch forwards the requests to different server farms by inspecting the application request.

Figure 10-21 *HTTP Header Load Balancing*

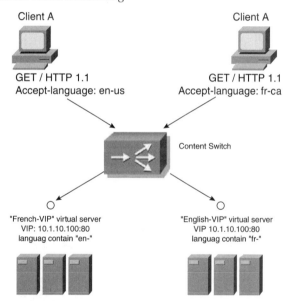

To configure your CSS with these two different virtual servers, use the configuration in Example 10-9. Browsers use character codes for specifying the language within the "Accept-Language:" HTTP header. Additionally, different dialects of the same language use a unique code. For example, the English language has dialect codes for Australian (en-au), Belize (en-bz), and many others. The example in Figure 10-21 uses United States English (en-us) and Canadian French (fr-ca), but you can catch all the available dialects by using the **contain** keyword in Example 10-9.

Example 10-9 *HTTP Header Load Balancing on the CSS*

```
header-field-group french-lang
 header-field french language contain "fr-" 20
```

continues

Example 10-9 *HTTP Header Load Balancing on the CSS (Continued)*

```
header-field-group english-lang
 header-field english language contain "en-" 20

service fr-web01
 ip address 10.1.10.10
 active
service en-web02
 ip address 10.1.10.11
 active

owner cisco
 content french-vip
  vip address 10.1.10.100
  header-field-rule french-lang
  protocol tcp
  port 80
  add service fr-web01
  active

 content english-vip
  vip address 10.1.10.100
  header-field-rule english-lang
  protocol tcp
  port 80
  add service en-web02
  active
```

You can also create Extension Qualifier Lists (EQL) to enable the CSS to inspect the URI for file extensions. For example, to configure a virtual server to service your static files, and another to serve your dynamic files, you can use the configuration in Example 10-10.

Example 10-10 *Using EQLs on the CSS*

```
eql static-files
 extension gif
 extension jpg
 extension jpeg
 extension asf
 extension rm
 extension qt
 extension mp4
 extension html
 extension htm

eql dynamic-files
 extension perl
 extension asp
 extension cgi
```

Example 10-10 *Using EQLs on the CSS (Continued)*

```
owner cisco
 content static-vip
  vip address 10.1.10.100
  url "/*" eql static-files
  protocol tcp
  port 80
  add service web01
  add service web02
  add service web03
  active

content dynamic-vip
  vip address 10.1.10.100
  url "/*" eql dynamic-files
  protocol tcp
  port 80
  add service web01
  add service web02
  add service web03
  active
```

To configure your CSM with these two virtual servers, use the configuration in Example 10-11. To configure the two language policies, you must associate the HTTP header maps ("french-lang" and "english-lang") to their respective server farms by using the **policy** command. Then, instead of applying the server farms to the virtual server, you apply the policies.

Example 10-11 *HTTP Header Load Balancing on the CSM*

```
mod csm 5
 map french-lang header
  match protocol http header language header-value "fr-"
 map english-lang header
  match protocol http header language header-value "en-"

serverfarm en-webfarm
 nat server
 no nat client
 real 10.1.10.10
  inservice

serverfarm fr-webfarm
 nat server
 no nat client
 real 10.1.10.11
  inservice
```

continues

Example 10-11 *HTTP Header Load Balancing on the CSM (Continued)*

```
policy french-policy
 serverfarm fr-webfarm
 header-map french-lang

policy english-policy
 serverfarm en-webfarm
 header-map english-lang

vserver french-vip
 virtual 10.1.10.100 tcp www
 policy french-policy
 persistent rebalance
 inservice

vserver english-vip
 virtual 10.1.10.100 tcp www
 policy english-policy
 persistent rebalance
 inservice
```

To switch content based on file extensions on your CSM, you must create a URL map with the **url-map** command in policy configuration mode, as Example 10-12 illustrates. The first matching policy that is configured within the virtual server content-vip wins. You should also consider configuring a default policy that catches requests that do not match any of your other policies.

Example 10-12 *Extension Matching on the CSM*

```
mod csm 5
 map static-files url
  match protocol http url *.gif
  match protocol http url *.jpg
  match protocol http url *.asf
  match protocol http url *.rm
  match protocol http url *.qt
  match protocol http url *.mp4
  match protocol http url *.html
  match protocol http url *.htm

 map dynamic-files url
  match protocol http url *.cgi
  match protocol http url *.perl
  match protocol http url *.asp

 map default-files url
  match protocol http url *.*
```

Example 10-12   *Extension Matching on the CSM (Continued)*

```
serverfarm stat-webfarm
 nat server
 no nat client
 real 10.1.10.10
  inservice

serverfarm dyn-webfarm
 nat server
 no nat client
 real 10.1.10.11
  inservice

serverfarm default-webfarm
 nat server
 no nat client
 real 10.1.10.12
  inservice

policy static-policy
 serverfarm stat-webfarm
 url-map static-files

policy dynamic-policy
 serverfarm dyn-webfarm
 url-map dynamic-files

policy default-policy
 serverfarm default-webfarm
 url-map default-files

vserver content-vip
 virtual 10.1.10.100 tcp www
 policy static-policy
 policy dynamic-policy
 policy default-policy
 persistent rebalance
 inservice
```

NOTE   Bear in mind that HTTP header load balancing is different from HTTP URL hashing. HTTP header load balancing is a method of selecting virtual servers. URL hashing is a method of deciding which real server to send the request to, after the content switch selects a virtual server.

Equal-Cost Multi-Path Router Load Balancing

Equal-Cost Multi-Path (ECMP) is similar to CEF load balancing. To configure per-flow load balancing, use the command

```
ip ecmp address
```

This command enables the CSS to hash the source and destination addresses of incoming packets together to ensure that your flows will traverse the same outgoing router. To enable per-packet load balancing, use the command

```
ip ecmp round-robin
```

By default, the CSS selects the same interface for return traffic of a flow as the incoming traffic came from. To disable this behavior for ECMP, you can use the command

```
ip ecmp no-prefer-ingress
```

Figure 10-22 illustrates ECMP.

Figure 10-22 *Load Balancing Packets Across Multiple Routers*

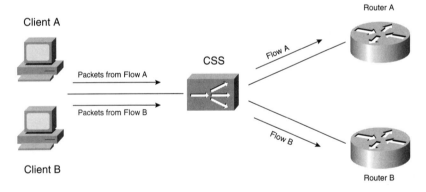

So far in this chapter, you've learned a lot about how content switches receive and forward requests to real servers from clients. As a result, you should now be able to configure and deploy a basic server farm in your production environment. Once you enable your configuration in production, moving forward, you may want to tweak the settings and make the server farm perform more efficiently by using enhanced application health checking. You may also have application requirements to ensure that users remain connected to the same real server for the duration of their sessions. Additionally, when the capacity of your server farms increase, you may find that your content switches start to fail—this is not an uncommon event in large server farm environments. To prevent your application from failing when your content switch fails, you should consider configuring content switch fault tolerance. The remainder of the chapter will provide you with the information you need to configure a robust and highly available server farm.

Health Checking

To determine the health of a real, content switches can perform either out-of-band or in-band health checks.

Out-of-Band Health Checking

With out-of-band (OOB) health checking, you configure the content switch to pose as an actual client and send mock requests to the real server. The content switch inspects the response of the request and changes the status of the real server accordingly. If the health check fails, the content switch temporarily removes the real from the pool, and does not issue any more connections until the health check succeeds. The health check parameters, such as ports, execution frequency, and timeouts, are highly tunable—you can adjust them to meet the specific requirements of your application.

You can configure the content switch to send TCP probes to a real server by opening a TCP connection to a configurable port. That is, the content switch sends a TCP SYN to the real, and if it receives a TCP SYN/ACK from the real within a configurable timeout value, the content switch deems the real to be healthy. To configure TCP probes on the CSS, you can use the configuration in Example 10-13.

Example 10-13 *Configuring TCP Keep-Alives on the CSS*

```
keepalive tcp-http
 type tcp
 port 80
 frequency 10
 retryperiod 5
 maxfailure 4

service web01
 ip address 10.1.10.11
 keepalive type named tcp-http
 active
```

Example 10-13 gives an example TCP keep-alive called "tcp-http" that you can assign to particular real servers by using the **keepalive** command in service configuration mode. This keep-alive sends a TCP SYN segment to port 80, waits 5 seconds for a response, and then retries three more times (that is, you have to subtract the initial attempt from **maxfailure** to get three retries) before taking the real server out of rotation. The CSS reattempts the keep-alive every 10 seconds.

To configure TCP probes on the CSM, you can use the configuration in Example 10-14.

Example 10-14   *Configuring TCP Keep-Alives on the CSM*

```
module csm 5
probe tcp-http tcp
 port 80
 interval 10
 open 15
 retries 3

serverfarm  web-farm
 real 10.1.10.11
  inservice
 probe tcp-http
```

You can also configure your content switch to send application-specific commands for various applications. Content switches contain a few built-in application layer checks, such as simple mail transfer protocol (SMTP), FTP, and HTTP. Content switches can send HTTP GET or HEAD messages to the real servers and then parse the response codes or the HTML page from the real server for errors. If you need to check for only particular HTTP response code, you should use the HTTP HEAD method to request only the HTTP headers, and avoid the real having to send the HTTP body in the message over the network.

To configure application layer keep-alives on your CSS, you can use the configuration in Example 10-15. By default, the CSS expects the HTTP 200 OK return code in response to HTTP HEAD method keep-alives.

Example 10-15   *Configuring HTTP Keep-Alives on the CSS*

```
keepalive keep-http
 type http
 method head

service web01
 ip address 10.1.10.11
 keepalive type named keep-http
 active
```

Example 10-16 illustrates HTTP keep-alives on the CSM. You must explicitly specify the successful HTTP status code in the CSM configuration.

Example 10-16 *Configuring HTTP Keep-Alives on the CSM*

```
module csm 5
probe keep-http http
 request-method head
 expect status 200

serverfarm  web-farm
 real 10.1.10.11
  inservice
 probe keep-http
```

With scripting languages, you can also write custom application layer probes that you can load and execute on the content switch, to send various application-specific commands to your real server. For example, you can write an application-specific probe to log in to your web application server with a set of known user credentials. Additionally, the CSM provides sample scripts on Cisco.com including an SSL-specific probe to check to see whether an SSL session can be opened to an SSL server. The script sends an SSL Client Hello message to the server, and waits to receive the Server Hello message from the server for successful probe execution. To enable a scripted keep-alive for a service on the CSS, use the service configuration command:

```
keepalive type script script-name "arguments"
```

NOTE The CSS uses a proprietary scripting language, and the CSM uses TCL scripting language to execute scripts. For more information on scripted keep-alives, refer to your product documentation on Cisco.com.

In the event of a real server failure, you can control what happens to the existing connections to the real on the CSM. You can either reassign the connections to new real servers or completely remove the connections from the CSM, using the following server farm configuration command:

```
failaction {purge ¦ reassign}
```

The drawback of OOB health checking is that it imposes a slight increase in load on your servers. Additionally, your content switch knows only the status of a server when it issues a keep-alive—your content switch is unaware of a failure if a real fails between probe intervals. Therefore, the content switch may send requests to a failed real for a maximum time equal to the probe interval. To help overcome these drawbacks, you should consider using in-band health checking in conjunction with OOB health checking.

In-Band Health Checking

You can configure the content switch to derive the status of a real server by inspecting live TCP connections and application transactions between the content switch and real servers. You can configure two forms of in-band health checking:

- **TCP connection monitoring**—If real servers are unable to complete the TCP handshake for a live request in a timely fashion, the CSM can retry the request a number of times. If the real does not complete its portion of the TCP handshake after a configurable number of retries, the content switch automatically removes the real from the pool. Once removed, the real remains out-of-service for a configurable amount of time.

- **HTTP return code monitoring**—The content switch can parse real servers' HTTP return codes. If the content switch receives numerous unexpected error codes from the real servers in response to valid requests, the content switch automatically removes the real from the pool. The number of erroneous return codes must first reach configurable thresholds to trigger removal from the pool.

NOTE The CSS does not support in-band health checking.

Figure 10-23 illustrates TCP connection monitoring in-band health checking.

Figure 10-23 *TCP Connection Monitoring In-band Health Checking*

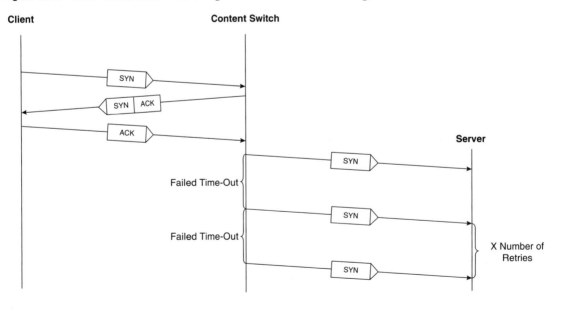

To configure TCP connection monitoring health checking on your CSM, use the following command in server farm configuration mode:

```
health retries count failed seconds
```

The retries is the number of TCP SYN requests that the CSM attempts to the real server before taking the real out-of-service. Once the CSM takes the real out-of-service with in-band health monitoring, the CSM continues issuing TCP connections to the real after the number of seconds you configure within the failed parameter. For example, the command **health retries 2 failed 20** reattempts the TCP connection twice before taking the real out-of-service for 20 seconds.

To configure HTTP return code checking on the CSM, use the following commands:

```
map name retcode
match protocol http retcode min max action [count ¦ log ¦ remove] threshold [reset
seconds]
```

You can specify the CSM to count, log the return codes to a Syslog server, or remove the real from service when it receives particular HTTP return codes. For example, you can configure a number of match entries with different actions with the configuration in Example 10-17.

Example 10-17 *Return Code Checking on the CSM*

```
module csm 5
map http-rets retcode
 match protocol http retcode 400 401 action log 5 reset 120
 match protocol http retcode 402 417 action count
 match protocol http retcode 500 500 action remove 3 reset 0
 match protocol http retcode 501 505 action log 3 reset 0

serverfarm webfarm
 real 10.1.10.11
  inservice
 retcode-map http-rets
```

NOTE   Because the error codes within the range 400–499 are client errors, you should not configure the CSM to take the real out-of-service when the server sends these return codes. See Chapter 8 for a list of the available return codes in HTTP 1.1.

You should not rely completely on in-band health checking because in-band catches only simple failures, such as a lack of SYN-ACK reply, RSTs, and unexpected HTTP return codes. Instead, you should use in-band health checking in conjunction with OOB health checking.

Session Persistence

When a client uses a load-balanced application, real servers sometimes store information about the client in memory for use throughout the session. For your applications that require your clients to remain connected for the duration of their session to the real server that contains the client's information, you can use one of the following content switching methods:

- Hash Load Balancing

- Source IP Sticky

- HTTP Cookies

- HTTP URL Sticky Strings

- SSL Version 3 Sticky

- Session Information Protocol (SIP) Caller ID and WAP Mobile Station International ISDN Number (MSISDN) Number Sticky

Hash Load Balancing

As you learned previously, content switches can perform a hash on source IP addresses, destination IP addresses, domain names, and URLs to distribute client requests across real servers. You should use hashing load balancing in the caching environments as discussed in Chapter 13. However, source IP hashing also provides a simple stateless way to stick a client to the same real server in SLB environments. To configure source IP hashing on your CSS, use the following content rule configuration command:

```
balance srcip
```

To enable source IP address hashing on the CSM, use the following command:

```
predictor ip-hash netmask source
```

You must specify the portion of the source address to hash with the address **mask** parameter.

IP Address Stickiness

IP address stickiness differs from hashing load balancing sticky because the content switch creates entries in a sticky table, whereas hashing is stateless. Additionally, with IP address stickiness, you configure the load-balancing method separately from the sticky method. Therefore, IP stickiness can determine when a server goes down or comes back online, whereas hashing cannot. To configure source IP sticky on the CSS, use the following command in content rule configuration mode:

```
advanced-balance sticky-srcip
```

To configure source IP and destination port stickiness on the CSS, use the following content rule configuration command:

```
advanced-balance sticky-srcip-dstport
sticky-mask netmask
sticky-inactive-timeout value
```

Use the sticky mask to modify the maximum amount of clients from a subnet that will stick to a single server. The inactive timeout value specifies how long the CSS waits with no activity to a sticky entry before invalidating it. To configure source IP sticky on the CSM, use the following command:

```
sticky sticky-group-id netmask netmask address source timeout sticky-time
```

You must associate this command to a policy and virtual server on the CSM in the same manner as Example 10-17 illustrates. The CSM does not support source IP in conjunction with destination port stickiness.

Both the CSS and CSM store entries for Layer 3 and 4 stickiness in a sticky table within RAM. When the content switch establishes a TCP connection between the client and server, it creates an entry in the table for subsequent application requests. When the client sends subsequent application requests over a separate TCP connection, the content switch performs a sticky table lookup to select the same real server for the client. To view the contents of the sticky table on the CSS, use the following exec command:

```
show sticky-table [all-sticky ¦ l3-sticky ¦ l4-sticky ¦ sip-callid-sticky ¦ ssl-sticky
¦ wap-sticky]
```

To view the contents of the CSM sticky table, use the following exec command:

```
show module csm mod-num sticky
```

You learned previously that some ISPs use mega-proxies to NAT several clients to the same source IP address, causing a large number of clients to stick to the same real server in the server farm. If you are concerned with the number of clients that originate from behind a mega-proxy, you should consider using HTTP Cookie, URL strings, SIP caller ID, or WAP MSISDN number sticky instead.

Some ISP proxies may also allow a single client to use multiple IP addresses throughout the duration of the client's session. For example, a client's Internet connection may temporarily disconnect, and then reconnect with a new IP address. Sticking on source IP address with a mask of 255.255.255.255 causes the content switch to send a client using multiple IPs to different real servers. If you are concerned with clients that may use multiple IP addresses, you should use a larger address mask, such as 255.255.255.0, to stick a larger amount of client IP addresses to a single real server.

HTTP Cookies

Recall from Chapter 8 that HTTP is not inherently stateful; however, servers may maintain state locally on behalf of clients visiting their site through the use of HTTP cookies. The server may then process any subsequent HTTP request using the stored client information, as a means to maintain the state of the HTTP "session." A typical example is an online shopping site that uses logical shopping carts to store items chosen by clients during their sessions.

Although most browsers support HTTP 1.1 connection persistence and pipelining, the majority of browsers open multiple TCP connections throughout the duration of a single user session to a website. In Chapter 1, "Introducing Content Networking," you learned the reason for opening multiple TCP connections to a site, to increase the effective bandwidth due to limitations of TCP over links with very high latency. Additionally, content switches can use HTTP rebalancing to distribute HTTP requests within the same TCP connection to different servers. In both cases, the content switch sends the client unknowingly to a real server that is unaware of the client's state information that is stored on the originally selected real server. To maintain client state, the content switch must send all requests during the client's session to the same real server, because this is where the client's information resides—Figure 10-24 illustrates this point.

You can accomplish session stickiness using HTTP cookies. You learned in Chapter 8 that two types of HTTP cookies are available. Real servers store persistent cookies in a text file on the hard disk of the client's computer, primarily to provide personalization and customization for the user on subsequent visits to the site. Real servers and clients store session cookies locally in RAM, and they exist only temporarily for the life of the session. The browser removes the cookie from RAM when the user closes the browser window(s) for the session, and the real server removes the cookie from RAM after a configurable timeout on your web server.

Figure 10-24 *Forwarding Client Requests to Multiple Reals While Maintaining Session State on Single Real Server*

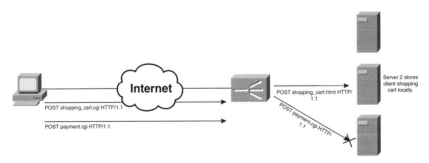

Content switches use session cookies to provide session stickiness for clients and can be set on the real server or, if the real server is not capable of setting cookies, the content switch can set the cookie on the real server's behalf. The session cookie is set by the server with the HTTP "Set-

Cookie:" header. The value of the cookie can be set to any attribute/value pair, such as "SESSION_ID=012321." For subsequent HTTP requests, either within the same TCP connection or across connections, the client uses the cookie as a handle for all communication during the session. You must configure your content switch to inspect cookies with a value starting with "SESSION_ID=," in this example, and store a mapping of the associated value to the real server originally chosen for the session. This way, the content switch does not load balance subsequent requests to new real servers—the cookie overrides the normal load-balance decision. Figure 10-25 illustrates how the CSM sticks a client to the same server.

Figure 10-25 *Session Persistence on the CSM*

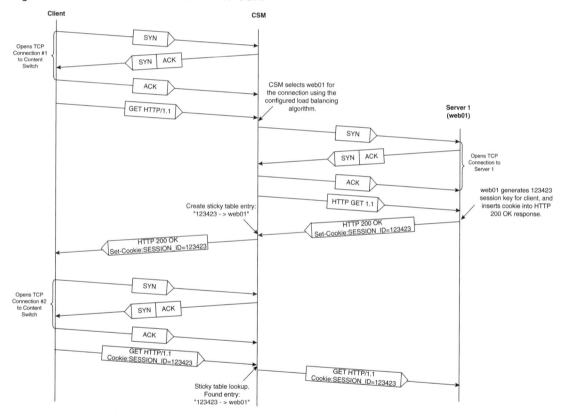

In Figure 10-25, the CSM selects the real server using the configured load balancing method, and forwards the GET request to that real. When the CSM receives the "Set-Cookie:" header from the real server, the CSM stores the association between the cookie value and real server in the sticky table. On subsequent requests from the client, the CSM performs a table lookup with the cookie that the client supplies to determine which real the client is stuck to. To configure your CSM to inspect HTTP cookies, you can use the configuration in Example 10-18. You must give the sticky configuration for "SESSION_ID" a unique identifier (for example, 1 in this case) and apply the sticky configuration to a policy using the **stick-group** command. You then apply the policy to the virtual server using the **policy** command.

Example 10-18 *Configuring Sticky Cookies on the CSM*

```
mod csm 5

sticky 1 cookie SESSION_ID time-out 100

serverfarm webfarm
 nat server
 no nat client
 real 10.1.10.10
  inservice
 real 10.1.10.11
  inservice

policy sticky-policy
 serverfarm webfarm
 sticky-group 1

vserver static-vip
 virtual 10.1.10.100 tcp www
 policy sticky-policy
 persistent rebalance
 inservice
```

To stick to only a portion of a cookie, as opposed to the entire cookie, use the following command:

```
cookie offset 5 length 8
```

This command benefits applications, such as Java 2.0 Enterprise Edition (J2EE), which store the real session ID only in certain bytes of the cookie value. If your origin servers do not support cookies, you can configure your CSM to insert a cookie in the server's response to the client, using the following command:

```
sticky 5 cookie mycookie insert
```

If you configure HTTP cookie stickiness on the CSS, it does not store entries in the sticky table. Instead, you can manually assign cookie string values to the services on the CSS. When a real server generates a cookie, the client uses that cookie in subsequent requests. The CSS inspects the cookie value and directs the request to the service configured with that value. With this configuration, the real server must generate the same cookie value for all clients, in order to identify itself to the CSS.

By default, the CSS uses manual service sticky strings. If you disable this feature and need to reenable it, you can use the following command:

```
string operation match-service-cookie
```

Because this is the default behavior for sticky cookies on the CSS, this command does not show in the configuration given in Example 10-19.

Example 10-19 *Configuring Sticky Cookies on the CSS*

```
service web01
 ip address 10.1.10.10
 string s001
 active
service web02
 ip address 10.1.10.11
 string s002
 active

owner cisco
 content sticky-vip
  vip address 10.1.10.100
  advanced-balance cookies
  string prefix "SESSION_ID"
  string skip-length 1
  string process-length 6
  protocol tcp
  port 80
  add service web01
  add service web02
  active
```

You can also configure the CSS to hash cookie values to stick to the same real server throughout the client's session. With cookie hashing, the CSS selects an original real server using the configured load-balancing method. The original real server generates a cookie, and the CSS responds to the client's request with the cookie, as normal. However, when the CSS receives subsequent requests from the client with the cookie, the CSS hashes the cookie to determine the sticky real server. Hashing the cookie assigns the client to the same real server for each request, but the sticky real server may be different from the original real server that generated the cookie. This should not be a problem, because the original real does not store any information about the client that is needed throughout the session—its sole task is to generate the cookie. With this configuration, the real servers can generate *unique* cookies for each requesting client, because you do not manually assign reals to predefined cookie values. To configure cookie hashing, use the following CSS content rule configuration command:

```
string operation [hash-a ¦ hash-crc32 ¦ hash-xor]
```

As mentioned previously, you can also configure your content switch to insert cookies into real server responses, which is transparent to both client and server, by using the following command:

```
advanced-balance arrowpoint-cookie
```

> **NOTE** You should use CSS cookies in a redundant CSS configuration. Because the sticky table is not used, failing over to the backup CSS does not cause the CSS to lose sticky information, whereas, with sticky mechanisms on the CSS that use the sticky table, sticky information is lost during the failover. For more information on CSS redundancy, see the section "Content Switch High Availability" at the end of this chapter.

URL Sticky Strings

Instead of setting a sticky string within a "Set-Cookie:" HTTP header of an HTTP 200 OK method, you can configure your real servers to send an HTTP 302 Object Moved method containing a sticky string within the URL of the "Location:" header. You must direct your content switch to inspect URLs from clients for the sticky cookie. For example, you can configure your real server to return the following URL in an HTTP 302 Object Moved method for client logins:

```
HTTP/1.1 302 Object Moved
Location: login.asp?session-id=201421
```

Clients use the value in the "Location:" header to request the login page. Your real servers must also embed the sticky string into the hyperlinks within all further HTML pages to which the client will have access during their session. To direct the CSS to inspect the client URLs to find the sticky string within your URL strings (after the "?" in the URL field), use the following content rule configuration command:

```
advanced-balance cookieurl
```

To configure your CSM to check the URL for the sticky string, use the sticky configuration command:

```
cookie secondary session-id
```

> **NOTE** The CSM combines URL strings with cookies in that it can search a cookie value in the URL after having learned it dynamically from a "Set-cookie:" message, to account for clients that reject the cookie sent by the server.

SSL Sticky

Recall from Chapter 8 that SSL version 3 provides a stateful session identifier in the SSL Handshake Protocol. SSL clients reference this session ID throughout the SSL communication between the client and server, even across TCP connections. Content switches create a mapping between the SSL session ID and real server, in the same way as with HTTP Cookies, and they store the mapping in their sticky tables. For every SSL packet, in any TCP session that is created within the main SSL session, the content switch uses the session ID as key into the sticky session lookup table. The content switch uses the resultant real server to which it forwards the clients' subsequent requests. The command **advanced-balance ssl** enables the CSS to use the SSL session ID to stick to clients.

Additionally, the **application ssl** command tells the CSS to not inspect the Layer 5–7 application. Once the CSS establishes the SSL flow, it cannot decipher the encrypted data, so there is no need for the content switch to inspect Layer 5–7 content. Example 10-20 shows you how to configure SSL sticky on the CSS.

Example 10-20 *Configuring SSL Sticky on the CSS*

```
service web01
 ip address 10.1.10.10
 active
service web02
 ip address 10.1.10.11
 active

owner cisco
 content sticky-vip
  vip address 10.1.10.100
  advanced-balance ssl
  application ssl
  port 443
  add service web01
  add service web02
  active
```

Example 10-21 gives a sample SSL sticky configuration for the CSM.

Example 10-21 *Configuring SSL Sticky on the CSM*

```
mod csm 5

sticky 1 ssl timeout 100

serverfarm webfarm
 nat server
 no nat client
 real 10.1.10.10
  inservice
 real 10.1.10.11
  inservice

policy ssl-sticky-policy
 serverfarm webfarm
 sticky-group 1
```

continues

Example 10-21 *Configuring SSL Sticky on the CSM (Continued)*

```
vserver static-vip
  virtual 10.1.10.100 tcp 443
  policy ssl-sticky-policy
  inservice
```

NOTE Both the CSM and CSS store SSL sticky entries in their sticky tables.

SIP Caller ID and MSISDN Number Sticky

You can also configure your CSS to perform sticky based on Session Information Protocol (SIP) caller identification using the **advanced-balance sip-call-id** content rule command.

Additionally, WAP gateways often add an HTTP extension header for the Mobile Station International ISDN Number (MSISDN). The extension header is "X-MSISDN:" and contains the unique identifier for the WAP client. You can configure your CSS to stick to clients based on the value in the "X-MSISDN:" header using the **advanced-balance wap-msisdn** content rule command.

NOTE The CSS uses its sticky table for both SIP and MSISDN sticky entries. The CSM does not support SIP caller ID or MSISDN number sticky.

Permanent Session Information Storage

With the stateful sticky methods you have learned so far (that is, HTTP cookies, URL sticky strings, SIP caller-id, and MSISDN numbers), if the sticky server that creates the cookie fails, the cookie is permanently removed from memory. Creating a permanent store of session information, such as an SQL database, is an alternative to stateful memory-based session information storage. If the original real server that a client connects to fails, the content switch can load balance subsequent requests to any available real server.

Because the session information is available through a separate back-end channel, the newly selected real servers can perform a lookup to the load the client's session information, based on the cookie or sticky string embedded within the client's request. A disadvantage of this method is the overhead of performing lookups across the network for every user request.

Content Switch High Availability

To ensure that your clients do not lose connectivity in the event of a content switch failure, you can configure high availability features. Both the CSS and CSM support high availability configurations.

CSS High Availability

To configure high availability on your CSS, you need to configure both redundant VIPs and interfaces with fate sharing and adaptive Session redundancy (ASR) as follows:

- **Redundant VIPs and interfaces with fate sharing**—You learned previously how to configure your client and server VLANs on the CSS. To configure redundancy, on your client VIPs and server interfaces you must configure the virtual routers that you want to be redundant. Using Virtual Router Redundancy Protocol (VRRP), your CSSs negotiate the master and standby CSS for a redundant VIP or interface, based on priorities you assign to your CSSs. The virtual routers you configure on two CSSs share the same IP and MAC address. When the two CSSs jockey for mastership, the CSS with the higher priority is assigned as master. The master for the virtual router responds to ARP requests for the VIP or interface, whereas the backup does not.

> **NOTE**   When CSSs first elect the master virtual router, the CSS containing the master sends a gratuitous ARP to indicate to all attached Layer 2 switches the address to which all requests for the redundant VIP or interface should be sent. That is, the CSSs use Gratuitous ARP as a way to advertise mastership to the connected Layer 2 switches.

To ensure that the client-side redundant VIPs and server-side redundant interfaces fail-over simultaneously, you must configure the VIPs and interfaces to share the same fate. When a VIP fail-over occurs on a CSS, the corresponding server-side interface should also fail-over. Otherwise, client-side TCP SYN segments will traverse one CSS, and their corresponding TCP SYN-ACK segments from the servers will traverse the other CSS, resulting in both CSSs dropping the connections.

- **Adaptive Session Redundancy (ASR)**—Once you configure your redundant VIPs and interfaces with fate sharing, you can enable ASR. With ASR, your redundant CSSs synchronize TCP-UDP flow information between each other. This way, when the CSS functioning as master fails, the standby can take over processing for existing flows transparently to your clients. The CSS does not synchronize its sticky table, so you should use stateless sticky with HTTP cookies if you want to enable the CSS high-availability features.

Figure 10-26 gives a sample redundant CSS configuration with a redundant client-side VIP, redundant server-side interface, and ASR.

To configure the high availability features given in Figure 10-26 on your CSS, you can use the configuration in Example 10-22. This configuration builds on the configuration you learned about previously in Example 10-4.

Figure 10-26 *CSS Virtual Router VIP and Interface Redundancy with ASR*

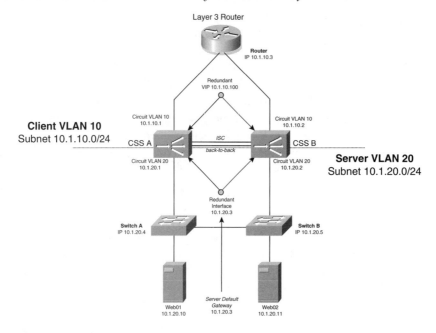

Example 10-22 *Configuring CSS High Availability*

```
CSS A
!*************************** INTERFACE *************************
interface e1
  bridge vlan 10
interface e2
  bridge vlan 20
interface e3
  isc-port-one
interface e4
  isc-port-two
!*************************** CIRCUIT *************************
circuit VLAN10
  ip address 10.1.10.1 255.255.255.0
  ip virtual-router 1 priority 101 preempt
  ip redundant-vip 1 10.1.10.100
  ip critical-service 1 share-fate

circuit VLAN20
  ip address 10.1.20.1 255.255.255.0
  ip virtual-router 2 priority 101 preempt
  ip redundant-interface 2 10.1.20.3
  ip critical-service 2 share-fate
```

Example 10-22 *Configuring CSS High Availability (Continued)*

```
!************************* SERVICE **************************
service web01
 ip address 10.1.20.10
 redundant-index 1
 active

service web02
 ip address 10.1.20.11
 redundant-index 2
 active

service share-fate
 ip address 10.1.10.3
 keepalive type script ap-kal-pinglist "10.1.10.3 10.1.20.4"
 active
!************************* OWNER **************************
owner cisco
 content http-vip
  vip address 10.1.10.100
  redundant-index 3
  protocol tcp
  port 80
  add service web01
  add service web02
  active
```
```
CSS B
!************************* INTERFACE **************************
interface e1
  bridge vlan 10
interface e2
  bridge vlan 20
interface e3
 isc-port-one
interface e4
 isc-port-two
!************************* CIRCUIT **************************
circuit VLAN10
  ip address 10.1.10.2 255.255.255.0
  ip virtual-router 1 priority 100
  ip redundant-vip 1 10.1.10.100
  ip critical-service 1 share-fate

circuit VLAN20
  ip address 10.1.20.2 255.255.255.0
  ip virtual-router 2 priority 100
  ip redundant-interface 2 10.1.20.3
  ip critical-service 2 share-fate
```

continues

Example 10-22 *Configuring CSS High Availability (Continued)*

```
!************************** SERVICE **************************
service web01
 ip address 10.1.20.10
 redundant-index 1

service web02
 ip address 10.1.20.11
 redundant-index 2

service share-fate
 ip address 10.1.10.3
 keepalive type script ap-kal-pinglist "10.1.10.3 10.1.20.5"
 active
!************************** OWNER **************************
owner cisco
 content http-vip
  vip address 10.1.10.100
  redundant-index 3
  protocol tcp
  port 80
  add service web01
  add service web02
  active
```

The interface section of the configurations of both CSS A and B contains the configuration for the client-side, server-side, and Inter-Switch Communications (ISC) interfaces. The CSS uses ISC to synchronize ASR flow and configuration information between the CSSs. To configure ASR between your CSSs, use the following command in service, content rule, or source group configuration mode:

> redundant-index *index-num*

You must assign unique index numbers to your items, as Example 10-22 illustrates.

Use of ASR provides stateful failover from the master to the standby CSS, by synchronizing flow information between CSSs to ensure that the standby CSS has the necessary flow information to seamlessly resume processing. You should use stateful failover for your mission-critical applications.

The circuit VLANs contain the VRRP configuration. To configure a virtual router, use the following circuit interface configuration command:

> ip virtual-router *vrid* {priority *number*} {preempt}

The VRID identifies the virtual router and must be unique between the circuit interfaces. You configure the virtual router's priority with the **priority** argument, and whether or not the CSS should preempt the current active CSS when it comes back online with the **preempt** argument. Notice that, in Example 10-22, the CSS A is configured with a higher priority and preempts CSS B when coming back online from a failure.

To configure a virtual router as a redundant VIP, use the command

```
ip redundant-vip vrid vip_address {range number} {shared}
```

Configure the range of IP addresses if you configured your VIPs to serve a range of IPs. The **shared** keyword indicates that both the active and standby virtual routers respond to requests to the same VIP. You will learn about this feature later in this section.

To configure a virtual router as a redundant interface, use the command

```
ip redundant-interface vrid ip_address
```

To ensure that both the redundant VIPs and interfaces fail-over simultaneously, you can configure critical services for your virtual routers. As the name indicates, critical services are critical to the functioning of the virtual router they are associated with. This means that, if the critical service fails, the CSS automatically fails the virtual router as well. In this case, the critical service fails if the ping tests fail to either the upstream router or downstream switch. For example, say that the client-facing physical interface Ethernet 0 of CSS fails. Then the ping test to the router will fail for both of the critical services that you configure for virtual routers with VRIDs 1 and 2 on CSS A. Therefore, the CSS will shut down both virtual routers simultaneously. CSS B will detect the failures to both virtual routers and take over as the active CSS for both.

> **NOTE**   To detect virtual router failures, VRRP periodically sends heartbeat packets between the CSSs you configure with VRRP to the multicast address 224.0.0.18 over the Layer 2 domain. The standby CSS detects a failure and takes over processing for the active virtual router when the heartbeat stops on the active virtual router.

The critical service "share-fate" in Example 10-22 uses the script "ap-kal-pinglist" that is available to you on your CSS. This script takes the IP addresses of the upstream and downstream devices that you want the CSS to ping to test for physical connectivity. You should also assign the "share-fate" service the IP address of the upstream router (that is, 10.1.10.3).

The CSSs also support an active-active configuration, by either load sharing traffic of multiple VIPs across CSSs, or by sharing traffic from a single VIP across CSSs. To configure load-sharing, you need to configure two or more VIPs with VRRP, as Example 10-23 illustrates.

Example 10-23   *VRRP Load Sharing with Multiple VIPs*

```
CSS A
!************************* CIRCUIT *************************
circuit VLAN10
  ip address 10.1.10.1 255.255.255.0
  ip virtual-router 1 priority 101 preempt
  ip virtual-router 2 priority 100
  ip redundant-vip 1 10.1.10.100
  ip redundant-vip 2 10.1.10.101
  ip critical-service 1 share-fate
  ip critical-service 2 share-fate

circuit VLAN20
  ip address 10.1.20.1 255.255.255.0
  ip virtual-router 3 priority 101 preempt
  ip virtual-router 4 priority 100
  ip redundant-interface 3 10.1.20.3
  ip redundant-interface 4 10.1.20.4
  ip critical-service 3 share-fate
  ip critical-service 4 share-fate
CSS B
!************************* CIRCUIT *************************
circuit VLAN10
  ip address 10.1.10.2 255.255.255.0
  ip virtual-router 1 priority 100
  ip virtual-router 2 priority 101 preempt
  ip redundant-vip 1 10.1.10.100
  ip redundant-vip 2 10.1.10.101
  ip critical-service 1 share-fate
  ip critical-service 2 share-fate

circuit VLAN20
  ip address 10.1.20.2 255.255.255.0
  ip virtual-router 3 priority 100
  ip virtual-router 4 priority 101 preempt
  ip redundant-interface 3 10.1.20.3
  ip redundant-interface 4 10.1.20.4
  ip critical-service 3 share-fate
  ip critical-service 4 share-fate
```

In Example 10-23, an additional VIP (10.1.10.101) and virtual redundant interface (10.1.20.4) is configured. You must configure your new real servers for the new VIP with the new virtual redundant interface as their default gateway. CSS A serves as master for VIP 10.1.10.100 and standby for VIP 10.1.10.101, and vice versa for CSS B.

You can configure active-active with only a single VIP using the **shared** keyword in the **ip redundant-vip** command. To share the load of a single VIP across two CSSs, use the configuration in Example 10-24.

Example 10-24 *VRRP Load Sharing with a Single VIP*

```
CSS A
!************************* CIRCUIT *************************
circuit VLAN10
  ip address 10.1.10.1 255.255.255.0
  ip virtual-router 1
  ip redundant-vip 1 10.1.10.100 shared

circuit VLAN20
  ip address 10.1.20.1 255.255.255.0
CSS B
!************************* CIRCUIT *************************
circuit VLAN10
  ip address 10.1.10.2 255.255.255.0
  ip virtual-router 1
  ip redundant-vip 1 10.1.10.100 shared

circuit VLAN20
  ip address 10.1.20.2 255.255.255.0
```

To distribute load across two CSSs for a single VIP, use the **shared** keyword of the **ip redundant-vip** command. This enables both CSSs to respond to traffic for the VIP. To distribute real server response traffic across the two CSSs, you must configure half of your real servers with 10.1.20.1 and the other with 10.1.20.2 as their default gateways. Also make sure you enable CEF per-flow load sharing on your upstream router. This way, the router will distribute incoming flow requests across your two CSSs, and thus preserve flow-state on your CSSs.

> **NOTE** If you do not require stateful fail-over or active-active load-sharing across your CSSs, you can configure CSS box-to-box redundancy. For more information on CSS box-to-box redundancy, refer to your product documentation.

CSM High Availability

To configure high availability on your CSM, you need to configure both fault-tolerant (FT) VLANS and redundant interfaces with Hot Standby Router Protocol (HSRP) tracking and connection and sticky table synchronization as follows:

■ **FT VLANS and redundant interfaces with HSRP tracking**—In contrast to the operations you perform with CSS, you need only configure your interfaces with redundancy. You do not need to explicitly configure your VIPs with redundancy. You configure CSMs with an FT

VLAN, which the standby CSM uses to learn the status of the active CSM. The CSMs use a proprietary multicast-based protocol to send heartbeat messages over the FT VLAN. The standby CSM detects when the active fails and takes over processing.

You also need to configure HSRP between the MSFC routers involved in the redundant configuration. You must configure the external client network interface with HSRP tracking to ensure that flows traverse the same path in both directions. This is similar in concept to fate sharing with the CSS.

■ **Connection and sticky table synchronization**—Once you configure your CSMs with FT VLANs and your routers with HSRP with fate sharing, you can enable connection and sticky table.

NOTE   You can use CSM high availability for active-backup only. The CSM handles connection and bandwidth loads such that support for an active-active (load-sharing) configuration is currently unnecessary.

Figure 10-27 gives a sample redundant CSM configuration.

Figure 10-27   *CSM High Availability*

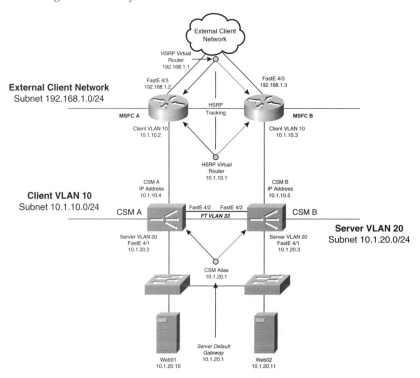

To configure the high availability features shown in Figure 10-27 on your CSM, you can use the configuration in Example 10-25.

Example 10-25   *Configuring CSM High Availability*

```
CSM A
interface fastethernet 4/1
 description *** Server VLAN 20 ***
 switchport access vlan 20

interface fastethernet 4/2
 description *** Fault-Tolerant VLAN 33 ***
 switchport access vlan 33

interface fastethernet 4/3
 description *** External Client Network ***
 ip address 192.168.1.2 255.255.255.0
 standby 1 priority 101 preempt
 standby 1 ip 192.168.1.1

interface vlan 10
 description *** CSM Internet Client VLAN 10
 ip address 10.1.10.2 255.255.255.0
 standby 2 priority 101 preempt
 standby 2 ip 10.1.10.1
 standby 2 track fastethernet 4/3 10

mod csm 5

 vlan 10 client
  ip address 10.1.10.4 255.255.255.0
  gateway 10.1.10.1

 vlan 20 server
  ip address 10.1.20.2 255.255.255.0
  alias 10.1.20.1 255.255.255.0

 vlan 33
 ft group 3 vlan 33
  priority 101
  preempt

vserver webvip
 virtual 10.1.10.100 tcp www
 serverfarm webfarm
 replicate csrp connection
 replicate csrp sticky
```

continues

Example 10-25 *Configuring CSM High Availability (Continued)*

```
 persistent rebalance
 inservice
CSM B
interface fastethernet 4/1
 description *** Server VLAN 20 ***
 switchport access vlan 20

interface fastethernet 4/2
 description *** Fault-Tolerant VLAN 33 ***
 switchport access vlan 33

interface fastethernet 4/3
 description *** External Client Network ***
 ip address 192.168.1.3 255.255.255.0
 standby 1 priority 100
 standby 1 ip 192.168.1.1

interface vlan 10
 description *** CSM Internet Client VLAN 10
 ip address 10.1.10.3 255.255.255.0
 standby 2 priority 100
 standby 2 ip 10.1.10.1
 standby 2 track fastethernet 4/3 10

mod csm 5

 vlan 10 client
  ip address 10.1.10.5 255.255.255.0
  gateway 10.1.10.1

 vlan 20 server
  ip address 10.1.20.3 255.255.255.0
  alias 10.1.20.1 255.255.255.0

 vlan 33

 ft group 3 vlan 33
  priority 100


vserver webvip
 virtual 10.1.10.100 tcp www
 serverfarm webfarm
 replicate csrp connection
 replicate csrp sticky
 persistent rebalance
 inservice
```

On both CSMs in Example 10-25, port 4/1 is configured in the server VLAN for back-end real server connectivity. Port 4/2 is used for the FT VLAN, and port 4/3 is for upstream connectivity to external clients. You must configure HSRP on the upstream interfaces and on the internal VLAN 10 client interfaces. Notice that the client interfaces are configured with HSRP tracking. You should configure tracking so that, when the upstream connectivity fails-over to the other Catalyst IOS switch, traffic flowing from the internal network will traverse the same switch.

Example 10-25 configures CSM A as the master CSM, because it has a higher priority (101) than CSM B (100) for its HSRP configuration (groups 1 and 2) and FT VLAN (group 3).

If you configure router-mode fault-tolerance, as shown in Example 10-25, you must also specify an HSRP-like default gateway for the server VLAN (with the **alias** command). When the active CSM fails, the standby will respond to ARP requests for the shared default gateway.

> **NOTE**   To configure bridge-mode fault tolerance, you can use the same configuration as in Example 10-25 with the exception of creating a shared default gateway on the server VLAN with the **alias** command. You also must specify the same IP address for the CSM client and server VLAN interfaces.

You configure the FT VLAN using the **ft group** command. To assign the CSM priority, you can use the **priority** FT configuration command. The CSM with the higher priority becomes master. The **preempt** command works in the same manner as with HSRP and VRRP—when the master fails and comes back online, it becomes master once again. As you learned previously, CSMs send multicast heartbeat messages to one another over the FT VLAN. When the standby CSM does not receive a heartbeat within the default of three seconds, it becomes the master CSM. You can modify this default by changing the fail-over value, using the **failover** FT configuration mode command. To change the time between heartbeats, you can use the **heartbeat-time** command.

Now that you know how to configure FT VLANS and redundant interfaces with Hot Standby Router Protocol (HSRP) tracking, you can configure connection and sticky table synchronization. To enable your CSMs to transfer their connection table entries across the FT VLAN to one another, use the **replicate csrp connection** virtual server configuration command, as Example 10-25 illustrates. If you enable session stickiness on your CSM and you want your CSMs to transfer their sticky table entries across the FT VLAN to one another, use the **replicate csrp sticky** virtual server configuration command.

> **NOTE**   The CSMs do not synchronize ARP table entries, but a standby CSM that becomes master will respond to ARP requests and learn the required ARP table entries automatically.

Summary

In this chapter you learned how content switches can accelerate your application, by exploring Cisco's content switch hardware and software features. Through sample configurations on the Cisco CSS and CSM, you learned how to configure your content switches to

- Distribute content requests using round robin, least connections, source IP address hashing, and server load algorithms.

- Apply Layer 5–7 rules to intelligently select appropriate groups of servers for client requests.

- Determine the health of real servers.

- Stick clients to the same server throughout the life of their application session.

- Apply high-availability features to your content switches.

Review Questions

1. What content switch hardware is responsible for providing in-band health checking? What about OOB health checking?

2. Why do content switches perform delayed binding?

3. What is involved in sequence-number remapping?

4. What is the major difference between router and bridge mode?

5. What is the major difference between relative and absolute load calculations?

6. What is the difference between HTTP header load balancing and HTTP URL hashing?

7. Why doesn't the CSS store its client to real server associations in the sticky state table with HTTP hash cookies?

8. What type of stickiness should you configure with CSS high availability?

9. What is the major difference between CSS and CSM high availability?

Recommended Reading

Mauricio Arregoces, Maurizio Portolani, *Data Center Fundamentals*, Cisco Press, 2003

Chandra Kopparapu, *Load Balancing Servers, Firewalls and Caches*, Wiley, 2002

Chapter Goals

You will learn how to configure content switching for the following security protocols in this chapter:

- **Secure Sockets Layer (SSL) Termination**—You can configure your content switch to terminate SSL connections on behalf of clients.

- **Firewall Load Balancing (FWLB)**—You can configure your content switch to distribute client traffic across multiple firewalls.

- **Virtual Private Network (VPN) Load Balancing (FWLB)**—You can configure your content switch to distribute client traffic across multiple VPN concentrators.

- **SYN-Cookies for SYN-Flood Protection**—You will learn how the CSM uses SYN-cookies to prevent SYN-flood attacks from flooding the CSM's connection table.

CHAPTER 11

Switching Secured Content

In Chapter 10, "Exploring Server Load Balancing," you learned how to configure content switching to accelerate your applications through the use of server load balancing. In this chapter, you'll learn four popular ways to accelerate secure content delivery by using content switching:

- **SSL Termination**— You learned about the operation of the SSL protocol in Chapter 8, "Exploring the Application Layer." Here, you will learn how content switches can off-load SSL computations from your origin servers to dedicated SSL devices and modules.

- **Firewall Load Balancing**— As you learned in Chapter 4, "Exploring Security Technologies and Network Infrastructure Designs," firewalls provide stateful packet inspection and maintain the context within and across TCP and UDP connections. In this chapter, you will learn how to load balance your traffic across multiple stateful firewalls.

- **VPN Load Balancing**— VPN devices can provide site-to-site or remote access for your corporate users. Content switches can also provide load balancing across multiple VPN concentrators.

- **SYN-Flood Protection**— The Content Switching Module (CSM) uses SYN-cookies to prevent SYN-floods from flooding its connection table.

SSL Termination

With SSL termination, a dedicated SSL termination device terminates the SSL connection, offloading CPU-intensive SSL computations from your origin servers. SSL termination devices have special hardware that can perform the SSL operations.

SSL termination also enables the content switch to parse cleartext application headers to intelligently load balance SSL requests. To provide SSL offloading, you can configure your content switch and SSL termination device to decrypt SSL traffic and forward the cleartext traffic to non-SSL real servers, as Figure 11-1 illustrates.

Figure 11-1 *SSL Offloading*

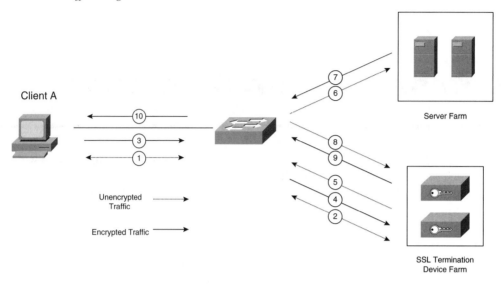

Because the content switch sees the request in cleartext, you can configure Layers 5–7 load balancing with SSL termination. Also, because the SSL module forwards traffic in cleartext to real servers, you should make sure that you secure your server farm switches to prevent sniffing of the cleartext traffic.

> **NOTE**   To encrypt traffic from your SSL termination device to your back-end real servers, you can configure Back-End Encryption on your Content Services Switch (CSS) and CSM. Refer to your product documentation on Cisco.com for more information on Back-End Encryption.

Based on Figure 11-1, a client's SSL transaction flows through the content network as follows:

1. The client generates a TCP SYN segment to initiate a TCP connection to the SSL port (443) on the content switch. The content switch receives the TCP segment, issues an HTTPS virtual server lookup, and opens the TCP connection with the client. The client generates a cleartext SSL Client Hello packet and forwards it to the content switch.

> **NOTE**   Refer to Figure 8-11 in Chapter 8 for more information on the SSL four-way handshake.

2. The content switch receives the SSL Client Hello and load balances the request to an available SSL termination device. If you configure SSL-sticky on the content switch, the content switch stores the Session ID associated with the connection. The SSL termination device then processes the Client Hello and completes the SSL four-way handshake with the client to establish an encrypted transport session.

> **NOTE**   If you have multiple SSL devices, you should configure SSL-sticky to ensure that each connection from within the SSL session is load-balanced to the same SSL device. This would be beneficial for clients who want to resume idle SSL sessions, as you learned previously from Figure 8-12 in Chapter 8.

3. The client generates an HTTPS application request and forwards it to the content switch over the encrypted SSL transport session. The content switch in turn forwards the encrypted request to the appropriate SSL termination device, based on the entry for the existing TCP connection in the content switch's connection table.

4. The SSL termination device receives the encrypted application request.

5. The SSL termination device decrypts the application request, optionally rewrites the URL or any HTTP headers in the request, and forwards it back to the content switch.

> **NOTE**   You will learn about URL and HTTP Header rewriting later in this chapter.

6. The content switch receives the cleartext application request, issues an HTTP virtual server lookup, stores any cleartext sticky information (for example, HTTP cookies and source IP addresses) that you configure, and load balances the request to an available real server. The content switch also performs destination Network Address Translation (NAT) on the packet to the real server IP address.

7. The real server processes the cleartext request and sends the HTTP 200 OK cleartext response to the content switch.

8. The content switch receives the HTTP 200 OK cleartext response and forwards it to the SSL termination device, based on the connection information in the content switch's connection table, thus overriding normal TCP/IP routing to the client source IP address. The content switch also reverses the destination NAT performed in Step 6.

9. The SSL termination device encrypts the response and forwards it to the content switch, again preserving the source and destination IP addresses.

10. The content switch routes the encrypted SSL packet to the client.

To configure SSL Termination, you can use either:

- **CSS with an SSL Module**—Recall from Chapter 10 that you can install an SSL encryption module in the CSS 11503 or 11506 or obtain a CSS 11501 with an embedded SSL module.

- **CSM with SSL Daughter Card Module (CSM-S)**—You can also obtain a CSM-S for terminating SSL connections. The daughter card module is not field upgradeable—you cannot purchase the daughter card separately for an existing CSM installation.

Configuring Your CSS for SSL Termination

To configure your CSS to offload your SSL connections to an SSL termination device, you must first load your keys and certificates to the SSL termination device. If you are already using public-key infrastructure (PKI) on your real servers and want to upgrade your system with SSL termination, you can import your existing private keys and server certificates to the SSL termination device. Otherwise, you can generate private/public key pairs and Certificate Signing Requests on the SSL termination device and request a server certificate from a Certificate Authority (CA). Once you enroll with a CA and receive the server certificate, you can import the server certificate to your SSL termination device.

> **NOTE** You can also use your own private CA to enroll certificates with Cisco CSSs and CSMs. For more information on configuring automatic certificate enrollment with private CAs, see your product documentation on Cisco.com.

Creating and Importing Keys and Certificates on the CSS

You learned about the SSL module that is available for the CSS in Chapter 10. To import pre-existing keys and certificates to your CSS SSL module, you can use the command:

```
copy ssl [protocol] ftp_record [import filename [format] "password" {"passphrase"}
```

The *passphrase* is the existing phrase created with the certificate for encrypting/decrypting. This phrase must be used anywhere you use the certificate, not just on the CSS. You must also create a new password as a second layer of security that the CSS will use to encrypt the imported certificate. This password is local to the CSS and prevents unauthorized administrators from accessing the certificate on the CSS. Before issuing this command, you should first create an FTP record where your certificate and private key is located. You can use the **ftp-record** command to create a record called **import-ssl**. You must include your FTP username, your password to the FTP server, and the home directory where the certificate and private key is located on the server. For example:

```
ftp-record import-ssl 10.1.1.1 cisco "cisco123" /home/sdaros
```

You can use the following **copy ssl** command to import a PEM file containing an existing server certificate and private key, called **sitecert.pem** and **sitekey.pem**, respectively:

```
copy ssl sftp import-ssl import sitecert.pem PEM "sanfran" "sanfran"
copy ssl sftp import-ssl import sitekey.pem PEM "sanfran" "sanfran"
```

You must indicate to the CSS whether the imported files contain a private key or a certificate by using the **ssl associate** commands:

```
ssl associate cert mycontentcert sitecert.pem
ssl associate rsakey mycontentkey sitekey.pem
```

> **NOTE** Make sure that you import your CA's root certificate. Additionally, if your CA issues you a chained certificate, make sure you also import any intermediary certificates within the chain.

Instead of importing existing keys, you can generate an Rivest, Shamir, and Adelman (RSA) public/private key pair for asymmetric encryption on the CSS using the following command:

```
ssl genrsa filename numbits "password"
```

This command stores both the private and public key in a single file that you must associate with a certificate name. For example, to generate a key called **mycontentkey**, use the following commands:

```
ssl genrsa mycontentkeyfile 1024 "sanfran"
ssl associate rsakey mycontentkey mycontentkeyfile
```

To generate a CSR for the key pair, use the following command in Example 11-1.

Example 11-1 *Generating a CSR on the CSS*

```
(config)# ssl gencsr mycontentkey
You are about to be asked to enter information
that will be incorporated into your certificate
request. What you are about to enter is what is
called a Distinguished Name or a DN.
For some fields there will be a default value,
If you enter '.', the field will be left blank.
Country Name (2 letter code) [US]US
State or Province (full name) [SomeState]California
Locality Name (city) [SomeCity]San Jose
Organization Name (company name) [Acme Inc]Cisco Systems, Inc.
Organizational Unit Name (section) [Web Administration]Network Engineering
Common Name (your domain name) [www.acme.com]www.cisco.com
Email address [webadmin@acme.com]admin@cisco.com

-----BEGIN NEW CERTIFICATE REQUEST-----
```

continues

Example 11-1 *Generating a CSR on the CSS (Continued)*

```
MIctCMtmZONOY+ybEHl/mX0RdqXFnivLBgNVBAYTAlVTMRAwDgYDVQQIEwdHZW9y
DQ kW6Pa6mbjeUV1wffn2dtbKsmz7DnK2BVbml2ZXJzaXR5IG9 yRPs36ywGwDK3
aWExNTAzBgNVBAsTLFVuaXZlcnNpdHkgQ29tcHV0aW5nIGFuZCBOZXR3b3JraW5n
IFNlcnZpY2VzMRYwFAYDVQQDEw13d3ctcy51Z2EuZWR1MIGdMA0GCSqGSIb3DQEB
AQUAA4GLADCBhwKBgQDh3yRPs36ywGwDK3ZS3qaOoNraOFHkSNTsielHUMHxV1/G
N1E43/bifEQJUvSw/nrkOQf3Ync8O/39lelUTJeP6QZkX9Hg1XtuSUov3ExzT53l
vbctCMtmZONOY+ybEHl/mX0RdqXFnivLpXohr7dJ5A1qHfjww/SLW8J/7UXj1QIB
A6AAMA0GCSqGSIb3DQEBBAUAA4GBAIEu35zoGmODCcwwNrTqZk3JQAjyONJxjjtd
uQ+QLQcckO4aghBpcqsgLckW6Pa6mbjeUV1wffn2dtbKsmz7DnK2fwnyaBtxXMvi
CC4o9uvW11i5TjdorfOdRI1lR0FrNAzf+3GQUl1S2a83wagvFjo12yUCukrxBgyU
bXbmNuJpkdsjdkjfkdjfkdfjdkfjdkfjdkfj
-----END NEW CERTIFICATE REQUEST-----
```

To apply for a server certificate, you must send the CSR to a CA of your choice. Most well-known CAs allow you to cut and paste your CSR to their websites and will issue you a server certificate via e-mail within a few business days. Once you receive your server certificate (called **sitecert.pem** in this example), you can import it using the **copy ssl** command that you learned previously:

```
copy ssl sftp import-ssl import sitecert.pem PEM "sanfran" "sanfran"
ssl associate cert mycontentcert sitecert.pem
```

> **NOTE** Make sure you keep track of when your certificates expire. You will need to obtain new certificates before they expire. Otherwise, clients will receive an error when they attempt to download the expired certificate.

Terminating SSL on the CSS

Now that you have a server certificate and a private key on your CSS, you can configure your CSS to terminate SSL connections on behalf of your real servers, as illustrated in Example 11-2.

> **NOTE** Note that there is no IP addressing and server destination-Network Address Translationing (DNATing) involved when configuring the CSS SSL module.

Example 11-2 *Configuring Your CSS to Terminate SSL Connections*

```
ssl-proxy-list ssl_proxy
 ssl-server 1
 ssl-server 1 vip address 10.1.10.1
 ssl-server 1 port 443
 ssl-server 1 rsacert mycontentcert
 ssl-server 1 rsakey mycontentkey
 ssl-server 1 cipher TLS_RSA_WITH_RC4_128_MD5 10.1.10.100 80 weight 5
```

Example 11-2 *Configuring Your CSS to Terminate SSL Connections (Continued)*

```
    ssl-server 1 cipher TLS_RSA_WITH_RC4_128_SHA 10.1.10.100 80 weight 10
    ssl-server 1 http-header session
    ssl-server 1 urlrewrite 1 www.cisco.com
    active

service ssl-serv1
 type ssl-accel
 add ssl-proxy-list ssl_proxy
 slot 5
 keepalive type none
 active

service ssl-serv2
 type ssl-accel
 add ssl-proxy-list ssl_proxy
 slot 6
 keepalive type none
 active

service web01
 ip address 10.1.10.10
 active

service web02
 ip address 10.1.10.11
 active

owner cisco
 content https-vip
  vip address 10.1.10.100
  protocol tcp
  port 443
  add service ssl-serv1
  add service ssl-serv2
  active

content http-vip
  vip address 10.1.10.100
  protocol tcp
  port 80
  add service web01
  add service web02
  active
```

Configuring URL and Header Rewrite on the CSS

You learned previously that, without back-end encryption, real servers receive cleartext requests and send HTML page responses in cleartext (in Steps 6–8 from Figure 11-1). However, if an HTML page includes embedded HTML references to other sites, you need to make sure that these links are prefixed by "https://" and not "http://"; otherwise, your browser may give you an error while accessing the secure site.

For example, your HTML page may include the following links:

<A HREF="**http:**//cisco.com/support.html">Support</A>
<A HREF="**http:**//cisco.com/services.html">Services</A>
<A HREF="**http:**//cisco.com/products.html">Products</A>

To inform your HTTP server that the current cleartext request is from the CSS SSL module (in Step 6) and is not a client request, you can configure the CSS SSL module to add an HTTP header to the HTTP request. For example, you can add an HTTP header including the SSL session information. To enable the CSS to insert SSL session information HTTP headers into requests that it proxies, use the following proxy list mode command, as Example 11-2 illustrates:

```
ssl-server number http-header session
```

You can then configure your HTTP servers to recognize these headers and supply an HTML page containing "https://" within the embedded links instead of "http:// ."

> **NOTE**   You can also configure the CSS to insert the client and server certificates as HTTP headers using the **client-cert** and **server-cert** keywords of the **ssl-server http-header** proxy list command.

Additionally, if your servers send HTTP 300 series redirects to your clients, then you should configure your CSS to rewrite the "http://" reference in the "Location:" header of HTTP 300 series redirect methods to "https://" with the proxy list command:

```
ssl-server number urlrewrite number hostname [sslport port {clearport port}]
```

This command enables you to specify particular URLs that you want to rewrite in HTTP 300 series redirects, by including the exact URL or by using wildcards. Entries without wildcards take precedence over wildcard entries, and prefix wildcards entries take precedence over suffix wildcard entries. For example, you can configure your CSS to rewrite all redirects for "*.cisco.com" (prefix wildcard) and "www.cisco.*" (suffix wildcard) with the commands:

```
ssl-server 1 urlrewrite 1 *.cisco.com
ssl-server 1 urlrewrite 1 www.cisco.*
```

You can also rewrite nonstandard cleartext HTTP ports (that is, any port other than port 80) with either the standard SSL port (that is, port 443) or nonstandard SSL ports. For example, the following command will rewrite "http://www.cisco.com:81" to "https://www.cisco.com":

```
ssl-server 1 urlrewrite 1 www.cisco.com clearport 81
```

The following command rewrites "http://www.cisco.com" to "https://www.cisco.com:444":

```
ssl-server 1 urlrewrite 1 www.cisco.com sslport 444
```

The following command rewrites "http://www.cisco.com:81" to "https://www.cisco.com:444":

```
ssl-server 1 urlrewrite 1 www.cisco.com sslport 444 clearport 81
```

> **NOTE**   Neither the CSM nor CSS supports rewriting HTTP URLs embedded directly within HTML pages.

Configuring Your Content Services Module with SSL

You can also configure your CSM-S for SSL termination. As with the CSS with an SSL module, you can import existing keys and server certificates to your CSM-S daughter card or generate new keys and request server certificates from a CA.

> **NOTE**   You can also configure SSL termination with the CSM using a separate SSL services module (SSLM). The configuration for the SSLM is the same as the CSM-S. For more information on the SSLM, refer to its product documentation on Cisco.com.

Creating and Importing Keys and Certificates on the CSM

To generate a private/public key pair on your CSM-S daughter card, use the command:

```
crypto key generate rsa general-keys label key-label [exportable] [modulus size]
```

For example, the **crypto key generate** command produces the output in Example 11-3 to generate a key pair called **mycontentkey** on the CSM-S. If you want to be able to export the private key from the SSL daughter card for future use outside the CSM-S, you can use the **exportable** keyword.

Example 11-3   *Configuring Your CSM to Generate an RSA Key Pair*

```
ssl-card(config)# crypto key generate rsa general-keys label mycontentkey exportable
The name for the keys will be: mycontentkey
Choose the size of the key modulus in the range of 360 to 2048 for your
General Purpose Keys. Choosing a key modulus greater than 512 may take
a few minutes.
```

continues

Example 11-3 *Configuring Your CSM to Generate an RSA Key Pair (Continued)*

```
How many bits in the modulus [512]: 1024
Generating RSA keys.... [OK].
```

To enter your organization's information for a CSR, you must create a trust point, as Example 11-4 illustrates.

Example 11-4 *Configuring a Trust Point on the CSM-S*

```
crypto ca trustpoint mycontent-trustpoint
 rsakeypair mycontentkey
 serial
 subject-name C=US, ST=California, CN=www.cisco.com, OU=Network Engineering, O=Cisco
Systems, Inc.
 enrollment url tftp://10.1.1.1/certificates
```

To generate a CSR for the key pair, use the command:

> **crypto ca enroll** *trustpoint-name*

For example, Example 11-5 shows the command output to generate a request for the key pair **mycontentkey** that Example 11-3 previously generated.

Example 11-5 *Creating a CSR on Your CSM-S*

```
ssl-card(config)# crypto ca enroll mycontent-trustpoint
% Start certificate enrollment ..

% The subject name in the certificate will be:CN=www.cisco.com, OU=Network Engineering,
O=Cisco Systems, Inc.
% The fully-qualified domain name in the certificate will be:www.cisco.com
% The subject name in the certificate will be:www.cisco.com
% The serial number in the certificate will be:B0FFF22E
% Include an IP address in the subject name? [no]:no
Display Certificate Request to terminal? [yes/no]:yes
Certificate Request follows:

MIctCMtmZONOY+ybEHl/mX0RdqXFnivLBgNVBAYTAlVTMRAwDgYDVQQIEwdHZW9y
DQ kW6Pa6mbjeUV1wffn2dtbKsmz7DnK2BVbml2ZXJzaXR5IG9 yRPs36ywGwDK3
aWExNTAzBgNVBAsTLFVuaXZlcnNpdHkgQ29tcHV0aW5nIGFuZCBOZXR3b3JraW5n
IFNlcnZpY2VzMRYwFAYDVQQDEw13d3ctcy51Z2EuZWR1MIGdMA0GCSqGSIb3DQEB
AQUAA4GLADCBhwKBgQDh3yRPs36ywGwDK3ZS3qaOoNraOFHkSNTsielHUMHxV1/G
N1E43/bifEQJUvSw/nrkOQf3Ync8O/39lelUTJeP6QZkX9Hg1XtuSUov3ExzT53l
vbctCMtmZONOY+ybEHl/mX0RdqXFnivLpXohr7dJ5A1qHfjww/SLW8J/7UXj1QIB
A6AAMA0GCSqGSIb3DQEBBAUAA4GBAIEu35zoGmODCcwwNrTqZk3JQAjyONJxjjtd
uQ+QLQcckO4aghBpcqsgLckW6Pa6mbjeUV1wffn2dtbKsmz7DnK2fwnyaBtxXMvi
CC4o9uvW11i5TjdorfOdRI1lR0FrNAzf+3GQUl1S2a83wagvFjo12yUCukrxBgyU
```

Example 11-5 *Creating a CSR on Your CSM-S (Continued)*

```
bXbmNuJpkdsjdkjfkdjfkdfjdkfjdkfjdkfj

---End - This line not part of the certificate request---

Redisplay enrollment request? [yes/no]:no
```

As you learned previously, to apply for a server certificate, you must send the CSR to a public CA of your choice (such as Verisign), or to your own private CA (such as Microsoft Certificate Services). If you use a public CA, once you receive the server certificate, you can TFTP it to the CSM-S using the **crypto ca import** command, as Example 11-6 illustrates. The CSM-S connects to the TFTP server specified previously in Example 11-4 using the **enrollment url** command. Make sure your certificate exists on a valid TFTP server before using the **crypto ca import** command.

Alternately, if you use a private CA, you can specify its URL with the **enrollment url** command, and the **crypto ca import** command will connect to the private CA to download the server certificate.

Example 11-6 *Importing a Server Certificate on Your CSM-S*

```
ssl-card(config)# crypto ca import mycontent-trustpoint certificate
% The fully-qualified domain name in the certificate will be: ssl-card.cisco.com
Retrieve Certificate from tftp server? [yes/no]:yes
% Request to retrieve Certificate queued

ssl-proxy(config)#
Loading mycontent-trustpoint.crt from 10.1.1.1 (via Ethernet0/0.172):!
[OK - 1608 bytes]

ssl-proxy(config)#
*Nov 25 21:52:36.299:%CRYPTO-6-CERTRET:Certificate received from Certificate Authority
ssl-proxy(config)# ^Z
```

> **NOTE** Make sure you load your CA's certificate (and intermediate certificate, if necessary) to the CSM-S using the **crypto ca authenticate** command. Also use the **enrollment url** command to make sure that the CA's certificate resides on the TFTP server you specify. If you are using your own private CA, the **crypto ca authenticate** command will load the CA certificate from the private CA.

Alternately, if you have existing private keys and certificates, you can import them into your SSL daughter card. For example, to import an existing PKCS#12 key, you need to have previously generated the PKCS#12 file using an external PKI system. Recall from Chapter 8 that a PKCS#12 file can contain a private key and server certificate chain.

Then, to import the existing private key and server certificate chain from the PKCS#12 file to your CSM-S, you can use the following command:

```
crypto ca import trustpoint_label pkcs12 {scp: | ftp: | nvram: | rcp: | tftp:}
[pkcs12_filename] pass_phrase
```

NOTE Using the **crypt ca import** command to import PKCS#12 certificates automatically generates the trust point configuration for use in your SSL proxy services. You will learn how to configure a proxy service on the SSL daughter card later in this section.

Terminating SSL on the CSM-S

Now that you have private keys and server certificates on your SSL daughter card, you can configure your CSM-S to terminate SSL connections. You can configure the content switch either in NAT-mode (that is, the content switch will destination-NAT the client's request to the SSL daughter card's IP address in Step 2 from Figure 11-1) or in dispatch mode (that is, the content switch will route the packet directly to the SSL daughter card without DNATing it). If you configure the content switch in NAT-mode, make sure you configure the SSL daughter card to DNAT the packet back to the virtual server IP address. Example 11-7 shows how to configure your CSM to terminate SSL connections in dispatch-mode, based on the network topology in Figure 11-2. For the example in this section, the SSL daughter card farm is in bridge-mode and the real server farm is in router-mode, as Figure 11-2 illustrates.

Figure 11-2 *Dispatch-Mode CSM with SSL Daughter Card in Bridge-Mode*

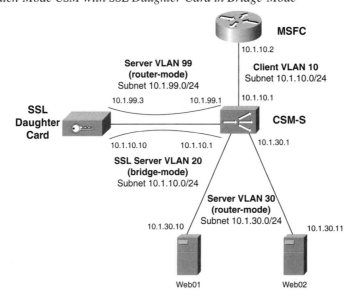

Example 11-7 *Configuring Your CSM to Terminate SSL in Bridge-Mode*

```
interface vlan 10
 description *** Client VLAN
 ip address 10.1.10.2


interface fastethernet 2/1
 description *** Web01
 switchport vlan 30

interface fastethernet 2/2
 description *** Web02
 switchport vlan 30

ip route 10.1.30.0 255.255.255.0 10.1.10.1
ip route 10.1.99.0 255.255.255.0 10.1.10.1
module csm 5

vlan 10 client
  ip address 10.1.10.1 255.255.255.0
  gateway 10.1.10.2

 vlan 20 server
  ip address 10.1.10.1 255.255.255.0

vlan 30 server
  ip address 10.1.30.1 255.255.255.0

vlan 99 server
  ip address 10.1.99.1 255.255.255.0

serverfarm ssl-accel-farm
 no nat server
 no nat client
 real 10.1.10.10 local
  inservice

serverfarm webfarm
 nat server
 no nat client
 real 10.1.30.10
  inservice
 real 10.1.30.11
  inservice

serverfarm forward-route
 no nat server
 no nat client
 predictor forward
```

continues

Example 11-7 *Configuring Your CSM to Terminate SSL in Bridge-Mode (Continued)*

```
vserver https-vip
 virtual 10.1.10.100 tcp https
 vlan 10
 serverfarm ssl-accel-farm
 inservice

vserver http-vip
 virtual 10.1.10.100 tcp www
 serverfarm webfarm
 persistent rebalance
 inservice

vserver direct-web
  virtual 10.1.30.0 255.255.255.0 any
  serverfarm forward-route
  inservice

vserver direct-ssl
  virtual 10.1.99.0 255.255.255.0 any
  serverfarm forward-route
  inservice
```

Here are some notes to help you understand the configuration in Example 11-7.

■ Recall from Chapter 10 that configuring bridge-mode requires that you give the client VLAN 10 and server VLAN 20 interfaces the same IP address (that is, 10.1.10.1 in Example 11-7).

■ Use the **no nat server** command to prevent the CSM from DNATing client requests to the SSL daughter card (thus enabling dispatch-mode processing).

■ The virtual server "http-vip" serves traffic from both cleartext client requests and from unencrypted traffic forwarded by the SSL daughter card.

■ The command **vlan 10** within the "https-vip" virtual server configuration indicates that the virtual server shall receive traffic from only VLAN 10.

■ You need to include the **local** keyword when configuring the SSL daughter card as a real server within a server farm. This keyword indicates to the CSM that the real server is the SSL daughter card and not an external real server.

■ The "direct-*type*" virtual server is necessary for you to be able to directly connect to your secure router-mode real servers for testing purposes. You also need to add a static route to the MSFC pointing to the CSM client IP address for the subnet of the router-mode reals (for example, **ip route 10.1.30.0 255.255.255.0 10.1.10.1**, in Example 11-7).

- VLAN 99 is for administering the SSL daughter card using Telnet.

- Because the SSL devices preserve the source IP address of the packet as the client's IP address, the CSM-S must use special routing for real-server return traffic. If the CSM-S uses normal routing, the cleartext real server return packets are routed to the client directly, bypassing the SSL daughter card. Therefore, the CSM-S routes the back-end real server return packets to the SSL daughter card by tracking the Layer 2 MAC address of the SSL daughter card during the connection flow.

Example 11-8 gives the corresponding SSL daughter card configuration for CSM-S termination. Whereas with the CSM-S you did not have to directly configure the SSL module with IP addressing, you must configure the CSM-S daughter card with an IP address and default gateway. The SSL daughter card is a separate TCP/IP host on the network and, as such, it responds to ARP requests. You must also administer it separately via Telnet through a separate command line interface.

Example 11-8   *Configuring Your SSL Daughter Card for SSL Termination*

```
ssl-proxy vlan 99
 ipaddr 10.1.99.3 255.255.255.0
 gateway 10.1.99.1
 admin

ssl-proxy vlan 20
 ipaddr 10.1.10.10 255.255.255.0
 gateway 10.1.10.1

ssl-proxy service ssl-termination
 virtual ipaddr 10.1.10.100 protocol tcp port 443 secondary
 server ipaddr 10.1.10.1 protocol tcp port 80
 no nat server
 certificate rsa mycontent-trustpoint certs-key
 inservice
```

Here are some notes to help you understand the configuration in Example 11-8.

- The **ssl-proxy service** command creates the virtual server called "ssl-termination." Virtual servers on the daughter card function in the same manner as on content switches. You must assign the same IP address and port to the virtual server. When the SSL proxy receives packets that match the virtual server, it decrypts the packets and sends them to the configured real server using the **server** command, which is simply its default gateway (that is, the CSM-S IP address 10.1.10.1). If there were multiple CSM-Ss, you would add them using the **server** command.

- Because this is a dispatch-mode configuration, you should disable server DNAT on the SSL daughter card using the **no nat server** command; otherwise, the request will be DNATed from the VIP to the IP address of the CSM.

- Specify the RSA certificate that you want to assign to the service by using the **certificate rsa** command. This example uses the certificate "mycontent-trustpoint" imported in Example 11-6.

- Because the SSL daughter card is in bridge-mode and is configured with the same virtual IP as the CSM-S, it receives the same ARP requests from the MSFC that the CSM-S receives. The **secondary** keyword prevents the SSL daughter card from responding to these ARP requests.

Configuring URL and Header Rewrite on the CSM

To enable the SSL daughter card to insert HTTP headers to inform the server that the SSL daughter card is proxying the connection, you can create an HTTP header policy on the SSL daughter card. Example 11-9 illustrates how to create an HTTP header policy and assign it to an SSL proxy service.

Example 11-9 *Creating an HTTP Header Policy*

```
ssl-proxy policy http-header insert-session-info
  session

ssl-proxy service ssl-termination
 virtual ipaddr 10.1.10.100 protocol tcp port 443 secondary
 server ipaddr 10.1.10.1 protocol tcp port 80
 no nat server
 certificate rsa mycontent-trustpoint certs-key
 policy http-header insert-session-info
 inservice
```

Similar to the CSS SSL daughter card, if your servers send HTTP 300 series redirects to your clients, then you should configure your CSM-S to rewrite the "http://" reference in the "Location:" header. To inspect the "Location:" header and replace "http://" with "https://" on the SSL daughter card, you can use the configuration in Example 11-10.

Example 11-10 *Creating an HTTP URL Rewrite Policy*

```
ssl-proxy policy url-rewrite rewrite-redirects
 url *.cisco.com
 url www.cisco.*
 url www.cisco.com sslport 444
 url www.cisco.com sslport 444 clearport 81

ssl-proxy service ssl-termination
```

Example 11-10 *Creating an HTTP URL Rewrite Policy (Continued)*

```
virtual ipaddr 10.1.10.100 protocol tcp port 443 secondary
server ipaddr 10.1.10.1 protocol tcp port 80
no nat server
certificate rsa mycontent-trustpoint certs-key
policy url-rewrite rewrite-redirects
inservice
```

Firewall Load Balancing

Firewalls can realize performance benefits from Cisco content switching by using Firewall Load Balancing (FWLB) technologies. Although most firewalls can be scaled inherently by supporting stateful failover to a standby unit, you can increase performance by load balancing requests across multiple active firewalls using the CSS or CSM.

CSS Firewall Load Balancing

To control traffic flowing in both directions across a group of firewalls, you must sandwich the group within two CSSs. The CSSs distribute requests over the firewalls and maintain the connection state flowing through the firewalls. The content switches use the state to intelligently switch packets from existing connections to the same firewall. Figure 11-3 illustrates how you can sandwich your firewalls between two CSSs.

Figure 11-3 *CSS Firewall Load Balancing*

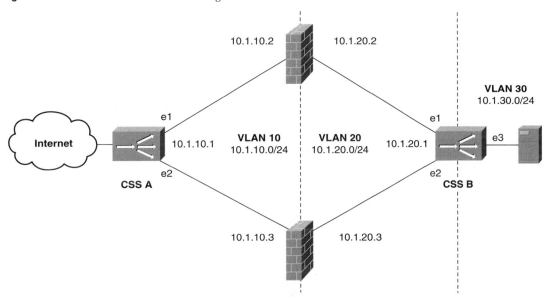

> **NOTE** You can provide CSS redundancy by installing two CSSs on both the inside and outside of the firewall group and configure the highly available features that you learned about in Chapter 10. This way you avoid having two single points of failure with the CSSs that are shown in Figure 11-3.

In Figure 11-3, consider an incoming TCP SYN segment from the Internet:

1. The CSS A decides which firewall to switch the request to, based on the configured SLB policy (for example, round-robin or hashing the source and destination IP addresses).

2. CSS A creates a connection entry for the request in its state table.

3. The selected firewall processes the request, creates a connection entry in its connection table, and forwards the TCP SYN segment to the CSS B.

4. CSS B simply forwards the packet to the destination: If the destination is a virtual server, the request is load-balanced to the server according to the rules specified for the server farm; otherwise, the packet is routed using the content switch's routing table.

5. CSS B also creates a connection entry in its connection table.

6. The server processes the request and sends a TCP SYN-ACK response back to CSS B.

7. CSS B looks up the connection in its connection table based on the information in the IP and TCP headers in the response, and updates the connection state with the SYN-ACK.

8. CSS B forwards the packet to the appropriate firewall based on the existing entry in its connection table.

9. The firewall updates its state with the SYN-ACK packet and forwards it to CSS A.

10. CSS A routes the request to the Internet per normal routing and updates its connection state.

11. The client's ACK then completes the TCP full-handshake over the same path as the original SYN segment.

Configuring FWLB differs slightly from configuring standard server load balancing (SLB) because the traffic is not destined to the firewall, but to services behind the firewall. To configure firewalls on the CSS, use the command:

```
ip firewall index local_firewall_address remote_firewall_address
remote_switch_address
```

You must configure the same index values on both CSSs. To add routes to back-end servers that you want to load balance across your firewalls, use the command:

```
ip route ip_address subnet_mask firewall index distance
```

Example 11-11 gives a sample FWLB configuration based on the topology in Figure 11-3.

Example 11-11   *CSS FWLB*

```
CSS A
ip firewall 1 10.1.10.2 10.1.20.2 10.1.20.1
ip route 10.1.30.0/24 firewall 1

ip firewall 2 10.1.10.3 10.1.20.3 10.1.20.1
ip route 10.1.30.0/24 firewall 2

interface e1
  bridge vlan 10

interface e2
  bridge vlan 10

circuit vlan 10
  ip address 10.1.10.1 255.255.255.0
CSS B
ip firewall 1 10.1.20.2 10.1.10.2 10.1.10.1
ip route 0.0.0.0/0 firewall 1

ip firewall 2 10.1.20.3 10.1.10.3 10.1.10.1
ip route 0.0.0.0/0 firewall 2

interface e1
  bridge vlan 20

interface e2
  bridge vlan 20

interface e3
  bridge vlan 30

circuit vlan 20
  ip address 10.1.20.1 255.255.255.0

circuit vlan 30
  ip address 10.1.30.1 255.255.255.0
```

> **NOTE**   Firewalls have drastically improved in performance over the past few years. The content switch must be at least X times more powerful than the firewalls being balanced, where X is the number of firewalls being balanced. Although the CSS supports FWLB, the CSM is preferable for FWLB for new deployments because its performance is better than the CSS in terms of bandwidth and flow-handling capabilities. Also, the CSS does not support reverse sticky for Active-FTP, as you will learn in the next section.

CSM Firewall Load Balancing

As you will quickly learn, with the CSM in router-mode, virtual servers are required for any traffic to pass through it. As a result, the configurations are generally more complicated than those of the CSS, but can be much more flexible. For example, the CSM enables you to configure complex designs, including single-CSM FWLB and stealth-firewall load balancing, which are not possible with the CSS.

Figure 11-4 gives a basic dual-CSM FWLB topology.

Figure 11-4   *Dual-CSM FWLB*

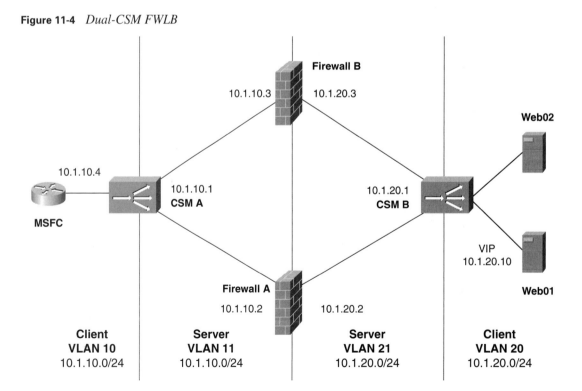

To achieve the FWLB design in Figure 11-4, you can use the configuration in Example 11-12.

Example 11-12 *Dual-CSM FWLB*

```
! MSFC shared by both CSMs
interface vlan 10
 ip address 10.1.10.4 255.255.255.0
 no shutdown
! CSM A
mod csm 5
vlan 10 client
 ip address 10.1.10.1 255.255.255.0
 gateway 10.1.10.4

vlan 11 server
 ip address 10.1.10.1 255.255.255.0

serverfarm forward
  description ** Used to forward outgoing connections from the web servers **
  no nat server
  no nat client
  predictor forward

serverfarm out-firewalls
 description ** Contains the outside interfaces of the firewalls **
 no nat server
 no nat client
 predictor hash address source 255.255.255.255
 real 10.1.10.2
  backup real 10.1.10.3
  inservice
 real 10.1.10.3
  backup real 10.1.10.2
  inservice

vserver in-connections
 description ** Distributes incoming connections from clients across firewalls **
 virtual 10.1.20.0 255.255.255.0 any
 vlan 10
 serverfarm out-firewalls
 inservice

vserver out-connections
  description ** Forwards outgoing connections from the web servers according to routing
table **
  virtual 0.0.0.0 0.0.0.0 any
  serverfarm forward
  vlan 11
```

continues

Example 11-12 *Dual-CSM FWLB (Continued)*

```
   inservice
! CSM B
mod csm 6

vlan 20 client
 ip address 10.1.20.1 255.255.255.0

vlan 21 server
 ip address 10.1.20.1 255.255.255.0

serverfarm in-firewalls
 description ** Contains the inside firewall interfaces **
 no nat server
 no nat client
 predictor leastconns
 real 10.1.20.2
  backup real 10.1.20.3
  inservice
 real 10.1.20.3
  backup real 10.1.20.2
  inservice

serverfarm web-farm
 description ** Contains the two web servers **
 nat server
 no nat client
 real 10.1.20.10

  inservice
 real 10.1.20.11
  inservice
vserver out-connections
 description ** Distributes outgoing connections initiated from the web servers across the
               available firewalls **
 virtual 0.0.0.0 0.0.0.0 any
 vlan 20
 serverfarm in-firewalls
 inservice

vserver web-vip
 description ** Distributes incoming connections initiated from external clients across web
               servers **
 virtual 10.1.20.100 255.255.255.0 www
 vlan 21
 serverfarm web-farm
 inservice
```

> **NOTE**   In Figure 11-4, CSM A and CSM B are installed within the same chassis as the MSFC, in slots five and six, respectively.

When a client initiates a connection from the Internet to the web server virtual IP (VIP) 10.1.20.100 on CSM B, CSM A is the first CSM to receive the packet and performs a virtual server lookup, matching the client's TCP SYN packet to the VIP called in-connections. This VIP distributes incoming connections from clients across the available firewalls in the server farm "out-firewalls" using the least connections predictor, which will produce even more distribution across your firewalls than source IP hashing. Single-connection TCP protocols, such as SMTP and BGP, require only one TCP connection for the application to work. As a result, you do not require hashing or sticking of subsequent application requests that occur over different TCP connections to the originally selected firewall.

The server farm "out-firewalls" contains the outside IP addresses of the firewalls you are load balancing. For example, say that CSM A selects Firewall B for the new connection. Then, CSM A creates a new connection in its connection table and forwards the packet to Firewall B. Firewall B also creates a new connection in its connection table and forwards the packet to CSM B. CSM B creates a new connection in its connection table and performs a virtual server lookup, matching the virtual server called "web-vip." CSM B then performs delayed binding with the client and eventually load balances the request to a real web server (for example, Web01). Web01 responds with a TCP SYN-ACK that traverses the same firewall as the original SYN did due to the existing connection entry in CSM B's connection table.

> **NOTE**   If your firewalls support stateful failover, you can use the **backup real** real server configuration command to specify the backup firewall.

When either back-end web server requires the initiation of a connection to the Internet, CSM B first receives the TCP SYN segment (assuming you configure the reals with CSM B as their default gateway), performs a virtual server lookup, and matches its VIP called "out-connections." This VIP distributes connections initiated from web servers across the available firewalls in the server farm "in-firewalls" using destination IP address hashing. As with using source hashing for incoming requests, you should use destination hashing for outgoing requests to distribute the connections across the firewalls more evenly.

> **NOTE**   The CSM also supports UDP-based protocols for FWLB.

Similar to "out-firewalls" configured on CSM A, the server farm "in-firewalls" on CSM B contains the inside IP addresses of the firewalls you are load balancing. In this case, say that CSM B chooses Firewall A. Then both CSM B and Firewall A create a connection state entry for the new connection in their connection tables and forward the segment upstream. When CSM A receives the TCP SYN, it matches the segment with the VIP called "out-connections" and forwards the packet to the Internet using its internal routing table, as the server farm "forward" stipulates.

Configuring Reverse Stickiness

Recall the sticky features that you learned in Chapter 10. You can configure stickiness when you require load balancing multiple TCP flows of a session to the same server as the original flow, to retain information stored about the flow on the server. The same principle is true with FWLB. For applications that require multiple connections in the same direction within the same application session, such as HTTP and Passive-FTP, you can use IP session stickiness or distribution via address hashing to ensure that multiple TCP sessions stick to the same firewall. That is, you can apply the same "forward" sticky configuration that you learned in Chapter 10 to FWLB.

However, for applications that open connections in both directions within the same session, such as Active-FTP, you must use IP reverse-sticky to ensure that TCP connections in the reverse direction take the same firewall. In the previous example, CSM A chose Firewall B for the client connection, but CSM B chose Firewall A for the server-initiated connection. With applications such as Active-FTP, you will require CSM B to choose Firewall B so that your firewall can reconcile the FTP data and control "buddy" connections for security purposes. Refer to Figure 11-5 to understand how IP reverse-sticky works.

Figure 11-5 *IP Reverse-Sticky*

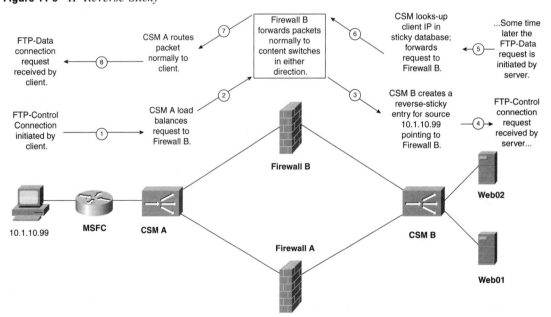

Configuring IP reverse-sticky on CSMB enables it to store a sticky entry in its sticky table during the initial connection made by the client. IP reverse-sticky forces CSMB to override its normal load balancing decision-making process for subsequent connection requests made by the real servers to clients located in its sticky database.

To configure IP reverse-sticky on CSMB, you can use the configuration in Example 11-13, as applicable to the previous HTTP configuration on CSM B; however, HTTP virtual servers do not normally require reverse-sticky—Active-FTP is the most common application to use reverse-sticky.

Example 11-13 *IP Reverse-Sticky*

```
sticky 77 netmask 255.255.255.255 address destination timeout 100

vserver out-connections
 virtual 0.0.0.0 0.0.0.0 any
 vlan 20
 serverfarm in-firewalls
 sticky 100 group 77
 inservice

vserver web-vip
 virtual 10.1.20.100 255.255.255.0 www
 vlan 21
 serverfarm web-farm
 reverse-sticky 77
 inservice
```

In Figure 11-5 you can see that, when the incoming client connection via Firewall B matches the virtual server "web-vip," CSM B creates a sticky entry with the client's source IP address (10.1.10.99) and the real server (Firewall B) in the sticky database. Subsequent TCP connections from the back-end real servers trigger CSM B to perform a sticky table lookup on the destination IP address of the request. If a real server initiates a connection to 10.1.10.99, CSM B forwards the TCP SYN request through Firewall B, thus overriding the normal outgoing load-balancing method of destination hashing.

Configuring Single-CSM FWLB

In a single-CSM FWLB configuration, as Figure 11-6 suggests, you must connect the inside and outside interfaces of the firewalls directly to the CSM.

Figure 11-6 *Single-CSM FWLB*

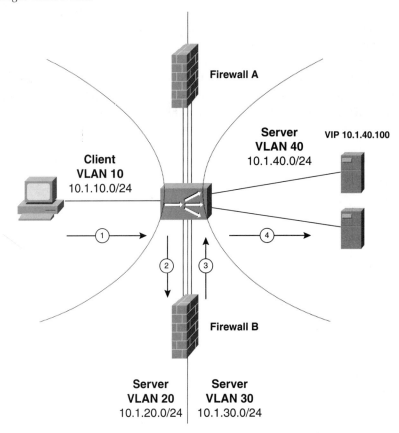

Example 11-14 gives a single-CSM FWLB configuration.

Example 11-14 *Configuring FWLB with a Single CSM*

```
mod csm 4
 vlan 10 client
  description *** Client's initiate connections from VLAN 10
  ip address 10.1.10.1 255.255.255.0

 vlan 20 server
  description *** VLAN 20 contains the firewalls outside interfaces
   ip address 10.1.20.1 255.255.255.0

 vlan 30 server
  description *** VLAN 30 contains the firewalls inside interfaces
  ip address 10.1.30.1 255.255.255.0

 vlan 40 server
```

Example 11-14 *Configuring FWLB with a Single CSM (Continued)*

```
  description *** Internal subnet for web servers
  ip address 10.1.40.1 255.255.255.0

serverfarm forward
 no nat server
 no nat client
 predictor forward

serverfarm in-firewalls
 description ** Contains the inside interfaces of the firewalls **
 no nat server
 no nat client
 predictor hash address source 255.255.255.255
 real 10.1.20.10
  inservice
 real 10.1.20.11
  inservice

serverfarm out-firewalls
 description ** Contains the outside interfaces of the firewalls **
 no nat server
 no nat client
 predictor hash address destination 255.255.255.255
 real 10.1.30.10
  inservice
 real 10.1.30.11
  inservice

serverfarm web-farm
 description ** Contains the web servers **
 nat server
 no nat client
 real 10.1.40.10
  inservice
 real 10.1.40.11
  inservice

vserver in-connections
 description ** Distributes incoming connections across the two firewalls **
 virtual 10.1.40.0 255.255.255.0 any
 vlan 10
 serverfarm out-firewalls
 inservice

vserver out-conns-20
 description ** Routes outgoing connections from the web servers from VLAN 20 to the
             Internet according to the routing table **
```

continues

Example 11-14 *Configuring FWLB with a Single CSM (Continued)*

```
   virtual 0.0.0.0 0.0.0.0 any
   serverfarm forward
   vlan 20
   inservice

vserver out-conns-40
  description ** Distributes outgoing connections from the web servers from VLAN 40 across
                 the two firewalls **
  virtual 0.0.0.0 0.0.0.0 any
  vlan 40
  serverfarm in-firewalls
  inservice

vserver web-vip
  description ** Distributes incoming connections from the Internet from VLAN 30 across the
                 two web servers **
  virtual 10.1.40.100 255.255.255.0 www
  vlan 30
  serverfarm web-farm
  inservice
```

When the CSM receives a client TCP SYN segment from the client VLAN 10 for the VIP
10.1.40.100, it performs a virtual server lookup and matches it to virtual server "in-connections."
The CSM then load balances the request across the two firewalls that are shown in Figure 11-6 and
chooses Firewall B. The CSM forwards the request out on VLAN 20, and Firewall B forwards it
back on VLAN 30. The CSM receives the request on VLAN 30, performs another virtual server
lookup, and matches the virtual server called "web-vip." The CSM load balances the request to the
real—return traffic from the real flows through the same firewall given the existing CSM
connection table entry.

Server-originated connections arrive to the CSM from VLAN 40, match the VIP "out-conns-40,"
and are load balanced to the firewalls. The firewalls forward the outgoing connection requests back
to the CSM on VLAN 20. The CSM matches the VIP "out-conns-20" and forwards the request to
the client using its routing table.

NOTE To configure stealth-mode FWLB, refer to your product documentation on Cisco.com.

VPN Load Balancing on the CSM

You can load balance VPN connections across the CSM to increase the performance and provide
redundancy to your VPN termination devices. Example 11-15 gives a dispatch-mode CSM VPN
load balancing configuration.

Example 11-15 *Configuring VPN Load Balancing on the CSM*

```
serverfarm vpn-farm
  no nat server
  no nat client
  real 10.1.10.10
   inservice
  real 10.1.10.12
   inservice

 sticky 5 netmask 255.255.255.255 timeout 60

 policy vpn-policy
  sticky-group 5
  serverfarm vpn-farm

vserver vpn-ah
  virtual 10.1.10.100 51
  slb-policy vpn-policy
  inservice

 vserver vpn-esp
  virtual 10.1.10.100 50
  slb-policy vpn-policy
  inservice

vserver vpn-ike
  virtual 10.1.10.100 udp 500
  slb-policy vpn-policy
  inservice
```

NOTE The CSS does not support VPN load balancing because it does not understand the IPSec protocols.

To configure your CSM for VPN load balancing, you must create virtual servers for the Authentication Header (AH), Encrypted Security Payload (ESP), and Internet Key Exchange (IKE) protocols. Similar to SSL, IPsec-based VPNs use multiple TCP connections to establish VPN sessions. Therefore, to ensure that clients stick to the same VPN concentrator across TCP connections, you should configure source IP address stickiness using the **sticky netmask** command.

NOTE If you want to configure directed-mode VPN load balancing, simply enter the command **nat server** in server farm configuration mode. Be cautious when rewriting fields within VPN traffic on your content switch because many VPN protocols have security features that protect the integrity of VPN messages.

Preventing Connection Table Flooding using SYN-Cookies

To avoid filling up its connection table during SYN-flood-based Denial of Service (DoS) attacks, the CSM uses SYN-cookies, which were covered briefly in Chapter 4. With SYN-flood attacks, the attacker sets random source IP addresses in numerous SYN packets that it sends to its victim. The victim receives the SYN packet, creates an entry in its connection table, responds with a TCP SYN-ACK packet, and awaits the final ACK segment from the sender. The final segment never arrives. Thus, the victim's connection fills very quickly with incomplete TCP connection entries.

However, with SYN-cookies, instead of allocating a record for every SYN segment from its clients, the CSM sends SYN-ACK segments with carefully constructed sequence numbers generated as a hash of connection's 4-tuple, the Maximum Segment Size, and a secret that continuously changes as time goes by. The connection 4-tuple contains the source and destination IP addresses and source and destination ports. When valid clients respond to the SYN-ACK with an ACK, they will include this special sequence number, which the CSM can verify before creating the connection entry. Without SYN-cookies, the CSM creates connection entries when it receives the initial SYN packet from clients. With SYN-cookies, the CSM creates the connection when it verifies the client's ACK segment to complete the connection. Because SYN-flood attackers typically do not respond to SYN-ACK segments, the SYN-flood traffic will not flood the CSM's connection table. Figure 11-7 illustrates SYN-cookies in practice.

Figure 11-7 *Using SYN-Cookies to Prevent SYN-Flood Traffic from Flooding the CSM Connection Table*

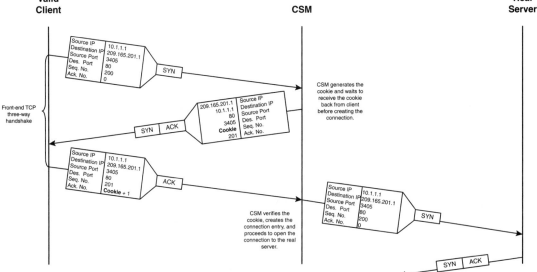

Summary

In this chapter, you learned how to configure the following technologies on your content switches:

- **Secure Sockets Layers (SSL) Termination**—You learned how to configure your CSS and CSM to terminate SSL connections on behalf of clients.

- **Firewall Load Balancing (FWLB)**—You learned how to configure your CSS and CSM to distribute client traffic across multiple firewalls.

- **Virtual Private Network (VPN) Load Balancing (FWLB)**—You learned how to configure your CSM to distribute client traffic across multiple VPN concentrators.

- **SYN-Cookies for SYN-Flood Protection**—You learned how the CSM uses SYN-cookies to prevent SYN-flood attacks from flooding the CSM's connection table.

Content switching enables you to increase the performance of your SSL, firewall, and VPN devices, in terms of packets per second, connections per second, and bandwidth. You can also increase the scalability of these devices with content switching technologies.

Review Questions

1. What sticky configuration should you perform in an SSL termination environment?

2. What is the purpose of HTTP header insertion and URL rewriting?

3. What is the purpose of IP reverse-sticky?

4. Why should you "sandwich" your firewalls with content switches when performing FWLB?

5. In Example 11-12, why should you configure source IP address hashing on incoming requests and destination hashing on requests initiated by the web servers?

6. How would you apply reverse-sticky in the single-CSM example in Example 11-14?

Recommended Reading

Chandra Kopparapu, *Load Balancing Servers, Firewalls, and Caches*. Wiley, 2002

RFC 2402. *"IP Authentication Header, IETF."* http://www.ietf.org/rfc/rfc2402.txt, 1998

RFC 2406. *"IP Encapsulating Security Payload (ESP)."* IETF, http://www.ietf.org/rfc/rfc2406.txt, 1998

RFC 2409. *"The Internet Key Exchange (IKE)."* IETF, http://www.ietf.org/rfc/rfc2409.txt, 1998

Chapter Goals

In this chapter, you will learn how to configure Global Server Load Balancing (GSLB). The chapter is divided into the following sections:

- **Introducing the Domain Name Service (DNS)**—You will learn about DNS resource records and iterative and recursive DNS.

- **Exploring Distributed Director (DD) Technologies**—You will learn how to configure the DD to distribute client traffic across multiple sites.

- **Exploring Content Services Switch (CSS) GSLB**—You will learn how to configure the CSS to distribute client requests across multiple sites.

- **Exploring Cisco Service Switching Module (CSM) GSLB**—You will learn how to configure the CSM to distribute client requests across multiple sites.

- **GSLB Stickiness**—You will learn about stateless DNS sticky (with source IP address hashing) and stateful DNS-sticky using a Global Sticky Database (GSDB).

CHAPTER 12

Exploring Global Server Load Balancing

In this chapter, you will learn how to resolve issues relating to disaster recovery, name resolution response times increases, and data center capacity increases. By mirroring your content across geographically distributed data centers and enabling the Global Server Load Balancing (GSLB) intelligent request routing capabilities discussed in this chapter, you can resolve many present and future redundancy, response time, and scalability issues.

You will learn about the following GSLB technologies in this chapter:

- DNS Round-Robin—Distributes requests across sites using round-robin with DNS servers only[md]no GSLB devices are required.

- BGP anycast—Advertises the site prefix from multiple locations into BGP; routers automatically distribute requests to the prefix based on BGP attributes, such as AS path.

- DNS GSLB—Distributes requests based on various metrics, such as proximity, and stickiness, across sites using GSLB devices enabled with DNS capabilities.

- HTTP Redirection—Distributes client requests across sites using the HTTP 301 Moved redirection method.

- Route Health Injection—Advertises host routes for healthy VIPs into the routing table, and routers select the VIP with the best routing metric for client requests.

You can enable one or more of these technologies in your network to achieve GSLB.

Domain Name Service Operation

The Domain Name Service (DNS) is the naming system on the Internet used by applications that require access to network resources via humanly recognizable names. Because GSLB systems can use DNS for distributed site selection, you should have a solid understanding of DNS before you tackle the load balancing concepts in this chapter.

The DNS system is a distributed hierarchical database of name-to-IP mappings. Figure 12-1 gives an example DNS hierarchy for some Cisco.com web servers.

Figure 12-1 *DNS Domain Hierarchy*

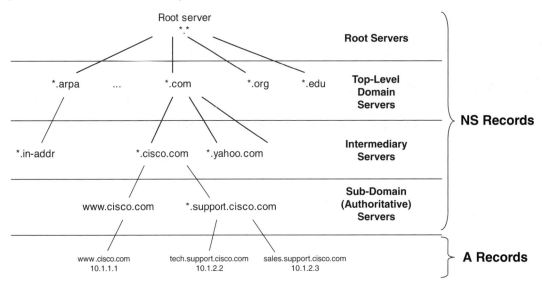

At the top of the hierarchy are the root name servers, as Figure 12-1 illustrates. The root servers are responsible for resolving all DNS requests on the Internet but delegate the resolution to the Top-Level Domain (TLD) servers for more specific domains. The TLD servers, in turn, delegate responsibility to intermediary DNS (IDNS) servers, which your enterprise or Internet Service Provider (ISP) may own and administer. The IDNS servers can be responsible (or authoritative) for specific domains or can further delegate resolution of subdomains to subdomain DNS servers. The subdomain servers may be responsible for one or more domain names, such as www.cisco.com. You can consider the GSLB devices in this chapter as subdomain DNS servers.

The Address (A) records reside at the leaves of the tree. In Figure 12-1, the www.cisco.com subdomain DNS server is responsible for the single subdomain www.cisco.com. The *.support.cisco.com DNS server is responsible for two domains for technical and sales support.

Nonprofit organizations administer the DNS root servers. They all behave identically in terms of DNS operation but have different hardware and software requirements, depending on the load on each server. Because the round trip time (RTT) to the root servers is a cause of additional delay in Internet transactions that require name resolution, the selection of the root server is important for reducing overall transaction times. As a result, the administrators of some of the busiest DNS root servers use Border Gateway Protocol (BGP)-anycasting for site selection. With BGP-anycast, the root DNS server is replicated across numerous sites, and the IP prefix of the server is advertised into BGP from each location. The BGP routing algorithm is then able automatically to select the best site for user requests on the Internet.

Introducing DNS Resource Records

A DNS server maintains configuration files that contain the resource records (RRs) for domains they are authoritative for. As an example, the IDNS server for *.cisco.com may contain the following resource records: Start of Authority (SOA), Address (A), Name Server (NS), and Mail Exchange (MX).

■   **Start of Authority (SOA) Records**—The DNS servers that are authoritative for a particular subdomain contain a Start of Authority (SOA) record. Example 12-1 gives a sample SOA record for the domain cisco.com that would reside on the intermediary DNS server for *.cisco.com.

Example 12-1   *A Sample SOA Resource Record*

```
CISCO.COM.    IN      SOA      ns1.cisco.com. ns2.cisco.com. (
                               1    ;    serno (serial number)
                               86400    ;    refresh in seconds (24 hours)
                               7200     ;    retry in seconds (2 hours)
                               2592000    ;    expire in seconds (30 days)
                               345600)    ;    TTL in seconds (4 days)
```

In the SOA record in Example 12-1, "IN" refers to the class of record. DNS currently supports only the Internet (IN) class. The type is SOA, and the primary and secondary authoritative intermediary DNS servers for the domain are ns1.cisco.com and ns2.cisco.com, respectively. These two name servers can both actively respond to DNS requests—the secondary remains synchronized with the primary by requesting zone transfers from the primary. Zone transfers contain all the available records on the primary DNS server. The SOA also contains the following:

— Current version (serial number) of the data file

— Number of seconds that the secondary name server should wait before checking for updates on the primary name server

— Number of seconds a secondary name server should wait before retrying a failed zone transfer

— Maximum number of seconds that a secondary name server can use data before it must either be refreshed or expire

The Time-to-Live (TTL) value enables you to specify the default amount of time that client DNS servers, when using iterative DNS, locally cache the A record responses. If you use recursive DNS, as you will learn in the next section, all DNS servers have access to the A record response and may cache the A record locally for subsequent requests.

Although each domain should be identified by two DNS servers, with one as the active DNS server and the other as the backup, the examples in this chapter reference only a single authoritative server for each subdomain.

- **Address (A) records**—A records define the association between each domain and IP address that your device is authoritative for. An example of an A record for Cisco.com is

  ```
  cisco.com.    3600 IN A 10.1.10.100
  ```

  In this resource record, the rightmost "." in the domain name indicates the root server; .com indicates the TLD server, and cisco.com refers to the authoritative domain containing all *.cisco.com subdomains. The www refers to the subdomain that your device is authoritative for. You can override the TTL value in the Start of Authority (SOA) record by specifying the TTL after the domain in the A record. The "A" refers to the type of record.

- **Name Server (NS) records**—DNS servers delegate authority to other DNS servers by using NS records. An example NS record for the domain Cisco.com, thus delegating the domain to the subdomain DNS server gslb.cisco.com, is

  ```
  www.cisco.com. IN NS gslb.cisco.com
  ```

  The A record to determine the IP address of the GSLB DNS server is

  ```
  gslb.cisco.com. IN A 10.1.10.101
  ```

  An NS record is also known as a referral record, because it refers client DNS servers to other DNS servers that are delegated to resolve more specific TLDs or subdomains.

- **Mail Exchange (MX) records**—MX records are the mail server domains that the DNS server is responsible for. An example MX record for the e-mail domain user@cisco.com is

  ```
  cisco.com. IN MX smtp.cisco.com
  ```

  The A record to determine the IP address of the mail server is

  ```
  smtp.cisco.com IN A 10.1.10.103
  ```

NOTE DNS uses UDP port 53 for standard DNS requests and responses. However, because zone transfer payloads are much larger, they require TCP (also on port 53) as a reliable transport.

Iterative DNS

With iterative DNS resolution, each server delegates the resolution responsibility to the next-level DNS server down the hierarchical tree you learned about previously in Figure 12-1. The DNS servers in the flow send an NS-record containing the next-level DNS server closer to the authoritative DNS server, as Figure 12-2 illustrates.

Figure 12-2 *Iterative DNS*

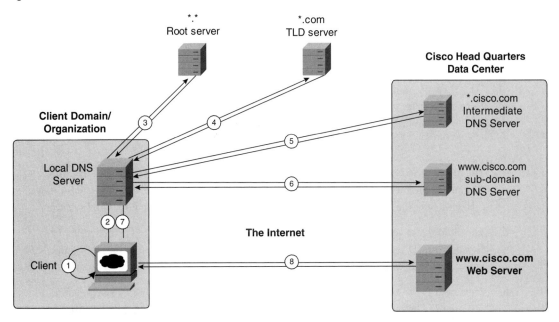

> **NOTE**   The Internet uses the iterative method for DNS resolution. The iterative method is beneficial in GSLB environments in which the client's DNS server IP address should be preserved throughout the flow for proximity load balancing and GSLB-sticky, as you will learn later in this chapter.

Consider the example from Figure 12-2 in which a client issues an A record request for Cisco.com.

1.   The client browser sends the A record request to the operating system. The operating system first checks its local hosts file for the requested A record. The hosts file is a text file to which you can manually add A records on your workstations or servers. If the host file contains the record, the client uses the entry for the connection. Additionally, if the client requested the same mapping in the recent past, the operating system may have a cached copy of the host-to-IP mapping in a local DNS cache. If so, the client uses the cached IP address for the connection.

2.   Otherwise, the client DNS server forwards the request recursively to the client DNS server. You can configure your local DNS server(s) either manually or dynamically via a Dynamic Host Control Protocol (DHCP) server.

> **NOTE**   In iterative DNS, clients send requests to their configured DNS server as recursive requests—the DNS server initiates and coordinates the iterative DNS flow. See the next section for more details on recursive DNS.

3. The local DNS server checks for a cached copy of the A record and responds directly to the client with the mapping, as a nonauthoritative answer. If it does not have a cached copy of the requested A record, the DNS server issues an iterative A record request to a root server, on behalf of the client. The root name server responds to the client DNS server with the NS-record of the *.com TLD server.

> **NOTE** You configure the list of root name servers and their IP addresses on the name server. Because the root servers change infrequently, maintaining a static list of root name server IP addresses is a trivial task that you can perform manually.

4. The client DNS server then extracts the TLD IP address from the NS-record response and formulates another A record request, which it sends to the TLD server. The TLD server responds with the NS record of the *.cisco.com IDNS server to the client DNS server.

5. The client DNS server sends an A record request to the *.cisco.com IDNS server. The *.cisco.com IDNS server responds with the NS record for the subdomain DNS name server authoritative for www.cisco.com.

6. The client DNS server sends the A record request to the subdomain DNS server. The subdomain DNS name server responds with the A record of the domain. To improve performance and reduce delay, the authoritative subdomain DNS server includes a TTL value in the A record response to the client DNS server. The client DNS server stores the A record in its cache for the length of time specified by the TTL.

7. The client DNS server sends the A record back to the client.

8. The client uses the IP specified in the A record for the TCP connection of the HTTP session to the Cisco.com web server.

> **NOTE** In Figure 12-2, the root and TLD DNS servers never see the A record response from the subdomain DNS servers. Therefore, using iterative DNS resolution, they cannot cache a copy of the A record locally.

Recursive DNS

With recursive DNS resolution, each server assumes responsibility of the resolution, in contrast to iterative resolution in which each DNS server passes the resolution responsibility to another DNS server. When a client sends an A record request for an IP address, recursive DNS requires that each DNS server in the hierarchy resolves the host name. When a recursive DNS server receives an A record request, it issues an A record request of its own to a server delegated to the domain at the next level down the DNS tree. This process continues until the request reaches the server authoritative for the domain, as Figure 12-3 illustrates.

Figure 12-3 *Recursive DNS*

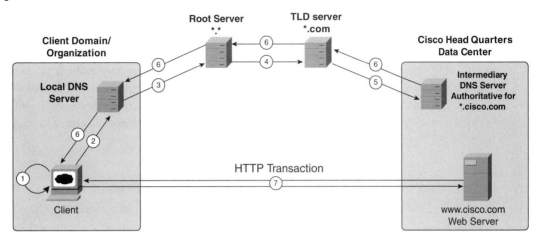

Consider an example of a user attempting to connect to Cisco.com from a web browser on the Internet.

1. The client checks for the A-record in its cache and hosts file.

2. The operating system sends the request in the form of a standard DNS A record request to its local DNS server, if the entry is not in its host file or cache.

3. The local DNS server checks for a cached copy of the A record and responds directly to the client with the mapping, as a nonauthoritative answer. If it does not have a cached copy of the requested A record, the DNS server issues a recursive A record request to a root server, on behalf of the client.

4. If the root server has a cached copy of the requested A record, it sends the answer to the client's DNS server. Otherwise, the root server issues an A record request to the name server that is authoritative for the TLD of *.com.

5. The TLD server checks for a cached copy of the mapping but sends the request to the iterative DNS server authoritative for cisco.com if the cache does not contain the mapping.

6. In this example, the iterative DNS server contains the A record for www.cisco.com. The responses ripple backward as DNS A record answer packets, in the reverse direction to which the requests arrived at the www.cisco.com name server.

7. Now that the application knows the IP address, it can open a TCP connection directly to the web server, to make an HTTP request for content.

NOTE   The Internet does not use the recursive DNS method for name resolution—this example is for illustration purposes only.

BGP-Anycast and DNS Round-Robin

The simplest GSLB that you can deploy is by creating exact replicas (or surrogates) of a site, including the services and IP addressing scheme. Then, to distribute load across the sites, simply advertise the IP prefix into BGP across the Internet from each site. You learned previously that this technique is commonly referred to as BGP-anycast. BGP routers that receive multiple prefixes install those routes in their routing tables that they deem are the most preferable using various BGP metrics, in particular the autonomous system (AS) path attribute. When requests arrive for content for the GSLB, BGP routes the packets to the nearest site at Layer 3, without any need for higher layers of intelligence.

The drawback to BGP-anycast is potentially uneven distribution of client requests across sites — the request distribution is dependant on the geographic location of your clients. If a large percentage of traffic comes from a particular geographic region, then those packets use the same route and thus the same site. Additionally, BGP-anycast lacks site health check capabilities.

Whereas you must use the same IP addressing scheme across your sites with BGP-anycast, other GSLB methods require a separate routable IP address space per site. For example, another simple GSLB involves installing multiple DNS A records in the domain's TLD DNS server (or the enterprise's intermediary DNS server, if available), with one entry for each location. Any readily available commercial DNS server software, such as Berkeley Internet Name Domain (BIND), can provide simple DNS round-robin load balancing between the entries. DNS round-robin evenly distributes client requests between the sites. An advantage of this design is that you do not need to manage a DNS server at each site. If your intermediary DNS server is delegated authority for the load-balanced domain replicated across your sites, you can locate it at the central location.

NOTE Recall that the TLD can delegate authority to an organization's intermediary DNS server, so that you can easily manage subdomains within your organization. If you do not use an intermediary DNS server, you will need the TLD entries to be updated with a single entry per replicated site.

Exploring Distributed Director Technologies

The drawback to DNS load balancing is that client DNS servers are blindly sent A records for each site, even if one of the sites is overloaded or goes down completely. Instead of using DNS load balancing, you can use the Distributed Director (DD) to intelligently distribute requests across your sites. The DD is the GSLB equivalent of the SLB Local Director (LD) device discussed in Chapter 10, "Exploring Server Load Balancing." As you learned, Cisco retired the LD and replaced it with the features and functionality of the CSS and CSM. Similarly, Cisco previously packaged the Distributed Director (DD) within a standalone GSLB hardware appliance. However, Cisco also retired the DD hardware appliance but ported the DD features to the Cisco IOS platform.

> **NOTE**   Future GSLB development is moving towards the Global Site Selector (GSS); therefore, you should consider using GSS in the place of the DD for GSLB. However, as Figure 12-4 suggests, a core GSS can be used with the CSS and CSM located at individual sites for site selection and request distribution using the Content Application Peering Protocol (CAPP).

Figure 12-4 shows how you can place a router running DD or a GSS in a multisite distributed network.

DDs do not contain full DNS server software but can respond to iterative DNS requests with A records for a small number of subdomains. To configure your DD to respond to A record requests, you must delegate authority of the domain of your distributed application from your iterative DNS server to your DD. To do this, you can add the following NS record and A record to your iterative DNS server, thus delegating the domain to the DD:

```
www.cisco.com. IN NS dd.cisco.com.
dd.cisco.com. IN A 10.1.10.1
```

You can locate your DD at your organization's headquarters, or at any one of the sites. To configure your DD to respond to A record requests from clients, first create the SOA record on the DD as follows:

```
ip dns primary www.cisco.com soa dd1.cisco.com gslb-admin@cisco.com
  21600 900 7776000 86400
```

> **NOTE**   With the design in Figure 12-4, if the central site containing the DD and IDNS server goes down, then your entire GSLB goes down. To avoid this, you can enable a DD and IDNS server at each site and configure the TLD DNS server to perform DNS load balancing across the IDNS servers (for the *.cisco.com domains), which in turn can DNS load balance across your DDs (for the www.cisco.com domain).

Figure 12-4   *Distributing DNS Requests Across Sites*

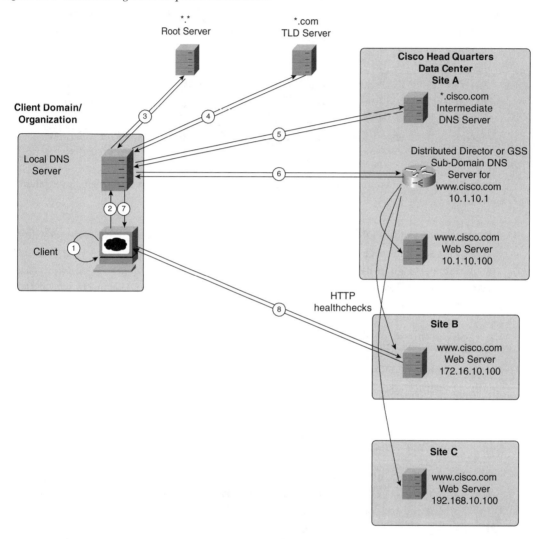

To enable the DD to respond to A record requests for www.cisco.com with IPs 192.168.10.100, 10.1.10.100, or 172.16.10.100 located at three different sites, enter the following command:

```
ip host www.cisco.com 192.168.10.100 10.1.10.100 172.16.10.100
```

Now that you have set up basic DNS functionality, you can configure your DD to select one of the available servers, based on one or more of the following DD metrics:

■   Randomized distribution

■   Proportional distribution

- Absolute preferences

- Routing protocol metrics

- Round Trip Times (RTT)

- Boomerang

If you specify more than one metric for a server, you can assign a priority that the DD uses to decide which metric to use in selecting a server. If there is a tie across the sites or if the metric fails to yield a result, the DD uses the next highest priority metric to select the site. To configure your DD to randomly select one of the IP addresses and assign the random metric a priority, you can use the command

```
ip director host www.cisco.com priority random 40
```

This command gives the random metric a priority of 40, but because it is the only metric configured thus far, the DD uses it for all requests for the domain. A metric with a lower priority number has an overall higher priority.

You can also proportionally divide requests among available sites using the commands

```
ip director server 192.168.10.100 portion 1
ip director server 10.1.10.100 portion 3
ip director server 172.16.10.100 portion 2
ip director host www.cisco.com priority portion 10
```

With these commands, the server 192.168.10.100 receives one of every six requests, 10.1.10.100 receives three of every six requests (that is, one half of the requests), and 172.16.10.100 receives two of every six requests. Additionally, the priority for the portion metric is 10.

Unlike standard BIND DNS servers, DDs have the ability to determine if the sites are available before answering the client's DNS A record request with an A record response. With this design, when the DD receives DNS requests from client DNS servers, the requests can be intelligently load balanced to the different sites, thus avoiding sending clients to sites that are unavailable. To ensure that the IP address that your DD selects is available, you can configure the DD to first attempt to connect to the available sites using the command

```
ip director host www.cisco.com connect 80 interval 300
```

This command attempts to connect to port 80 every 300 seconds—the DD caches each IP address that it successfully connects to for 60 seconds. Additionally, if you configure random selection, the DD randomly selects among the cached IP addresses for 60 seconds for each subsequent request for the domain.

To configure a primary/backup setup (that is, absolute preference), you can use the **preference** keyword to direct clients to a backup site if the primary site(s) is down.

```
ip director server 192.168.10.100 preference 3
ip director server 10.1.10.100 preference 3
ip director server 172.16.10.100 preference 5
ip director host www.cisco.com priority admin 15
```

This configuration assigns 192.168.10.100 and 10.1.10.100 as primary sites and distributes requests across the two using the portions you configured previously (that is, 1/6 and 1/2, respectively). If either of these two sites fails, the backup site 172.16.10.100 will take over. The primary/backup metric is called **admin** and is given the priority 15 in this example.

Director Response Protocol and Boomerang Protocol

Cisco developed Director Response Protocol (DRP) as a simple way for the DD to communicate with routers at remote sites. Based on information exchanged between the DD router and DRP agent routers, the DD can select the site with the best routing metrics and shortest round-trip time (RTT—the sum of the forward and return paths to/from the client DNS server). Additionally, using the Boomerang protocol in conjunction with DRP, the DD can use the site with the shortest *return* path time to the client.

To determine the routing metrics for the individual sites, the DD can learn the following routing protocol information from the remote routers using DRP:

■ **DRP external (drp-e)**—Number of BGP autonomous systems between the DRP agent and the client DNS server.

■ **DRP internal (drp-i)**—The IGRP or EIGRP routing distance between the DRP agent and the closest Autonomous System Border Router (ASBR).

■ **DRP server (drp-s)**—The IGRP or EIGRP routing distance between the origin server and DRP agent. You shouldn't use DRP-I or DRP-S if you use an IGP other than IGRP or EIGRP.

Figure 12-5 illustrates what each of these metrics means.

When the central DD receives an A record request from a client, it queries the DRP agents at each site to look up the DRP-E, DRP-I, and DRP-S routing metrics based on the client and origin server IP addresses. The sum of these three metrics gives the total routing distance between the origin server at each site and the client. The DRP agents then respond to the central DD, which then compares the returned metrics from each site and decides which site's A record to send to the client. In Figure 12-5, the DRP-S and the DRP-I are the same for both sites, but the DRP-E values are different and thus break the tie. To configure a router as a DRP agent, use the command

Figure 12-5 *The DRP-E, DRP-I, and DRP-S Routing Metrics*

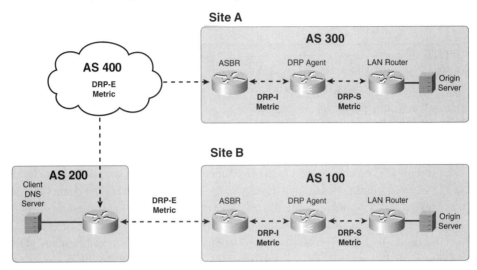

```
ip drp server
```

To configure DRP on the central site DD, you must associate the server IP addresses with router DRP agents located at the individual sites

```
ip director server 192.168.10.100 drp-association 192.168.10.1
ip director server 10.1.10.100 drp-association 10.1.10.1
ip director server 172.16.10.100 drp-association 172.16.10.1
ip director host www.cisco.com priority drp-e 20 drp-i 25 drp-s 25
```

If you do not have access to a router at each site that has the necessary routing information to supply routing metrics for the site, you can use RRT calculations or Boomerang instead. The DD supports the following stateless time-based metric calculations:

■ **ICMP probes**—If you use ICMP probes, the DD directs all the DRP agents to send an ICMP echo request to the client DNS server. When a DRP agent receives the ICMP echo response, it calculates and reports the RTT to the coordinating DD using the DRP protocol.

> **NOTE** DD's usage of RTT is stateless because the DD does not store per-client RTT information. Alternately, the CSS uses a stateful Proximity Database (PDB), which you will learn about later in this chapter.

■ **TCP probes**—If you use TCP probes, the DD directs all the DRP agents to send TCP SYN/ACK segments to the client DNS server on TCP port 53. When the client DNS server receives the SYN/ACK for an invalid connection, it should send a TCP RST packet in response. The

DRP agent uses this response to calculate the RTT to report to the coordinating DD. Use the keyword **drp-r** to specify the priority of the ICMP or TCP probe metric using the **ip director host priority** command.

> **NOTE**   As you learned previously, most DNS servers use TCP port 53 for zone transfers to achieve reliable delivery of zone files. As a result, most DNS servers listen on TCP port 53. If the DD cannot access the DNS server on TCP port 53, the proximity calculations for the particular client DNS server will not succeed.

- **Boomerang DNS racing**—If you use Boomerang DNS racing, the coordinating DD forwards the A record request to the DRP agents. In response, the DRP agents formulate a DNS A record response to send directly to the client DNS server. The client DNS software uses the first A record response it receives as the response for the requesting client. With the Boomerang metric, the coordinating DD must know the RTTs between itself and other sites in advance in order to ensure that each DRP agent sends the A record response at the same time. Use the keyword **boomerang** to specify the priority of the Boomerang metric using the **ip director host priority** command.

> **NOTE**   To make sure that the DRP agents receive the A record request from the DD at the same time, you can configure the Boomerang protocol to synchronize the clocks between the DD and the DRP agents using the **ip director drp synchronized** command. With synchronized clocks, the DD can specify an absolute wallclock time to send the A record responses. If this command is disabled, which is the default, the DD specifies a relative time to the individual DRP agents based on the measured delay between the DD and the DRP agents.

To configure RRT ICMP or TCP probes, you can use the following command (TCP is the default):

```
ip director drp rttprobe [tcp ¦ icmp]
```

Like the CSS load calculations that you learned in Chapter 10, the DD differentiates between RTT times using a tolerance value similar to the load step/sensitivity value on the CSS. The tolerance is the percentage difference between RTT values at which the DD deems the RTTs as being different. You can change the tolerance percentage from the default 10 percent to 20 percent using the command

```
ip director host www.cisco.com drp-rtt tolerance 20
```

You can also change the number of probes that the DRP agents use to calculate the RTTs using the command

```
ip director host www.cisco.com drp-rtt probes 2
```

You can also use the Boomerang protocol to determine which site has the shortest return path time to the requesting client. Figure 12-6 shows you how Boomerang works.

Figure 12-6 *Boomerang Protocol Operation*

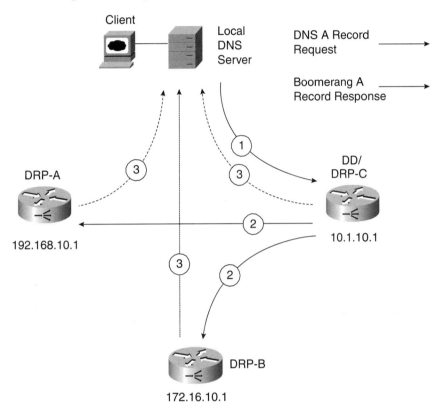

Consider the example shown in Figure 12-6 in which a client sends an A record request that ends up at the DD subdomain DNS server for the domain www.cisco.com.

1. The client request arrives at the DD.

2. The DD sends a DRP packet to each DRP agent. If you configured clock synchronization, the packet includes the wallclock time at which each DRP agent should send its request. If not, the DD staggers the DRP packets such that the DRP agents receive the packets at the same instance in time.

3. The DRP agents sends the A record responses for the subdomain www.cisco.com to the client DNS server.

> **NOTE** The Boomerang protocol, ICMP, and TCP probes assume that the client is in close proximity to its local DNS server, which is the case in the vast majority of DNS environments. Otherwise, proximity-based DNS does not provide any added value to your clients. If possible, evaluate the proximity of clients that are using your application to their DNS servers before enabling a proximity-based solution.

To configure your DRP agents to use the Boomerang protocol, you can use the following command:

```
ip drp domain www.cisco.com
```

To configure the DD to use the Boomerang protocol and set its priority to 1, use the following command:

```
ip director host www.cisco.com priority boomerang 1
```

As a security measure, your firewall or router may contain filters that block packets with source IP addresses outside the range you allocated within your network. For example, this measure would prevent someone from maliciously using your network for sourcing Distributed Denial of Service (DDoS) attacks. Because the DD spoofs the client's DNS server IP address, these packets may be blocked before leaving the DD's subnet. To determine whether such filters exist, use a sniffer and the **boomerang send-packet** command to send a packet with a source address outside the subnet on which the DD resides. The sniffer should be installed on one of your other sites or somewhere on the outside interface of your firewall to see if the firewall blocks the packet. If the sniffer detects the packet, you know that the firewall did not block the packet containing the boomerang-altered source IP address.

> **NOTE** The GSS also supports DRP. Refer to your GSS product documentation on Cisco.com for more information on configuring the GSS with DRP.

HTTP Redirection

HTTP redirects can provide GSLB functionality with less involvement of the DNS infrastructure than methods described in previous sections—the DD uses HTTP redirects to inform the client of the most suitable site to which to send their requests. If you use HTTP redirection, each site not only requires a separate routable IP address space but also requires a separate domain name. You can use HTTP redirection by having the client issue the HTTP request directly to the DD. The DD then chooses the most appropriate server, using the DNS metrics that you learned about so far (except the Boomerang protocol), to send an HTTP 301 Moved response to.

In the previous example, you could assign sites as follows:

- **Headquarters site (Site A)**—Domain site-a.cisco.com and IP address 10.1.10.100

- **Site B**—Domain site-b.cisco.com and IP address 172.16.10.100

- **Site C**—Domain site-c.cisco.com and IP address 192.168.10.100

When the DD receives the HTTP GET request, it uses the metrics you configured to determine the most suitable site and sends an HTTP 301 Moved with the selected site name in the "Location:" header. The client then issues a regular DNS query for IP address of the new domain to connect to with HTTP. If you want to avoid this additional DNS resolution, you do not have to use site-specific domain names but bear in mind that your clients will see the IP address of the site in the URL field of their web browsers instead of a domain name.

With HTTP redirection, you do not delegate your subdomains to your DD (with NS records). Instead, you must create the A record for your DD directly on your IDNS server:

```
www.cisco.com. IN A 10.1.10.101
```

NOTE   HTTP redirection is used for HTTP traffic only—you cannot use this method for distributing non-HTTP requests, such as FTP and SMTP, across your sites.

Now your clients can establish an HTTP session directly to your DD. To configure your DD to use HTTP redirects to distribute requests across your sites, you first need to enable the HTTP server on the DD and specify the main IP address that clients use to connect to your domain:

```
ip director ip-address 10.1.10.101
```

You then specify your DD host as having this IP address:

```
ip host www.cisco.com 10.1.10.101
```

NOTE   HTTP redirection occurs after the DNS resolution occurs. Additionally, with HTTP redirection the DD sees the source IP address of the client, and not the IP address of the client's DNS server.

You then create an additional hidden domain (that is, www-servers.cisco.com) to allocate to the group of sites, and specify the site IP addresses to this domain. Note that this domain will be used only in the DD configuration.

```
ip host www-servers.cisco.com 10.1.10.100 172.16.10.100 192.168.10.100
ip dns primary www-servers.cisco.com soa dd1.cisco.com gslb-admin@cisco.com
```

Now you can specify the names you wish to assign to your sites, which the DD uses to redirect your clients to

```
ip director server 10.1.10.100 server-name site-a.cisco.com
ip director server 172.16.10.100 server-name site-b.cisco.com
ip director server 192.168.10.100 server-name site-c.cisco.com
```

> **NOTE**   The Content Switching Module (CSM) and the Content Services Switch (CSS) also support HTTP redirection. For more information on configuring HTTP redirection on the CSS and CSM, refer to the technical documentation on Cisco.com.

A Robust Distributed Director Configuration

Example 12-2 shows you the complete central DD configuration that you have learned about so far (except the Boomerang protocol). For the DRP agents, you simply need to enable the DRP agent using the **ip drp server** command.

Example 12-2   *Sample DD Configuration*

```
ip host www.cisco.com 10.1.10.101
ip host www-servers.cisco.com 10.1.10.100 172.16.10.100 192.168.10.100
ip host dd1.cisco.com 10.1.10.1
!
ip dns primary www.cisco.com soa dd1.cisco.com gslb-admin@cisco.com
ip dns primary www-servers.cisco.com soa dd1.cisco.com gslb-admin@cisco.com
!
ip director ip-address 10.1.10.101
ip director server 10.1.10.100 portion 3
ip director server 10.1.10.100 preference 3
ip director server 10.1.10.100 drp-association 10.1.10.1
ip director server 10.1.10.100 server-name site-a.cisco.com
!
ip director server 172.16.10.100 portion 2
ip director server 172.16.10.100 preference 5
ip director server 172.16.10.100 drp-association 172.16.10.1
ip director server 172.16.10.100 server-name site-b.cisco.com
!
ip director server 192.168.10.100 portion 1
ip director server 192.168.10.100 preference 3
ip director server 192.168.10.100 drp-association 192.168.10.1
ip director server 192.168.10.100 server-name site-a.cisco.com
!
ip director host www.cisco.com drp-rtt tolerance 20
ip director host www.cisco.com drp-rtt probes 2
ip director host www.cisco.com priority drp-r 5 portion 10 admin 15 drp-e 20 drp-i 25
  drp-s 25 random 40
ip director drp synchronized
ip director host www.cisco.com connect 80 interval 300
```

Exploring CSS Global Server Load Balancing

Cisco has numerous products capable of GSLB processing, giving Cisco the ability to fit GSLB functionality into virtually any content networking design. Due to the increase in demand for cross-site redundancy and RTT reduction, Cisco includes GSLB features in the CSS. Just as with the DD, you can configure your CSSs in your distributed network to act as DNS servers and respond to DNS queries for particular subdomains.

> **NOTE**   You should consider using the GSS at the headquarters site in the place of the CSS, a consideration which is similar to that you make when working with the DD. The GSLB principals of the GSS are similar to those of the DD, CSS, and CSM. Refer to the product documentation on Cisco.com for more information on the GSS.

CSS Multisite Load Distribution

The CSSs in your GSLB network can exchange load and status information for your virtual and real servers (you learned to configure ACA load in Chapter 10), using the Keep-Alive Appliance Protocol (KAL-AP) over reliable Application Peering Protocol (APP) connections. You must first create an APP peer mesh in order to disseminate information throughout your distributed network. You can then configure the A records on your CSSs for the virtual IPs (VIP) that they serve and NS records to delegate authority to other lower-level CSSs. The CSSs exchanges these A and NS records with one another using APP, in addition to the load and status information via KAL-AP mentioned previously.

When a CSS receives an A record request from the TLD or IDNS server via the DNS infrastructure (with round-robin load balancing, if necessary), it determines the best site using the load and status information learned through APP. The CSS then responds to the client's DNS server with the A record of the best site.

For example, say that the subdomain www.cisco.com is replicated at two sites, with three real servers at each site. You should delegate the subdomain www.cisco.com to the CSSs across the two sites, by updating your intermediary DNS servers with two NS records associated with the two content switches, which you learned how to do previously.

You then configure your CSSs to respond to queries to the subdomain www.cisco.com, as Figure 12-7 illustrates. When the intermediate DNS server receives the client DNS request, it chooses either CSS using round-robin—say that it chooses CSS-B for the request in this example. When CSS-B receives the request, it determines that CSS A is more capable of fielding the request, based on the load of the real servers for the VIP. As a result, CSS-B responds to the client's DNS server with the VIP of CSS-A. The client DNS server forwards the A record to the client, which uses the VIP address of CSS-A for the connection. Figure 12-7 illustrates this example.

Figure 12-7   *GSLB Using the CSS*

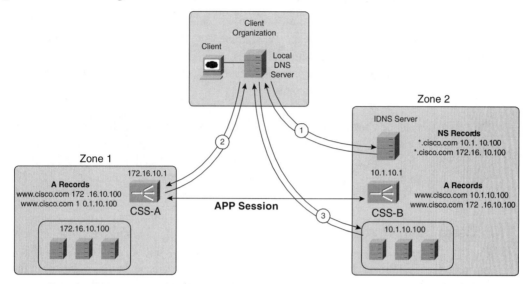

> **NOTE**   The DD does not support APP and therefore do not have the ability to track the load of remote servers to base the load balancing decision on. The CSM does support APP for use with GSS.

To configure the zone for your individual sites, use the following command on each CSS:

```
dns-server zone zone_index {tier1 ¦ tier2 {"description" {weightedrr ¦ srcip ¦
   leastloaded ¦ preferlocal ¦ roundrobin ¦ ip_address {weightedrr ¦ srcip ¦
   leastloaded ¦ preferlocal ¦ roundrobin } {weight}}}}
```

You must specify the tier and the load-balancing method for the zone with this command. You can create nested zones using tiers in a CSS proximity environment. You will learn about CSS proximity later in this chapter. If you configure the least-loaded load balancing method, you must configure ACA for your real servers as you learned previously in Chapter 10.

To modify the way in which the CSS uses the load information, you can use the command

```
dns-server zone load [reporting ¦ frequency seconds ¦ variance number]
```

The **frequency** keyword modifies the time between processing the load information and advertising it to APP peers. The **variance** keyword modifies the range of load numbers that the CSS considers different. This number is similar to the load step, which you learned about in Chapter 10.

Example 12-3 shows you a sample CSS GSLB configuration. Notice that you do not manually configure the A records for the other sites, because the CSS advertises these to one another using APP.

Example 12-3 *Sample GSLB Configuration Using the CSS*

```
CSS A
app-udp
 app
 dns-server zone 1 tier1 "Site A" weightedrr
 app session 10.1.10.1
 dns-server

 dns-record a www.cisco.com 172.16.10.100 3600 single kal-ap weight 5
CSS B
app-udp
 app
 dns-server zone 2 tier1 "Site B" weightedrr
 app session 172.16.10.1
 dns-server

 dns-record a www.cisco.com 10.1.10.100 3600 single kal-ap weight 10
```

The configuration in Example 12-3 creates an APP connection between the two sites, "Site A" and "Site B," across which it sends KAL-AP keep-alive messages. If you do not configure KAL-AP with the **kal-ap** keyword in the **dns-record** command, the CSS uses ICMP keep-alives (KAL-ICMP) by default.

Example 12-3 uses WRR to distribute the load across the two sites. APP-UDP is required for the CSS Proximity Database (PDB) that you will learn about later. Additionally, you can specify the TTL for the A record (that is, 3600 seconds in this example) after the domain name in the **dns-record a** command.

The **single** keyword specifies that the CSS will return only a single A record to the client DNS server. If you instead specify **multiple**, the CSS will return all available A records (there are two of them in this example) to the client DNS server. Then the client DNS server can cache the multiple A record answers for the time specified in the TTL and round-robin load-balance subsequent requests for the domain. If you enable multiple records, the client DNS server may load balance clients to sites that are unavailable. Be sure to understand how your sites behave before enabling multiple records.

CSS Proximity-Based Load Balancing

The CSS uses a stateful Proximity Database (PDB) to store RTTs for client DNS servers, resulting in better overall response times for clients than the stateless proximity DD solutions that you learned about previously. In a CSS proximity configuration, each site contains a PDB and a Proximity DNS (PDNS) server. PDNS servers maintain the health of their local virtual servers and advertise their health to peer PDNS servers located at different sites. For the PDB to work efficiently, make sure that your DNS requests are load-balanced between the PDNS servers by the DNS infrastructure (that is, by the TLD or your IDNS servers). Figure 12-8 illustrates the PDB flow.

When a PDNS server receives a DNS request, it sends a lookup request via APP-UDP to the PDB for the site closest in proximity to the requesting client DNS server. If the PDB does not have an entry for the client IP, it coordinates a probe of the client DNS server between itself and the other sites in the GSLB (Steps 3 and 4 in Figure 12-8), through a mesh of peer APP connections. The PDB server sorts the resulting list of RTT values from its peers and sends the list to the requesting PDNS server. When the PDNS server receives the ordered list, it determines the health of each entry through its APP peer connections (Steps 7 and 8 in Figure 12-8) and decides which site is best suited for the request. The example in Figure 12-8 takes the following steps for a client A record request for "www.cisco.com."

Figure 12-8 *Proximity Database DNS Resolution Flow*

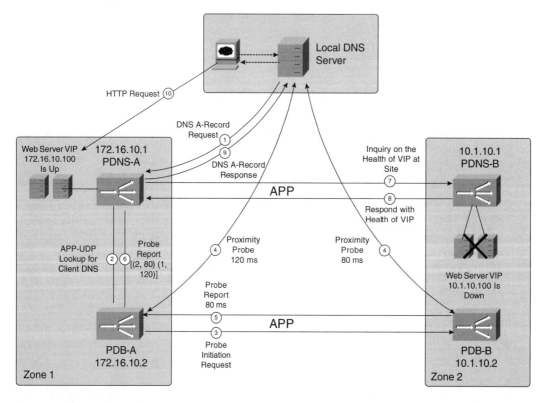

1. The client's DNS server receives the NS-record of PDNS-A from the DNS infrastructure. The client DNS server then sends a DNS request to PDNS-A.

2. PDNS-A then queries the PDB-A server for the site closest to the client DNS server.

3. Because PDB-A does not have the entry for the client DNS server, it coordinates probes with PDNS-B to the client DNS server.

4. PDB-A and PDB-B both send probes to the client DNS server to determine the RTTs. Unlike with the Boomerang protocol, they do not need to send the probes at the same instant in time.

5. PDB-B sends the RTT between itself and the client DNS server (80 ms) to PDB-A.

6. PDB-A sends the ordered list of RTTs to PDNS-A. The list contains two entries in the form of (zone-id, RTT). Therefore, the ordered list appears as [(2, 80) (1, 120)]. That is, the RTT calculated by PDB-B is less than that calculated by PDB-A.

7. PDNS-A then requests the health of the VIP for the requested domain from PDNS-B.

8. PDNS-B returns the status of the VIP for domain www.cisco.com. In this example, PDNS-B advertises the VIP as being unavailable.

9. Because the VIP for the domain is down, even though the RTT is less for Zone 2, PDB-A sends its local web VIP within the A record to the client DNS server.

10. The client establishes a TCP connection with the VIP in Zone 1 and sends the HTTP request to the VIP.

The CSS determines proximity using ICMP or TCP probes, in the same fashion as the DD determines proximity using ICMP and TCP probes. That is, with TCP probes, the CSS sends a TCP SYN/ACK to port 53 of the client's DNS server. The client's DNS server recognizes the faulty TCP segment and sends a TCP RST to the requesting PDB, enabling the PDB to calculate the RTT. If the above PDB probes fail for any reason, the PDNS chooses a configurable default load-balancing method for the request, such as least connections. For example, if the client DNS server is behind a firewall that blocks TCP SYN/ACK segments without first receiving a TCP SYN segment, TCP probes may fail to a client DNS server.

> **NOTE**   Because the Boomerang protocol sends only DNS responses, it is unable to determine the RTT to client DNS servers. Therefore, you cannot use Boomerang with PDB. However, you can use the Boomerang protocol outside stateful proximity with the CSS functioning as a Content Routing Agent (CRA), but you need the Global Site Selector (GSS) to coordinate the Boomerang operation. You will learn how to configure your CSS as a CRA in the section called "Configuring Content Routing Agents" in this chapter.

The PDBs periodically synchronize their RTT information over the APP peer mesh to retrieve complete ordered lists of RTT values for every request. In this example, after synchronization, both PDBs have the RTT that the other PDB calculated for the client DNS server; that is, they will both have the ordered list [(2, 80) (1, 120)]. If later a DNS request for the domain from the same client DNS server is sent to PDNS-B by the DNS infrastructure, PDB-B will not have to coordinate probes between itself and PDB-A.

A PDNS is not required at every site, but PDBs are in order to probe client DNS servers during initial RTT calculations for a particular client DNS server. If you do not have a PDNS server at every site, make sure that the DNS infrastructure has NS records for only those sites that contain a PDNS server. Figure 12-8 illustrates a fully redundant solution, with both PDNS and PDB servers located at each site.

To configure your PDBs, you can use the configuration in Example 12-4.

Example 12-4 *Configuring the CSS Proximity Database*

```
! PDB A
app-udp
 app
 app session 10.1.10.2

 proximity db 1 tier1 "Site A"
! PDB B
app-udp
 app
 app session 172.16.10.2
 proximity db 2 tier1 "Site B"
```

To configure your PDNS servers, you can use the configuration in Example 12-5.

Example 12-5 *Configuring the CSS Proximity DNS Server*

```
! PDNS A
app-udp
 app
 dns-server zone 1 tier1 "Site A" 172.16.10.2
 app session 10.1.10.1
 dns-server

 dns-record a www.cisco.com 172.16.10.100 single kal-icmp
! PDNS B
app-udp
 app
 dns-server zone 2 tier1 "Site B" 10.1.10.2
 app session 172.16.10.1
 dns-server

 dns-record a www.cisco.com 10.1.10.100 single kal-icmp
```

You create the zone using the **dns-server zone** command, similarly to the way you configure the zone in nonproximity configurations, but in a proximity configuration you must specify the IP address of the PDB. Additionally, this example uses KAL-ICMP to determine the health of the VIPs on the peer PDNS servers (that is, Steps 7 and 8 in Figure 12-8).

Multitiered Proximity

To scale your CSS proximity environment, you can nest additional zones within your existing zones. To create a nested zone, you must assign the PDNS servers of the nested zones as a second-layer tier server using the **tier2** keyword in the **dns-server zone** command. You must also create NS records for the second layer tier on your Tier 1 PDNS CSS, thus delegating the required domains to the Tier 2 PDNS CSS (using the **dns-record ns** command). When your Tier 1 PDNS CSSs receive a client DNS request for a Tier 2 domain, they perform a recursive DNS lookup by issuing an A record request to the Tier 2 PDNS CSS you specified in the NS record. When the Tier 2 PDNS CSS receives the request, it performs the same flow that you learned previously in Figure 12-8 among its Tier 2 APP peers. When the Tier 2 finds the best-suited A record, it stores the A record locally in its PDB server and sends the A record to the Tier 1 PDNS server. The Tier 1 PDNS server then responds to the client DNS server with the A record.

Configuring Content Routing Agents

Like the CSS, the Global Site Selector (GSS) maintains a PDB, but behaves like the Distributed Director in determining proximity. That is, the GSS uses DRP to instruct IOS-based routers to probe client DNS servers for calculating RTTs to store in the PDB. The GSS also supports Boomerang DNS racing but, as you learned, Boomerang precludes calculating RTTs; therefore, the GSS PDB cannot work in conjunction with Boomerang. Hence, you must use CRAs on a CSS or a DRP agent on an IOS router at each site for Boomerang DNS racing.

You learned how to configure DRP for Boomerang previously. However, to enable the CSS as a CRA for GSS Boomerang DNS racing, you can use the configuration commands

```
dns-boomerang client enable
dns-boomerang client domain www.cisco.com 10.1.10.100
```

NOTE   For information on configuring your GSS for GSLB, refer to its product documentation on Cisco.com.

Exploring CSM Global Server Load Balancing

The CSM supports GSLB by enabling participating CSMs to respond to A record requests from client DNS servers. As you learned in previous examples, you should specify your CSMs in NS records that you configure in your IDNS or TLD DNS servers.

The CSM does not maintain APP connections between GSLB peers and therefore does not support DNS proximity or the DNS sticky features discussed in this chapter. However, the CSM can maintain APP connections to the GSS, which can send KAL-AP requests to the CSM to determine the load of the CSM's virtual servers.

> **NOTE** You should consider using the GSS at the headquarters site in the place of the CSM, just as you considered using GSS for DD and CSS. As mentioned previously, the GSLB principals of the GSS are similar to the DD, CSS, and CSM. Refer to the product documentation on Cisco.com for more information on the GSS.

To configure your CSM based on the topology in Figure 12-9, you can use the configuration in Example 12-6.

Figure 12-9 *GSLB Using the CSM*

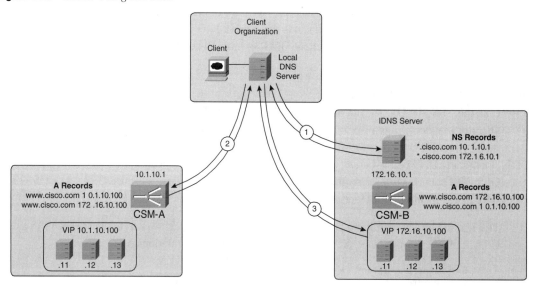

Example 12-6 *Configuring the CSM for GSLB*

```
CSM A
 serverfarm web-farm
  predictor leastconn
  real 10.1.10.11
   inservice
  real 10.1.10.12
   inservice
  real 10.1.10.13
```

Example 12-6 *Configuring the CSM for GSLB (Continued)*

```
    inservice

 serverfarm gslb-farm dns-vip
  predictor leastconn
  real 10.1.10.100
   inservice
  real 172.16.10.100
   inservice

 map dns-map dns
  match protocol dns domain www.cisco.com

policy dns-policy dns
 dns map dns-map
 serverfarm primary gslb-farm ttl 60 responses 1

vserver dns-virtual dns
 dns-policy dns-policy
 inservice

vserver web-virtual
  virtual 10.1.10.100 tcp www
  serverfarm web-farm
  inservice
```
CSM B
```
serverfarm web-farm
  predictor leastconn
  real 172.16.10.11
   inservice
  real 172.16.10.12
   inservice
  real 172.16.10.13
   inservice

 serverfarm gslb-farm dns-vip
  predictor leastconn
  real 10.1.10.100
   inservice
  real 172.16.10.100
   inservice

 map dns-map dns
  match protocol dns domain www.cisco.com

policy dns-policy dns
 dns map dns-map
 serverfarm primary gslb-farm ttl 60 responses 1
```

continues

Example 12-6 *Configuring the CSM for GSLB (Continued)*

```
vserver dns-virtual dns
 dns-policy dns-policy
 inservice

vserver web-virtual
   virtual 172.16.10.100 tcp www
   serverfarm web-farm
   inservice
```

In Example 12-6, both CSMs are configured to respond to DNS A record requests. The CSMs match incoming A record requests with the virtual server called **dns-virtual**. The policy **dns-policy** specifies the server farm containing the available VIPs for the A record request, the TTL (that is, 60 minutes), and the number of responses to return to client DNS servers. You specify the domain that the CSM will match A record requests against within the DNS map called **dns-map**.

When the CSM receives an A record request from a client DNS server, it selects among the VIPs that you specify in the server farm called **gslb-farm**. You must specify the local and remote VIPs and the load-balancing method in this server farm. You can use round-robin, least connections, ordered list, domain hash, and source IP address/domain hash. The ordered list method is unique to GSLB, where the CSM uses the first address in the list of VIPs you specify in the server farm until it becomes unavailable or overloaded, and then moves to the next address in the list. The CSM repeats this process for every subsequent entry in the list.

You can also use Route Health Injection (RHI) for distributing requests to multiple CSM VIPs in the following scenarios:

■ Within the same data center LAN across different Catalyst 6500 chassis. For all intents and purposes, you can effectively consider this scenario the same as a local SLB environment.

■ Across different sites containing CSMs connected by private WANs within an enterprise organization.

■ Across different sites containing CSMs over the Internet.

CSM performs RHI in the first two scenarios by advertising healthy VIPs as host routes (that, is /32 routes) into the local MSFC routing table. A VIP is considered healthy if it is configured within at least one healthy virtual server that contains at least one healthy real server. The MSFC advertises the host route, using an IGP routing protocol that you configure, throughout the network. Other CSMs may advertise the same VIP, resulting in multiple host routes for the VIP. As you learned in Chapter 3, "Introducing Switching, Routing, and Address Translation," when multiple routes exist within an IGP, routers select a single route to forward packets. Routers choose the route with the best distance or metric or both, depending on the IGP used. If the routes have the same cost, you learned how CEF per-flow load balancing shares the load equally across the VIPs.

If a CSM determines that the advertised VIP is no longer available or is overloaded, it removes the route from its MSFC routing table. The remaining VIP(s) located at another site(s) takes the full load of requests, until the failed VIP comes back online. To configure your virtual servers with RHI, use the following virtual server configuration command:

```
advertise active
```

You can also use RHI for Internet GSLB by effectively providing BGP-anycast routing discussed previously. The CSMs at each site install host routes in the MSFC routing tables. The MSFC can then advertise the host routes using an IGP to the Autonomous System Border Router (ASBR). The ASBRs can then summarize the host route and advertise it to their BGP peers. When a client requires access to the VIP, the DNS infrastructure returns the VIP address advertised by all sites. The BGP protocol handles distributing requests across the sites, using various metrics, including AS path.

Because BGP does not propagate host routes to other autonomous systems, you need to make sure that the host routes are summarized before being advertised to remote BGP peers in different autonomous systems. For greater control of summarization boundaries, manual summarization on the ASBRs may be desirable, depending on your IP addressing scheme at the different sites.

> **NOTE**   Route Health Injection can also be achieved on the CSS using OSPF. For more information on configuring RHI on the CSS, refer to the CSS technical documentation on Cisco.com.

GSLB Stickiness

Recall from Chapter 10 that some e-commerce applications require that clients remain connected to a server across TCP connections. The same principle pertains to GSLB in which clients must remain connected to a site even when the client refreshes its DNS entry for the site (some browsers refresh their DNS entries every 30 minutes, which may not be long enough for users to complete their transactions). However, because DNS is not extensible, as HTTP is, it cannot inherently simulate stateful connections through the use of such structures as cookies. Alternately, DNS sticky uses source IP sticky to enable your GSLB to remember the site at which a client DNS server was originally directed. If a client issues additional DNS queries for the domain throughout its session, it receives the same IP address from your content network.

You can configure DNS sticky with either source IP hash load balancing method, or by using a stateful DNS sticky table. Recall from Chapter 10 that source IP hash is a stateless load-balancing method in which the content switch hashes the source IP address for every new request to choose an available server. Hashing the source IP address results in the same site for every request from that source IP address. Therefore, hashing ensures that locally cached DNS entries that are refreshed before the end of a transaction are assigned to the same server as the original request.

As you learned from Chapter 10, the drawback to the source hashing method is an uneven selection of sites from client DNS requests. For example, source hashing can cause users in a source NAT environment to all stick to the same site, thus creating an uneven distribution of requests across the sites. The sticky database solution provides a more robust stateful sticky solution than simple hashing. With a sticky database, you can use other, more effective load-balancing methods, such as the proximity methods discussed previously, ordered lists, least connections, or weighted round-robin (WRR).

With CSS DNS-Sticky, you can store the Global Sticky database (GSDB) on a single CSS located at any site and accessed by other CSSs at your other sites. The GSDB is initially empty, and the CSS populates it with mappings of client DNS server IP address to zone indexes as the CSS receives client requests. Figure 12-10 illustrates DNS sticky using the CSS.

Figure 12-10   *DNS Sticky*

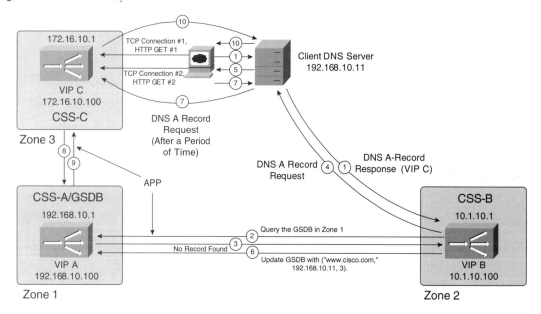

When a CSS at a site receives a client request for a sticky domain from the DNS infrastructure, it sends a lookup request to the GSDB, using the combination of the client's DNS server IP address and the sticky domain name as the key. If an entry exists for the client DNS server and domain in the GSDB, the GSDB returns the appropriate IP address to the requesting CSS. Otherwise, the GSDB CSS indicates that the entry does not exist to the requesting CSS. The requesting CSS then chooses a site using the configured load-balancing method and notifies the GSDB of the selected site. The GSDB stores the client DNS IP-to-zone index mapping so that future requests from the client DNS server for the domain will use the same A record.

The flow for the client request in Figure 12-10 to www.cisco.com is as follows:

1. The client issues an A record request for the subdomain www.cisco.com to CSS-B in Zone 2.

2. CSS-B first queries the GSDB stored in CSS-A through its APP connection to CSS-A.

3. Because the GSDB is empty, CSS-A returns a null answer and CSS-B selects VIP C, using the least-load load balancing method and load information obtained over the APP connection to CSS C. In this example, CSS C is the least loaded when CSS-B receives the client's request

4. CSS-B sends the A record response to the requesting client DNS server.

5. The client DNS server informs the client of the IP address of the domain, and the client connects to the VIP on CSS C.

6. CSS-B sends a database update to the GSDB in CSS-A containing the requested domain, the client DNS server source IP address, and the zone index of CSS-C; that is, CSS-B sends CSS-A the entry ["www.cisco.com," 192.168.10.11, 3].

7. After a period of time, the client refreshes the DNS entry for www.cisco.com, which in this instance the DNS infrastructure sends to CSS-C.

8. CSS-C first queries the GSDB on CSS-A, which now contains the entry for the client DNS server/domain/zone index tuple—["www.cisco.com," 192.168.10.11, 3].

9. CSS-A sends its query response to CSS-C.

10. CSS-C sends the A record of the VIP that it serves to the client DNS server, which was the most appropriate server for the original request in Step 4. The client DNS server then sends the response to the client. Even if CSS-C is considered overloaded in terms of the configured load-balancing algorithm, the stickiness feature overrides the load thresholds for the sake of maintaining session persistence. However, when the original site is completely down, the CSS overrides the DNS-sticky feature with a new site that it chooses based on the configured load-balancing method.

For each CSS, you can manually configure sticky to apply only to the domains you want, using the configuration in Example 12-7.

Example 12-7 *Configuring DNS-Sticky on the CSS*

```
CSS A
app-udp
 app
 dns-server zone 1 tier1 "Site A" weightedrr
 app session 172.16.10.1
 app session 10.1.10.1 dns-server

 dns-record a www.cisco.com 192.168.10.100 3600 single kal-ap weight 5 sticky-enabled
 gsdb
 gsdb ttl 14400
```
```
CSS B
app-udp
 app
 dns-server zone 2 tier1 "Site B" weightedrr
 app session 172.16.10.1
app session 192.168.10.1
 dns-server

 dns-record a www.cisco.com 10.1.10.100 3600 single kal-ap weight 10 sticky-enabled
 gsdb-interface primary 192.168.10.1
```
```
CSS C
app-udp
 app
 dns-server zone 3 tier1 "Site C" weightedrr
 app session 10.1.10.1
 app session 192.168.10.1 dns-server

 dns-record a www.cisco.com 172.16.10.100 3600 single kal-ap weight 15 sticky-enabled
 gsdb-interface primary 192.168.10.1
```

In the configuration in Example 12-7, the GSDB is enabled on the CSS-A using the **gsdb** command. CSS-B and CSS-C are each configured with a GSDB interface pointing to CSS-A using the **gsdb-interface** command. CSS-B and CSS-C query the GSDB configured with this command for all A records configured as sticky. You can configure your A records as sticky by adding the keyword **sticky-enabled** to the **dns-record** command. The **gsdb ttl** specifies the time that sticky entries exist in the GSDB. When a new request arrives for an entry, the GSDB resets the TTL for that individual entry to the value you specify with this command.

> **NOTE** The TTL you configure with the **gsdb ttl** is the time during which the GSDB stores the sticky A record in its database—this TTL does not affect the TTL that the CSS advertises to client DNS servers in A record answers. Alternately, you can modify the TTL value in CSS A record answers for domains using the TTL option in the **dns-record** command.

You can also configure stateful DNS sticky in your proximity environment. The CSS containing the PDB houses the GSDB database and answers sticky queries from CSSs that you configure as PDNS servers. When the PDNS receives the client request for a sticky domain, it first queries the GSDB for the client DNS server IP address. If the GSDB contains the queried IP address, the PDNS formulates the DNS response for the returned site. If the site specified in the GSDB is down, the PDNS contacts the PDB for the client DNS server IP address. If the PDB does not contain the client DNS server IP address, it coordinates probes across the available sites, as described previously, and informs the GSDB of the new mapping.

Summary

In this chapter, you first learned about DNS resource records and how DNS operates iteratively and recursively. The Internet DNS system primarily uses iterative DNS, but you learned how to incorporate recursive DNS in a multitiered GSLB environment by using NS records and zones on the CSS.

You also learned how to configure GSLB load-balancing methods, such as round-robin, ordered-list, least-connections, Boomerang, HTTP redirection, proximity-based, and DNS-sticky load balancing.

Review Questions

1. What is the difference between iterative and recursive DNS?

2. What type of answer occurs in this situation: your local DNS server responds to your A record request with a cached copy of the A record?

3. What is the purpose of SOA DNS records?

4. What are the various DD metrics you can use to select among your available sites?

5. What are stateless RTT calculations?

6. Why should you disable Boomerang when using HTTP redirects with the DD?

7. Why is stateful proximity beneficial?

8. Why is stateful DNS-sticky beneficial?

Recommended Reading

Scot Hull, *Content Delivery Networks*, McGraw-Hill/Osbourne, 2002

RFC 1591, *Domain Name System Structure and Delegation,* IETF, http://www.ietf.org/rfc/rfc1591.txt, 1994

Part VI: The Application and Content Networking System: Content Caching, Streaming, Routing, and Distribution

Chapter Goals

In this chapter, you will learn how to configure caching and streaming media by covering the following topics:

- **Redirection Methods**—You will learn how to redirect your client's requests to your content engines.

- **Enabling Value-Added Services to your content engines (CEs)**—You will learn how to configure your content engines for web-based caching.

- **Delivering Streaming Media**—You will learn how to configure your content engines for Windows and RealMedia caching and streaming.

CHAPTER 13

Delivering Cached and Streaming Media

The nature of content requests from Internet users tends toward the 80/20 axiom in network computing, where 80 percent of client requests are for 20 percent of your content. To deliver content to your users in a more efficient manner, you can configure your network to cache frequently requested objects in closer proximity to your users.

In this chapter, you will learn primarily how to deliver unmanaged content to your internal users more efficiently. Unmanaged content is content that is sourced from an origin server that you do not manage yourself, such as a server on the Internet. However, you can use most of the concepts in this chapter to deliver content that you manage, such as content from an intranet HTTP or streaming media server. In Chapter 14, "Distributing and Routing Managed Content," you will learn strictly how to deliver your managed content more efficiently. As the name suggests, managed content is content that you or another person or group in your organization has full control over creating and maintaining.

Redirecting Application Requests

Cisco content edge delivery provides redirection capabilities, enabling transparent delivery of cached content to your clients. Transparent redirection is useful in caching environments because routers or content switches can direct requests for content to a cache, which then can field the request on behalf of your unknowing clients. You can configure transparent redirection using either of the following methods:

- Web Cache Control Protocol

- Content Switch redirection

Introducing Web Cache Control Protocol

Web Cache Control Protocol (WCCP) is a Cisco proprietary protocol aimed at optimizing content delivery between clients and CEs, by redirecting client requests to appropriate CEs transparently. WCCP does not inspect the URL or HTTP request to classify traffic for redirection. Otherwise, delayed binding would be required by WCCP to complete the TCP connection on behalf of the server to allow the client to send the HTTP request to the WCCP router. Instead, the WCCP router inspects packets on incoming or outgoing interfaces and matches them against service groups that you configure for WCCP inspection. WCCP defines service groups by port numbers—WCCP looks no further into the payload of the packet than the TCP/UDP packet header.

To configure WCCP on your router, first you must specify the version that you wish to enable, using the command

```
ip wccp version [1 ¦ 2]
```

WCCP version 2 includes some enhanced features over version 1, including support for multiple redundant routers, improved security, Layer 2 redirection, and redirection of applications other than HTTP over TCP port 80.

To configure a service group on your router, you can use the command

```
ip wccp {web-cache ¦ service-number ¦ outbound-acl-check} [group-address multicast-
address] [redirect-list access-list] [group-list access-list] [password password [0 ¦ 7]]
```

With WCCP version 2, you can configure either well-known or user-defined groups, by specifying a service number within the **ip wccp** command. You can use well-known service groups for inspecting protocols whose ports are predefined (for example, in an RFC) and are therefore known by both the CE and WCCP router without manually configuring the desired ports. For example, as the name indicates, you can use the well-known service group called **web-cache** (service 0) for caching HTTP port 80 objects. In contrast, you must configure the ports of the user-defined service groups (services 90–97) on the CE—the CEs advertise the ports you configure to the router using WCCP signaling. Table 13-1 lists the available WCCP service groups.

Table 13-1   *Available WCCP Service Groups*

Service Group Name	Service Group Number	Description	Default Ports
Web-cache	0	HTTP protocol	80
DNS	53	DNS protocol	53
FTP-Native	60	FTP	21
HTTPS-Native	70	HTTPS protocol	443
RTSP	80	Real Time Streaming Protocol (RTSP)	554
MMST	81	Microsoft's MMS protocol over TCP	1755
MMSU	82	Microsoft's MMS protocol over User Diagram Protocol (UDP)	1755
WMT-RTSPU	83	Microsoft's implementation of the RTSP over UDP	5005

Table 13-1   *Available WCCP Service Groups (Continued)*

Service Group Name	Service Group Number	Description	Default Ports
CIFS-cache	89	Supports caching Common Internet File System (CIFS) traffic on ports 139 and 445	139 and 445
User-Defined	90-97	A custom protocol that you want to redirect	You can define up to eight ports per user-defined service.
Custom-Web-Cache	98	You can define nonstandard ports for redirecting HTTP traffic (without using up one of your "user-defined" service groups)	You can define up to eight ports for the custom web cache service.
Reverse-Proxy	99	The well-known reverse proxy protocol	80

NOTE   The difference between the reverse-proxy service and the web-cache service is that web-cache service uses the destination IP address to determine which hash bucket to use when distributing client requests across multiple CEs. Whereas, reverse-proxy hashes the source IP address to select an available hash bucket. You will learn about hash buckets later in this chapter.

Other parameters that you can specify in the **ip wccp** command are

- For outbound WCCP, the **outbound-acl-check** keywords enable the router to process any outbound ACLs before the WCCP outbound configuration classifies the packets.

- The **group-address** keyword enables you to configure a multicast address that the WCCPv2 cluster routers and CEs communicate with.

- The **redirect-list** keyword enables you to configure an ACL to control the traffic that the router will redirect within the service group that you configure.

- The **group-list** keyword enables you to configure an ACL to restrict the CEs that the router can learn about.

- To configure a Message Digest 5 (MD5) password for the WCCP routers to authenticate messages received from the service group, you can use the **password** keyword.

To enable WCCP on your CE, you can specify the WCCP version with the **wccp version** command:

```
wccp version 2
```

Then you must specify the WCCP routers that the CE will communicate with, by using the command

```
wccp router-list list-num IP-Address1 .. IP-AddressN
```

Then, you associate the service group that you configured on your router with the command

```
wccp [web-cache ¦ service-number service-group] router-list-number list-num
[l2-redirect] [mask-assign]
```

If you configured a user-defined service group on your router, you must associate the ports on your CE that you want the WCCP router to redirect to the CE, with the command

```
wccp port-list list-num port-num
```

For example, to enable the standard **web-cache** service group on your CE, you can use the commands

```
wccp version 2
wccp router-list 1 10.1.20.2
wccp web-cache router-list-num 1
```

Redirecting Traffic at Layer 2 and Layer 3 with Web Cache Control Protocol

Once you enable WCCP on your router with the **ip wccp** command, you can enable Layer 2 or 3 traffic redirection on the router's interfaces. With Layer 2 redirection, the WCCP router rewrites the MAC address in the Ethernet frame to redirect traffic transparently to a different destination IP address (that is, the CE) than specified by the destination IP address in the IP packet header. Not all router platforms support Layer 2 redirection—the Catalyst 6500 Multilayer Switching Feature Card (MSFC)/Policy Feature Card (PFC) contains hardware acceleration for WCCP Layer 2 redirection. This feature is negotiated between directly connected Cisco Content Engines and the MSFC/PFC. The Ethernet frame is forwarded to the transparent cache, which in turn processes the request. To configure Layer 2 redirection, you can configure your CEs with the **l2-redirect** keyword in the **wccp service-number router-list-number** command that you learned previously—no configuration is required on the MSFC/PFC.

WCCPv2 uses generic routing encapsulated (GRE) tunneling with Layer 3 application redirection, which leaves the original IP packet intact. The WCCP router encapsulates the packet with an additional GRE packet header containing the source IP as the WCCP router and the destination IP as the CE device. WCCPv2 uses GRE so that the WCCP router can communicate directly with the CE over IP while retaining the original packets of the client. This is beneficial if the CE is any number of Layer 3 hops away from the WCCP router.

> **NOTE**   Layer 2 redirection provides a more efficient redirection mechanism by avoiding additional packet encapsulation and processing at Layer 3. However, your CEs must be visible at Layer 2 from the MSFC.

With Layer 3 redirection, the client sends a request for content to an origin server, by first sending a SYN segment to the origin server. The packet contains the source IP of the client and the destination of the origin server. In the case of redirecting web traffic, the WCCP router inspects the TCP header within the IP packet for port 80 in the destination port field and matches the "web-cache" service group. The WCCP router then chooses an available CE for the request and encapsulates the IP packet in a GRE packet with its interface as the source address and the selected CE's IP address as the destination. When the CE receives the packet, it decapsulates the GRE header and responds directly to the client with a TCP SYN/ACK segment, by spoofing the source address of the origin server. This way, the client is unaware that the TCP response was sent by the CE. The client then sends the TCP ACK packet to complete the TCP handshake and application layer content request to the origin server, which the WCCP router forwards to the CE over the GRE tunnel. The CE then decides whether or not the content is cached and proceeds with the transaction.

Input Redirection Vs. Output Redirection

You can enable your WCCP router to redirect packets as they either arrive or leave a router interface, using the interface configuration command:

```
ip wccp [web-cache ¦ [service-number service-group redirect [in ¦ out]
```

You can configure either input or output redirection with the following commands:

- **Input Redirection**—With input redirection, the router matches incoming traffic against a WCCP service group that you configure and redirects the traffic immediately to the CE. The WCCP router does not perform a routing table lookup before matching traffic, even when using Layer 3 redirection. You must configure input redirection if you decide to use Layer 2 redirection.

  For example, to configure input redirection for the web-cache service on an interface, you can use the command

  ```
  ip wccp web-cache redirect in
  ```

> **NOTE** WCCP classifies only the first packet of a flow and redirects the packet to the CE. All subsequent traffic of the flow is Cisco Express Forwarding (CEF)-switched to the CE.

- **Output Redirection**—With output redirection, the router routes traffic from its incoming interfaces to the outgoing interface that you configure for outgoing redirection, and then matches the traffic against its configured WCCP service groups. For example, to configure output redirection for the web-cache service on an interface, you can use the interface configuration command:

  ```
  ip wccp web-cache redirect out
  ```

Output redirection is less efficient than input redirection because

— The router performs a CEF trie lookup to determine the next-hop address based on the destination IP address of the incoming traffic. Avoiding these additional CEF lookups for Layer 3 redirection can be beneficial in high traffic environments.

— WCCP inspects traffic from all incoming interfaces that are routed to the outgoing interface. WCCP uses the fastest switching path that you configure (for example, CEF switching) for processing traffic on outgoing interfaces. However, WCCP still imposes unnecessary overhead to the switching path when applying policies to all your outgoing traffic—especially to traffic from incoming interfaces that will never contain WCCP traffic. Fortunately, you can exclude incoming interface traffic from being classified by WCCP on outgoing interfaces by using **ip wccp redirect exclude in** on incoming interfaces.

WCCP Load Distribution Using Hash Buckets

To scale your caching environment, you can install multiple CEs and distribute requests across them using WCCP. The WCCP router distributes the incoming requests using hash buckets or address mask assignments.

Recall the IP address hash load-balancing method that you learned about previously in Chapter 10, "Exploring Server Load Balancing." To select an available real server, the content switch computes a numeric hash value based on the source or destination IP address in the IP header of the request. The content switch then divides the hashed value by the number of reals N, with the remainder giving the resultant real to forward the request to. This mechanism works fine for an SLB with content replicated across your real servers. However, you want to avoid replicating content across available CEs. For example, using simple destination IP address load balancing, when a cache fails, the hash values are divided by $N-1$. The remainder of the division then results in a cache, different from the one receiving previous requests for the same content, receiving the new request, causing a sudden redistribution of content across all of the CEs. The redistribution of content across CEs results in major bursts of cached content misses by your clients.

The solution to this problem is the use of a series of data structures called hash buckets—you learned previously how CEF switching uses hash buckets in Chapter 3, "Introducing Switching, Routing, and Address Translation." When the first request arrives at the WCCP router, the router computes a hash on the various fields in the IP and TCP headers, resulting in a range of predetermined values, usually a pool of CEs that is relatively larger than reasonable. For illustration purposes, assume that the hash function produces a 3-bit value. Therefore, a maximum of eight hash buckets are available. In actuality, WCCP uses 256 hash buckets—recall from Chapter 3 that the CEF load-sharing table uses 16 hash buckets (with a 4-bit hash function).

WCCP intelligently assigns the available CEs to the hash buckets based on CE load and availability. CEs with a lower load are assigned to more buckets than CEs with higher loads. For example, say WCCP assigns the hash buckets according to Figure 13-1. The hash function can then produce a hash value of 5 for an originating TCP SYN segment of a flow. Because bucket number 5 is assigned to CE 2, the router sends the request to that CE for this and all subsequent packets in the flow. This way, only CE 2 maintains a copy of the requested file, thus avoiding file duplication across the pool of caches.

> **NOTE**   The designated CE sends WCCP policy information for the selected service group to the WCCP router(s) on behalf of the cache cluster (WCCP elects the CE with the lowest IP address as the designated CE). The policy information includes the load-balancing method (hash buckets or mask assignment) and the mask/hash table. The designated CE distributes the buckets among the available CEs, based on the load of the CEs, before advertising the hash or mask bucket table to the WCCP router(s).

Figure 13-1 illustrates how WCCP uses hash buckets for CE assignments.

Figure 13-1   *Using WCCP Hash Buckets*

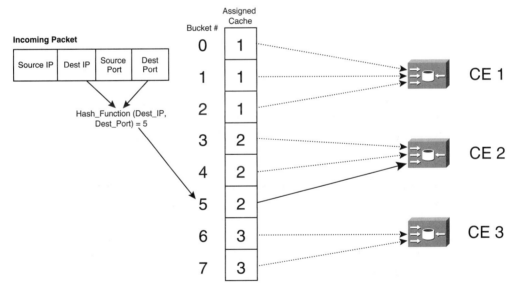

Recovering from a CE Failure

When a CE fails, WCCP reassigns to the other available CEs the buckets to which the failed CE was assigned—only the files from the failed CEs are redistributed among the remaining CEs, as Figure 13-2 illustrates. All other CEs remain assigned to their respective hash buckets, thus avoiding the system-wide file redistribution that occurs when a CE fails when using straight hashing. When a CE fails using hash buckets, requests only for the content held in the failed CE experience cache misses.

Figure 13-2 *Recovering from a CE Failure Using Hash Buckets*

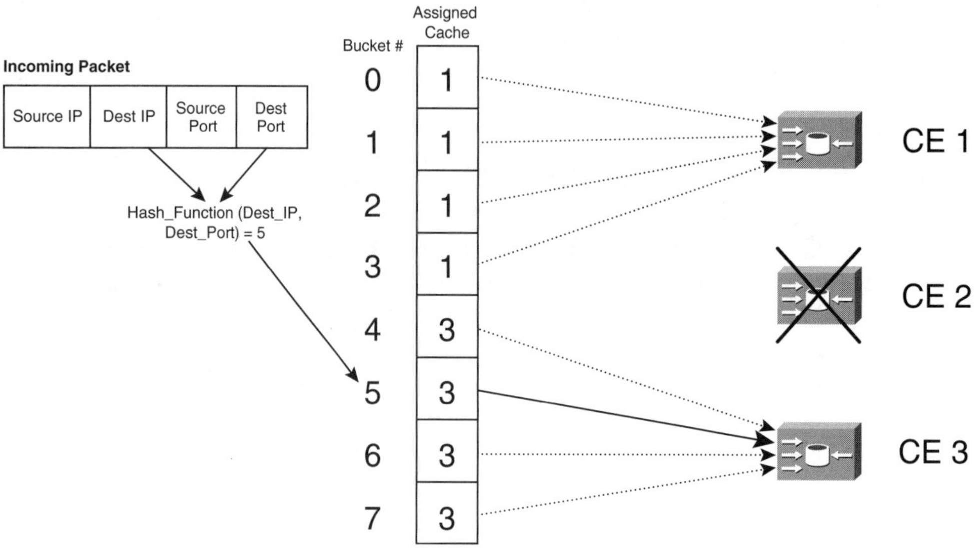

Adding a New CE

Unlike with CE failures, when you add a new cache to the pool, the cached objects in the entire pool require redistribution among the available caches. The hash bucket assignments need to be adjusted to fit the new CE in the available buckets. For example, Figure 13-3 adds a fourth CE to the cluster. If WCCP assigns buckets 6 and 7 to the new CE, the other buckets need to be reorganized to ensure that the load is distributed across the CEs. Fortunately, in this example, bucket 5 is still assigned to CE 3, so existing files for the illustrated flow are not affected.

To help reduce the likelihood of a flood of cache misses, the new CE attempts to satisfy incoming requests by querying the other CEs in the cluster for the content before sending the request to the origin server to retrieve the original content. This technique is called cache healing. Cache healing enables a CE that receives a request for an object that was previously served by another CE, referred to as a "near miss," to query the other CEs for the file. You can enable healing mode on your CE by using the following command:

```
http cluster {heal-port number ¦ http-port number ¦ max-delay seconds ¦ misses number}
```

By using the **http cluster** command, you can specify the port from which the CEs listen to content requests from other CEs (the default is 14333). You can also specify the actual port for the request by using the **http-port** keyword (the default is port 80). The **max-delay** keyword specifies the number of seconds that the healing client (that is, the newly added CE) waits before it sends the request to a healing server (the default is zero seconds). You can configure the total number of misses before the CE disables healing mode, by using the **misses** keyword.

Figure 13-3 *Inserting a New Cache*

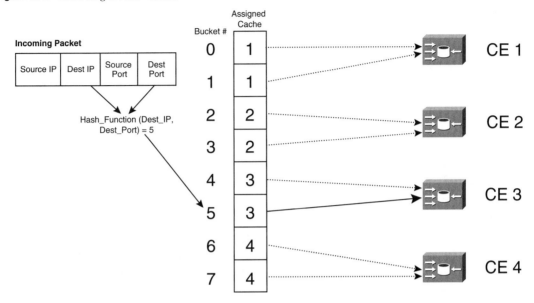

To ensure that existing flows to working CEs do not disconnect when adding a new cache to the cluster, you should enable WCCPv2 flow protection by using the following command on your CEs:

```
wccp flow-redirect enable
```

To ensure that a newly added CE is not overwhelmed with connections when it is first added to the cluster, you can enable WCCPv2 slow start with the command

```
wccp slow-start enable
```

Slow start ensures that the CE will be assigned buckets at smaller increments during the CEs bootup process, enabling the CE to completely boot before assigning it a full load.

WCCP Hot Spot Handling

When WCCP hashes requests for a frequently requested file or small group of files to the same bucket, the CEs assigned to the bucket become overloaded. Because WCCP version 1 is traditionally assigned a single CE per bucket, WCCP version 1 sends all requests for the requested file(s) to the same CE. This situation is called a hot spot, and it can cause undesirable effects in a pool of CEs, such as CE overloading. WCCP version 2 automatically detects hot spots in the hash buckets and will assign more than one CE to the bucket, thus distributing the load across the available CEs.

WCCP CE Load Shedding

You may find that CEs sometimes become overloaded within a CE cluster, even with the WCCP hash bucket hot spot handling feature. If so, you can configure the CE overload bypass feature. With the bypass feature, when a CE becomes overloaded, it instructs the router to bypass the bucket that the router used to send the current request to the CE—the router will redirect the request to another CE. If the CE load does not decrease when it receives the next request from the WCCP router (on a different bucket), it instructs the router to bypass the bucket that the router used to send the current request to, and so on until the CE load decreases. To configure overload bypass, use the command

```
bypass load {enable ¦ in-interval seconds ¦ out-interval seconds ¦ time-interval
    minutes}
```

The command **bypass load enable** enables the bypass feature. The command **bypass load in-interval** indicates the interval between bypassed buckets coming back online (default of 60 seconds) after the CE's load starts to decrease. The command **bypass load out-interval** specifies the time during which the CE will bypass another bucket after the previous bypass (default of four seconds). Last, the command **bypass load time-interval** indicates the time during which the CE will wait before enabling a bypassed bucket.

WCCP Load Distribution Using Mask Assignment

Address mask assignment load distribution is similar to hash assignment, except that, instead of hashing the IP address or ports, WCCP applies a mask to the IP addresses to determine a value to use as an index into a "mask" table. WCCP applies the masks you specify to the incoming packet header fields, by performing a bitwise-AND operation using the mask among the source IP address, destination IP address, source TCP/UDP port, and destination TCP/UDP port fields. The result of the mask is an index into a table of 127 entries. The entries contain pointers to the available caches. You can configure the masks yourself on your caches, using a total of seven bits within the four fields mentioned previously. Table 13-2 gives the default values for the four available masks—the CE applies the value given in the Mask column to the field specified in the Field column.

Table 13-2   *Default WCCP Version 2 Masks*

Field	Mask (in Hex)	Mask (in Binary)
Source IP address	0000	0000000000000000
Destination IP address	1741	0001011101000001
Source Port	0000	0000000000000000
Destination Port	0000	0000000000000000

To enable mask assignment, you must specify the **mask-assign** keyword in the **wccp service-number router-list-num** command that you learned about previously. Notice that the masks in Table 13-2 use only six of the possible seven bits (only on the destination IP address field), resulting in only 64 possible entries. To manually adjust the mask values on your CE, you can use the command

```
wccp service-number mask {[dst-ip-mask hex_num] [dst-port-mask port_hex_num]
[src-ip-mask hex_num] [src-port-mask port_hex_num]}
```

Table 13-3 gives alternate masks across three of the four fields, using all seven available bits in total, thus giving 127 possible values.

Table 13-3   *Sample WCCP Version 2 Masks*

Field	Mask (in Hex)	Mask (in Binary)
Source IP address	2480	0010010010000000
Destination IP address	0208	0000001000001000
Source Port	0003	0000000000000011
Destination Port	0000	0000000000000000

To configure the values in Table 13-3 for the web-cache service group, you can use the command

```
wccp web-cache mask src-ip-mask 0x2480 dst-ip-mask 0x0208 src-port-mask 0x0003
```

For illustration purposes, Figure 13-4 masks on the destination IP address using 0x0460, which gives eight possible mask table entries. Figure 13-4 gives the resulting mask assignments for a sample request using the destination mask 0x0460. This mask in binary is 0b10010000001, which gives a result of 0b101 when masked against the destination IP address 192.168.10.1. Using 0b101 (that is, 7 in decimal) as an index into the table results in selecting CE 4.

You can apply the same rules to mask buckets that you learned previously with *hash* buckets—that is, how hash buckets deal with failed caches, bucket overload, and the addition of a new cache. Refer to sections "Recovering from a CE Failure," "Adding a New CE," "WCCP Hot Spot Handling," and "WCCP CE Load Shedding" for more information.

> **NOTE**   Like Layer 2 redirection, the mask assignment method requires special hardware and is currently supported on the Catalyst 6500 MSFC2/PFC2 and above.

Figure 13-4 *Sample Mask Bucket Assignment*

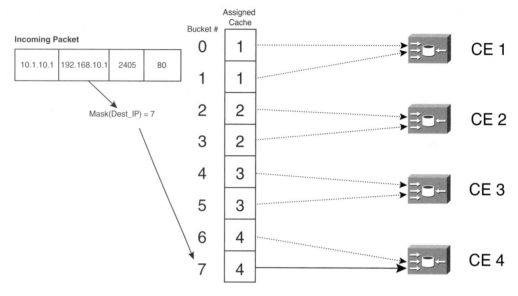

Layer 4–7 Content Switch Redirection

Content switches can provide robust redirection capabilities using Layer 4–7 redirection. Because content switches perform delayed binding, they can inspect the HTTP headers to obtain load-balancing criteria. This enables you to use the following features:

■ You can use HTTP header load balancing to match cache virtual servers and manually configure certain types of files for redirection.

■ The content switch can hash URLs to ensure that requests for the same file are forwarded to the same caches.

■ Intelligent in-band health probes and real-time load calculations are available for you to configure.

■ Content switches do not redirect content that is marked as non-cacheable ("no-cache") in the HTTP "Cache-Control:" header. The content switch instead forwards the request directly to the origin server.

With content switch redirection, you create virtual servers for traffic flowing in the direction of the cacheable requests. You can then create policies within the virtual servers to match the types of traffic you want cached—you should use Extension Qualifier Lists (EQL) for specifying the file types to be cached. All other types of flows in the same direction traverse the content switch per normal routing policies.

As with WCCP, content switches can perform redirection that is transparent to your clients. That is, clients send requests directly to the origin server, but when the content switch matches a request to a virtual server for a CE farm, the content switch can forward the request to the selected cache, using either NAT- or dispatch-mode forwarding. The cache processes the request and initiates a connection to the origin server on a cache-miss using its IP address as the source of the request, or by spoofing the client's IP address.

> **NOTE**   Later you will learn how to configure content switch redirection in the "Request Redirection Topologies" section of this chapter.

Content Switch Load Distribution

You can use one of the following CSS-balancing methods to distribute requests across your pool of CEs:

- **Source IP address hashing**—Sticks a client to the same CE for every request from the client. Source IP address hashing may cause duplication of content across your pool of CEs because, if two different sources request the same content, the CSS directs them to different CEs based on their source IP address. Use the content rule command **balance srcip** to configure source IP address hashing.

- **Destination IP address hashing**—Directs all client requests to the same destination IP address to the same CEs. Destination IP address hashing is useful in forward caching environments and some reverse caching environments in which a large number of servers are being cached. The method ensures that the CSS does not replicate content across caches. Use the content rule command **balance destip** to configure source IP address hashing.

- **Domain or URL balancing**—With these methods of balancing, the CSS divides the 26 letters of the alphabet evenly between the caches. With domain balancing, the CSS uses the first four letters after the first dot (".") of the domain in the "Host:" header of the GET request to determine which CE to select. To configure domain balancing, use the **balance domain** content rule command.

  With URL balancing, the CSS takes the first four letters in the "Host:" header after the URL that you configure in your content rule (for example, if you configure "\support\" the CSS would use the first four letters immediately after the last "\"). To configure domain balancing, use the **balance url** content rule command. Both of these methods may cause duplication of content across your pool of caches.

- **Domain or URL Hashing**—With these methods of balancing, the CSS uses an exclusive-OR (XOR) hash function to reduce the domain name or URL into an index to identify an available cache. To configure URL hashing, use the **balance urlhash** content rule command. To configure domain hashing, use the **balance domainhash** content rule command.

Recall from Chapter 10 that the CSS distributes all GET requests within an HTTP-persistent TCP connection to the same server (unless the CSS matches the request to a different virtual server that does not contain the originally selected real server). To ensure that the CSS distributes the requests evenly across the caches, you should disable persistence (using the **no persistence** content rule command) and enable request rebalancing (using the **persistent reset remap** global command).

> **NOTE** You can also use the traditional load balancing methods that you learned about in Chapter 10, such as least connections, weighted round robin, and response times, for CE load distribution.

Adding and Removing CEs When Using CSS Redirection

A drawback to CSS redirection is that, when you add a new CE manually or when the CSS adds a recovered CE to the pool, the CSS must redistribute content across the pool of CEs. To circumvent content redistribution when a failed cache recovers and comes back online, you can configure your CSS to direct all subsequent requests destined to the failed CE to the origin server instead. Once the CE comes back online, the CSS will resume sending requests to the CE. To configure the CSS to bypass a failed CE, you can use the **failover bypass** content rule command.

With this command, if a client establishes a new TCP connection to the CSS and sends a request for a file residing on the failed CE, the CSS redirects the client to the origin server instead. When the CE recovers, the CSS directs new clients to the recovered CE. However, in the case of existing clients that are using HTTP-persistent TCP connections, if the CE later recovers, and the client sends a subsequent request to the virtual server containing the recovered CE, the CSS bypasses the entire virtual server. This behavior is called bypass persistence. To ensure that persistent connections use virtual servers containing the recovered cache, you can disable bypass persistence with the **bypass persistence disable** command. If you disable bypass persistence, you must direct the CSS to either redirect or remap the persistent connection using the **persistent reset** global command. These commands will make sure that the CSS resumes sending requests within a HTTP-persistent TCP connection to virtual servers containing the recovered CE, including the recovered CE itself.

As an alternative to configuring **failover bypass**, you configure your CSS to distribute subsequent requests that were originally designed for the failed CE to the next configured CE in your content rule using the **failover next** command. You can also direct the CSS to distribute requests for files residing on the failed CE across the remaining CEs using the **failover linear** content rule command. If you do not configure a failover mechanism using the **failover** command, the content switch redistributes all content across your pool of CEs. If you do not configure a failover mechanism, you should consider configuring CE healing on your CEs, to avoid content redistribution.

Request Redirection Topologies

In this chapter, you learn how you can configure your Cisco CEs to add value to networked applications. To do so, you must first learn about the three common caching topologies: proxy, forward, and reverse caching.

Proxy Caching

You can configure proxy caching by placing a CE in close proximity to your clients and explicitly configuring your client's web browser or media player to send content requests directly to the CE for all external access. Under normal circumstances, the client would formulate a content request with the IP packet's destination IP address set to the IP address of the origin server. However, if you use a proxy cache, your browser or media player would send the IP packet with the proxy cache's IP address set as the destination IP address in the IP packet. The client will establish a TCP connection directly to the proxy cache to send the application request over.

When the proxy cache receives the request, it processes the request and responds directly to the client. If the cache has a copy of the requested object (known as a cache-hit), the cache responds directly to the client with the requested object. Otherwise, the proxy cache generates an identical request, but with its own IP address as the source of the packet, and sends the request to the origin server (known as a cache-miss). The proxy caches require your browser or media player to include the requested host domain name in either the URI field or within an HTTP "Host:" header in the client's HTTP GET request. Using DNS, the proxy cache resolves the domain name, for use as the destination IP address of the packets sent to the origin server.

When the proxy receives the origin server's response, it caches a copy of the object, unless the "Cache-Control:" header prevents the object from being cached before sending it the client. As you learned in Chapter 8, "Exploring the Application Layer," the values "no-store" or "no-cache" in the "Cache-Control:" header prevent the cache from storing the object. With either a cache-hit, -miss, or near-miss, from the client browser or media player's perspective, the object appears to be coming directly from the proxy cache, which is where the client sent its request in the first place. From the end-user's perspective, the transaction appears to be occurring directly with the origin server.

Because the client's browser or media player addresses its requests with the proxy's IP address, you do not need to configure network redirection on your routers or content switches. The intermediary routers simply route the packets directly to the client per normal routing policies. However, to create a redundant array of proxy caches, you require a content switch. You can create a virtual server containing the VIP to which you point client's browsers and media players. The proxy cache requests are then load-balanced to the various caches. Figure 13-5 illustrates forward proxy caching.

Figure 13-5 *Forward Proxy Caching*

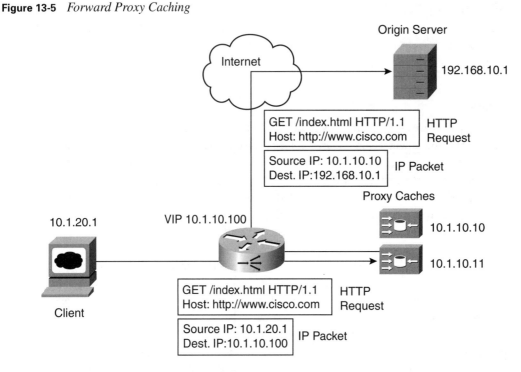

To configure your CSS to load balance client requests among multiple proxy caches, you can use the configuration in Example 13-1. You cannot use WCCP for proxy cache load balancing.

Example 13-1 *CSS Forward Proxy Load Balancing*

```
service proxy-1
 ip address 10.1.10.10
 type proxy-cache
 active

service proxy-2
 ip address 10.1.10.11
 type proxy-cache
 active

eql static-files
 extension gif
 extension jpg
 extension jpeg
 extension asf
 extension rm
```

Example 13-1   *CSS Forward Proxy Load Balancing (Continued)*

```
 extension qt
 extension mp4
 extension html
 extension htm

owner cisco
 content proxy-vip
  vip address 10.1.10.100
  url "/*" eql static-files
  protocol tcp
  port 80
  balance domainhash
  failover bypass
  add service proxy-1
  add service proxy-2
```

To enable forward proxy caching, you need to assign your proxy caches as **type proxy-cache**. This command tells the CSS to destination-NAT client requests to the proxy cache's IP addresses. It also prevents the CSS from matching requests originated from the proxy caches against configured virtual servers, to avoid loops between the CSS and proxy caches.

> **NOTE**   The EQL in Example 13-1 is not exhaustive. Make sure that you understand what file types you should redirect to your proxy cache before enabling redirection on your CSS.

Because you must explicitly configure your client's browser with the proxy IP address, you can use proxy caching only in an enterprise environment in which you have administrative access to the clients that are requesting the content. As an alternative to manual proxy configuration, you can use dynamic proxy auto-configuration to help automate the proxy setting changes on your client's browser or media players. Dynamic PAC is a method in which the user's browser is configured with a URL to a ".pac" file that contains information on the proxy. To change all your user's proxy settings, you need only change this single file, not every browser or media player in your organization. You will learn more about how to configure PAC files in Chapter 14.

> **NOTE**   The Cisco CE caches FTP, HTTP, HTTPS, MMS, and RTSP in proxy mode by default—you do not need to configure any special settings to cache these protocols on their standard ports.

Transparent Caching

As with proxy caches, you place transparent CEs in close proximity to the client. However, as the name indicates, transparent caching is transparent to the client program because you do not need to configure client browsers or media players with the proxy IP address. When a client sends a request, the destination of the packet remains as the origin server, but the transparent cache is programmed to accept the request nonetheless. If the object is available in the transparent CE's cache file system (CFS), the cache spoofs the origin server IP address before sending the request back to the client. If the object is not available in the cache, the transparent cache opens a separate TCP connection to the origin server with its IP address as the source and sends the request unmodified. Figure 13-6 illustrates forward transparent caching.

Figure 13-6　*Forward Transparent Caching*

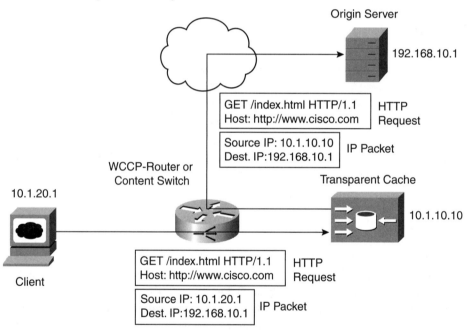

> **NOTE**　Transparent caching is also known as forward caching and forward transparent caching.

When you configure forward transparent caching using the web-cache service, the WCCP router hashes the destination IP address to select a hash bucket for determining to which CE the request should be forwarded. Because the IP address space used on the Internet is much vaster than the source IP address space that you use in your organization, WCCP can more evenly distribute content across the available CEs through use of destination IP address hashing.

To configure your CSS to redirect requests to a farm of transparent caches, you can use the configuration you learned previously in Example 13-1 with the exception of assigning the cache's services as **type transparent-cache**, which indicates to the CSS that it should not destination-NAT the client requests to the cache's IP address. This command also prevents the CSS from matching requests originated from the proxy caches against configured virtual servers, to avoid loops between the CSS and proxy caches.

Reverse Transparent Caching

With reverse caching, you locate your CE(s) in close proximity to your origin servers, as opposed to proxy and transparent caching, in which you locate the CE in close proximity to your clients. Figure 13-7 illustrates reverse transparent caching.

Figure 13-7 *Reverse Transparent Caching*

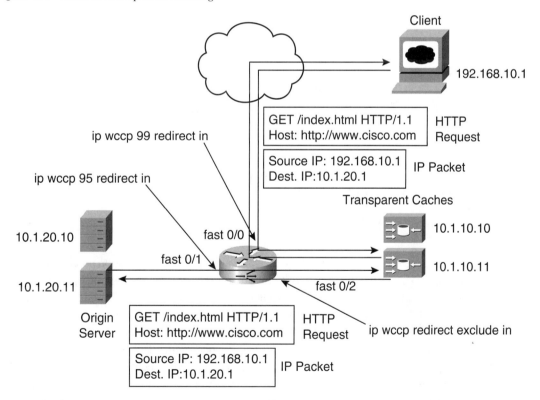

When retrieving content from an origin server, you can configure the CE to use as the source either its own IP address or the IP of the requesting client—Figure 13-7 illustrates how the CE spoofs the client IP address to source the connection. You should configure spoofing on your caches with reverse caching so that your origin server can use the client's source IP address for auditing and logging purposes. To configure the CE to spoof the client's IP address, use the command **wccp spoof-client-ip enable** on your CE. If you use this command on the CE, you must also configure the WCCP router to redirect the return packets from the origin server to the CE, in addition to redirecting packets from the client to the CE, as Figure 13-7 and Example 13-2 illustrate.

Example 13-2 *WCCP Reverse Proxy Load Balancing with Client IP Spoofing*

```
WCCP on the Router
ip wccp 99
ip wccp 95

interface fastethernet 0/0
 ip address 192.168.10.2 255.255.255.0
 ip wccp 99 redirect in

interface fastethernet 0/1
ip address 10.1.20.1 255.255.255.0
 ip wccp 95 redirect in

interface fastethernet 0/2
 ip address 10.1.10.1 255.255.255.0
 ip wccp redirect exclude in
```
```
WCCP on the CE
wccp version 2
wccp router-list 1 10.1.10.1
wccp port-list 1 80
wccp service-number 95 router-list-num 1 port-list-num 1 application cache
   hash-destination-ip match-source-port
wccp reverse-proxy router-list-num 1
wccp spoof-client-ip enable
```

As you learned previously, by default the WCCP router inspects the destination port of packets for the service group port (for example, port 80 for HTTP traffic). However, with IP spoofing, you must tell the WCCP router to redirect the origin server's return packets as the source port, not the destination port. For example, when the CE receives the client's HTTP requests, it establishes a TCP connection to the origin server using the client's IP address by sending a TCP SYN request to the server. The server receives the TCP SYN and responds with a TCP SYN-ACK packet to the client with port 80 as the source address. When the WCCP router receives the server's TCP SYN-ACK, it must inspect the source port to check for the port that you configured in service group 95 (that is, port 80 in this example). When the router receives return packets with the source port of 80, it redirects them to the CE. To instruct the WCCP router to inspect the source port instead of the destination port, use the **match-source-port** option, as Example 13-2 illustrates.

Once the router matches traffic against the service group, it performs a hash to determine the hash bucket for the request. Because the reverse-proxy service hashes incoming requests on the source IP address (that is, the client's IP address), you must configure the WCCP router to hash the server's responses on the destination IP address. You should configure this hash argument swap to make sure that the WCCP router sends the server's response back to the same CE as the client's original request. To do this, you must create another service group on the CE (that is, service group 95) and assign the destination address as the hash argument with the **hash-destination-ip** keyword.

Additionally, to avoid the spoofed packets originating from the CE from being classified and redirected by the WCCP router, you must configure the router interface with **ip wccp redirect exclude in**.

To use a CSS instead of WCCP for reverse transparent caching, you can use the configuration in Example 13-3.

Example 13-3 *CSS Reverse Proxy Load Balancing Without Client IP Spoofing*

```
service proxy-1
 ip address 10.1.10.10
 type transparent-cache
 no cache-bypass
 active

service proxy-2
 ip address 10.1.10.11
 type transparent-cache
 no cache-bypass
 active
service web01
 ip address 10.1.20.10
 active

service web02
 ip address 10.1.20.11
 active

eql static-files
 extension gif
 extension jpg
 extension jpeg
 extension asf
 extension rm
 extension qt
 extension mp4
 extension html
 extension htm
```

continues

Example 13-3 *CSS Reverse Proxy Load Balancing Without Client IP Spoofing (Continued)*

```
owner cisco
 content cache-miss-vip
  vip address 10.1.10.101
  protocol tcp
  port 80
  add service web01
  add service web02

 content transparent-vip
  vip address 10.1.10.100
  url "/*" eql static-files
  protocol tcp
  port 80
  balance srcip
  failover bypass
  add service proxy-1
  add service proxy-1

 content web-vip
  vip address 10.1.10.100
  protocol tcp
  port 80
  add service web01
  add service web02
```

To use your CSS for redirection, you need to include the command **http l4-switch enable** on your CE. Additionally, in the event of a cache-miss, you must use the **http proxy outgoing host** command to direct all cache-miss traffic to a new VIP on the CSS. For example, the following command directs the CE to forward all requests for files that it does not serve to the IP 10.1.10.101:

```
http proxy outgoing host 10.1.10.101
```

Example 13-2 shows a new virtual server called "cache-miss-vip" that contains this VIP. This new virtual server in turn directs all cache misses to your web server farm. Under normal circumstances, the CSS will not match any requests originating from CEs against its configured virtual servers. However, in a reverse proxy configuration, you must configure the command **no cache-bypass** on your services, for the CSS to allow CEs to originate cache-miss requests to the CSS.

For all client requests that do not match the EQL in virtual server "transparent-vip," the CSS matches the virtual server called "web-vip." This virtual server simply forwards the client's requests to your server farm for processing.

Ensuring Content Freshness

Recall from Chapter 8 that HTTP uses the implicit control conditional HTTP header "IF-Modified-Since:" (IMS) to determine whether the content residing on the origin server has been changed since the content was originally obtained. On a cache-miss, the CE requests the object from the origin server. The response from the origin server includes a timestamp indicating the time when the origin server issued the fresh piece of content, which the CE stores along with the object in its cache file system. On subsequent hits to the object, the CE populates the "IF-Modified-Since:" header with this timestamp. If the content has been modified on the origin server after the content was loaded on the CE, the origin server sends an "HTTP 200 OK" response to the CE including the latest copy of the requested object. Upon receiving this response from the origin server, the CE generates a new timestamp for the cached object and forwards the object to the client. If, on the other hand, the origin server determines that the requested object has not been modified, it responds with "HTTP 304 Not Modified" to the CE. To ensure that the "If-Modified-Since:" header is accurate, when possible, make sure that your CE and origin server clocks are synchronized.

To enable HTTP request revalidation, use the command

```
http reval-each-request {[all] ¦ [none] ¦ [text]}
```

Preloading Content

CEs populate themselves on demand by storing copies of content inline with client's requests. For noncached objects, the clients must wait for the content from the origin server—the CE serves all subsequent requests for the object from its cache. To avoid having your clients wait for downloads from external HTTP or FTP sites or Windows Media Technology (WMT) media servers, you can preload your CE with content—you cannot preload Real Media files on your CE.

To preload content to your CE, you can create a preload URL list containing the URLs that the CE will traverse. Upon traversal, the CE caches the files for subsequent client requests. A sample URL list is given in Example 13-4.

Example 13-4   *Sample Preload URL List*

```
http://www.cisco.com 3
http://www.cnn.com 2
mms://10.1.10.2 1
ftp://ftp.cisco.com 4
```

Each entry contains the depth, indicating the depth of URLs that the CE will recursively visit within the main URL. The default depth is 3. You can store this URL list on an HTTP, FTP, or HTTPS server, or to the local disk on the CE called "local," and configure the CE to retrieve the list using the command

```
pre-load url-list-file path
```

To enable preloading on your CE, you can use the command

```
preload enable
```

You can also limit the number of concurrent connections that the CE will issue when traversing the URLs in the list, by using the command

```
pre-load concurrent-requests num-requests
```

To mark the Type of Service (ToS) or Differentiated Services Code Point (DSCP) values for preloaded packets that the CE serves, use the command

```
pre-load dscp [set-tos ¦ set-dscp] value
```

Transparently Delivering Authenticated Content

Internet applications often require authentication of users before supplying private content to the requesting client. To ensure that authentication between origin servers and clients takes place, the CE performs end-to-end authentication that is transparent to the client and origin server. Once the user authenticates with the external site, the CE can optionally cache the object and the user's credentials for the object, only if the object is authenticated using HTTP Basic authentication. In contrast, the CE does not cache Kerberos, Windows NT LAN Manager (NTLM), or Digest-protected objects, because these methods encrypt the user's passwords using a one-time nonce value. Therefore, they cannot be used for verification more than once—the CE simply forwards the authentication information and objects transparently between the client and origin server. Figure 13-8 illustrates end-to-end authentication.

Figure 13-8 *End-to-End HTTP Authentication*

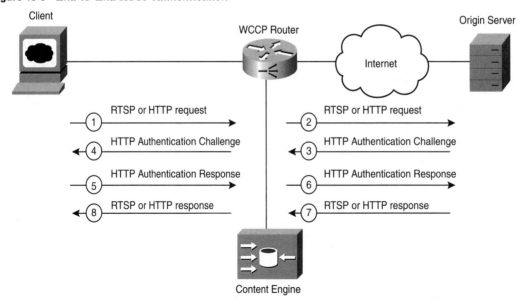

Consider the example that is shown in Figure 13-8 of a client requesting authenticated content from an origin server:

1. The client sends an HTTP request to an origin server.

2. The CE intercepts the request and determines that the requested object is not available in its cache file system. The CE then creates another connection to the origin server over which it sends the client's GET request.

3. The origin server challenges the CE for Basic authentication.

4. The CE then challenges the client for Basic authentication.

5. The web browser or media player prompts the client for credentials in a pop-up window and sends them to the CE. The CE stores the credentials for future requests.

> **NOTE**   If your clients were located at a branch office and the origin server was located at your central office, the origin server might challenge the user for NTLM or Kerberos authentication. In this case, the browser would automatically provide the user's Windows login credentials to the CE.

6. The CE responds to the origin server with the user's credentials.

7. The origin server responds to the CE with the requested object along with a timestamp for the object.

8. The CE stores the requested object, along with the user's credentials, in its cache file system. The CE then responds to the client with the requested object.

On future requests for the Basic authenticated object, the CE sends a conditional IMS request to the origin server containing the timestamp and the user's locally cached credentials, without challenging the client again. If neither the object nor credentials have changed, the origin server sends the message "HTTP 304 Not Modified" to the CE. If different users request the object, the process described previously is repeated. For NTLM- or Kerberos-authenticated objects, only the object is cached, and the user is rechallenged for credentials before the cached object is provided to the requesting client.

Enabling Transparent Value-Added Services on Your CEs

Cisco renamed the CE from "cache engine" to "content engine" because CEs provide much more than just basic web caching services. In this section, you will learn how to enable value-added services on your CEs, such as

- Content authentication and authorization

- SSL caching

- Content adaptation using Internet Content Adaptation Protocol (ICAP)

- URL filtering
- TCP/IP parameter value adjustments

Content Authentication and Authorization

With content request authentication and authorization, the CE can authenticate and authorize client requests before supplying access to cached or remote objects. With content request authentication, the CE ensures that your internal enterprise users requiring external Internet access are who they claim to be, by authenticating them with an external Authentication Authorization and Accounting (AAA) server. Once the CE authenticates those users, it can use authorization to ensure that the users have the privilege rights to access the requested objects.

For example, when a user requests an object, the CE sends their credentials to the AAA server. The AAA server verifies the user's credentials and responds to the CE with a pass or failure message. If the user's credentials pass authentication, the AAA server may also indicate the Windows-based groups that the user is a member of. The groups may be associated with the user's department or employment status (for example, regular or temporary). The CE can then make a determination, based on the group the user belongs to, of whether to supply the content to the requesting client. Figure 13-9 illustrates how content authentication and authorization with AAA works.

Figure 13-9 *HTTP Authentication of Client Requests*

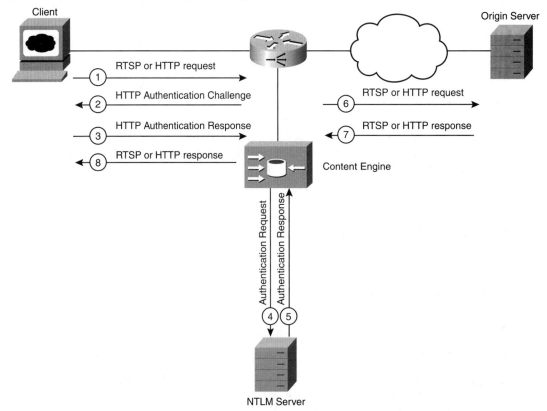

For example, say that your organization does not offer web access to temporary contract employees, but only to regular full-time employees. Figure 13-9 could represent the following process:

1. When a user requests an object, the CE intercepts the request, using either proxy-mode configuration or transparently through WCCP or a content switch.

2. The CE then challenges the client for credentials using the same TCP connection, by spoofing the origin server IP address.

3. The client responds to the challenge with the user's credentials.

4. The CE then opens a separate TCP connection to the AAA server to send the user's credentials for verification. The AAA server may be running TACACS+, RADIUS, LDAP, or NTLM.

5. The AAA server processes the request and determines whether the username/password combination is correct. The AAA server includes the configured group to which the user belongs in its response to the CE.

6. The CE then matches the content to the rules that you configure for the particular group. If the rules indicate that the group is authorized to receive the requested content, and if the CE contains a fresh copy of the requested object, it serves the object directly to the client. Otherwise, the CE opens a connection to the origin server, with its own IP address as the source, to retrieve a fresh copy of the content.

7. The origin server provides a fresh copy of the content to the CE.

To configure authorization rules for Windows-based groups, you can use ACLs containing permit or deny rules for particular groups. For example, you can use the ACL commands given in Example 13-5 to permit only employees who are members of the "fulltime" Windows group and deny all other employee access to the Internet. Example 13-5 configures an NTLM server at IP address 10.1.10.1 for authentication and group-based request authorization.

Example 13-5 *AAA Request Authentication and Authorization*

```
ntlm server host 10.1.10.1
ntlm server enable

access-lists 300 permit groupname mydomain/fulltime
access-lists 300 deny groupname any
access-lists enable
```

SSL Caching and Tunneling

You can also use CEs to cache SSL-encrypted objects, thus effectively offloading SSL computations and SSL object delivery from origin servers to the CE. To configure your CE to terminate SSL connections and cache SSL objects, you must install the origin server certificates and private keys on the CE whose secure sites you want to offload. You must use the SSL caching feature on SSL content that you manage yourself.

Alternatively, the CE can perform SSL tunneling for unmanaged objects. The Internet Draft "Tunneling TCP-based protocols through Web proxy servers" specifies the HTTP CONNECT method for a client to indicate to a CE that it should tunnel a TCP connection to the requested origin server. This draft is not protocol dependent; therefore, the CE does not need to be SSL-aware to coordinate the tunnel. The CE does not participate in the SSL handshake, and it does not supply a server certificate to requesting clients. The CE simply initiates a TCP connection to the server on behalf of the client. You can use either transparent redirection or proxy mode to perform SSL tunneling.

To create the SSL tunnel using the CONNECT method, the client opens a TCP connection over the SSL port and sends an HTTP CONNECT method (for example "CONNECT www.cisco.com HTTP/1.0"). If required, the CE can authenticate the client, using HTTP authentication and authorization that you learned about previously, before establishing the tunnel. The CE then establishes a TCP connection between itself and the origin server, and sends an "HTTP/1.0 200 Connection Established" to the client.

The benefit of SSL tunneling using the CONNECT method is that you can apply authentication and authorization to your client's SSL requests. You cannot perform filtering of the content because you do not install the server's certificate and private key on the CE with SSL tunneling—the traffic remains encrypted between the client and the server.

The CE can also tunnel SSL traffic from clients that do not explicitly use the CONNECT method. The CE simply intercepts TCP connections to the SSL port and establishes another TCP connection to the SSL origin server. As with the CONNECT method, the client and server complete the TCP handshake without intervention from the CE. However, with this transparent SSL tunneling method, you cannot configure the CE to perform HTTP authentication and authorization with the client.

Internet Content Adaptation Protocol

You can configure Internet Content Adaptation Protocol (ICAP) to transparently adapt content for your clients. You can use third-party ICAP server applications in conjunction with your CE to perform the following value-added services to clients at the edge of your network:

- Human language translation

- Content transformation (for example, XML to HTML)

- Advertisement insertion

■   Virus scanning

■   Spam filtering

In an ICAP design, the CE performs the role of an ICAP client. The ICAP client encapsulates the client's HTTP requests or responses, or both, into an ICAP request and sends them to an ICAP server for processing. An ICAP server can be a dedicated server that performs any of the previous functions separate from the caching functions of the CE, or is integrated within the CE as a third-party plug-in. Refer to your third-party ICAP server documentation for more details.

ICAP is a TCP/IP-based protocol and uses the default TCP port 1344. As with RTSP, ICAP is based on the HTTP protocol and shares many semantics with HTTP. For example, the ICAP response methods are the same as the HTTP response methods. However, there are currently three request methods that ICAP uses:

■   **REQMOD**—Used for request modification requests

■   **RESPMOD**—Used for response modification requests

■   **OPTIONS**—Used by the client to learn about supported methods of the ICAP server

As with other caching services, you can use WCCP, a content switch, or direct proxy configuration to direct user requests to the CE. Figure 13-10 illustrates the flow of ICAP requests and responses between an ICAP client (that is, a Cisco CE) and an ICAP server (for example, a virus scanner) for ICAP RESPMOD processing.

Consider the ICAP RESPMOD example that is shown in Figure 13-10 in which a virus scanner ICAP server is used:

1.   The client browser unknowingly sends an HTTP request for an infected file from a website.

```
GET /virus.exe HTTP/1.1
Host: www.infectedsite.com
```

2.   The CE determines that the requested file is not cached and sends the request to the origin server.

3.   The origin server sends the response to the CE.

```
HTTP/1.1 200 OK
< data of executable containing the virus >
```

4.   The CE encapsulates the headers of the HTTP response into an ICAP request and sends to the ICAP server.

```
REQMOD icap://icap.cisco.com/ ICAP/1.0
  HTTP/1.1 200 OK
 <data of executable containing the virus >
```

5. The ICAP server processes the origin server's response, determines that the file contains a virus, and formulates an error message for the client's web browser.

```
ICAP/1.0 200 OK
Connection: close
HTTP/1.1 403 Forbidden
Sorry, the requested file contains a virus.
```

6. The CE decapsulates the ICAP response from the ICAP server and sends the ICAP server-generated HTTP message to the client browser.

Figure 13-10 *ICAP RESPMOD Processing*

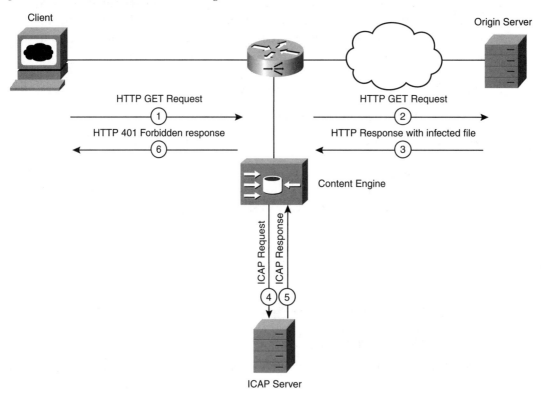

URL Filtering

You can configure your CE to filter URLs within HTTP, HTTPS, FTP, RTSP, or MMS requests. The CE can apply local rules to the URLs or forward the client's requests to a third-party Employee Internet Management (EIM) URL filtering application for authorization. Following are the URL filtering applications that the Cisco CE supports:

- **Local URL list files**—You can manually configure "good lists" and "bad lists" containing URLs that you want the CE to filter against incoming client requests.

- **SmartFilter** — You can directly enable this local third-party plug-in on your CE.

- **Websense and N2H2** — These are external third-party URL filtering applications. As with SmartFilter, you can also enable a local plug-in for Websense filtering.

You can direct client request packets to the CE by either WCCP, by a content switch, or by way of manual proxy configuration on the browser or media player. When the CE receives a TCP SYN request from a client through WCCP, it completes the TCP three-way handshake with the client to inspect the HTTP URL before sending the request to the origin server. Depending on what method you configure, the CE can then either check its local lists or forward the request to a third-party filtering application. If you use an external third-party filtering application, the CE forwards the request to the application and awaits an authorization response. The external application then inspects the URL and performs a lookup into its URL database. If the filtering application contains the URL in its database, it sends an authorization failure response to the CE. The CE then spoofs the connection to the client and sends a page to the client indicating that the user does not have permission to access the URL. If the URL is not within its database, the URL server sends an authorization success message to the CE. The CE then originates the client's request to the origin server, per normal caching procedures.

Adjusting TCP/IP Parameter Values

Another valuable function of a CE is its ability to fine-tune the TCP protocol to accelerate flows from an end-to-end perspective. As you learned previously in this chapter, CEs interact with clients and origin servers in either proxy or transparent mode. In either mode, the CE establishes two TCP connections between itself and both client and origin server (that is, one TCP connection to the origin server and one to the client). In transparent mode, for the client-side connection, you learned that the CE spoofs the origin server's IP address. For the server-side of the connection, you learned how the CE can either use its own IP address or spoof the client's IP address.

Because the CE is involved in both the client and server sides of the TCP connection, you can configure your CE to adjust the following TCP parameters that you learned about in Chapter 2, "Exploring the Network Layers," in order to streamline the TCP flow:

- **Send windows size** — You can adjust the advertised client and server send window sizes using the following commands:

  ```
  tcp server-send-buffer KB
  tcp client-send-buffer KB
  ```

- **Receive windows size** — You can adjust the advertised client and server receive window sizes using the following commands:

  ```
  tcp server-receive-buffer KB
  tcp client-receive-buffer KB
  ```

■   **Initial congestion window (CWND) value**—You can adjust the initial CWND value using the command

```
tcp cwnd-base segments
```

■   **Initial slow start threshold**—You can adjust the initial slow-start threshold using the command

```
tcp initial-ss-threshold segments
```

■   **Transmit timer**—You can adjust the transmit timer value using the command

```
tcp increase-xmit-timer-value value
```

■   **Client and server Maximum Segment Size (MSS)**—You can adjust the MSS using the commands

```
tcp server-mss maxsegsize
tcp client-mss maxsegsize
```

Additionally, the CE can enable the following TCP features that are not enabled by default for most applications:

■   **IP Type of Service (ToS) field**—You can enable ToS processing on your CE using the command

```
type-of-service enable
```

■   **Enable TCP-over-Satellite**—You can enable TCP-over-Satellite using the window scale option (WSopt) on your CE using the command

```
tcp server-satellite
tcp client-satellite
```

■   **Enable Explicit Congestion Notification (ECN)**—You can enable your CE to inspect and use the ECN field, if available, using the command

```
ecn enable
```

Delivering Streaming Media

As you learned from Chapter 9, "Introducing Streaming Media," streaming media solves major issues with viewing audio-video media directly from an origin server. That is, without streaming, users have to wait for the video-file downloads to complete before viewing the content in their video players. With video streaming, the client video player displays video frames directly to the user as packets arrive on the network, which is similar to standard television broadcasting.

The Cisco CE can deliver Windows or RealNetworks streaming media:

> **NOTE**   Make sure you understand the concepts from Chapter 9 before configuring on your CEs the streaming media services that you will learn about in this section. You will learn how to stream MPEG1/2/4 and Apple QuickTime in Chapter 14.

- **Windows Media Technologies (WMT)**—WMT uses the Windows Media Encoder (WME) for capturing live audio and video feeds and the Windows Media Server (WMS) for scheduling and delivering video on demand (VoD) or live presentations to clients. The CE can serve cached WMT VoDs, split live broadcasts, and schedule VoD rebroadcasts.

- **Real Networks**—Real uses the RealProducer for capturing live audio and video feeds and the Helix Universal Server for scheduling and delivering VoD or live presentations. The CE can serve cached Real Media VoDs and split live broadcasts.

Figure 13-11 illustrates the relationship between these encoders and origin servers in the context of the streaming media components that you learned about in Figure 9-1 from Chapter 9.

Figure 13-11   *Windows Media Technology and Real Media Streaming*

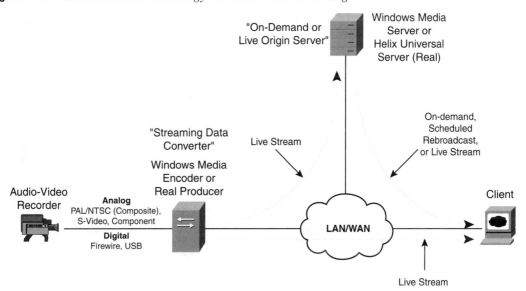

Streaming Video-on-Demand

VoD is a multimedia presentation that users can request and view at their convenience. As you learned in Chapter 9, VoDs are files that are encapsulated in the specific streaming container file format of the vendor software within which you author the presentation.

To stream RTSP VoDs, the Cisco CE runs an RTSP gateway to which it sends incoming RTSP requests. Upon receiving an RTSP request, the RTSP gateway selects a back-end streaming media proxy to which it will forward the request. The CE supports either the WMT or Real Media RTSP back-end proxies, as Figure 13-12 illustrates. By inspecting the browser type in the "User-agent:" header of the RTSP request and the media type of the file requested, the RTSP gateway selects a back-end proxy to which it will forward the request. Figure 13-12 illustrates an example in which a client sends an RTSP PLAY method request for an employee product training VoD called "prod-train.rm."

NOTE   In Figure 13-12, you can assume that the client has already directly requested the Session Description Protocol (SDP) file or Synchronized Multimedia Integration Language (SMIL) file from the origin server by using HTTP. You learned about this process previously from Figure 9-3 in Chapter 9. Bear in mind that, if you configure HTTP web caching, the CE may also cache and serve the SDP or SMIL file to clients. Additionally, assume that the client has already issued the SETUP RTSP command through the RTSP gateway, in the same manner as the PLAY method that was shown in Figure 13-12.

Figure 13-12   *Video-on-Demand Streaming Using the RTSP Gateway*

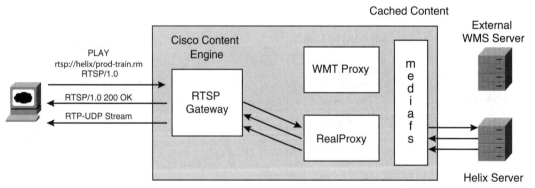

NOTE   The CE can also cache MMS VoDs. MMS requests need not be processed by the RTSP Gateway—the CE passes MMS requests directly to the WMT proxy.

When a client requests an RTSP or MMS VoD, the CE first determines whether it has the entire VoD that the client requested in its media file system (mediafs). If not, the CE determines which back-end proxy to send the RTSP request to or sends the MMS request directly to the WMT proxy. In the example in Figure 13-12, an RTSP request is destined to the RealProxy back-end server. The RealProxy server then connects to the origin server and requests the streaming object on behalf of the client. The RealProxy server attempts to request the file using HTTP streaming over TCP, by specifying the HTTP protocol in the RTSP SETUP method, to ensure that the CE reliably receives the object without errors that the network may introduce. If only a partial object exists in the mediafs, the CE waits for the rest of the file before sending it to the client. In the event that a client cancels or aborts the transfer early, the CE attempts to back-fill missing content, by continuing the download from the origin server to ensure that the VoD object is available for subsequent requests.

When the CE receives the entire file, it disconnects from the origin server and originates the VoD to the client itself. If the CE already has the entire file, it connects to the origin server only to determine that the file is the most up-to-date version of the presentation or to authenticate the client. The CE disconnects from the origin server immediately. In other words, with VoD streaming, there is no dependency on the origin server for delivery of the content, other than to verify the freshness of the content or when end-to-end authentication is required on the origin server.

Splitting Live and Prerecorded Broadcasts

As you learned from this chapter, CEs provide services for video streaming, content adaptation, authentication, URL filtering, and server SSL acceleration. Additionally, CEs offer stream splitting services to requesting clients for delivering scheduled live and prerecorded broadcasts from your WMS or Helix-origin servers. The CE treats live streams that you schedule on the WMS or Helix origin servers no differently from prerecorded streams.

NOTE   Prerecorded broadcasts are also known as scheduled rebroadcasts, or simply rebroadcasts.

With stream splitting, a CE receives an incoming stream and fans it out to requesting clients, as Figure 13-13 illustrates. Stream splitting saves bandwidth and network resources by avoiding the origin server having to originate a single stream per user.

Figure 13-13 *Live and Rebroadcast Stream Splitting*

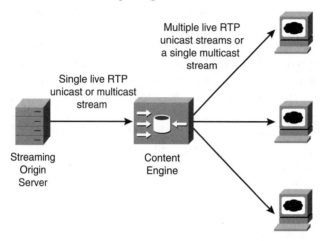

> **NOTE** Caching of live broadcasts is not available because streaming servers do not format live streams as actual files. Alternatively, they encode the media from the source and send it in data packets directly to clients.

During a live presentation, the presentation always originates from the origin server as a single stream to the incoming interface of the CE. Both front- and back-end streams can be either multicast or unicast, resulting in the four combinations of stream delivery outlined in Table 13-4.

Table 13-4 *Stream Splitting Combinations*

Origin Server to CE	CE to Client
Unicast	Unicast
Unicast	Multicast
Multicast	Unicast
Multicast	Multicast

In a unicast-to-unicast configuration, the CE receives the live or rebroadcast stream as unicast and splits it to clients as individual unicast streams. In a unicast-to-multicast configuration, the CE generates a multicast stream from the single unicast input stream and sends it to a multicast group that you can configure on your CE. As long as you enable multicast on the downstream network, as you learned in Chapter 5, "IP Multicast Content Delivery," the routers will forward the multicast group traffic to group members without duplication of the stream. For unicast-to-unicast streams, each client receives a distinct live stream causing potential duplicates of traffic streams on the network, depending on the location of the requesting clients. These first two methods in

Table 13-4 are also known as *pull-splitting* because client requests trigger the CE to proactively "pull" the unicast stream from the origin server on behalf of the requesting clients.

Instead of simply having clients request a multicast stream directly from the origin server, you can configure multicast-to-multicast as listed in Table 13-4. Multicast-to-multicast is beneficial because you can perform the value-added services on your CE that you learned about previously in this chapter, such as content authentication, URL filtering, and ICAP services. These last two methods are known as *push-splitting* because the CE simply joins the upstream live multicast stream to split the stream to clients. That is, the origin server blindly "pushes" the stream to the network for the CE to receive by joining the multicast group.

Streaming Windows Media Technology

To enable the WMT streaming server on your CE, you must purchase a separate WMT license key from Cisco. To view and accept the Cisco license agreement on your CE, enter the following commands:

```
show wmt license-agreement
config terminal
wmt accept-license-agreement
```

You can then install your WMT key onto your CE to enable WMT, by using the following command on your CE:

```
wmt license-key licensekey
```

To enable the WMT on your CE, use the following command:

```
wmt enable
```

Alternatively, you can evaluate the WMT license for 60 days, by using the command

```
rtsp proxy media-real evaluate
```

Now that you have a WMT license installed, you can configure either VoD or live/rebroadcast streaming.

Configuring Windows Media Video on Demand

You can configure your CE to cache and stream Windows Media VoD files to your requesting clients, on behalf of the origin WMS server. To enable the WMT proxy that you learned about previously for VoD caching on your CE, you can use the following command:

```
wmt cache enable
```

You also learned previously how to configure your router to redirect MMS and RTSP traffic to your CE using WCCP. The CE accepts both Windows MMS and RTSP requests for content, similar to the following URLs:

```
mms://wms.cisco.com/tac/cetraining.asf
rtsp://wms.cisco.com/tac/cetraining.asf
```

Recall with transparent redirection that your clients specify the origin server IP address or domain name in the URL. However, if you are using direct proxy mode, you must specify the CE IP address or domain name in the Windows media player proxy settings.

By default, the CE caches WMT objects to its streaming media file system (mediafs) by listening to the MMS port 1755 and RTSP port 554. You can disable or reenable WMT VoD caching using the **no wmt cache enable** or **wmt cache enable** commands, respectively.

As you learned previously, you can preload WMT files to your CE by using URL lists. To save peak-hour WAN network bandwidth to your branch offices, you can preload WMT VoD files to your branch office CEs during off-hours. You can then inform your branch office users of the URL to view the VoD.

Configuring the CE Internal WMS Server for Live and Scheduled Rebroadcast Presentations

The Cisco CE supports both the WMS server and proxy for live stream splitting:

- **Internal WMS Server**—You can manually configure your CE to receive live content from the WME or external WMS servers directly and serve the content to your clients, thus providing WMS server capabilities on your CE. You then create publishing URLs for clients to connect to by configuring broadcast aliases or multicast stations on the CE. The client Windows media player can reference the CE broadcast alias or multicast station directly—the CE splits the incoming stream from the WME or external WMS servers to multiple requesting clients. You can use the internal WMS server as a highly flexible way to split and schedule rebroadcasts of your managed WMT content.

    NOTE The CE does not implement the full WMS server software, so you cannot completely replace the functionality of your external WMS origin server using the internal WMS server on your CE.

- **WMT Proxy**—You can program your external WMS server to unicast-pull the live content from a WME server, which can then broadcast the live event to your requesting clients. Without any configuration, the WMT proxy on your CE splits the live streams to your requesting clients, on behalf of the WMS origin server. Windows media player requests must reference the WMS origin server directly, but you can redirect the requests to the CE for the WMT proxy to process and split the stream via unicast to requesting clients. The WMT proxy does not support multicast-push splitting. The WMT proxy can also proxy requests for content from public WMS servers on the Internet. The WMT proxy is meant primarily for splitting unmanaged WMT content, but you can use it to automatically split your managed content as well. When you enable WMT on your CE (with the **wmt enable** command), both the WMT proxy and internal WMS server are enabled. They are actually the same software, but you can consider them logically as separate entities.

NOTE   The WMT proxy, internal WMS server, and RealProxy are available for standalone CE streaming. However, the RealSubscriber (for streaming prepositioning Real Media VoDs) and the Cisco Streaming Engine (for streaming prepositioned Apple QuickTime [QT] and MPEG4 VoDs and splitting live Apple QT and MPEG4 streams) are available within only a full ACNS deployment using a Content Distribution Manager (CDM). See Chapter 14 for more information.

Configuring Unicast-to-Unicast Live Splitting

To configure unicast-to-unicast stream splitting with the internal WMS server, you must define a broadcast alias that points to the source of the live unicast stream from the WME or external WMS server. The broadcast alias is also known as a publishing point. The WME captures audio and video from the live inputs, such as a video camera and microphone, and "publishes" the encoded output to the unicast publishing point that you configure on the external WMS server for clients to view. In other words, publishing points are simply a way to assign to live unicast streams a unique name that clients can use to make requests for the live stream. Figure 13-14 shows how the internal WMS server on the CE can acquire the live stream either directly from the WME or from an external WMS server.

Figure 13-14   *Live Broadcasting from the Internal WMS Server*

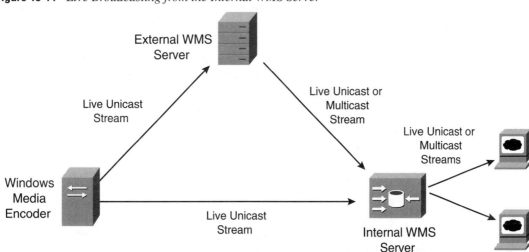

To create the broadcast alias, you can use the following command:

```
wmt broadcast alias-name broadcast-alias source source-url
```

> **NOTE** You cannot create scheduled WMT rebroadcasts on the CE for delivery via unicast. However, you can create scheduled rebroadcasts and deliver them to clients using multicast. You will learn more about scheduled rebroadcasts in the section "Configuring Unicast- or Multicast-to-Multicast Scheduled Rebroadcasts."

For example, if you want to create a broadcast alias called "myceolive" for the external WMS source located at "mms://wms.cisco.com/ceo-live," you can use the command

```
wmt broadcast alias-name myceolive source mms://wms.cisco.com/ceo-live
```

Notice that the source URL also contains a publishing point called "ceo-live," which you must configure on the external WMS server itself. Additionally, you can use "rtsp://", "rtspu://" for retrieving the stream from the origin server. Refer to your WMS server and WME product documentation for more information on how to encode and deliver live audio–video streams.

Now that you have created a broadcast alias, clients can request the live unicast presentation from their Windows media player using a URL containing the protocol, CE IP address, or domain name and the broadcast alias as follows:

```
mms://ce1.cisco.com/myceolive
```

Configuring Multicast-to-Unicast Live Splitting

To configure multicast-to-unicast live stream splitting with the internal WMS server, you must also create a broadcast alias on your CE for the live multicast stream from the external WMS server (WME servers do not support multicast streaming). However, you must specify the source of the multicast by referring to the multicast description file of the source stream. WMS uses multicast description (.nsc) files to describe live multicast streams. The .nsc file provides information about the multicast stream, such as IP multicast addresses, ports, and streaming formats, so that requesting clients can receive and decode the live stream. Clients that wish to receive a multicast stream can first request the .nsc file. The client media player then extracts information from the file to join the multicast group and decode the streaming content. The CE does the same to receive the multicast stream from the external WMS server. For example, to configure a broadcast alias to split a live multicast stream from "http://wms.cisco.com/ceo-live.nsc" into individual unicast streams, you can use the command

```
wmt broadcast alias-name myceolive source http://wms.cisco.com/ceo-live.nsc
```

You must be sure to create the multicast description file "ceo-live.nsc" on the external WMS server. Once you have done that, your clients can request a unicast stream using the same URL as before with unicast-to-unicast in their media player:

```
mms://ce1.cisco.com/myceolive
```

NOTE Because clients use the IP address or domain name of the CE to make requests for the live internal WMS server content, you do not need to configure WCCP redirection or the client media player's proxy settings.

Configuring Multicast-to-Multicast Live Splitting

To enable your CE to split a live multicast or unicast stream into a multicast stream with the internal WMS server, you must create a multicast station on your CE. To configure a multicast station, use the command

```
wmt multicast station-configuration station-name multicast-dest-IP dest-port
    stream-source-url
```

For example, to create a station called "myceolive" that multicasts the stream to the IP 238.1.1.1 on UDP port 4321, from the external WMS multicast source at "mms://wms.cisco.com/ceo-live.nsc," you can use the command

```
wmt multicast station-configuration myceolive 238.1.1.1 4321
    http://wms.cisco.com/ceo-live.nsc
```

You must start the multicast station on the CE with the command

```
wmt multicast-station start myceolive
```

NOTE To configure multicast on your CE, you must obtain a separate multicast license and install it on your CE.

The CE collects the information in the "ceo-live.nsc" from the external WMS server along with the IP multicast addresses that you specify with this command to dynamically create another .nsc file called "myceolive.nsc." Your clients use the CE-generated .nsc file as the publishing URL in their Windows media players:

```
http://ce1.cisco.com/myceolive.nsc
```

Configuring Unicast-to-Multicast Live Splitting

To configure a unicast-to-multicast live stream with the internal WMS server, you must specify the unicast publishing point that you created on the external WMS server as follows:

```
wmt multicast station-configuration myceolive 238.1.1.1 4321
    mms://wms.cisco.com/ceo-live
```

With both unicast- and multicast-to-multicast configurations, the client media players extract information from the "myceolive.nsc" file (that the CE creates) to join the multicast group. Using the multicast technologies that you learned about in Chapter 5, "IP Multicast Content Delivery," and the streaming media technologies that you learned about in Chapter 9 the client then can receive and decode the live multicast stream.

Configuring Unicast- or Multicast-to-Multicast Scheduled Rebroadcasts

To schedule a rebroadcast of the live stream with the internal WMS server, you can configure your WME server to unicast-push the live stream to your external WMS server (or configure your external WMS server to unicast-pull the live stream from the WME server). You can then configure the external WMS server to convert that live stream into the WMS streaming container format (.asf), to schedule and distribute the file as a rebroadcast VoD on your CE. The command to schedule a rebroadcast event is

```
wmt multicast schedule-start station-name minute hour day month
```

You can specify the scheduled rebroadcast of the streaming container file called "ceo-rebroad.asf" sourced from your WMS server at 1:55 PM, September 29th, using the **wmt multicast** commands as follows:

```
wmt multicast station-configuration myceolive 238.1.1.1 4321
    mms://wms.cisco.com/ceo-rebroad.asf
wmt multicast station-configuration myceolive schedule-start 55 13 29 9
```

With this configuration, branch office clients can, starting at 1:55 PM, September 29th, request the rebroadcast using the publishing URL "mms://ce1.cisco.com/myceolive.nsc" in their media players. You can also preload the "ceo-rebroad.asf" file to your branch-office CEs ahead of time during off-hours to save peak-hour WAN bandwidth at the time of the scheduled rebroadcast.

Streaming Real Media

To stream VoDs and split live Real Media, you can enable the RealProxy on your Cisco CEs. You can use the RealProxy for caching and splitting both unmanaged and managed VoDs and live streams. As with the WMT proxy, when you simply enable RealProxy, the CE caches VoDs and splits live Real Media streams to your clients automatically, without any additional configuration.

To enable RealProxy on your CE, you must purchase a separate RealProxy license key from Cisco. To view and accept the license agreement, enter the following commands:

```
show rtsp proxy media-real license-agreement
config terminal
 rtsp proxy media-real accept-license-agreement
```

You can then install the RealProxy key onto your CE, using the following command on your CE:

```
rtsp proxy media-real license-key licensekey
```

Once you install the key, you can enable RealProxy using the command

```
rtsp proxy media-real enable
```

Like the WMT proxy, the RealProxy feature on the Cisco CE supports both VoD caching and live unicast stream splitting, by default. However, to configure advanced options on the RealProxy server, such as multicast splitting, you must use the CE web interface. To log in to the CE secure web interface, enter the CE domain name or IP address into your browser URL field, and specify port 8003. Entering the CE username and password takes you to the CE home page shown in Figure 13-15.

Figure 13-15 *The Cisco CE Web-Interface Home Page*

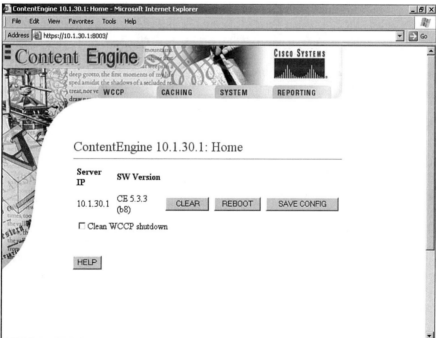

To configure the RealProxy, under the "Caching" tab, select "Real Proxy." If you enabled RealProxy in the previous configuration step with the **rtsp proxy media-real enable** command, you can click the "ADMIN" button to enter the RealProxy configuration interface, as Figure 13-16 illustrates.

Figure 13-16   *The Cisco CE Web-Interface RealProxy Admin Page*

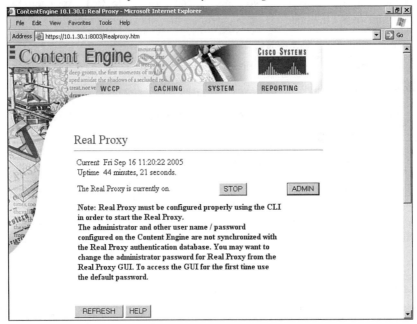

Figure 13-17 shows the screen that you first see in the RealProxy web interface.

Figure 13-17   *The RealProxy Web-Interface Home Page*

RealProxy Video-on-Demand Caching

To enable or disable VoD caching, choose the "Cache" option in the left control pane, as Figure 13-18 illustrates. VoD caching is enabled by default.

Figure 13-18   *Configuring RealProxy VoD Caching*

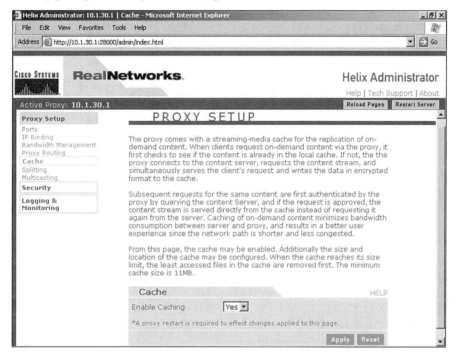

Like the WMT proxy, clients use the IP address or the domain name of the origin server in the publishing URL to request the live stream from the RealProxy. Therefore, you must configure WCCP redirection or configure the client media player's proxy settings to point to the CE for RTSP requests (using service group 80). Then, to request a VoD from the Helix Universal Server, you can use a publishing URL similar to the following URL:

```
rtsp://helix.cisco.com/sales_training.rm
```

RealProxy Pull-Splitting

RealProxy supports unicast-pull for live stream splitting. That is, when users request a live stream, the RealProxy requests the live stream from the Helix origin server using unicast and splits the stream to clients using either unicast or back-channel multicast delivery. Like the WMT proxy, the RealProxy does not support multicast-to-unicast or multicast-to-multicast. However, as you learned previously, you can manually configure these combinations using the internal WMS server.

To enable live stream splitting on the RealProxy, make sure you enable splitting in the "Splitting" screen, as Figure 13-19 illustrates. Live stream splitting is enabled by default.

Figure 13-19 *Configuring RealProxy Live Splitting*

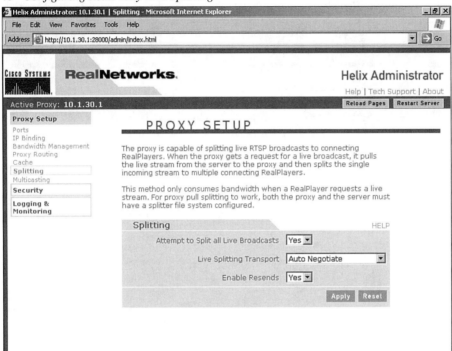

To request a live stream from the Helix Universal Server, which you can configure your WCCP router to redirect to your CE, you can use a publishing URL similar to the following URL:

```
rtsp://helix.cisco.com/broadcast/live
```

Users can use this URL to request the stream for either unicast or multicast delivery—the type of delivery depends on how you configure the RealProxy. To deliver the live stream using multicast, the RealProxy uses back-channel multicast. With back-channel multicast, a control connection is maintained between the client and RealProxy. The client uses the control connection for authentication, for sending RTSP commands, and for providing statistics to Helix Universal Server. Figure 13-20 illustrates how to configure back-channel multicast. Back-channel multicast is enabled by default, but you must configure multicast addresses for back-channel multicast to work.

Figure 13-20   *Configuring RealProxy Back-Channel Multicast Splitting*

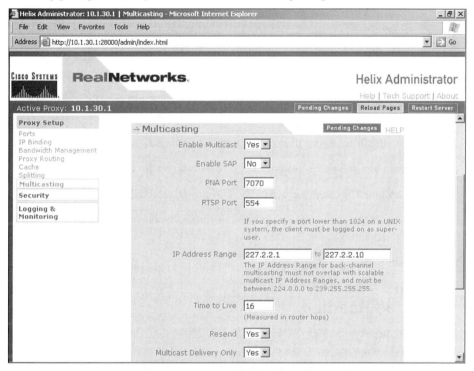

> **NOTE**   If you want to enable standard multicast (without maintaining the back-end multicast control connection), you can configure your Helix server to multicast directly to your clients. Refer to your Helix documentation for more information on configuring unicast or multicast live broadcasts.

Summary

In this chapter, you learned how to configure WCCP and content switch application redirection techniques, within various caching topologies, including proxy, transparent, and reverse caching.

You learned about the additional services that CEs can provide to your network outside of basic object caching services. Value-added services, such as SSL caching, ICAP, URL filtering, and TCP/IP parameter adjustments, are some of the features that are available within the CE that you can enable in your network environment. These features are transparent to your clients and origin servers. You also learned how to configure Windows and RealMedia streaming services on standalone CEs.

Review Questions

1. What is the difference between the standard web-cache and reverse-proxy WCCP service groups?

2. Is it possible to configure IP spoofing with forward caching?

3. Does the CE always require spoofing the origin server for client requests?

4. Why can't the CE cache Kerberos-, NTLM-, or Digest-authenticated objects?

5. What transparent value-added services can you enable on your Cisco CEs, other than standard caching services?

6. What are pull- and push-splitting?

Recommended Reading

Duane Wessels, *Web Caching*, O'Reilly, 2001
http://www.realnetworks.com/products/
http://www.microsoft.com/windows/windowsmedia/

In this chapter, you will learn how to configure content distribution and routing by covering material that is organized into the following sections:

- **Introducing Content Distribution and Routing**—You will learn the difference between pre-positioned, cached, and live content.

- **Initializing and Registering Your ACNS Network Devices**—You will learn how to initialize and register devices in your Application and Content Networking System (ACNS) network.

- **Setting Up Your ACNS Network for Acquisition and Distribution**—You will learn how to create location trees and content channels.

- **Acquiring Content to Preposition**—You will learn how to configure your ACNS network to acquire content that will be prepositioned throughout your network by distributing the content to the content engines (CE).

- **Configuring Content Prepositioning**—You will then learn how to configure content prepositioning.

- **Content Request Routing**—You will explore how simplified hybrid routing and dynamic proxy autoconfiguration can be used to route client's content requests.

- **Configuring Streaming Media**—You will learn how to configure video on demand (VoD) prepositioning and live/scheduled-rebroadcast programming using ACNS.

CHAPTER **14**

Distributing and Routing Managed Content

In this chapter, you will learn how to efficiently deliver managed content to accelerate your enterprise applications. You can use content distribution, routing, and streaming media for a number of enterprise applications, including:

- E-learning and Corporate Communications

- Software and File Distribution

E-learning and Corporate Communications

The explosive growth of the Internet economy in the past decade has led many companies to raise their expectations of employee levels of information intake. Due to advances in technology, mergers, acquisitions, market volatility, and competitive pressures, today's employees must be empowered to respond effectively to these increasing demands. Ensuring that employees are able to learn new skills and assimilate vast amounts of new information on top of existing skills will guarantee a company's success in tough markets.

Areas that benefit from a robust e-learning and corporate communications solution are

- **Product Sales**—Sales employees' knowledge of their organization's current and upcoming products and those of the competition is important to winning a potential sales opportunity. If a formidable competitive vendor is also involved in the account and has the necessary competitive ammunition, it may win the sales opportunity.

- **Customer Support**—Customer support representatives must be kept abreast of their departments' methods and procedures that may change very frequently.

- **Quality Assurance**—For quality assurance employees, applying quality control mechanisms in dynamic manufacturing settings can offer a challenge with respect to keeping quality levels of their products sustained.

To facilitate the learning process, your organization must implement a solution that affords quick retrieval of relevant information and enables employees to learn material most suited for them at their leisure. Traditional training methods, such as CD- or DVD-ROM-based Computer

Based Training (CBT) and classrooms have proven costly and time consuming in today's Internet culture.

The goals of e-learning are reduced training costs, easy access to educational content, increased collaboration, and improved accountability. Reduced corporate training costs are a major testament to the benefits of e-learning. E-learning solutions reduce these types of training expenses: travel costs, accommodations, training facilities, and time spent away from the office for numerous employees to meet at a headquarters.

E-learning is a way for organizations to provide education through networks. Today's networks provide the medium that classrooms, boardrooms, and lecture halls provided in the past. E-learning solutions can provide educational content live or on-demand. Live solutions can provide an experience similar to a classroom setting, including interactive verbal discussions, online whiteboards, instant messaging questions, and answers between teacher and student or student-to-student discussions.

Some users may be unable to attend training due to schedule constraints, or users may learn at different paces or have differing levels of knowledge of the material. For these reasons, on-demand e-learning may be beneficial. On-demand content can be viewed at any time by the learner but with the same components and effectiveness as a classroom or live e-learning solution.

Software and File Distribution

For large organizations with mobile staff located at branch offices, organizing corporate files and software is a complicated task. File servers normally store data files and software for client access at the corporate headquarters. Incremental operating system patches and hot-fixes are downloaded from Microsoft's Windows Update site directly by the client or to a centrally located systems management server, from which the updates are pushed to the client stations automatically. Antivirus updates are loaded in a similar fashion, resulting in each branch office containing numerous clients downloading the same file (virus definitions) across expensive WAN links.

File sizes vary from extremely large, for entire hard disk images for PC ghosting purposes, to very small, for antivirus definition or security hotfix updates. File compression is of limited use for large images, so scalability is a major issue for most organizations with limited WAN bandwidth available to the branch office. Files that benefit from file compression, such as text files, are not normally as large, so they do not have a major effect on WAN bandwidth.

Typical large-scale software distribution processes involve a third-party systems management application to build and distribute content. For large organizations with mobile staff located at branch offices, the penetration of software distribution is often low. Furthermore, the servers themselves are Windows-based in the vast majority of enterprise environments. Windows-based file servers are as vulnerable to malicious code as the clients they are protecting; therefore, they, too, must be included in the update process. Because Cisco's software distribution platform is a hardened content network appliance, it is not vulnerable to Windows-based malicious code or security exploits.

This type of solution is beneficial—one that pre-positions content to your branch office directly to avoid replicated client requests from consuming valuable WAN bandwidth, especially during peak hours of traffic. Additionally, the solution must be able to intelligently route content to the closest source, normally at the branch office where the client is located, instead of pointing every workstation or server in the organization to the origin server, which is located at the headquarters. The solution must be able to scale with company growth and be easily administered, allowing for bandwidth throttling. A user must be able to work from any remote location and have content requests automatically directed to the local content. If possible, you can add beneficial features of the solution that include scheduling off-hours or staggered content updates across the WAN to branch office remote locations. Overall bandwidth consumption will be reduced as a result.

Introducing Content Distribution and Routing

In addition to the on-demand caching and live stream splitting that you learned about in Chapter 13, "Delivering Cached and Streaming Media," an ACNS network can allow you to enable the following rich multimedia features on your network:

- **Pre-Positioned On-Demand Channels**—ACNS provides you the ability to distribute objects within the network in advance of client requests. You learned previously how CEs populate themselves on-demand by caching copies of content inline with clients' requests. With ACNS, you can pre-position streaming or nonstreaming channels of organized static files, such as HTML, Macromedia Flash, Shockwave, JPEG, Windows Media, Apple QuickTime, and RealNetworks, to CEs in advance of client requests during off-peak hours.

- **Scheduled Live or Rebroadcasted Channels**—ACNS provides integration with the Cisco IP/TV streaming media solution and third-party streaming server software, such as Windows Media Technologies (WMT), RealNetworks, and Apple QuickTime, for scheduled live or rebroadcast events.

The ACNS system comprises the following elements:

- **Content Distribution Manager** (CDM)—The CDM is the heart of the ACNS network solution. The CDM is the central management console of an ACNS network and is responsible for facilitating the pre-positioning of on-demand content and for scheduling live streaming programs. The CDM does not directly store any of the content locally. Alternately, for on-demand content the CDM uses manifest files, which are XML files that you can write to instruct the CEs on the following: the origin servers that the content resides on and what content on the origin servers should be distributed in the ACNS network.

For live or scheduled rebroadcast content, the CDM schedules programs and organizes the distribution of the streaming content to your users.

- **CEs**—If the CDM is the heart, then CEs are the limbs of the ACNS network. They do the work in distributing files and providing caching and streaming services to requesting clients. As you learned in Chapter 13, through third-party licensing, the CE can run both WMT and RealNetworks proxies for splitting and caching of streaming content. However, this feature is unique to the ACNS system—you can serve streaming content directly from both Windows Media Server (WMS) and RealNetworks *server* software that you can license and enable on your CEs. Additionally, with ACNS, you can enable the Cisco Streaming Engine. The streaming engine is a standard Real-Time Streaming Protocol (RTSP) server and can be used to proxy and directly stream Motion Picture Experts Group (MPEG)1/2/4 and Apple QuickTime streaming content. The Cisco Streaming Engine does not require a separate third-party license.

- **Content Routers (CR)**—The Cisco Content Router is the nose of the ACNS network, used to sniff for the best location of the content to serve to clients. CRs use Domain Name Server (DNS) and HTTP/RTSP redirection for routing client's content requests. As with the Global Server Load Balancing (GSLB) devices that you learned about in Chapter 12, "Exploring Global Server Load Balancing," the subdomains that the CR responds to must be delegated to the CR by the DNS servers that are responsible for the domain.

To source your own MPEG1/2/4 or Apple QuickTime live or VoD streams, you can use Cisco IP/TV streaming solution, instead of using a third-party solution. You can use the Cisco IP/TV system either on its own or within an ACNS system. Used with the ACNS system, you can distribute and route IP/TV content much more efficiently than as a stand-alone system. The Cisco IP/TV 3400 series video server solution consists of the following elements:

- **IP/TV Program Manager**—To schedule live IP/TV streams, you must use the IP/TV Program Manager. The IP/TV Program Manager software runs on the Cisco CE hardware in separate device modes that you can configure via the CE command-line interface (CLI).

- **IP/TV Broadcast servers**—To source live streams, you must use the IP/TV broadcast server. This server is capable of encoding and delivering MPEG1/2/4 and Apple QuickTime live streams for live or on-demand delivery. The IP/TV broadcast server requires a dedicated Cisco-branded IP/TV hardened appliance or a generic standalone server. You acquire this appliance or server yourself and install the broadcast server IP/TV software on it. If you use your own hardware, make sure that your capture cards are supported by the IP/TV Broadcast software first.

- **IP/TV Viewer**—To view content that is created with the IP/TV Broadcast server, you can use the Cisco IP/TV viewer.

Figure 14-1 illustrates a typical ACNS network topology that will be used throughout illustrations and examples in this chapter.

Figure 14-1 *A Content Distribution and Routing Topology*

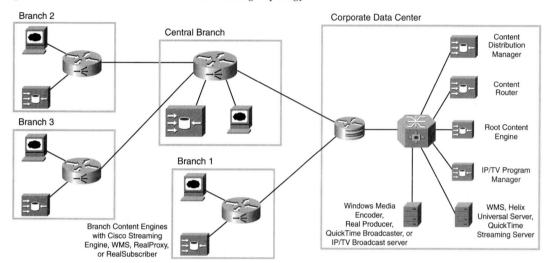

Initializing and Registering Your ACNS Network Devices

The Cisco CE can run in four different modes, corresponding to the ACNS elements you learned about previously: CDM, CE, CR, and IP/TV Program Manager. These four modes are available as separate personalities within the same ACNS operating system. To change the device mode, you simply need to enable the mode and reboot the CE for the changes to take effect. The CE command to change the mode of a CE is

```
device mode {content-router | content-engine | content-distribution-manager |
   program-manager}
```

The following series of CEs is available for enabling the three ACNS device modes:

■ **Content Engine Network Modules**—CE network modules for the Cisco 2600 and 3600 series multiservice platforms and the Cisco 2800 and 3800 series integrated services routers. You can enable these service modules as CEs only.

■ **Content Engine 511 series**—The CE 511 is an entry-level platform for small branch offices. Like the CE network module, you can enable these devices as CEs only.

- **Content Engine 566 and 7326 series**—These are higher-end series CEs, with faster CPUs and more storage capacity than the CE 511. These series CEs can support the CDM, CE, CR ACNS device modes.

If you are configuring your device for the first time, you should allocate disk space appropriately for the following disk regions on your ACNS devices:

- **System File System (sysfs)**—Allocated for system use.

- **Cache File System (cfs)**—Allocated for caching unmanaged HTTP and FTP objects on standalone CEs, which you learned about in Chapter 13. Unmanaged objects are sourced from public Internet origin servers.

- **Media File System (mediafs)**—Allocated for unmanaged VoD proxy caching, using the WMT proxy or RealProxy, that you also learned about in Chapter 13.

- **Content Delivery Network File System (cdnfs)**—Allocated for pre-positioning managed content, which you centrally administer with a CDM. Managed content is content that you source from an origin server that you manage yourself (for example, an intranet web or FTP server or an enterprise WMS server).

To allocate the percentage of disk space for each region, use the command

```
disk config sysfs sys-percent cfs cache-percent mediafs stream-percent cdnfs
    cdn-percentage
```

For example, for CEs primarily used for prepositioned content, you can weight the allocation more toward the cdnfs, as follows:

```
disk config sysfs 10% cfs 15% mediafs 15% cdnfs 60%
```

As mentioned previously, you must configure and enable your ACNS devices from the CDM GUI. For devices to be configurable on the CDM, you must first register them using DHCP or with the CE command

```
cdm ip {ip-address | hostname}
```

For more information on registering your CEs using DHCP, refer to your product documentation.

To enable the ACNS process on your device, which will enable you to configure your device with the CDM, enter the following command:

```
cms enable
```

This command enables a management database that contains the device configuration you create and modify using the CDM. Without this command, you cannot manage the device with the CDM.

Setting Up Your ACNS Network for Acquisition and Pre-Positioning

To configure your ACNS network, you must first create channels of content that you want to pre-position to your CEs. Channels conceptualize the mapping of content located on your origin servers to the content pre-positioned to your CEs. The CDM sends the channel information to the CEs that you subscribe to the channel, so they will know how to receive the pre-positioned content.

> **NOTE**   Pre-positioning content simply means that you place it somewhere ahead of time, so that it is ready when needed.

You then associate a manifest file to the channel, which is an XML file that you host on an external origin server that specifies objects within your origin servers that will be pre-positioned to your CEs.

You then create a location tree for the channel from your CEs, which will house the channel's pre-positioned content for upcoming client requests. Figure 14-2 shows how you can create a location tree containing five locations, based on the network diagram in Figure 14-1.

Figure 14-2 *A Three-Level Location Tree Containing Five Locations.*

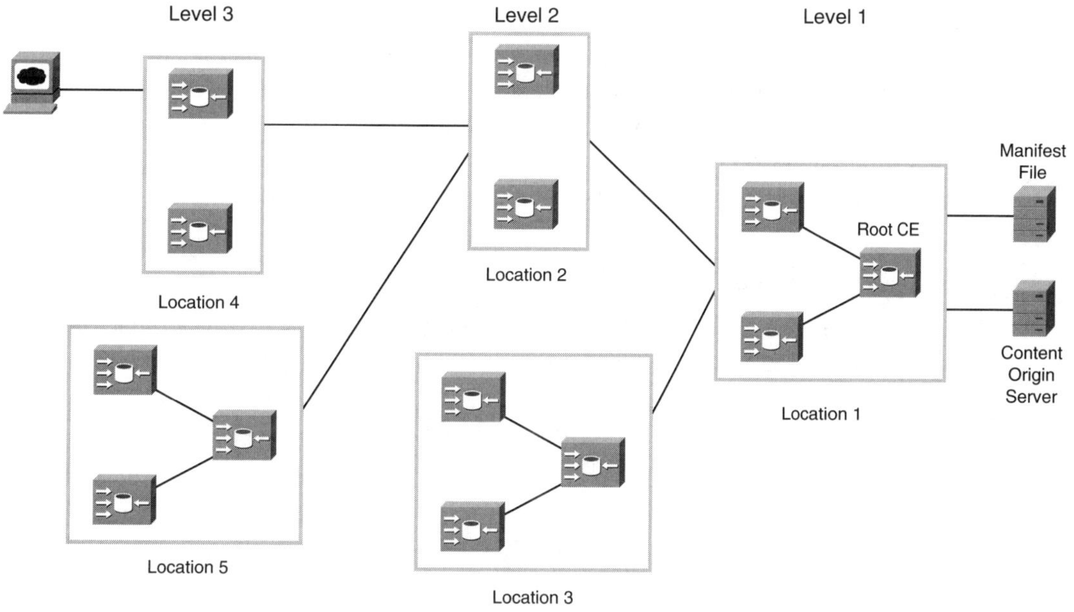

Content distribution is divided into two pieces: content acquisition and pre-positioning. The root CE of the tree, which you should choose as being in close proximity to your origin servers, first acquires the content by retrieving the external manifest file. The root CE parses the XML manifest file, crawls the origin servers for the content specified in the manifest entries, and acquires the content into its cdnfs. Once acquired, the root CE can then pre-position the content to the CEs located downstream in location tree by using either unicast-pull or multicast-push distribution, depending on your preference. As you learned in Chapter 5, "IP Multicast Content Delivery," multicast conserves bandwidth consumption by delivering content to end-devices with only a single flow of the content on any link in the network at a given time. In contrast, the CEs themselves can unicast-pull the content directly from the origin servers, potentially replicating content on individual links on the network. Unicast-pull is desirable for networks with few CEs; whereas, in large networks with numerous CEs, you should use multicast to avoid flooding resources during content distribution.

In Chapter 13, you learned how to accelerate static and streaming content delivery by configuring your CEs to cache origin server content on-demand, to the benefit of subsequently requesting users. That is, the CE inspects live client requests and unicast-pulls content directly from your origin servers located on the Internet or within your corporate resources. Additionally, you learned how to configure your CEs to preload content in advance of user requests by unicast-pulling objects from specific origin servers in anticipation of future user requests for the preloaded content.

In contrast, with the content pre-positioning model, the root CE of the location tree acquires content that you specify in the manifest file, previous to any client requests. If you configure unicast-pull pre-positioning, receiver CEs initiate the distribution of the content throughout the location tree (that is, they "pull" the content from the root-CE); with multicast-push distribution, the root-CE proactively multicasts the content down the location tree.

Creating Location Trees

Figure 14-3 shows you how to configure a location in the CDM. You link the locations together into the form of a tree by specifying the parent location in the configuration.

To assign CEs to your locations, you specify the location when you create the CE in the CDM, as Figure 14-4 illustrates.

Figure 14-3 *Configuring a Location*

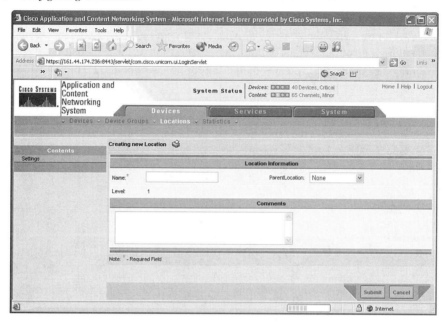

Figure 14-4 *Assigning a Content Engine to a Location*

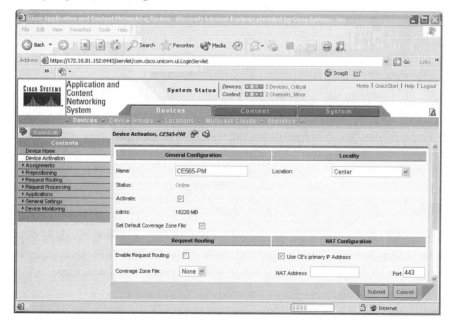

Configuring Content Channels

To create a content channel, you must first create a content provider and a website to associate to the channel for the particular content that you want to pre-position. A content provider is an individual or group of individuals within your organization that is responsible for creating and maintaining the content that you are configuring for pre-positioning. Figure 14-5 illustrates how to configure a content provider in the CDM.

Figure 14-5 *Configuring a Content Provider*

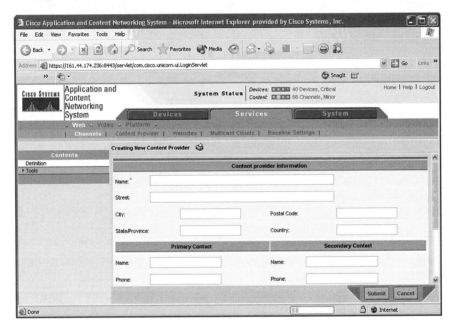

A website specifies the location of the content that the content provider is responsible for creating and maintaining. To integrate Cisco IP/TV into your ACNS network, select the website as the IP/TV Program Manager IP address or hostname. For more information on IP/TV and ACNS integration, see the section called "Creating Scheduled Live and Rebroadcast Programs in ACNS" later in this chapter.

Figure 14-6 illustrates how to configure a website in the CDM.

To create the channel, you must specify the content provider and website you created previously. For live channels, make sure that you click on the "Live Channel" checkbox in the channel configuration. You also specify the channel quota in terms of cdnfs disk space, as Figure 14-7 illustrates.

Figure 14-6 *Configuring a Website*

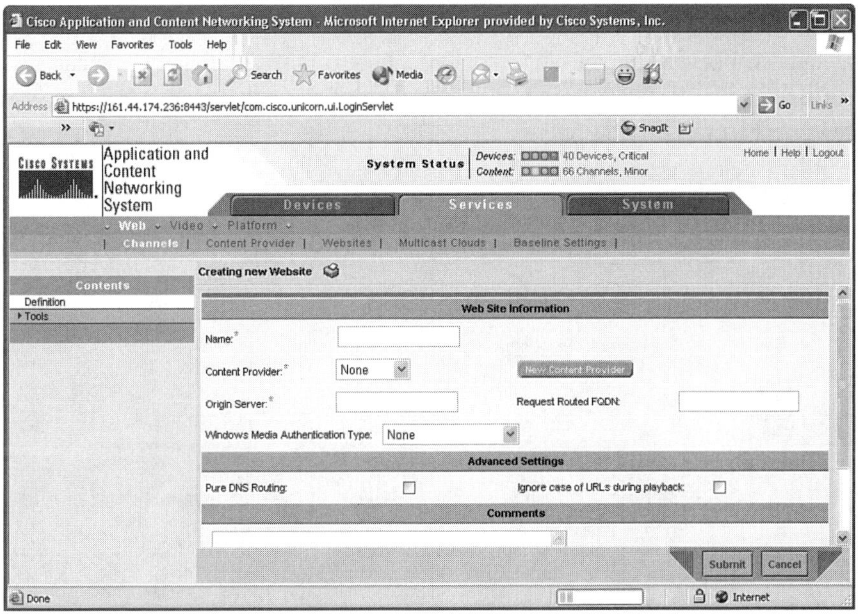

Figure 14-7 *Configuring a Content Channel*

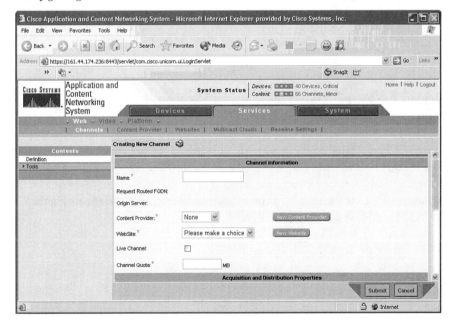

You should set the priority of the channel, so that the root-CE knows which channels are of higher importance and therefore which channels it should distribute before the others. The priorities are High, Normal, and Low. You can configure the root-CE to mark packets with DSCP values for individual channels within the configuration in Figure 14-7. Alternately, you can also have the root-CE mark the IP DSCP value for packets, depending on the priority that you assign to the channel, as Figure 14-8 illustrates.

Figure 14-8 *Packet Marking Based on Channel Priority*

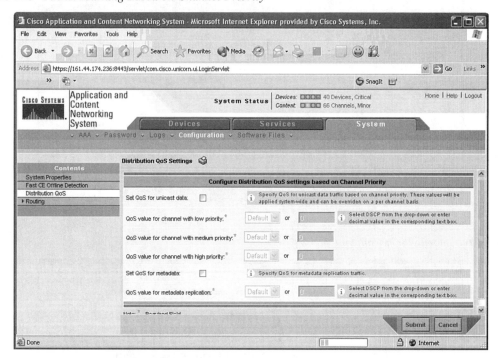

CEs in your location tree exchange meta-data describing the content being pre-positioned. You can also mark these packets from the CDM GUI in Figure 14-8.

You subscribe CEs to the channel's content by assigning CEs to the channel in the CDM. Figure 14-9 shows how to subscribe CEs to a channel.

Figure 14-9 *Subscribing CEs to a Channel*

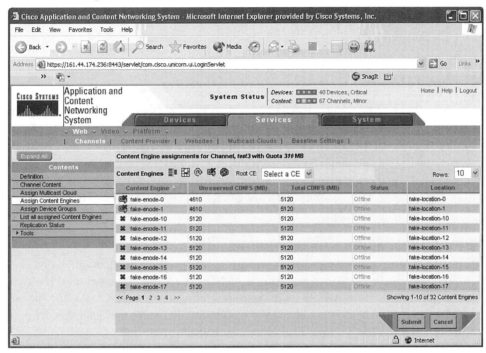

You can assign a root CE to a channel when you assign CEs to the channel, as Figure 14-9 illustrates.

Acquiring Content to Pre-Position

Now that you've learned how to set up a location tree, you can pre-position content to the CEs located within the tree, so that the tree can provide content to the clients requesting content from the network. The content acquisition model of content networking begins at the origin server containing the channel's content. You should choose the root CE for the channel as a CE in close proximity to the channel's origin server because, as you learned previously, the root CE acquires the content for the channel by unicast-pulling the content from the origin server.

The type of content determines the protocols that you can use to fetch the content, which are as follows:

■ HTTP for acquiring content from a website

■ FTP for files from an FTP server

- Windows Common Internet File System (CIFS)

- UNIX Network File System (NFS) for retrieving content from Windows- and UNIX-based file servers

- Microsoft Media Servics (MMS) or RTSP for acquiring streaming content for live or on-demand viewing.

Keep in mind that the protocols used to acquire the content into the ACNS network need not be the same as those used by clients for viewing or downloading the content. For example, the acquirer can use FTP to pull Apple QuickTime streaming files from an FTP server, whereas clients can use their Apple media player to view the content using RTSP and RTP.

You can configure content acquisition using either the CDM GUI or with external manifest files.

Configuring Acquisition Using Manifest Files

You should use manifest files if you have content developers in your organization who would like to specify what content to preposition to the ACNS network from their websites. These content developers are resources who do not have administrative access to the CDM GUI. They simply need to write the manifest file and let you know of the URL where they published it for you to specify when you configure the channel for their content.

The manifest file instructs the root CE for the channel to pull either individual items of content or to crawl through entire directories of content. You write manifest files in XML using tags specific to ACNS acquisition. Example 14-1 gives a sample manifest file for acquiring content in an ACNS network.

Example 14-1 *Sample Manifest File*

```
<CdnManifest>
  <server name="cisco">
    <host name="http://www.cisco.com" />
  </server>
  <crawler
    server="cisco"
    start-url="tac/docs.html"
    depth="10"
    prefix="tac"
  </crawler>
  <item src="sales/docs.pdf" />
</CdnManifest>
```

You can use the following tags in your manifest file:

- **<CdnManifest>...</CdnManifest>**—Indicates the beginning and end of the manifest file.

- **<server>...</server>**—Enables you to identify a server for applying crawler tags to. This way, you do not need to write the entire URL for the server in every crawler job.

- **<crawler.../>**—Crawls a directory starting at the location specified in **start-url** for a specific **depth**, within the given **prefix**. In Example 14-2, the acquirer will crawl the URL http://www.cisco.com/tac for a depth of 10, starting with http://www.cisco.com/tac/docs.html.

- **<item>.../>**—Specifies the URL source of an individual item to pull.

> **NOTE**   Refer to your ACNS documentation for the XML schema that outlines the entire manifest XML file specification.

Figure 14-10 shows how to assign the manifest file to a channel.

Figure 14-10 *Assigning a Manifest File to a Channel*

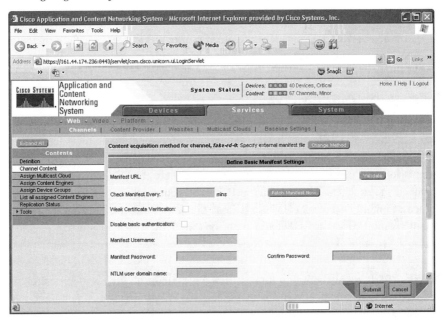

Configuring Acquisition Using the CDM GUI

The CDM GUI enables you, as an ACNS administrator, to configure content acquisition directly by creating Quick Crawl Filters, as Figure 14-11 illustrates.

Figure 14-11 *Configuring Content Acquisition from the CDM GUI*

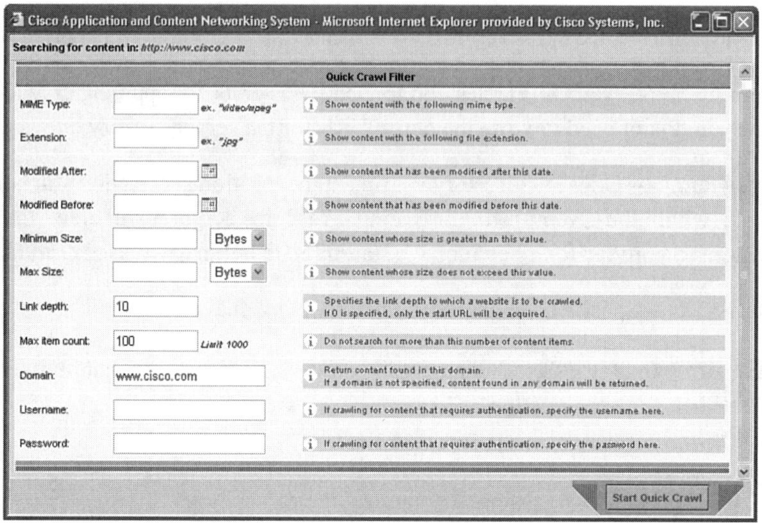

Configuring Content Pre-Positioning

As you learned previously, you can configure your root-CE to distribute the content that you want to pre-position using either multicast-push or unicast-pull.

Multicast-Push Distribution Trees

Because multicast was designed for real-time applications with high tolerance to packet loss, User Datagram Protocol (UDP) was chosen for the transport protocol—multicast cannot run over TCP. However, file transfers have no tolerance for lost packets and therefore require a reliable transmission mechanism. To reliably distribute content to the CEs registered to the channel, you can enable Pragmatic General Multicast (PGM) on your CEs. As you learned in Chapter 5, "IP Multicast Content Delivery," PGM is a reliable multicast protocol. The root CE sends the channel content to a multicast address that you define on the CDM, which registered CEs join to to receive the channel content.

> **NOTE** To distribute with IP multicast, you must enable all your routers within the ACNS network with IP multicast. You can also enable the PGM router-assist feature to minimize negative acknowledgement (NAK) and NCF flooding.

To configure multicast in your ACNS network, you must create a multicast cloud. Figure 14-12 illustrates how to configure a multicast cloud.

Figure 14-12   *Configuring a Multicast Cloud*

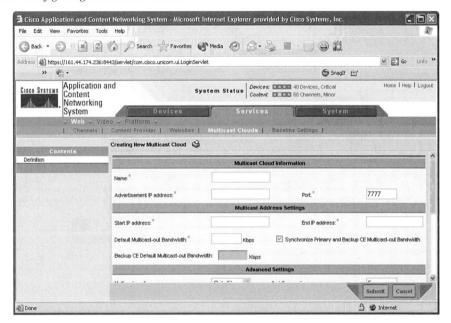

Unicast-Pull Distribution Trees

Like multicast-push trees, the concept of distribution trees can also be used for pre-positioning content in a unicast-only environment. The unicast distribution trees are created from the location trees that you created previously.

With unicast-pull distribution, each location is elected a location leader. The location leader unicast-pulls the channel's content from the forwarder of its parent location. The leader of a location is in turn the forwarder for other CEs within its location. The forwarder for child locations can be any of the CEs within the location.

For example, in Figure 14-13, the receiver CE in Location 4 determines the forwarder in Location 2 and establishes a TCP connection, over which it sends the request. The forwarder in Location 2 then establishes a TCP connection with the location leader in Location 2 and sends the request. The location leader in Location 2 determines the forwarder in Location 1, which happens to be the root CE in this example, and receives the requested object. The forwarders then forward the requested object down the unicast tree using the existing TCP connections established previously.

Figure 14-13 *Unicast Distribution Trees*

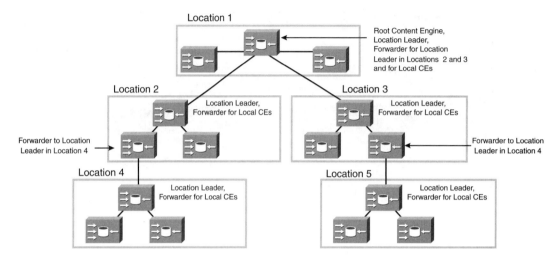

You can influence which CEs become the forwarders and location leaders from the CDM, as Figure 14-14 illustrates.

Figure 14-14 *Configuring Location Forwarder Probability and Leader Preference*

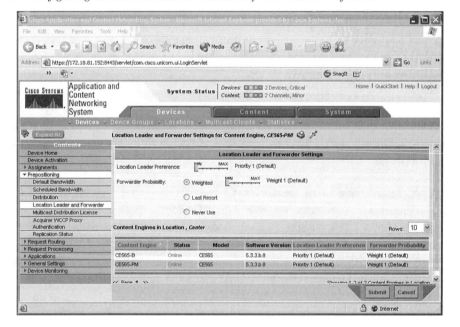

Content Request Routing

To send client requests to the best-suited CE, you have three options using ACNS:

- **Web Cache Communication Protocol (WCCP)**—You learned how to configure WCCP to redirect clients to their local CE in Chapter 13. With this method of request routing, you can configure the user's branch router to direct their requests to the CE located in their branch.

- **Simplified Hybrid Routing (SHR)**—SHR uses HTTP redirection and coverage zones to determine the best-suited CE. With coverage zones, you have the flexibility to assign users manually to any CE in your ACNS network.

- **Dynamic Proxy Autoconfiguration (PAC)**—Dynamic PAC also uses coverage zones to determine the best-suited CE, and dynamically adjusts client's proxy settings with the best-suited CE URL or IP address.

Simplified Hybrid Routing

With SHR, your CR decides which CE to route client requests to, using coverage zone information you specify with an XML file. The coverage zone file includes the mapping of source IP subnets to CE IP address. When you register your CEs with the CDM, the CDM creates a default coverage zone file including the subnet that the CE resides on and the IP address of the CE. For example, based on the zones in Figure 14-15, the CDM will create the coverage zone file in Example 14-2. You can manually adjust the default coverage zones in the coverage zone XML file if you need to—in this example, the second entry for 10.1.30.0/24 with metric 30 was manually added as a backup to the entry with metric 20. This way, the central branch CE can server Branch 2, if necessary.

Figure 14-15 *Simplified Hybrid Routing*

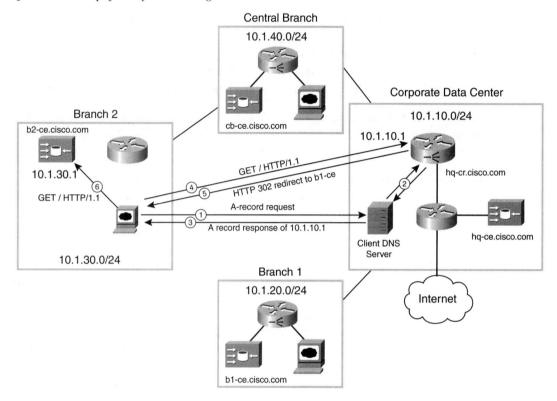

Example 14-2 *Sample Coverage File*

```
<?xml version="1.0"?>
<CDNNetwork>
  <coverageZone>
    <network>10.1.10.0/24</network>
    <CE>hq-ce.cisco.com</CE>
    <metric>20</metric>
  </coverageZone>

  <coverageZone>
    <network>10.1.20.0/24</network>
    <CE>b1-ce.cisco.com</CE>
    <metric>20</metric>
  </coverageZone>

  <coverageZone>
    <network>10.1.30.0/24</network>
    <CE>b2-ce.cisco.com</CE>
```

Example 14-2 *Sample Coverage File (Continued)*

```
      <metric>20</metric>
  </coverageZone>

  <coverageZone>
    <network>10.1.30.0/24</network>
    <CE>cb-ce.cisco.com</CE>
    <metric>30</metric>
  </coverageZone>

  <coverageZone>
    <network>10.1.40.0/24</network>
    <CE>cb-ce.cisco.com</CE>
    <metric>20</metric>
  </coverageZone>

</CDNNetwork>
```

> **NOTE**   In order for your CR at the headquarters to receive the client A record requests, you must delegate authority to the CR for the appropriate subdomains.

Based on Figure 14-6, the following sequence takes place:

1. With SHR, the client sends its DNS request to its local DNS server.

2. The DNS server sends an iterative DNS request to the root DNS server, which eventually ends up at the CR delegated to the pre-positioned subdomain. The CR responds to the local DNS server with its own IP address in an A record response.

3. The local DNS server responds to the client with the A record of the CR.

4. The client sends the HTTP GET request to the CR, which determines the most suitable CE for the requesting client from the coverage zone file.

5. The CR sends an HTTP 302 redirect for the selected CE.

6. The client reissues the request to the CE.

Recall from Chapter 12, "Exploring Global Server Load Balancing," that most GSLB solutions use the client DNS server to select a site to it, which sends the client's request. GSLB assumes that the client DNS server is in close proximity to the requesting clients. However, SHR does not make this assumption, because most often clients issue DNS requests to the organization's DNS server, which is located in the corporate headquarters—the same location as the CR. This is why the CR uses the HTTP GET request from the client to determine which CE to redirect to.

Dynamic Proxy Auto-Configuration

Recall from Chapter 13 that you can configure your client browsers with direct proxy routing, by specifying the proxy that the client should use for requests. With Dynamic Proxy Autoconfiguration (PAC), you instead specify the IP address of the PAC proxy server in client browsers or media players. The PAC proxy server returns a script that the browser executes to determine which proxy to use for requests.

With Dynamic PAC in ACNS, you configure a CE as a PAC file server, create a PAC file template, and associate a coverage zone file to the template. When a user opens a browser, the browser sends a request for the PAC file to the PAC file server CE, which populates the PAC file on-the-fly with edge-CE IP addresses from the coverage zone file, based on the source IP address of the requesting client. The client browser executes the script in the PAC file for each request that the client makes, to select the CE to which it sends the request. Figure 14-16 illustrates the traffic flow for Dynamic PAC.

Figure 14-16 *Dynamic PAC*

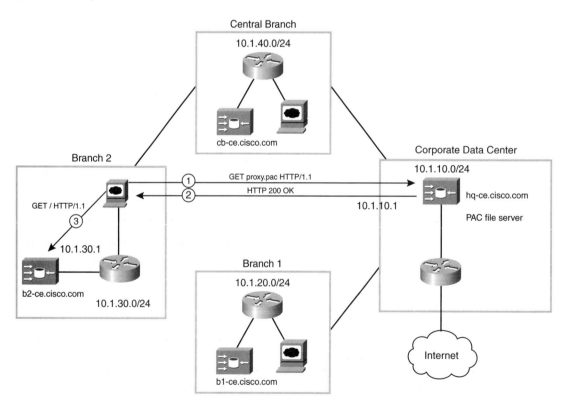

When you write the PAC file template for the PAC file server, you must specify a function called FindProxyForURL. When executed by the client browser, FindProxyForURL returns a list of the closest IP addresses to use as the proxy for all browser requests. Two examples of resulting strings returned from this function are

> PROXY 10.1.30.1:80; 10.1.40.1:80; DIRECT
> PROXY b2-ce.domain.com:80; cb-ce.domain.com:80; DIRECT

The client attempts to connect to the entries from left to right until it finds a CE that is available or when it reaches the DIRECT keyword. Then the browser sends the request directly to the origin server. These sample strings are based on the two coverages for clients that are located within Branch 2 subnet 10.1.30.0/24, in Example 14-2. The coverage with the lower metric is listed first in the "PROXY" string, and therefore the client browser attempts to connect to this CE first.

You can use the following macros in the PAC template that the PAC file server substitutes with CEs from the coverage zone file, where n can be a value between 1 and 5.

- **CE_NAME_n**—The hostname of the CE in nth closest proximity to the requesting client. For example, CE_NAME_1 would generate "b2-ce" for the previous example.

- **CE_IPADDR_n**—The IP Address of the CE in nth closest proximity to the requesting client. For example, CE_IPADDR_1 would give "10.1.30.1."

- **NEAREST_PROXIES_n**—The PAC server generates a string including a list of IP address of CEs up to the nth closest CE. For example, NEAREST_PROXIES_2 would give "PROXY 10.1.30.1; 10.1.40.1."

You can use these macros in the template as literal constants within the FindProxyForURL function. For example, you can use the simple function in Example 14-3 to return the IP addresses of CEs that are ranked in terms of proximity to the client. If no proxy is available, clients go directly to the origin server.

Example 14-3 *Sample PAC File Template*

```
function FindProxyForURL (url, host)
ce1 = CE_NAME_1;
ce2 = CE_NAME_2;
if (ce1 != "") {
  ce1 = "PROXY " + ce1 + ".cisco.com:80; ";
}
if (ce2 != "") {
  ce2 = ce2 + ".cisco.com:80; ";
}
return ce1 + ce2 + "DIRECT";
```

The parameter called **url** is the requested URL within the client's HTTP GET request. The host parameter is the domain name within the requested URL (for example, **http://www.cisco.com** is a URL, and **www.cisco.com** is the associated host). You can use these parameters if you need to handle certain URLs differently from others, but you may not need to use these parameters at all in your PAC file template, as demonstrated with Example 14-3.

If a client browser in Branch 2 requests the PAC file, the headquarters CE returns the file in Example 14-4 based on the source IP address of the client.

Example 14-4 *Sample PAC File*

```
function FindProxyForURL (url, host)
ce1 = "b2-ce";
ce2 = "cb-ce";
if (ce1 != "") {
  ce1 = "PROXY " + ce1 + ".cisco.com:80; ";
}
if (ce2 != "") {
  ce2 = ce2 + ".cisco.com:80; ";
}
return ce1 + ce2 + "DIRECT";
```

When the client at Branch 2 runs this function, the following value is returned:

PROXY b2-ce.cisco.com:80; cb-ce.cisco.com:80; DIRECT

You should include checks in the script to ensure that the PAC file server populates the macros with data from the coverage file (that is, "if (ce2 != "")"). For example, if you did not include these checks and the coverage had only a single entry for the specific requesting source, the resultant PROXY string would contain an erroneous entry:

PROXY b2-ce.cisco.com:80; .cisco.com:80; DIRECT

Dynamic PAC is useful in roaming office environments, where clients move from office-to-office or home-to-office but still require pre-positioned content. A disadvantage with Dynamic PAC is that you still have to configure all browsers with the central PAC file server URL.

Configuring Streaming Media

With regards to streaming media, an ACNS solution administered with a CDM offers the benefits detailed in Table 14-1 over the streaming services provided in standalone CEs.

Table 14-1   *Using Standalone CEs Versus a CDM-Administered ACNS Solution*

Feature	Standalone CE	CDM ACNS Solution
WMS proxy/server live splitting and conventional prerecorded VoD caching	✓	✓
RealProxy live splitting and conventional prerecorded VoD caching.	✓	✓
RealSubscriber prerecorded VoD pre-positioning.		✓
MPEG4 live/scheduled-rebroadcast ACNS programs and prerecorded VoD pre-positioning.		✓
Apple QuickTime live/scheduled-rebroadcast ACNS programs and prerecorded VoD pre-positioning.		✓
WMS live/scheduled-rebroadcast ACNS programs and prerecorded VoD pre-positioning.		✓

To provide MPEG4 and Apple QuickTime live and scheduled rebroadcasts, you can use either of the following:

- **Apple QuickTime**—Apple QuickTime uses the QuickTime Broadcaster for capturing live audio and video feeds and the QuickTime Streaming Server for Apple OS X (or Darwin server open source that you can compile for Windows and UNIX platforms) for scheduling and delivering Apple QuickTime and MPEG4 VoDs or live presentations to clients.

- **Cisco IP/TV**—Cisco uses the IP/TV Broadcast Server for capturing live audio and video feeds and delivering MPEG4 VoDs. You must use the IP/TV Program Manager to schedule live or rebroadcast events on the IP/TV Broadcast server.

Figure 14-17 illustrates how you can include these components into your streaming media ACNS network.

Figure 14-17 *Available Streaming Media Servers for ACNS*

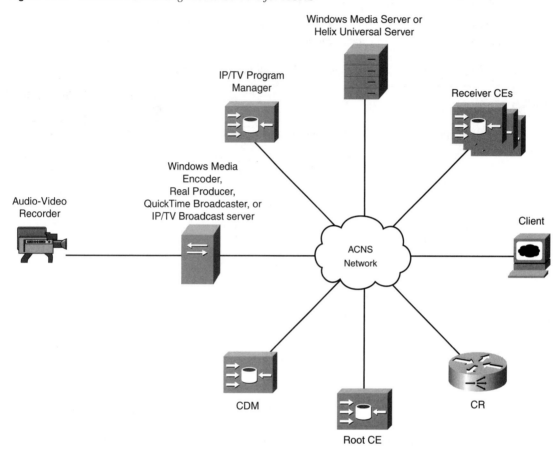

Streaming Prepositioned Video On-Demand Content

Recall from Chapter 13 that you can use the RealProxy and WMS proxy for VoD caching on a standalone CE. Figure 13-12 in Chapter 13 illustrates conventional streaming media caching. Additionally, with a CDM-administered ACNS solution, you can configure MPEG4 and Apple QuickTime VoD pre-positioning by enabling the Cisco Streaming Engine on CDM-registered CEs. The Cisco Streaming Engine is another back-end server that the RTSP gateway can forward requests to, as Figure 14-18 illustrates.

Figure 14-18   *The RTSP Gateway for CDM-Administered ACNS Solutions*

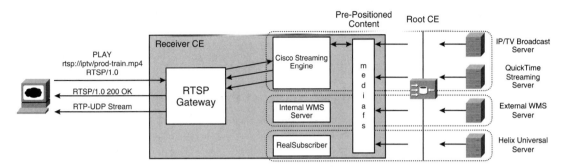

To configure pre-positioned VoD streaming, you need to first pre-position your VoD files to your CEs, as you learned previously in this chapter. When you enable the Cisco Streaming Engine and configure request redirection or direct proxy routing to the RTSP gateway, the RTSP gateway inspects and forwards requests for MPEG4 or Apple QuickTime VoDs to the Cisco Streaming Engine. The RTSP gateway can recognize these formats based on the file extension in the request (for example, .mov for QuickTime format and .mp4 for MEG4 format). The Cisco Streaming Engine responds to the request by streaming the prepositioned VoD from cdnfs.

To pre-positioned IP/TV MPEG4 VoDs, the CDM sends channel information to IP/TV Program Manager and all the Content Engines subscribed to that channel. You then create a program on the IP/TV Program Manager and assign it to the channel you created on the CDM. The IP/TV Program Manager creates the manifest file for the program that the root CE uses to acquire the content from the IP/TV Broadcast server using FTP. The root CE then distributes the IP/TV VoD to the subscribed CEs.

You can also stream prepositioned WMS and Real VoD content to your CEs. For pre-positioned WMS VoD streaming, you must enable the WMS server on your CE—you learned how to do this in Chapter 13, with the CE CLI, but you can also complete the same configuration centrally for individual CEs using the CDM GUI.

To stream your pre-positioned RealNetworks VoD files, you must enable the RealSubscriber on your CEs from the CDM GUI. The RealSubscriber is a full-blown Helix Universal Server system and requires a separate license. Previous versions of ACNS required that you install a Helix "publisher" origin server running on dedicated hardware that would issue stream-based licenses to the "subscribers" running on your CEs. The publisher would allow a fixed number of total streams to be shared across all your CEs. However, you can now obtain bandwidth-based licenses from Cisco that you can install on a CE-by-CE basis from the CDM GUI. As a result, you do not need to install a dedicated Helix publisher to issue the subscriber licenses. The bandwidth licenses available for your RealSubscribers are dependant on the model of your CE.

> **NOTE** The RealSubscriber on the CE also supports Synchronized Multimedia Integration Language (SMIL) streaming. You can pre-position your SMIL files to your CEs along with the RealMedia files, and the CEs will stream the presentation according to the flow specified in the SMIL file.

Creating Scheduled Live and Rebroadcast Programs in ACNS

You can schedule the following live or rebroadcasted events in ACNS:

- **Cisco Streaming Engine live and rebroadcast**—Sourced from IP/TV Broadcast and Program Manager servers or Apple QuickTime Streaming Servers. Your users can view these events using the Cisco IP/TV viewer or Apple QuickTime client media players.

- **Windows Media live and rebroadcast**—Sourced from WMS or WME servers. Your users can view these events using the Windows media players.

- **TV-out and export**—These programs can be sourced from WMS, WME, IP/TV, or QuickTime Streaming Servers. The TV-out programs are viewed using a TV directly attached to the CE. Export programs are exported to an external set-top box using HTTP.

> **NOTE** Scheduled live or rebroadcast of RealNetworks is not supported by ACNS; however, you can pre-position your Real VoDs and make them available to your clients, as you learned previously.

To schedule a live event, you must first set up your origin server for the live broadcast. If you are using the IP/TV Broadcast server, you must use the IP/TV Program Manager to create and schedule the program and import it into your ACNS network. The IP/TV Program Manager sends the program information to the CDM, and the CDM sends the IP address of the root CE to the IP/TV Program Manager. The CDM then sends the program information to the CEs subscribed to the channel that you configured previously with the IP/TV Program Manager as the origin server. The IP/TV Program Manager sends the root CE IP address to the IP/TV Broadcast server, which can then send the live traffic to the root CE. The root CE then distributes the live event down the location tree for the channel.

For non IP/TV programs, you configure a live channel in the CDM and associate a root CE that will acquire the event via unicast from the streaming origin server directly—you learned how to configure channels previously. You then configure a program in the CDM and associate the live channel with a day and time that you want the root-CE for the channel to acquire the live content from the origin server via unicast.

Figure 14-19 shows you how to add a program using the CDM GUI.

Figure 14-19 *Adding a New Program*

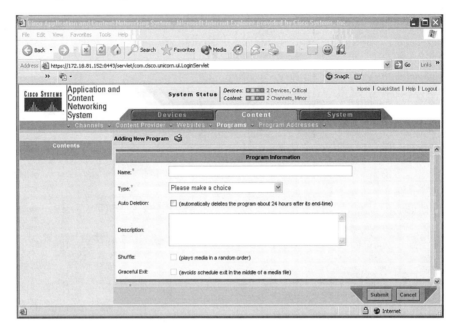

Figure 14-20 shows you how to configure a schedule for the live channel.

Figure 14-20 *Scheduling a Live Program*

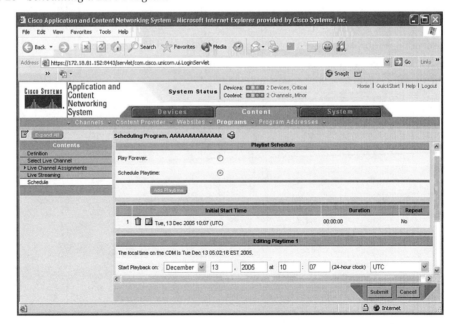

The root-CE can then distribute the live traffic to subscribed CEs using the unicast location tree you created previously. When that scheduled time arrives, the CEs subscribed to the channel can request and split the live event to requesting clients using either unicast or multicast splitting. Figure 14-21 shows you how to enable multicast delivery to your clients.

Figure 14-21 *Streaming Settings For a Live Program*

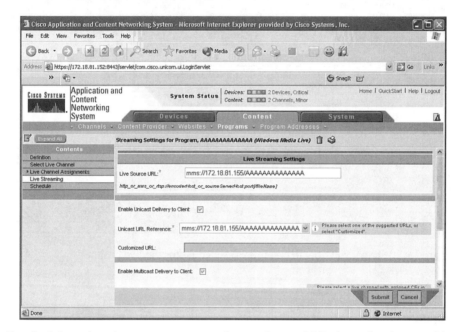

To schedule a rebroadcast event, you must first configure a VoD channel and pre-position the VoD to your CEs. You can then schedule a day and time from the CDM GUI that the pre-positioned content will be available for requesting clients.

Summary

In this last chapter, you combined numerous technologies that you learned about throughout this book, such as content switching, application layer protocols, DNS, GSLB, QoS, and streaming media, to explore the following content distribution and routing technologies:

- **Content Distribution**—Content distribution is divided into acquisition and pre-positioning. The root-CE first acquires the content using a manifest, then prepositions the content to downstream CEs.

- **Content Routing**—You learned how to route client requests using WCCP, Simplified Hybrid Routing, and Dynamic Proxy Autoconfiguration (PAC).

- **Enhanced Streaming Media**—You learned how you can enable enhanced streaming services, such as the Cisco Streaming Engine and RealSubscriber, with a CDM-administered ACNS solution.

Review Questions

1. From which file system do edge CEs serve pre-positioned content?

2. What is a manifest file used for and why wouldn't you use the CDM GUI instead?

3. What is the criterion for choosing the root-CE?

4. What is the relationship between a location leader and a location forwarder?

5. What do you require to stream pre-positioned RealMedia formatted files?

Recommended Reading

Markus Hofmann and Leland Beaumont, *Content Networking: Architecture, Protocols, and Practice*, Elsevier, 2005

David Flanagan, *JavaScript: The Definitive Guide*, O'Reilly, 2001

Answers to Review Questions

Chapter 1

1. In which layers of the OSI model does content networking reside?

   Answer: Content networking devices technically work at Layers 1–7, but true content networking services can be considered to reside in Layers 5–7 of the OSI model.

2. What are the four main purposes and goals of content networking?

   Answer: The four main purposes and goals of content networking are to:

   — Perform scalability and availability services for applications.

   — Increase available network bandwidth and decrease application response times.

   — Provide customization and prioritization of content within your network.

   — Enable security, auditing, and management of a network.

3. Estimate how many servers are required to provide "four nines of availability" for an application known to fail 11.5 percent of the time?

   Answer: Five servers are required for the application to achieve "four nines of availability":

   $$1 - (0.115)^5 = 0.99998 = 99.99\%$$

4. What is the difference between application scalability and availability?

   Answer: Application availability requires replication to ensure data recovery, whereas scalability simply increases the capacity of a system.

5. How are bandwidth and response times reduced in a content network?

   Answer: Bandwidth and response times are reduced by placing content in closer proximity to requesting clients.

6. What is the main difference between an ICDN and an ECDN?

    Answer: An ICDN is owned and operated by a third-party provider and often requires content-based billing software to track and charge for customer bandwidth and content usage. An ECDN is often owned, operated, and used by the same organization, and therefore no usage billing is required.

7. Name four scenarios in which content can be switched.

    Answer: Content can be switched in the following four ways: SLB, Global SLB, FWLB, and VPN load balancing.

8. Name four solutions that Cisco ACNS can provide.

    Answer: Cisco ACNS can provide the following four solutions: point-of-sale videos and Web kiosks, software and file distribution, e-learning, and corporate communications.

Chapter 2

1. How many wire pairs does 100BASE-T use of a UTP copper cable? How many does 1000BASE-T use?

    Answer: The 100BASE-T standard uses two pairs (four wires in total), one pair for transmitting and another for receiving. The 1000BASE-T standard uses all four pairs (eight wires in total) of the UTP cable. Using echo cancellation, each pair is capable of transmitting and receiving simultaneously.

2. What are the physical differences between step and graded index multimode fiber?

    Answer: Step index multimode fiber has the same physical fiber properties throughout the core, which results in a sudden reflective "step" into the fiber cladding. In contrast, variations are imposed in the composition of graded index glass in the core, which results in a gradual increase in refraction toward the center of the core.

3. For 100BASE-FX, why is NRZ-I signaling used with 4B/5B encoding and not just straight NRZ?

    Answer: In Table 2-3, quite a few of the 5-bit codes have more ones than zeros. The reason that 100BASE-FX uses NRZ-I with 4B/5B is that more transitions are performed during long strings of ones using NRZ-I than with straight NRZ.

4. What error checking is performed with IP, UDP, and TCP?

    Answer: IP checks for errors in the IP packet only. UDP and TCP check for errors in the UDP header and segment payload, but only TCP retransmits erroneous segments.

5. What is the purpose of the TCP three-way handshake?

   Answer: The TCP three-way handshake is used to synchronize TCP sequence numbers and exchange TCP options between TCP devices.

6. How is packet loss detected by TCP senders?

   Answer: Outstanding segments are detected by the sender with either a timeout or by receiving duplicate ACKs from the receiver.

7. Why is TCP bandwidth limited over satellite links? How can TCP bandwidth over satellite be accelerated?

   Answer: The TCP window size limits bandwidth over satellite connections due to high latency. Use of multiple TCP connections or the window scaling option (WSopt) or both are ways to accelerate the TCP bandwidth over satellite links.

8. What is the lowest level of content awareness in TCP/IP?

   Answer: The TCP urgent pointer is the lowest level of content awareness of the TCP/IP protocol suite.

Chapter 3

1. How are MAC address tables built in Layer 2 switches?

   Answer: Layer 2 switches build MAC address tables by inspecting ARP traffic flowing across the switch.

2. Do Layer 3 switches maintain an ARP cache or a MAC address table?

   Answer: Layer 3 switches maintain both an ARP cache and a MAC address forwarding table. The MAC forwarding table is used to forward frames between ports within a single VLAN, and the ARP cache is used to route frames between VLANs.

3. What is the purpose of VTP?

   Answer: VTP saves time configuring VLANs and saves NVRAM space in large network environments. The network administrator needs only to add VLANs to the VTP server before assigning VLANs to switch ports across the entire network. VTP is also used to give VLANs human-readable names.

4. What is the difference between distance-vector and links-state dynamic routing protocols?

    Answer: Distance-vector algorithms send periodic routing updates and use hop count metrics. Link-state algorithms send triggered updates when changes occur and use metrics based on the state of the links (that is, based on the bandwidth, delay, reliability, load, and MTU of the link).

5. What is a RIB? Give a few examples of protocols that use RIBs.

    Answer: The routing information base stores routing information learned by link-state and hybrid-dynamic routing protocols. The best RIB routes are installed in the main routing table. OSPF, EIGRP, and BGP routing protocols maintain their own RIBs.

6. What is a FIB? Give a few examples of switching paths that use FIBs.

    Answer: A forwarding information base is efficient data structure containing forwarding information used by routers to bypass slow(er) routing tables and ARP cache lookups. Examples of switching paths that use RIBs are fast and CEF switching. Process switching does not use a RIB.

7. What form of NAT do content switches use to load balancing requests across server farms?

    Answer: Destination NAT is used by content switches to perform server load balancing.

Chapter 4

1. What is the difference between stateful and stateless ACLs?

    Answer: Stateful ACLs track transport state information, such as IP addresses, TCP/UDP ports, TCP sequence numbers, and TCP flags. Stateful ACLs do not track any transport information.

2. How do stateful ACLs track transport state information?

    Answer: Basic ACLs track transport state simply by checking to see if the ACK or RST TCP flags are set in the TCP header. IP session filters create temporary ACL entries for return traffic. CBAC and PIX firewalls store transport state information for each connection in a state table. The table includes IP addresses, TCP/UDP ports, TCP sequence numbers, and TCP flags.

3. How can you approximate UDP connections?

    Answer: You can approximate UDP connections by tracking packets with the same source and destination IP addresses and ports that transit the firewall over the same time frame.

4. How can you achieve supervisor redundancy?

   Answer: Supervisor redundancy is achieved by installing two supervisors in a single chassis, or by using two chassis with a single supervisor installed in each.

5. How can you achieve switch fabric redundancy?

   Answer: For active backplanes, two chassis are required for redundancy. For passive backplanes (that is, SFMs or integrated switch fabrics), either two modules in a single chassis or two chassis with a single module each are required for redundancy.

6. What is one benefit of sandwiching public servers between two firewalls?

   Answer: Both single and dual firewall configurations secure internal resources from the public resources. However, server sandwiching enables firewalls of different vendors to secure internal resources.

7. What content networking solutions do remote branch users benefit from?

   Answer: Remote office users benefit from content edge delivery, distribution, and routing in order to place content closer to the client.

Chapter 5

1. What is the difference between the ISM and SSM multicast models?

   Answer: With the ISM model, the routers in the network maintain source information. However, with SSM the receivers are responsible for specifying the desired source. The receiver application obtains knowledge of the source unicast IP address or URL through methods external to the multicast protocol, such as the user selecting the source from a list of available sources supplied by a web page.

2. How many possible globally scoped multicast addresses are available for ISM? For SSM?

   Answer: The IANA allocates multicast addresses within the range 232.0.0.0 – 232.255.255.255 to SSM.

   For the entire multicast range 224.0.0.0 – 239.255.255.255, there are $16 * 2^{24} = 16 *$ 16,777,216 = 268,435,456 possible addresses available. Therefore, to calculate the available addresses for ISM applications, subtract the locally scoped addresses (that is, $2^8 = 256$ addresses for the range 224.0.1.0 – 224.0.1.255) and the SSM addresses from this number. The result is 268,435,456 – 16,777,216 – 256 = 251,657,984. You have to divide this number by 32 because of the 32-to-1 mapping of addresses to Ethernet MAC addresses. The result is

251,657,984 / 32 = 7,864,312 possible addresses available for ISM and 16,777,216 / 32 = 524,288 for SSM. Because multicast applications randomly assign multicast addresses, the chances of having frames with duplicate MAC addresses on an Ethernet LAN are very low.

3. What is the difference between source and shared distribution trees?

   Answer: With source trees, the source of the multicast stream is at the root of the tree, providing the shortest possible path between the source and receivers of the content. Rendezvous Points are the root of shared trees and often cause the multicast stream to take a suboptimal path to the receivers.

4. How does dense-mode multicast differ from sparse-mode multicast?

   Answer: Dense-mode routers periodically flood the multicast stream to the entire network, even to last-hop routers that do not have active receivers for the group. Sparse-mode routers send the multicast stream only to last-hop routers that contain multicast receivers for the stream.

5. How do multicast routers route multicast packets downstream?

   Answer: Multicast routers use reverse path forwarding (RPF) to forward frames to last-hop routers.

6. How do multicast routers route multicast packets upstream?

   Answer: For forwarding PIM Join messages up the distribution, instead of checking to see if the source of the packet (the last-hop router, in this case) is reachable from the RP interface using RPF, the router checks its outgoing interface (OIF) list. If the router receives the packet from an interface in the OIF list, then the router forwards the packet out its RPF interface.

   For forwarding multicast stream data up the distribution tree, you need to configure Bidir-PIM.

7. What is the difference between Auto-RP and BSR?

   Answer: Auto-RP distributes the RP candidate information using dense-mode multicast, forcing you to enable PIM sparse-dense mode on all Auto-RP routers. BSR uses a hop-by-hop method, allowing you to configure only PIM sparse mode on all BSR routers.

8. What are the differences between Auto-RP, BSR, and Anycast RP?

   Answer: The Auto-RP and BSR protocols do not allow you to configure load-balancing of streams within the same group between multiple active RPs. Anycast RP allows per-group load balancing.

9.   What are the differences between CGMP and IGMP snooping?

Answer: Both CGMP and IGMP snooping provide you with the ability to restrict multicast traffic in a Layer 2 switched network to only those ports with active receivers attached. However, you must configure CGMP on the router to signal to the switch which ports to forward the traffic to. You do not need to configure IGMP snooping on the router because the switch inspects the IGMP messages directly.

Chapter 6

1.   What tools can you use to mark IP precedence and DSCP?

Answer: You can mark DSCP with class-based packet marking only. You can mark the IP Precedence of a packet using Policy-Based Routing, QoS Policy Propagation via Border Gateway Protocol, Committed Access Rate/Class-Based Policing, Network Based Application Recognition, and Class-Based Packet Marking.

2.   If a router has 100,000 concurrent connections on average, approximately how much memory does NBAR use to store information for those connections?

Answer: NBAR uses approximately 15 MB of memory.

3.   Why is WFQ not scalable to high-speed links?

Answer: Because WFQ uses a single queue per flow, the number of required queues would grow too high for high-speed links, and potentially flood the router's memory.

4.   What is the difference between standard WFQ and CBWFQ?

Answer: Standard WFQ automatically classifies traffic into flows, and you require only a single interface configuration command (**fair-queue**). In contrast, CBWFQ allows you to configure classes of traffic and allocate bandwidth to the classes through the MQC. Furthermore, because each flow in standard WFQ is tracked in memory, WFQ is not as scalable as CBWFQ.

5.   How many egress queues do Catalyst 29xx/35xx/37xx/4xxx series switches have? What about Catalyst 6500 series switches?

Answer: Catalyst 29xx/35xx/37xx/4xxx series have four egress queues. To determine the number of egress queues on your Catalyst 6500 series switches, use the **show port capabilities** command.

6.   What is the difference between traffic shaping and policing?

Answer: Traffic policing drops packets when the token buckets are full, whereas shaping queues packets when the token buckets are full for transmission during periods of lower congestion.

7.   How does RSVP differ from other QoS congestion avoidance mechanisms?

Answer: With RSVP, the hosts signal their QoS requirements to the network. However, with traffic shaping, policing, and BGP policy propagation, you need to evaluate the application's QoS requirements and configure them on your routers manually.

Chapter 7

1.   What are the disadvantages of using procedural markup languages?

Answer: Procedural markup languages are inflexible, information retrieval is difficult, and they require multiple documents for files that require different formats.

2.   What is PDATA?

Answer: PDATA indicates that the parser should inspect the data that follows for tags. For example, the footer in the book outline example in this chapter uses the PDATA "**Copyright © Cisco Press 2005**." The **&#xA9** indicates to the parser to insert the copyright (©) symbol into the data.

3.   What is the purpose of the Document Type Definition (DTD) file and XML schemas?

Answer: You can use DTDs and XML schemas to declare custom elements and define the overall structure and flow of your XML documents. You can then validate your XML files to ensure that they use the valid elements.

4.   What are the benefits of XHTML over HTML?

Answer: You can specify custom tags using XHTML. Because XHTML forces you to adhere to the strict rules of XML, browsers will gradually become less complex to develop.

5.   What are your two options for transforming XML content into a displayable or printable form?

Answer: You can transform XML into XHTML or HTML and apply CSS. Or you can transform XML into XSL-FO to generate displayable or printable output using a third-party XSL-FO processor.

6. What is an XML namespace?

    Answer: Namespaces are tag prefixes that distinguish between elements of the same name defined within different DTDs or XML schemes.

7. What is the benefit of CSS?

    Answer: CSS is beneficial for rendering a large number of documents into a standard format. CSS also has powerful and intuitive formatting tools that were previously unavailable to you.

8. What is the purpose of the **position()** function in the XSLT examples in this chapter?

    Answer: The **position()** function outputs the line number of the current goal.

Chapter 8

1. What is an application layer protocol?

    Answer: An application layer protocol is any process, either custom or well-known, that has a structured mechanism for communicating between clients and servers.

2. What is the difference between HTTP persistence and pipelining?

    Answer: Within both HTTP persistence and pipelining, clients open up a single connection for multiple requests-responses, but with pipelining, the client does not wait for the HTTP responses from the server before sending additional requests.

3. What is the HTTP header and value that servers use to issue session cookies to clients?

    Answer: To issue a session cookie to a client, the server does not include the value within the "expires=value" parameter in the "Set-Cookie:" header. For example, the following header will issue a session cookie "Session-ID=020313214" to clients:

    Set-Cookie: Session-ID=020313214

4. What is the difference between basic and message digest authentication?

    Answer: Basic authentication does not encrypt your username and passwords before sending them on the network—your passwords are encoded using Base64 encoding, but Base64 is a two-way encoding algorithm, meaning that you can easily reverse the encoded value. Message digest encoding hashes your username, password, and a nonce value issued by the server. Message digest hash algorithms are one-way, meaning that you cannot obtain the original value when given the hashed value.

5. What is the difference between explicit and implicit cache controls?

    Answer: Implicit cache controls are the responses sent by origin servers to conditional requests from caches. Explicit controls are sent by the origin servers to caches to control the way that the caches store and yield content.

6. List the three types of security schemes and the available algorithms that PKI systems commonly use.

    Answer:
    Public key algorithms—PKI uses Digital Signature Algorithm (DSA) and Rivest Shamir Adleman (RSA) to encrypt a random number between client and server used to generate a bulk encryption secret key.

    Secret key algorithms—PKI uses Data Encryption Standard (DES), Triple DES (3DES), Rivest Cipher 2 (RC2), and Rivest Cipher 4 (RC4) for encrypting bulk data with its secret key.

    Hash key algorithms—PKI uses Message Digest 5 (MD5) and Secure Hash Algorithm 1 (SHA-1) for integrity checking during SSL sessions and for authenticating certificates.

7. How do Certificate Authorities (CAs) generate digital signatures for signing a server's certificate?

    Answer: The CA creates a digital signature by first computing a hash on the contents of the certificate. The CA then encrypts the hashed value using its private key to produce its digital signature.

Chapter 9

1. What is progressive download?

    Answer: Progressive download enables you to view streaming content as it is downloaded to your media player. With progressive downloads, you can watch live events as they take place. In addition, you do not have to wait for an on-demand stream to download before viewing it. The player delays displaying the content for a few seconds to create a content buffer in order to alleviate packet jitter.

2. What are the three major streaming media vendors?

    Answer: Windows, RealNetworks, and Apple are the three major streaming media vendors.

3. What is the purpose of a streaming meta-file?

   Answer: Instead of embedding the URLs of the media files directly into your HTML, you can point your users to the URL that houses the meta-file. The media player uses the metafile to synchronize the different clips of your presentation. The media player can then request the session description file for each stream specified in the meta-file.

4. What is the relationship between "streaming containers," "codecs," "FourCCs," and "RTP-UDP"?

   Answer: You package streaming media into streaming container files before transmitting over the network. Codecs are algorithms used to encode and decode streaming media, such as MPEG, H.323, and G.711, before transmitting over the network. FourCCs are codes used to identify vendors, such as DivX, that implement the available codec algorithms. RTP is the application layer protocol, and UDP is the transport protocol that the application uses to deliver the streaming media over the network to requesting clients.

5. What is the difference between the way Apple/MPEG and Windows/RealMedia structure their container files?

   Answer: Windows/RealMedia structure their container files into data packets and synchronize the streams by interleaving the data packets within the file itself. Apple/MPEG leave the streams intact and use hint tracks stored within the file to synchronize the streams upon transmission. Therefore, when an Apple/MPEG4 server sends packets over the network, there is no Apple QuickTime- or MPEG4-related information embedded in the packets, just the standard application transport header and payload format information.

6. Does RTP provide sequence numbers to reorder out-of-sequence packets?

   Answer: No. RTP sequences packets in order to detect and drop out-of-sequence packets. Reordering packets would result in too much delay between the sender and receiver.

7. What is the difference between RTCP and RTSP?

   Answer: RTCP is the sister protocol of RTP. RTCP groups and synchronizes the RTP-UDP streams within an RTP session. In contrast, clients use RTSP to instruct streaming servers to play, pause, rewind, and fast-forward streaming media.

8. What port numbers does RTP use? What about RTSP, WMT, and ReaMedia?

   Answer: RTP uses the RTP UDP port range 16384–32767. RTP uses the even numbers in this range; RTCP uses odd numbers within the range. RTSP uses TCP port 554. RealMedia also uses RTSP port 554 on TCP for control and synchronization and uses RTP for data transmission. WMT uses MMS on UDP/TCP port 1755 for control and UDP ports 1024–5000 for data.

9. What is the purpose of streaming media session description files? How do they differ from meta-files?

   Answer: You can use session description languages to inform requesting clients of the session that they desire to participate in. This way, your users need know only the URL of the session beforehand to participate in the session, not the container file formats, IP addresses, ports, and transport protocols. A web server supplies the client browser with a meta-file to hide from the browser the information that is specific to the media-player specific information. The browser passes the meta-file to the player, and the player requests the session description file for each stream within the meta-file. Note that you can use SMIL for both meta-files and for session description files.

Chapter 10

1. What content switch hardware is responsible for providing in-band health checking? What about OOB health checking?

   Answer: The connection processor is responsible for providing in-band health checking. The control processor is responsible for providing OOB health checking.

2. Why do content switches perform delayed binding?

   Answer: A content switch must delay the binding of front-end and back-end TCP connections to make load-balancing decisions based on application content. By proxying the front-end TCP connection, the content switch can inspect the application request and select the virtual server that best fits the request.

3. What is involved in sequence-number remapping?

   Answer: Because the content switch performs delayed binding, the real server's sequence numbers are unknown when the content switch establishes a connection with the client. The content switch selects a virtual server and establishes the back-end TCP connection with a real server. To bind the front- and back-end TCP connections together, the content switch must overwrite the real server's sequence numbers with the sequence numbers that the content switch previously synchronized with the client.

4. What is the major difference between router- and bridge-mode?

   Answer: Bridge-mode enables you to configure your VIPs on the same subnet as your real servers, whereas in router-mode your VIPs and serverfarm subnets must be different.

5.   What is the major difference between relative and absolute load calculations?

Answer: Relative load normalizes your real server load calculations with the best-performing real server, whereas, absolute load calculates each real server's load individually.

6.   What is the difference between HTTP header load balancing and HTTP URL hashing?

Answer: HTTP header load balancing is a method of selecting virtual servers. URL hashing is a method of deciding which real server to send the request to after the content switch selects a virtual server.

7.   Why doesn't the CSS store its client to real server associations in the sticky state table with HTTP hash cookies?

Answer: Because hashing is stateless in nature, the CSS can simply recalculate the hash to determine the associated real that should receive the request. However, with source IP sticky, the content switch cannot calculate the originally chosen real server on the fly, so it must store the association in the sticky table for later use.

8.   What type of stickiness should you configure with CSS high availability?

Answer: Because ASR does not synchronize state across redundant CSSs, you should use HTTP cookie-stickiness—it is a stateless sticky mechanism by nature, and therefore does not require state synchronization.

9.   What is the major difference between CSS and CSM high availability?

Answer: The CSM does not require support for an active-active configuration because of its high concurrent connection and bandwidth support. However, you may benefit from an active-active scenario with the lower-end CSS models; therefore, the CSS supports an active-active configuration.

Chapter 11

1. What sticky configuration should you perform in an SSL termination environment?

   Answer: If you have multiple SSL offloading modules, you must configure SSL sticky to ensure that the content switch chooses the same SSL module for each connection of a session. If you also want your client to stick to the same back-end real server and you don't have back-end SSL configured, you must also configure a cleartext sticky method, such as HTTP cookie or source IP address sticky. Otherwise, you should consider configuring back-end SSL.

2. What is the purpose of HTTP header insertion and URL rewriting?

   Answer: You can use HTTP header insertion to inform real servers that the client requested an SSL page, in order for your real server to make sure that all embedded URLs include "https://" links. URL rewriting automatically rewrites the "Location:" header in HTTP redirects from your real servers with "https://" URLs.

3. What is the purpose of IP reverse-sticky?

   Answer: If you have applications that originate connections in both directions (that is, from client-to-server and server-to-client, such as FTP), you should use IP reverse-sticky to ensure that connections originating from a real server traverse the same firewall as the client-originated connections.

4. Why should you "sandwich" your firewalls with content switches when performing FWLB?

   Answer: You should sandwich your firewalls to ensure that return traffic and connections that originate from real servers flow through the same firewall as incoming traffic. Return traffic of existing connections is forwarded to the same firewall using the inside content switch's connection table. Additionally, you can configure reverse-sticky to ensure that outgoing buddy connections originating from the real servers are forwarded to the same firewall as incoming connections.

5. In Example 11-12, why should you configure source IP address hashing on incoming requests and destination hashing on requests initiated by the web servers?

   Answer: You should hash on the source IP address for incoming connections because the client IP address space on the Internet introduces more variability to the hash function than the IP address space of your origin servers, decreasing the chances of one firewall receiving more connections than the other. The same concept pertains to connections initiated from your origin servers.

6. How would you apply reverse-sticky in the single-CSM example in Example 11-14?

   Answer: You can apply the command **reverse-sticky 77** to the virtual server called "web-vip" and the **sticky 100 group 77** command to the virtual server called "out-conns-40" to enable reverse-sticky in to Example 11-14.

Chapter 12

1. What is the difference between iterative and recursive DNS?

    Answer: With iterative DNS, the client's DNS server is responsible for determining the IP address associated with a domain. To achieve this, the DNS servers send NS (or referral) records to the client DNS server until it reaches the DNS server authoritative for the requested domain. With recursive DNS, each DNS server in the system is responsible for determining the IP address for the domain, by recursively issuing A record requests until the authoritative DNS server is reached.

2. What type of answer occurs in this situation: your local DNS server responds to your A record request with a cached copy of the A record?

    Answer: When you request an A record, your local DNS server may cache it for the length of time specified in the TTL by the authoritative DNS server. If you request the A record again before the TTL expires, the answer from your local DNS server is called a nonauthoritative answer.

3. What is the purpose of SOA DNS records?

    Answer: SOA records tell a DNS server that it is authoritative for the particular domain.

4. What are the various DD metrics you can use to select among your available sites?

    Answer: You can use random, portion, preference, routing protocol, RTT, and Boomerang metrics to select from your available sites.

5. What are stateless RTT calculations?

    Answer: When the Distributed Director calculates the best RTT between the client's DNS server and the available sites, it does not store the RTT state associated to the requesting client for subsequent DNS queries from that client for the requested domain.

6. Why should you disable Boomerang when using HTTP redirects with the DD?

    Answer: When you use the Boomerang protocol, the client DNS server is the only entity that knows which site has the shortest return path to the client DNS server (based on which A record it receives first from the available sites). Therefore, the DD cannot determine which site to include in the "Location:" header of the HTTP 301 Moved method.

7. Why is stateful proximity beneficial?

    Answer: Use of stateful proximity reduces overall response times by avoiding client DNS server probes for every request.

8.   Why is stateful DNS-sticky beneficial?

Answer: Stateless DNS-sticky using source IP hashing may provide an uneven distribution of requests across your sites. However, using a stateful GSDB enables you to use intelligent load balancing methods to distribute client requests across your sites, such as the least-loaded and proximity methods.

Chapter 13

1.   What is the difference between the standard web-cache and reverse-proxy WCCP service groups?

Answer: In a cache cluster environment, the web-cache service group tells the router to hash the destination IP address and source port to select a CE in the cluster. However, with the reverse-cache service group, the router hashes the source IP address and source port to select an available CE. With reverse caching, hashing on the source IP addresses from clients on the Internet provides a wider distribution of hash values, as compared to the finite number of IP addresses for your data center origin servers.

2.   Is it possible to configure IP spoofing with forward caching?

Answer: If you need to preserve your client's source IP address for requests across your WAN or onto the Internet, you can configure IP spoofing in a forward caching. However, bear in mind that, if you do not configure spoofing, your client's source IP addresses are hidden from the Internet, which is a security measure against hacking.

3.   Does the CE always require spoofing the origin server for client requests?

Answer: Yes, the CE must spoof the origin server IP address in both forward and reverse proxy environments for at least the duration of establishing the TCP connection. Because the client sends its TCP SYN segment to the origin server IP address, it drops any TCP SYN/ACK packets from any other IP address. However, once the TCP connection is established, the CE may send the HTTP/RTSP method "305 Use Proxy" to redirect client media players or browsers to send their requests directly to the CE IP address instead of the origin server.

4.   Why can't the CE cache Kerberos-, NTLM-, or Digest-authenticated objects?

Answer: As you learned in Chapter 8, "Exploring the Application Layer," these protocols use a one-time nonce value with the user's credentials to prevent replay attacks, thus preventing the CE (or anyone else) from re-using the client's credentials.

5. What transparent value-added services can you enable on your Cisco CEs, other than standard caching services?

    Answer: You can enable content authentication and authorization, SSL caching, content adaptation, URL filtering, and TCP parameter value adjustments. Live stream splitting is also a transparent value-added service that Cisco CEs can provide to your clients, origin servers, or both.

6. What are pull- and push-splitting?

    Answer: With pull-splitting, the client requests trigger the CE to proactively pull the live stream via unicast from the origin server. With push-splitting, the origin server pushes the live stream via multicast to the network for the CE to actively join.

Chapter 14

1. From which file system do edge CEs serve prepositioned content?

    Answer: CEs serve prepositioned content from the cdnfs file system.

2. What is a manifest file used for and why wouldn't you use the CDM GUI instead?

    Answer: A manifest file is an XML document that web developers can use to specify the content that they want prepositioned to the ACNS network. Because web developers do not normally administer the ACNS network, the XML manifest file provides them a standard interface into the ACNS network.

3. What is the criteria for choosing the root-CE?

    Answer: Primarily, the root CE should be the closest CE to the origin server containing the content. You should also make sure that the root CE has the CPU, memory, and disk capacity to handle distributing channel content through your ACNS network.

4. What is the relationship between a location leader and a location forwarder?

    Answer: The location leader unicast-pulls content of a channel from the forwarder of its parent location.

5. What do you require to stream prepositioned RealMedia formatted files?

    Answer: You need to obtain a license for RealSubscriber to stream prepositioned RealMedia formatted files. In contrast, to stream RealNetworks format from on-demand cache (non-prepositioned), you need to obtain the RealProxy license.

Index

Numerics

J-L

Cisco Press

Learning is serious business.

Invest wisely.

Cisco Press

3 STEPS TO LEARNING

STEP 1

First-Step

STEP 2

Fundamentals

STEP 3

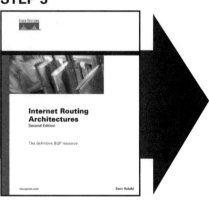

Networking Technology Guides

STEP 1 **First-Step**—Benefit from easy-to-grasp explanations. No experience required!

STEP 2 **Fundamentals**—Understand the purpose, application, and management of technology.

STEP 3 **Networking Technology Guides**—Gain the knowledge to master the challenge of the network.

NETWORK BUSINESS SERIES

The Network Business series helps professionals tackle the business issues surrounding the network. Whether you are a seasoned IT professional or a business manager with minimal technical expertise, this series will help you understand the business case for technologies.

Justify Your Network Investment.

Look for Cisco Press titles at your favorite bookseller today.

Visit **www.ciscopress.com/series** for details on each of these book series.

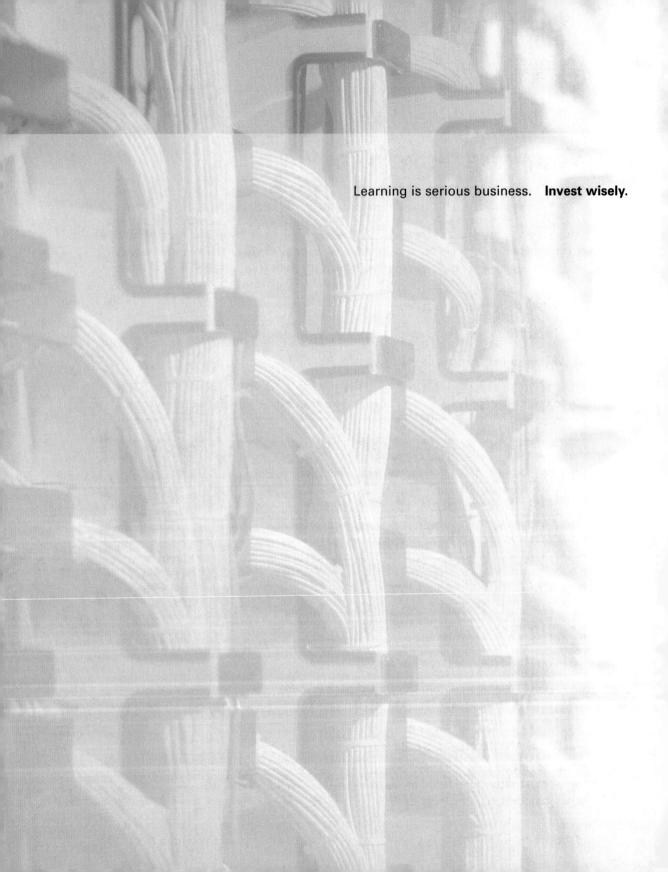
Learning is serious business. **Invest wisely.**

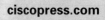

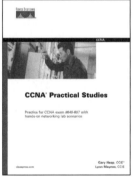

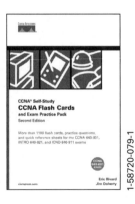

SEARCH THOUSANDS OF BOOKS FROM LEADING PUBLISHERS

Safari® Bookshelf is a searchable electronic reference library for IT professionals that features more than 2,000 titles from technical publishers, including Cisco Press.

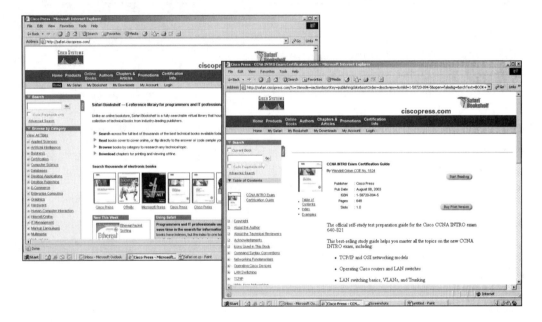

With Safari Bookshelf you can

- **Search** the full text of thousands of technical books, including more than 70 Cisco Press titles from authors such as Wendell Odom, Jeff Doyle, Bill Parkhurst, Sam Halabi, and Karl Solie.

- **Read** the books on My Bookshelf from cover to cover, or just flip to the information you need.

- **Browse** books by category to research any technical topic.

- **Download** chapters for printing and viewing offline.

With a customized library, you'll have access to your books when and where you need them—and all you need is a user name and password.

Cisco Press

Learning is serious business.

Invest wisely.

Cisco Press

NETWORK BUSINESS SERIES

JUSTIFY YOUR NETWORK INVESTMENT

Understand the business case for technologies with Network Business books from Cisco Press. Designed to support anyone **searching for optimal network systems,** Network Business titles help you justify your network investments.

1-58720-121-6

Look for Network Business titles at your favorite bookseller

The Business Case for E-Learning
Kelly / Nanjiani • ISBN: 1-58720-086-4

The Business Case for Network Security
Paquet / Saxe • ISBN: 1-58720-121-6

The Business Case for Storage Networks
Williams • ISBN: 1-58720-118-6

The Case for Virtual Business Processes
Young / Jude • ISBN: 1-58720-087-2

IP Telephony Unveiled
Brown • ISBN: 1-58720-075-9

Power Up Your Small-Medium Business
Aber • ISBN: 1-58705-135-4

The Road to IP Telephony
Carhee • ISBN: 1-58720-088-0

Taking Charge of Your VoIP Project
Walker / Hicks • ISBN: 1-58720-092-9

Coming in Fall 2005

The Business Case for Enterprise-Class Wireless LANs
Castaneda / Alasdair / Vinckier • ISBN: 1-58720-125-9

MPLS for Decision Makers
Sayeed / Morrow • ISBN: 1-58720-120-8

Network Business Series. **Justify Your Network Investment.**

Visit **www.ciscopress.com/netbus** for details about the Network Business series and a complete list of titles.

CISCO SYSTEMS

Cisco Press

SAVE UP TO 30%

Become a member and save at **ciscopress.com**!

Complete a **user profile** at ciscopress.com today to become a member and benefit from **discounts up to 30% on every purchase** at ciscopress.com, as well as a more customized user experience. Your membership will also allow you access to the entire Informit network of sites.

Don't forget to subscribe to the monthly Cisco Press newsletter to be the first to learn about new releases and special promotions. You can also sign up to get your first **30 days FREE on Safari Bookshelf** and preview Cisco Press content. Safari Bookshelf lets you access Cisco Press books online and build your own customized, searchable electronic reference library.

Visit **www.ciscopress.com/register** to sign up and start saving today!

The profile information we collect is used in aggregate to provide us with better insight into your technology interests and to create a better user experience for you. You must be logged into ciscopress.com to receive your discount. Discount is on Cisco Press products only; shipping and handling are not included.

 Learning is serious business.
Invest wisely.

Safari®
BOOKS ONLINE
ENABLED

THIS BOOK IS SAFARI ENABLED

INCLUDES FREE 45-DAY ACCESS TO THE ONLINE EDITION

The Safari® Enabled icon on the cover of your favorite technology book means the book is available through Safari Bookshelf. When you buy this book, you get free access to the online edition for 45 days.

Safari Bookshelf is an electronic reference library that lets you easily search thousands of technical books, find code samples, download chapters, and access technical information whenever and wherever you need it.

TO GAIN 45-DAY SAFARI ENABLED ACCESS TO THIS BOOK:

- Go to **http://www.ciscopress.com/safarienabled**

- Complete the brief registration form

- Enter the coupon code found in the front of this book before the "Contents at a Glance" page

If you have difficulty registering on Safari Bookshelf or accessing the online edition, please e-mail customer-service@safaribooksonline.com.